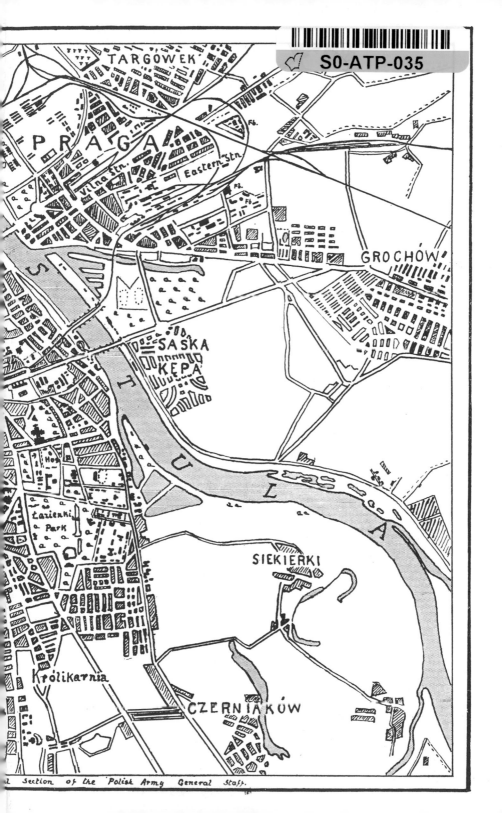

TARGÓWEK

PRAGA

Vilna Stn.

Eastern Stn.

Fₜ.

GROCHÓW

SASKA KĘPA

WISTULA

Łazienki Park

SIEKIERKI

Królikarnia

CZERNIAKÓW

Section of the Polish Army General Staff.

THE SECRET ARMY

THE SECRET ARMY

by

T. BOR-KOMOROWSKI

THE BATTERY PRESS
NASHVILLE

First U.S. edition published by

THE BATTERY PRESS, INC.
P.O. Box 3107, Uptown Station
Nashville, Tennessee 37219 U.S.A.

Second in the Allied Forces Series

Originally published in Great Britain
by Victor Gallancz Ltd.

Printed and Bound in the U.S.A.

ISBN: 0-89839-082-6

FOREWORD

The Warsaw Uprising of August, 1944 was one of the most tragic events in Poland's modern history. Yet, it was a time of tremendous national sacrifice and serves as an inspiration to succeeding generations who search for freedom. This struggle is carried on today by Solidarity, the embodiment of the unquenchable spirit of the Polish Nation.

The story of the Polish resistance and its epic stand in Warsaw is largely unknown in the English-speaking world. Formed almost immediately after the German victory in 1939, the Polish Home Army was the largest, and most active, of the European resistance forces in World War II. It carried out extensive sabotage operations and provided the allies with vital intelligence information. Largely self-sufficient, the Polish Home Army had to maintain its morale in the face of uncompromising repression. It drew its strength from all quarters; women and children played an active part in most of its clandestine operations.

Today, with the hindsight of 40 years, it is all too easy to see that Poland's fate was sealed in the field of politics, not on the battlefield. But the struggle was not in vain; it stands as a living testimony to the fact that the price of freedom is a high one. It is a price that the Polish Nation has never shrunk from paying.

To the memory of the Home Army Soldiers
who gave their lives for the liberty of Poland

The rural population near Wilno join in prayer with Home Army soldiers, January 1944.

An underground press. Half an hour later the pistol and a good run saved the printer's life from the Gestapo.

"Street kitchens" for the feeding of those rendered homeless by the fighting.

The Headquarters of a district command in Warsaw.

New recruits for the Home Army.

Theater Square

Soldiers of the Home Army appear from sewers and basements after two months of grim fighting.

A poster proclaims "Long Live the Polish Army."

CONTENTS

MAP OF THE PARTITION
OF POLAND 1939

1:8 000,000

PART ONE

CHAPTER I

THE BIRTH OF THE UNDERGROUND, CRACOW

As a colonel in the Polish Army at the outbreak of war on September 1st, 1939, I had been involved in continuous fighting, during which the German armoured columns had driven deep into Poland from west, north and south. It was then that the news reached us that the Russians had crossed the Polish frontier in the east. Some people were still in doubt whether they were coming as friends or foes. In any case, it was clear to us that we could not withstand the German onslaught much longer, and we therefore planned to break through the enemy's lines and reach the Hungarian border.

In the morning on September 19th, a strange incident occurred on the Wieprz River. From the mass of civilian refugees on the road one man suddenly came forward and insisted on speaking to me.

"I am an official from the President's office," he said, "and I have a large sum of public money with me which I want to hand over to someone, preferably a military authority. Would you agree to take it and give me a receipt?"

"I don't see why I should take money belonging to the Treasury. What is it you really want?"

"I've lost touch with my head of department. I am only an ordinary refugee now. This agreement between the Russians and the Germans seems to leave us no hope, and yet I am certain the struggle will go on. That is why I want to give this money to an officer."

"What agreement between the Russians and the Germans?" I asked impatiently.

"Do you mean to say you have not heard? The Russians have invaded the country in support of Hitler. They must be in Lwów by now. This is a new partition of Poland."

The last few weeks had tired me out. I had not had a moment's sleep for several nights past, and this news drove me into a frenzy.

"Who told you all this? This is just defeatist gossip, which you should not repeat!"

In silence, he opened his dispatch-case and pulled out a typewritten slip of paper, which he handed to me without comment. It was the text of a joint communiqué issued over the Soviet and German wireless:

"In order to avoid all kinds of unfounded rumours concerning the respective aims of the Soviet and German armies operating in Poland, the Government of the U.S.S.R. and the German Government declare that these operations have no aim contrary to the interests of Germany or the U.S.S.R. or to the spirit and letter of the Russian-German Pact of Non-aggression. On the contrary, the aim of their armies is to restore peace and order destroyed by the collapse of the Polish State."

I was stunned. Was all this a tremendous lie, and was this man simply one of the German fifth columnists? The country was riddled with spies at that moment. But no, his papers convinced me of his identity. Thoughts were racing through my head. Suddenly I remembered that our troops had no money with which to buy food, so I took the bundle. It contained 36,000 zlotys.

We did not reach the Hungarian frontier, although we broke through the German lines again and again, while the Luftwaffe attacked ceaselessly. When we realised that we were encircled, we decided to disband our units, and tried to escape captivity singly or in small groups. That night I was riding through a dense forest with about fifteen of my officers and men when we fell into a German ambush. We scattered, and after an hour only a few of us were still at liberty. We then decided to abandon our horses, and began to make our way on foot towards Cracow, from where we hoped to make another attempt to cross the frontier into Hungary. We could, of course, only march at night; by day we had to keep hidden in the undergrowth or woods. Peasants gave us food and supplied us with civilian clothes. Little did I suspect then that the money I was carrying on me was to be the first funds of the future Underground Army.

After many narrow escapes, my companion and I—there were only two of us left then—reached Cracow late one evening.

It was already dark. At the station I learned that we had

roughly an hour before curfew, when all Poles had to be indoors. We were tired out, and it was with an effort that we dragged ourselves out of the station to search for a place in which to spend the night. We chanced on a little hotel quite near. When we inquired for the rooms, the porter at once asked to see our papers. We showed him the passes we had got at Bochnia, authorising us to travel to Cracow, which were all we had; but the porter did not think it was enough. All hotels in Cracow were under Gestapo supervision, and sometimes they were searched more than once in twenty-four hours. Should a hotel guest be discovered without identity papers, naturally he, the hall porter, would be arrested along with the suspect.

We had no choice. I gave the hall porter a searching look; his face seemed honest. "You know what will happen if we are stopped by a patrol?" I asked him. He nodded understandingly and, after a moment's hesitation, led us up the stairs and into an attic, where at last we were able to have a decent wash and shave—the first since our wanderings began. There was no question of clean linen, as we had nothing beyond what we stood up in.

In the morning, well rested after a good sleep, we discussed our next move. So far we had carefully avoided all towns, and our experiences in the country had told us nothing of the conditions which we now had to face in the streets of Cracow. I decided to go and have a look round and try to find a lodging with friends.

Looking over Cracow now, I saw the swastika flying from the Wawel, for centuries the residence of Polish kings. The walls of the houses were covered with German notices and orders. A couple of phrases seemed to recur in all of them insistently; one was "strictly forbidden" and the other "penalty of death." There was one poster which appeared every few paces. Above the words, "England, this is your work," was the picture of a wounded Polish soldier lying in rags against a background of Warsaw in ruins; the soldier's fist was raised against the picture of the British Prime Minister, Neville Chamberlain.

Propaganda and the Gestapo had followed hard on the heels of the German front-line troops, taking immediate control of the whole territory. A newspaper, printed in Polish by the Germans, was already appearing in Cracow. German military police patrolled all over the town, mostly in threes or fours, moving slowly with an apparently bored expression on their faces. In reality, they kept a keen watch in all directions. They continually stopped passers-by, searching any parcels they might be carrying and checking documents. In accordance with new orders, every Jewish shop had a David's star painted on the front, together with the inscription: "*Nicht Arisch*" (non-Aryan). Jews were forbidden to show themselves in the centre of the town and, when walking past a German, were required to step aside and bow.

Walking through the streets, I met an old friend of mine.

"Where have you been hiding?" was his first question.

"In a hotel," I smiled back.

"A hotel? Without papers? Well . . . of course, it's certain arrest. You'd better come to my flat at once. As a matter of fact, I've got Germans there too—Wehrmacht officers." He smiled wryly. "Still, I think even so you'd be safer there than in a hotel."

We agreed that I should go to his flat that evening and spend the night there.

But my luck was out. Most of the flat, as my friend had warned me, was occupied by Germans. However, he squeezed me in for the night. It was in the morning that things began to go wrong.

By chance it happened that an old photograph of mine stood on the writing desk in the sitting-room. As I left the flat next morning, I passed the German batman in the garden and I noticed that he stared at me rather hard. While I was out, he approached the maid:

"Who's the officer in uniform in that picture on the writing desk?"

The maid shrugged her shoulders. "How should I know?" she replied. "I've never set eyes on him."

"I suppose it isn't that man who was in the flat this morning?" persisted the batman.

But the maid kept her wits about her and saved the situation by maintaining that this man had been the carpenter who had just put in new window panes; the others having been broken during the air raids.

All this happened while I was out. Had I met the batman again, the encounter might well have ended in disaster both for my friend and myself. When I returned from town, he met me at a neighbouring street corner and explained what had happened. Obviously, the next night had to be spent elsewhere.

My lack of papers complicated things a good deal. Both indoors and out, I could be arrested at any moment. And it was not my risk alone; it was shared by whoever afforded me refuge and hospitality. There was, of course, no possible chance of smuggling myself across the frontier without documents, and my plan to leave seemed doomed to failure. The whole of Sub-Carpathia was seething with Gestapo agents. A newcomer arriving there had to be in possession of some sort of papers unless he wanted to get arrested at the first street corner.

A woman doctor, a friend of mine, came to my rescue. She arranged with the senior doctor of the Bonifratow Hospital that I should be admitted there as a chronic lumbago case. I had to share a room with a member of the Cracow Town Council who had broken his leg in an accident. He had a steady stream of visitors, and it was from them that I was able to form a picture of the situation in town and country.

One day the Councillor's son brought news of a proclamation which had been posted up. It was worded in typical German style:

"Inhabitants of the General Government!

"Victorious German arms have, once and for all, put an end to the Polish State. Behind you lies an episode in history which you should forget forthwith; it belongs to the past and will never return.

"Inhabitants of the General Government!

"The Fuehrer has decided to form a General Government of part of the territory of the Polish State and to place me at its head. The General Government can become the refuge of the Polish people if they will submit loyally and completely to the orders of the German authorities and accomplish the tasks set them in the German war effort. Every attempt to oppose the new German order will be ruthlessly suppressed."

The proclamation was signed by the newly appointed Governor-General, Hans Frank. It was accompanied by a notice of the compulsory call-up for work. Men and women were called upon to register.

The same afternoon, the Councillor's son again brought us news, but this time the joyful news that we had a new Government and a new Army. He showed me the carbon copy of a radio communiqué issued a few days earlier. It announced the formation of the Polish Government in Paris under the Premiership of General Sikorski. President Raczkiewicz had succeeded President Moscicki. The first step taken by General Sikorski's Government was the formation of Polish fighting units in France. My relief was enormous. So my premonitions had been correct! The battle which we had lost in Poland would be taken up again in France, and service in the uniform of a Polish officer would now be continued. The efforts to get through to Cracow and avoid capture had not been in vain! I now had a definite aim: to reach France as quickly as possible.

Now I had to get some documents. I soon learned that this was not so easy, since they would have to be faked. At this juncture, help again arrived quite unexpectedly and freed me from my enforced stay in hospital.

Two of my Army comrades, Colonels Rudnicki and Godlewski, came to see me. They had arrived from Warsaw with the same end in view—to cross the frontier into Hungary—and they proposed that I should join them. My lack of documents was a hindrance, but a few days later an old friend, Maria Krzeczunowicz, brought me, with justifiable pride, a Polish identity card complete with the correct stamp and signature of the authorities. A good deal of mystery was attached to its origin, but I was not over-curious. She filled it in for me with an assumed name, Tadeusz Korczak. It was the first of numerous pseudonyms which I was to use in the years ahead.

I left hospital that same day and moved into a room which "Maria" had found me. There we held a meeting—Maria, the other two and myself—to decide on the next step in our plan. Before leaving, Rudnicki was anxious to go into Soviet-occupied Poland to find out what had happened to his family left behind in Lwów. He also promised to see my wife. We agreed to await his return, for we needed rest and strength to cross the mountains to Hungary and there was plenty to do.

Meanwhile, events were developing in Cracow. One day the German authorities invited all professors, lecturers and assistants to a lecture to be held in the Aula Magna of this oldest Polish University, founded in 1364. "The Attitude of the National Socialist Movement towards Science and Learning" was the title of the lecture. Nearly all the professors came. When the hall was crowded, the chief of the Cracow Gestapo marched up to the chair and declared that, as this University had always shown anti-German tendencies, everybody in the hall was under arrest. At the same moment the Collegium Novum, the building where the assembly took place, was surrounded by S.S. men, who immediately marched into the Aula Magna and began to belabour the professors savagely with their rifle butts. One hundred and sixty-seven professors, lecturers and assistants, a few students, and other persons who by chance happened to be present, were sent to the Cracow Prison. From there the professors went to the concentration camp of Sachsenhausen-Oranienburg. Fourteen, some of them scholars of international fame, died of ill-treatment. Others survived, only to die immediately after returning home, while others remained alive, but never recovered their previous health.

But then we still knew nothing of what was yet to come. We were thunderstruck. A whole university arrested and deported was a thing we had never heard of before! However, this was only the beginning of our experiences with the *Kulturträger*. Two days later a big block of flats belonging to the University, where many of the professors lived, was invaded late in the evening. The families of the deported had to leave their homes at once. They had twenty minutes to pack their belongings. During this time the electric light was switched off for the whole block, so that the families could not find the things they wanted to take with them. When they were gone, the light came on and German families moved in the same evening. Later on whole districts were treated in this way.

All this happened while I was waiting for Rudnicki's return. Then one evening in Maria's flat I met Mr. Surzycki, a member of the National Party, who had already been very active in helping other groups to get away to France.

"So you want to go to France, do you?" he began. "Why? So that you can go on fighting the Germans, of course. I can tell you one thing: nobody wants to sit down under the new order. On the contrary, they *all* want to fight against it. It's only a few weeks since we suffered the greatest defeat in our history. We lost our Army and our State, and the country was divided between two invaders. In a situation like this, you might argue that the best course would be to adapt oneself as best one could and see what the future would bring forth. But the whole population, the entire nation, has decided on one policy: *to continue the fight!* This is the right decision. All our hopes for the future depend on inter-Allied obligations, because our fight with the Germans is the only way we can fulfil our own obligations to the Allies. Therefore we must fight.

"One can hardly envisage the possibility of everyone going to France, though. We must fight in *this* country, as well as in France. That is why we have started a military organisation here—headed by Colonel Epler. By very bad luck, the Gestapo have got on his trail and, as his family is here in Cracow, he has to leave at once. I shall have to help him to France with all the means at my disposal. As for you, I propose you should remain here and take over his work."

Surzycki explained that he thought I should do it because I had never meddled in politics and had not belonged to the régime in power before the war (which he looked upon as one of the factors responsible for our defeat).

Here I must explain that at the time of this conversation the responsibility for our military defeat was put almost entirely on the previous Government, and it was for this reason that political antagonism was then so strong. After the collapse of France, which gave the second proof of Germany's strength, it became clear that the reasons for our defeat went far deeper than had appeared at the beginning, and political differences almost disappeared in the common effort.

When Colonel Rudnicki turned up from the Soviet-occupied zone, he had much to tell us of conditions there. They were very different from ours. Soviet methods of police procedure were more refined and efficient than those of the Germans. A general fear of the N.K.V.D. reigned among the people of eastern Poland and there was a mutual distrust of which the greatest use was made. Political meetings, gatherings and elections organised by the Soviet authorities showed "unanimity." This was forced upon the people not so much by blood and terror as by the spy system, which was organised to perfection. It permeated into all social spheres through the medium of specially trained agents. The result was a psychological tension in the atmosphere which became almost unbearable.

Rudnicki had not seen my wife. This was an immense

disappointment to me. He had heard only that she had left for a little town on the San River. From this I realised that she was trying to cross the river and the border of the occupation zones to reach me.

I repeated the gist of Surzycki's words to Rudnicki and discussed the matter with him. Regular officers were pouring into France in such numbers that those who remained behind would undoubtedly be needed far more in Poland than abroad. We heard from Rudnicki that in Soviet-occupied Poland and in all ranks of society a great many secret organisations were springing into existence; the need to organise and centralise them for the whole of the Republic was becoming obvious.

We therefore had another meeting with Surzycki. He wanted us to set up a military organisation for his party. I was opposed to this and said so. As a Regular Army officer, I recognised only one authority—my Commander-in-Chief, General Sikorski, in Paris. It was quite impossible to place myself under the orders of any political party. I maintained that there should be only one military organisation, common to all and independent of political opinion.

Finally, everybody agreed to my point of view and our decision was made. Convinced that we should be of more use in Poland, we had determined to stay. Thus it was that I began the work of organising military units in south-west Poland. It was then December, 1939. Events had forced us to realise that we could not be simply passive sufferers, that German terror had to be opposed by every means at our disposal.

On December 27th one of my men was returning to Warsaw after having visited his family in the suburbs. At the station he was held back by the whispered warning: "Don't travel."

At the next station, Wawer, the Germans were taking everyone off the trains. Something serious was happening there. He learnt that mass executions were taking place near the Wawer depot in retaliation for the murder of a German in a nearby inn. It was not till several hours later that he gathered it was safe to take a train. As he passed Wawer, he could see clearly from the train a wall splashed with blood. A heap of corpses still lay there, most of the victims obviously having been taken from their homes in night attire. Naturally, the public shooting was the only subject of conversation on the train. It was in this way that he heard the whole story.

Two German policemen had walked into the inn, where they found two criminals wanted by the police. To avoid arrest, the criminals opened fire, killing one policeman and wounding the second. Soon after, a German patrol arrived at the inn. Their first act was to hang the innocent innkeeper over his own door. The dragging forth and execution of people lasted all night. One hundred and seventy people perished in this way. There was one characteristic incident. Among those put to death there was a man named Goering. Because of his name, the Germans had three times given him fifteen minutes to declare himself a German and thus save his life. He stood with his face to the wall, his hands above his head, and refused each time. His reply to them was simple and direct:

"I was born a Pole and I shall die a Pole, regardless of how I die."

He was finally shot along with the others, and his name can still be seen on one of the crosses in Wawer Cemetery.

The shooting of Poles in smaller groups had by then become a habit of the invaders. In the citadel of Cracow alone daily executions of ten or twenty peasants picked up in the neighbourhood was a common occurrence. The reaction of Poland as a whole was unanimous and passionate: the nation resolved to take up the fight and show the world that the enemy could kill our bodies, but never the immortal spirit of freedom, which had been bred in us over a thousand years.

I don't think it has often happened in history that the leaders of a people could be so very certain of fulfilling the will of a whole nation. This time, a country completely overrun by two invaders and torn in half had decided to fight. No dictator, no leader, no party and no class, had inspired this decision. The nation had made it spontaneously and unanimously.

Once I knew I was to stay and work out a plan for the organisation of the Underground Army in south-west Poland, practical methods to execute this plan had to be decided upon. None of us had any experience in these matters. Every day officers, civilians—once even a monk from a remote monastery—turned up, reporting to me the numbers and other details of their local organisations. Often they had sworn in a few hundred people, mostly youths determined to fight to the last. They were all coming for instructions and orders.

Rudnicki and I worked out the main principle of our conspiracy. We instructed our people to form groups of five. Each member of a group was allowed to know only his four fellow members, each one of them in his turn creating a new group of five.   In this way the pyramid, with me at the top, was constantly growing. The use of real names was forbidden and pseudonyms introduced. The whole area was subdivided into sectors, corresponding to the pre-war administrative divisions. Each sector was to have its own local commander.

Most of our men, except for a few older commanders, were untrained, as most of the Polish Regular Army, mobilised in 1939, had been taken prisoner by the Germans or Russians. We had to train them immediately in the use of such arms— Polish and German—as were at our disposal. This was the beginning of the eventual secret military schools.

I formed a small staff of officers in Cracow, and with their aid I fixed a series of meeting places, each of which was known by some such name as "Monastery," "Dining-Room" and so on. In this way no addresses were put on paper when meetings were arranged. Code words were always used. The Gestapo had a far-flung net of spies and agents in Poland and had at their disposal the most up-to-date police apparatus. No Pole ever knew when his name would figure on the list of suspects, or when he would be shadowed. We had to keep our activities a complete secret, especially with regard to meeting places. Usually, people whose flats were contact points knew nothing about their callers except their pseudonyms and the password. This was the nucleus of the liaison net.

We had to create a separate intelligence system and carry out counter-espionage so that we might warn our own people, and so on.

Enormous deliveries of materials pouring ceaselessly from Russia to Germany provided us with a good chance to weaken the German war-potential. We created a special organisation for sabotage, which we had to equip with explosives and arms as well as a special intelligence system. In this way constant acts of sabotage were perpetrated on the long communication lines and in the new factories which the Germans were putting up in Poland. At the same time began the systematic destruction of railways, rolling stock and stores of war material.

Poland was at that time completely cut off from any source of information other than Hitler's propaganda. Anyone found to have a radio set was put to death; the entire pre-war Polish Press had been liquidated. The Germans published newspapers printed in Polish. It became vital to put up secret wireless stations where Allied and neutral news could be heard. The various news items had to be taken down and then printed in secret bulletins, first by mimeographs, later by secret printing presses. Finally, they had to be distributed throughout Poland. In this way we created our own Underground Press, which provided an adequate commentary on events in order to oppose the enemy's lies and keep up the morale of the nation. Later on we were also to print instructions and manuals for secret training courses and schools.

In the first year the stream of officers and reservists toward the Hungarian frontier grew to mass proportions, in spite of the tremendous difficulties and risks. Often the Carpathian Mountains had to be crossed in weather of 54 or more degrees below freezing-point (– 30° C.), through deep snow and snow-storms. German police with dogs guarded the frontier and the whole area forty miles deep. Those who tried to reach Hungary and those who helped them were often tracked down and killed.

In the beginning names and addresses of guides, as well as their pass-words, were handed from one person to another with little or no restriction. The result was that as many as twenty people would attempt to get across at a time, with the inevitable result of a mass arrest. Frequently the Germans would arrange an ambush in the house of a guide they had caught, thus succeeding in arresting numerous unsuspecting people who turned up to ask for the guide. Sometimes such an ambush would be kept up for weeks.

All those men were compelled to use the one narrow route through Slovakia. In an attempt to reduce the number of arrests, we set up transfer posts which could only be reached by those directed to them through our organisation. Even then, things were anything but easy, as the men had to be led by experienced and well tried guides across the mountains by little-known paths.

Every Pole had to make his own individual decision about the way he chose to continue the fight. No one exercised any authority over him. He could go to France or join the Underground. I did, however, introduce priority for airmen and sailors and those wanted by the Gestapo to leave the country.

One of our first needs was to get arms. Many had been buried in secret hiding-places after the campaign. I had them dug up, cleaned, protected against rust and reburied.

In all our work we always had to reckon with the danger that any secret of ours might at any moment be revealed under torture. The men who embarked on the road of conspiracy—above all, the officers—constantly searched for by the Gestapo, which threatened with the death penalty anyone who hid them, had to be provided with aliases and false personal documents as well as indispensable working papers. A certain number of secret institutions, therefore, had to come into existence to produce such documents. Often these did not prove effective in case of arrest, so we had to improve our system of forgery. People whom we could trust absolutely had to procure for us genuine documents of men and women who had disappeared during the war.

As our organisation was constantly growing and developing, new tasks and problems emerged and had to be dealt with daily. Our ever-broadening experience had to battle with new situations, and thus it was life itself which shaped our movement. It took a long time—from 1939 to 1944—and the road was irksome and dangerous, but it led to the fully organised "Secret State" with about 380,000 men in the fighting units.

For my own part, I avoided all contact with relations and pre-war friends from the beginning. I let it become known that I had got safely abroad.

In an effort to change my appearance, I shaved off my moustache, and when I went into the street I put on glasses with heavy rims. At first I used plain lenses, because there was nothing wrong with my sight. But later I heard that the Germans were stopping people who wore glasses, inspecting the lenses and, if these were of plain glass, arresting them, so I began to use convex lenses. The result of these precautions was satisfactory. Acquaintances more often than not failed to recognise me in the street.

As a further security measure, I asked a medical friend to provide me with a dose of efficient poison. Next day he gave me a small glass capsule. It was very fragile. The mere act of swallowing fractured the glass, which then pierced the skin of the throat, thus bringing cyanide and blood into direct contact. The immediate effect was apparently rather like that of splitting the skull with a battle-axe. I concealed this capsule in its small casing in the lining of my jacket and felt ready for anything. It had a most comforting moral effect on me.

Another important thing was to avoid everything which could attract attention. The hardships of everyday life made this easy, as we were all getting thinner and thinner and our clothes grew shabbier all the time. The address of my lodging was guarded with the utmost secrecy and only a very few specially selected people knew of it. I always left the house in the morning when the streets were filled with people going to work, and I did that every day, whether I had anything to do that morning or not. The people in my flat were to think that I had a normal full-time job. Avoidance of the centre of the city and public restaurants became an absolute necessity.

But all these primitive security measures would never have been sufficient. You had to keep your eyes open continuously, and watch what was going on around you. You could at any moment be taken in a mass street-raid, run into a police patrol or enter a watched house.

When our work had been developed on a large scale, I decided to send a courier to the Polish authorities abroad. I chose one of the younger officers, Lieutenant Ledochówski. I gave him a written report on the situation and told him: "You will see General Sikorski's representative in Hungary. You will tell him that it was my intention to report to General Sikorski in Paris. I am doing this now from Cracow, placing myself and the men who have accepted my leadership at his disposal, in the conviction that the fight should continue on our home territory. You will ask him, in my name, for further orders. You will direct his attention to the fact that military organisations are springing up all over the country and that their efforts should be co-ordinated."

He was back in a few weeks, after an exhausting secret journey. He had had to get over the mountains, which were then covered with snow-drifts; they were not easy to negotiate in normal times. In that same year Ledochówski crossed the frontier several times as a courier to and from Hungary.

Soon after, we decided, with Rudnicki, to contact the organisation being built up in Warsaw by General Tokarzewski and to accept his orders, as we learned that he had subordinated himself to the Commander-in-Chief. We were all taking such careful precautions by now, however, that it was extremely difficult to get into touch with another organisation without contact addresses and passwords. I succeeded, however, in contacting Colonel "Rog," who had been sent from Warsaw by General Tokarzewski to start a section of their organisation in Cracow. We agreed that there should be only one military organisation, so Rudnicki and I left for Warsaw.

The journey between Cracow and Warsaw was very difficult in those days. The Germans were putting into practice their plans for forced labour by a general call-up. All men without so-called legal documents were held, after country-wide check-ups. Searches were especially frequent and concentrated on the railways. Documents once again became of primary importance.

I was furnished with a certificate stating that I was an agent dealing in the purchase of wood for coffins. It was useful to a certain extent, as it covered my movements around Cracow; but the alleged work was not the sort to exempt me from deportation for forced labour in the Reich. Still less would it justify a journey from Cracow to Warsaw: it would have been difficult to explain why coffin wood was more procurable in the capital than elsewhere.

Colonel Rudnicki and I then decided that a certain measure of risk was unavoidable, and we chose to take it. Our German was good, and accordingly we bought two tickets for Warsaw at the booking office reserved for Germans. Our tickets were for sleeping cars, also strictly reserved for Germans. Obviously, no Pole would ever dare infringe this law. In consequence, we travelled in comfort and peace and were well looked after by the German waiters and attendants.

This was my first visit to Warsaw since the September siege. The city still bore marked traces of the fighting and presented a sad sight. About a fifth of the capital had been destroyed. Squares and courtyards were filled with graves of people killed during the bombing and fighting.

There was no electricity, no gas, no fuel. After dusk, the city was plunged into complete darkness. Piles of uncleared rubble lay everywhere. Trams were replaced by horse-drawn carts which for a fee took people from one side of the city to the other.

Rudnicki and I made our way to the art dealer who had been recommended to us by Colonel Rog. There were two girl assistants in the shop. I approached one of them; she was a fair girl whose appearance corresponded with Rog's description.

"I have come about drawing——" I began.

"Do you want a water colour or a pastel?"

"No. I have come about drawing lessons."

After this exchange of passwords, she led us to a room behind the shop, where a liaison girl turned up to fetch us. She took us to our lodging for the night, which was in a flat facing the destroyed Parliament Building. Like everywhere else in Warsaw that winter, it was unheated, and we sat in overcoats and gloves. The owner of the flat, although a member of the Underground and in all probability sworn in, asked us no questions. She did, however, try to warm us with hot supper, for which we were heartily grateful.

Next morning, the same liaison girl came and took me to a private flat. I had again to wait, all the time without the least idea whom I was actually waiting to see. At last the door opened to admit an old friend, Colonel Rowecki. It turned out that he was General Tokarzewski's Chief of Staff.

He had much to tell me. It appeared that he was already in receipt of orders from France. He explained that General Tokarzewski had been ordered by General Sikorski to go to the Soviet-occupied zone, and was busy preparing for his departure to Lwów and his work as Underground commander in the Soviet zone. He would take Rudnicki with him as Chief of Staff.

The German-occupied zone was to be taken over by Rowecki. Both territories, according to General Sikorski's orders, were to come under the command of General Sosnkowski, who was in Paris working on the organisation of the Underground Army in Poland. This army was then known as "Zwiazek Walki Zbrojnej" (Union of Armed Warfare). It was destined to continue our fight at home and to be an integral part of the Polish armed forces. It was then, also, that the wording of the oath we all had to take was brought from France:

"Before God the Almighty, before the Holy Virgin Mary, Queen of the Crown of Poland, I put my hand on this Holy Cross, the symbol of martyrdom and salvation, and I swear that I will defend the honour of Poland with all my might, that I will fight with arms in hand to liberate her from slavery, notwithstanding the sacrifice of my own life, that I will be absolutely obedient to my superiors, that I will keep the secret whatever the cost may be."

The member of the Underground Army who was swearing in the new soldier had to answer:

"I receive thee among the soldiers of Freedom. Victory will be thy reward. Treason will be punished by death."

I was very happy to have this wording for the national oath. The many small organisations had sworn in their people with various words. Now we had one oath for all and a new bond uniting us—a very important one in a country as religious as Poland.

I told Rowecki that I was ready to serve under his orders. When he had thanked me, he expressed concern over the present situation.

"There are too many different military organisations in Warsaw," he said. "This desire to organise resistance is spontaneous and general. People from various political, professional or social groups are now forming separate centres. Sometimes they link up together. But they have all gone underground and formed para-military groups. It is an excellent symptom, but the splitting of effort is a potential danger. Just imagine a general uprising by numerous different groups, each acting independently," he concluded rather desperately. He paused and then continued: "My orders are to unite them all under my command. But I have no means of enforcing such a measure. There are no steps I can take towards it. All I have is the authority of the Polish Government abroad, and this is of necessity a moral authority only, and the future alone can show whether it is sufficiently strong to overcome political differences as well as personal ambitions and unite the whole nation."

I replied, in all sincerity, that I had no doubts as to the outcome, and based my optimism on the fact that the attitude of the nation had so far, even without guidance, been homogeneous. No political group had shown the slightest inclination to remain passive towards the new order, let alone to collaborate with the Germans. Clearly, no quislings were forthcoming. The Sikorski Government would therefore be the only authority—unmolested by any rival. True, the Communists might try to organise some rival faction. But their numbers had been small, even before the war, and since the agreement between Germany and Russia they had maintained complete silence and shown no activity of any sort against the Germans. Perhaps this was due to the fact that the majority of the Communist leaders had, in fact, moved into the Soviet zone of occupation, where they took important posts in the Soviet administration. Their ranks, never strong, were thus further weakened. In these circumstances, I concluded, no division of the nation was discernible, and the military unification of the country was therefore bound to meet with success.

In general, the aims of our Army were to prepare for an armed rising and, more immediately, to support the Allied effort by sabotage and diversionary activity and above all by maintaining an intelligence service. Rowecki offered me command of Warsaw, which he wanted me to take over in a few weeks. Rog was to take the command of the Cracow province. We fixed another meeting a few weeks ahead, and arranged our means of liaison.

On my return to Cracow, new tasks awaited me. A courier came from Hungary bringing an order signed by General Sikorski and General Sosnkowski, entrusting me with the command of the German-occupied southern region of Poland. I went back to Warsaw to see Rowecki, who agreed to obey the orders from France. He then made Colonel Rog Commander for Cracow, and an officer with the *nom-de-guerre* of "Starosta," Commander for Silesia. Both were to act under my orders.

Silesia had been incorporated into the Reich by the Germans and was separated from Cracow by a police frontier, which it was extremely difficult for a Pole to cross legally. Before the war the population of Silesia had included a German minority speaking both languages. The presence of this minority, now strengthened by elements from Germany, enabled the Gestapo to keep a close watch on the Polish population. Any stranger attracted the immediate attention of the authorities. The post of commandant of the province was not an easy one to fill or to operate.

This was why Starosta, himself a Silesian, was chosen. Remarkable for his exceptional courage and self-sacrifice, he entered Silesia armed with the papers of a Gestapo officer. He was obliged to change his headquarters incessantly. The Silesians sheltered him. Roughly once a month he used to come to Cracow and report on his progress, at the same time receiving further orders.

In Cracow my immediate associates were necessarily few,

my Chief of Staff being Cichocki, a major who went by the name of "Jaś."

One evening in January, 1940, to my astonishment, Rudnicki opened the door of my lodging to me. He said there was a lady waiting in my room. I assumed that it must be Maria. We had arranged that she should call at my place only when danger was threatening. I was therefore rather apprehensive as I entered the room, only to find Renia, my wife, sitting on the sofa!

It had been difficult for her to get to me. From our estate near Lwów she had been evacuated to the east; then, after the arrival of the Bolsheviks, she had returned to Lwów. She had no news of me. At last she heard I had gone to Hungary. She immediately tried to do the same, was caught by the Russian secret police, interrogated and freed as by a miracle, because she told them that she was an artist, and Soviet propaganda makes much of the protection extended to artists. She left Lwów again soon after and spent a few rather difficult weeks in a small place on the San, without being able to cross the river. It was not until January that she succeeded in getting over. And there she was.

She gave me many details about what was going on beyond the San. What she said was not very comforting. Both invaders had one aim in common—to finish off the Poles. But while the Germans were trying simply to exterminate us, the methods of the Russians were very different. It was not the physical existence but the morale of a free-born and free-bred nation they were trying to weaken and to break. They were penetrating into private life in an amazingly cunning way. Those they could not hope to influence were not hanged or shot in market places, but simply disappeared into prisons or were deported to Russia. There had been no mass deportations till then, though there was some talk of them. So far there had only been mass arrests of reserve officers, but the outlook was very black.

When Renia found me in Cracow, she understood at once what I was doing without my having to tell her much about it. It was quite clear that we could not live under the same roof. In my work everything had to be subordinated to safety. But Renia was very firm on one point: she wished to serve in the Underground—if only in the most modest capacity. I refused. Cracow was not a large city and we were known to many people there. It was obvious that the Gestapo would soon trail my wife, once they had tracked me down. I considered it would be safer if she kept quite clear of the Underground. But she would not give in. "I have no children, I can take the risk," she explained. So she stayed—and worked.

She evolved a type of work of her own invention. Many of our friends were then in P.O.W. camps in Germany. Their only source of information, if it can be called such, was German propaganda. Every line of their letters revealed melancholy depression.

My wife embarked on a very active and large-scale correspondence with these men. At first, the letters were quite innocuous. Later, in addition to the letters, she started to send the prisoners books, a step permitted by the Germans. Then she began a simple code. In place of the date on postcards, she would insert the number of a page in a book. On the page indicated, faint, inconspicuous dots were put over letters, so that whole sentences were gradually built up. By this means real news got through.

Many of the initial efforts to send them the truth were wasted. They did not grasp the ruse at once. But a friend of ours in one camp had been a cryptographer in the Intelligence Service before the war, and he was the first to catch on.

Renia and I met rarely. We had stolen moments on occasional Saturdays and Sundays. At that time we had little to eat, although the shops were full of excellent food—"for Germans only." All that Poles could get on ration cards was little more than a piece of revolting bread, made with something more like clay than flour, and the black market was too expensive for us.

When Renia was asked where I was, she spread the news that I was abroad with the army in France. The wife of an officer who was in France triumphantly brought her a piece of news one day: "Your husband has already arrived where he wished to be," she whispered.

"You don't know how happy you make me," said Renia promptly, "but how in the world did you get to know it? I have no news whatever."

"Oh, that's quite simple. I got the news through the International Red Cross from my husband, who is in France. '*My former commander is with us,*' he wrote."

My wife kissed the good lady without saying a word. The

latter, evidently thinking she was speechless with joy, pressed her hand and went off proud and happy. From that day on we had proof positive that I was abroad with the Army, owing to the lucky circumstance that her husband had more than one former commander. . . .

Soon after this Rudnicki left us, after completing his preparations for the work ahead of him in the Soviet-occupied zone. I well remember the night he turned up at Maria's flat to bid us farewell. He was dressed in a workman's clothes, as he planned to move about in the Soviet zone thus. He was normally a gay person, but that evening he was ominously subdued and depressed, as though he felt a premonition of what lay ahead. His money for the trip consisted of two 20-dollar gold pieces, one in the heel of each shoe.

I never saw him again on Polish territory. Our next meeting was to be in 1945, when he was commanding the 1st Polish Armoured Division with the British armies invading Germany and reported to me, lately liberated from a P.O.W. camp in Germany, as his Commander-in-Chief. His intended journey to Lwów led him much further than he expected. Very soon after crossing the frontier into the Soviet zone, he was arrested by the N.K.V.D. while trying to board a train at his first railway station. He had his story ready: he was a worker fleeing from the Germans to the Soviet zone. A long and arduous interrogation failed to prove anything against him. But he was condemned to several years' deportation to Siberia for having crossed the border illegally. There he worked in a brick factory, cutting wood for the furnaces, until the outbreak of war between Russia and Germany and the Soviet-Polish Pact in 1941 set him free. He reported to General Anders, who was then forming a Polish army on Russian soil, and accompanied him through the Italian campaign. Our reunion in 1945 was typical of many Poles whose war activities led them far afield before throwing them together again. General Tokarzewski also was arrested after having reached the Soviet occupation zone. He too went through great sufferings before he was freed in 1941.

In Cracow, one of the greatest difficulties of our organisation at the outset was money. It was not until the very end of 1939 that the first financial help reached us from outside, when the Polish authorities in Hungary sent in a considerable sum by a special courier patrol. The party crossed the Hungarian

B

frontier successfully, but while negotiating the Slovakian border into Poland they ran into a German frontier patrol. The Germans sent out police dogs and our men had to jettison their valuable packages. Some of them were thrown into a cottage garden belonging to an old peasant woman. The Germans threw a cordon round the whole district and conducted a minute search, but the only money they succeeded in finding was in the packets discarded on the main road.

Later, when things had calmed down, the farm woman retrieved the packages and took them by night to the house of a large estate nearby. The lady of the house had no connection with the Underground and had no idea how to set about delivering the money to its rightful destination. After some hesitation, she took the money to Archbishop Sapieha in Cracow. She told him the circumstances in which the money had been found and asked him either to keep it safely or to give it to some charity. The Archbishop had no means of knowing the origin of the money, and he feared it might be the proceeds of some robbery. Accordingly, he refused to accept it. It was just as she was leaving the Archbishop's house that the lady, quite by chance, met an old friend of hers, Maria Krzeczunowicz, who listened eagerly to the story. She then told her friend the true story of the money and persuaded her to hand it over to its rightful owners, the Underground. Thus it was that we received our first official funds, amounting to about 250,000 zlotys—a considerable sum in those days. The Germans got the rest.

Later on we had help again in a rather surprising form. Maria was visited one day by an elderly, very corpulent nun, beaming with jollity and good humour. On entering, she asked a question which increased Maria's astonishment. It was the password of the couriers coming from Hungary. Then she smiled at a man who happened to be in the room and said, "Would you mind going out?" When he had done so, she said to Maria, "I really cannot undress in a man's presence."

"But why in the world do you want to undress?" Maria burst out.

The visitor beamed again. "Wait and see." And she began to unfasten and to unbutton the different and rather intricate parts of her voluminous habit, producing bit by bit a lot of flat parcels with which she was padded. When she had finished a lot of money was lying on the table.

"But where did you get them from?"

"That's quite simple. From the Hungarian frontier. Who would suspect a poor old nun?" she went on. "And then, after all, if they had caught me, it would not have mattered so much. Only it would have been a pity to lose such a lot of money."

Then, a little less corpulent, and smiling once more, "God bless you all," she left the flat. So we again had money, but, what was worse, the Germans became aware of the fact that a large part of the pre-war Polish notes, which had been taken out of the country by the administrative officers and private individuals, was now being brought back secretly. An order was issued: all notes of 100- or 500-zloty denominations were to be restamped.

This put our funds in jeopardy. The money had to be saved, so I went for help to Surzycki, who was manager of an alcohol manufacturing company. He acted promptly. He picked out one of his cashiers and took him into the secret. Part of his duties consisted in taking large sums of money daily to the bank, and the idea was that over a period he should try to smuggle our notes in as well. As this was not sufficient, we had to find other illegal ways to save our funds. During one of these visits to the bank, one of our men was discovered, arrested and sent to a concentration camp.

The German authorities became more suspicious, and gradually became convinced that the headquarters of the regional organisation might well be in Cracow. They were helped considerably by careless talk. In those early days, people had not yet learned to recognise the danger of talking. Conspiratorial discipline, so necessary to any underground movement, had not yet been achieved.

We were hardly surprised, in the circumstances, to see a new poster on the walls of Cracow; it appeared simultaneously in Warsaw and other places. Part of it ran as follows:

"To the non-German inhabitants of the General Government:

"The same men who provoked this war and dragged you to the depths of misery have now started to organise a conspiracy against German authorities and wish to bring fresh misfortunes upon you. You are hereby warned that every attempt at rebellion will be drowned in a sea of blood."

At the same time, all Polish officers were ordered to register with the German authorities on pain of death. The same threat faced all those who sheltered officers.

I forbade officers under my command to comply with this German demand. It was not easy for them, though. They were placed in a most difficult position with regard to the families with which they were living. In some cases, in an effort to reconcile their position with their conscience, they told the people with whom they were living the truth about their rank and present activity. In no cases did I hear of any officer being refused shelter. All my officers were provided with false documents and pseudonyms. The forging of personal papers had now reached a high standard of efficiency.

In those days danger approached me closely for the first time. The Germans arrested Captain Poziomski at Kielce, where he was working in the Underground. A few days after his disaster, I heard that 400 hostages, drawn from every walk of life, had been arrested in Kielce—landowners, lawyers, teachers, priests and smallholders. The whole town was deeply stirred. Four hundred families lived in anxiety and despair over the fate of the hostages. Naturally, I did not connect this news in any way with myself.

The Gestapo beat and tortured Poziomski, but he defended himself as best he could, trying to betray or say as little as possible. After a certain time, he was taken from his cell and appeared before the chief of the Gestapo in Kielce, who offered him his freedom for a week in order to locate my whereabouts. Four hundred Polish hostages would pay with their lives for his failure.

Poziomski was then taken to the market place in Cracow in a prison van and released for the week. He was, quite understandably, plunged into deep despair; there seemed to be no way out of the terrible quandary. In his dilemma, he decided to seek the advice of an old friend, a retired officer. By chance, the officer's daughter, "Mary," was at home, and she, quite unknown to her family, was a member of the Underground. Poziomski arrived in a state of complete exhaustion, both physical and mental, and told them his story. Mary listened breathlessly, trying not to show her intense agitation. When she had heard it all, she decided on immediate action.

That same evening my wife was surprised to hear a knock at the door, and even more astounded when she admitted Mary, trembling with nervous excitement.

"What on earth are you doing out on the streets after curfew time?" she asked.

Mary cut her short. "Your husband is in immediate danger," she burst out. "He must leave Cracow at once—disappear altogether."

My wife tried to calm her while in short, excited phrases, Mary told her story. Poziomski, after all, did not know my address. All the same, I was very grateful to Mary for her prompt warning, for it gave me time to review the situation. I considered that Poziomski would not try to find me. Even if he did, he would not succeed. That, however, did not alter the fate of the 400 hostages. I had now to face the question squarely: had I the right to save my own life and continue working at such a price? I put the problem on a broader basis, since it was clearly not I who mattered. I asked myself whether the fight against the Germans, in the circumstances which were now arising (and were likely to grow in dimension and intensity), was not too costly to be continued. For a considerable time I wrestled with my thoughts. But my final conclusion was quite definite.

Put it this way: Supposing I gave myself up to the Germans. Would it help? In a month or two, possibly sooner, the same diabolical blackmail would be applied to my successor—for a successor there would certainly be. If once this method of terror were allowed to succeed, it would be used with increasing frequency until we were forced into complete submission. A few months of German rule had made it quite clear what such submission would mean. Faced with a totalitarian régime, there were only two alternatives: to fight or to surrender. There was no possibility of halfway measures. If we ceased resistance, we should be completely absorbed into the German war machine; that was abundantly evident. Such a step would be tantamount to serving German aims and would be working against our allies. No; this could not be done, whatever the price.

After some time, news reached me that Poziomski had fled; he had been told by Mary that I had gone to Hungary a few months earlier. I was to meet him again, years later, in the Warsaw Underground. After his flight, twenty or thirty hostages were shot according to the German threat, and considerably more were deported to concentration camps; a few were released.

Some days later, I left for Warsaw to meet Rowecki and remained with him a week. Every morning, and sometimes in the afternoon too, I was visited by various chiefs of departments from our G.H.Q. We discussed plans for future activities and the general situation in the country.

German policy towards the Polish people was simple in its ruthlessness. It aimed at the complete annihilation of the more outstanding elements of the Polish nation. The rest was to be reduced to unconditional servitude for the greater glory of the Reich. Private property was deliberately destroyed. Factories, industry, even modern buildings and blocks of flats belonging to individuals were taken over by the Germans. Every means of education was abolished. Universities were closed, secondary schools disbanded. Only lower vocational schools were tolerated so that boys and girls could learn some manual trade—Germany was in need of trained workers. The youth of Poland would have been entirely deprived of education if it were not for the initiative of the Polish people themselves, who, at the risk of great sacrifice and danger, had organised clandestine schooling.

Under German occupation, a Pole had no right to own property, no right to participate in any sort of cultural activity, no right to study. He was only to sweat and labour under the supervision of German slave-drivers. Even so he could never feel safe or be sure to survive. This included everybody, not only the members of the Underground organisation, but also those whose existence was perfectly regular from the German point of view. There was no family in Poland that did not suffer, not one that did not mourn somebody dear, either killed or imprisoned or held in a concentration camp.

All this is difficult to imagine for anyone who was not then in Poland. Only those who, day after day, lived through the tragedy can understand. We in Poland never met the so-called "good Germans." Towards us they were always ruthless tyrants and murderers, intoxicated with victory and out to drain every drop of profit from our subjugated country.

The main topic of our conversations was, however, the question of the German policy of hostages. The Germans had two aims in imposing this system of communal responsibility. In the first place, they tried to force the members of the Underground to consider the fight not worth the appalling cost. And, secondly, they expected to drive a wedge between the population and the Underground; to discredit the leaders of the latter in the eyes of the nation by representing them as responsible for the mass reprisals. Terror is, however, a dangerous weapon. Mass reprisals amounted to the indiscriminate use of terror which affected everybody and produced a feeling of universal danger independent of whether the individual was playing an active part in the fight or not. It was all a matter of luck, since the choice of subjects for the arrests, deportations to concentration camps and executions was made without the slightest discrimination.

In fact, a member of a secret organisation could actually feel safer than others in the circumstances. He had the protection of his organisation's intelligence service, which was often in a position to warn him of approaching danger, and, with his false documents, he was much safer. The method of imposing mass responsibility, striking as it did at the population as a whole, produced a result quite opposite to the one intended. It developed a strong tendency to strengthen the bond uniting the whole nation, increased the general feeling of solidarity and opened all eyes to the necessity for universal co-operation. The results thus produced were ideal for the development of conspiracy.

On the other hand, these particular German methods forced us to act carefully and to adopt widespread precautions. The rule that poison and not revolvers should be used in self-defence, came as a necessary consequence. In such circumstances, a man is not protecting his own life so much as those of the others whom he might betray under torture. The second principle which had constantly to be borne in mind was that every act directed against the Germans had to be of vital importance and be necessitated by a strong reason clearly understandable to every Pole. We were forced to avoid any action dictated merely by desire for revenge or inspired by hatred and deprived of any deeper military significance.

A representative type of work undertaken by the Underground during the first period of occupation was sabotage on the railways. The number of railway engines to be sabotaged each month was fixed by headquarters in Warsaw in a monthly programme. It became necessary to create special units for that purpose. Special instructions for this work were developed and printed with the collaboration of engine-drivers and engineers. Only such methods as could not be proved to have been sabotage were adopted, and they were gradually improved upon. In 1940, the average period of disablement for each engine damaged was fourteen hours; in 1942 the period had risen to five days; by 1943 to fourteen days.

A specially prepared chemical product was added to the grease in the greasing-box. Only ten days later, our observers in railway maintenance shops all over Poland reported that about 200 engines had had to be withdrawn from circulation, some for three days, some for three months, according to how soon the engine-driver in each case realised that something was out of order. The Germans were quite unable to diagnose the cause. For nearly three weeks, rail traffic in Poland was completely disorganised; a large number of trains had to be withdrawn, and delays in the timetable often passed the twenty-four hour mark.

Another railway objective was the material being sent by Russia across Poland to Germany. At that time Russia was helping Hitler considerably in his fight against the West. Russia's main exports to Germany were oil, coal, cotton wastes and ores. One of the regular lines used for this traffic ran through Przemyśl, Cracow and Breslau—that is to say, across my region. The Germans had developed this line and made it capable of an increased turnover in order to get the supplies through more quickly. Przemyśl Station (on the demarcation line fixed by the Molotov-Ribbentrop Agreement) had been rebuilt and enlarged, and here, therefore, the Germans had made special installations for loading supplies.

Two or three trains of petrol wagons passed along the line every day. For the destruction of these, we used incendiary bombs of our own production. A container charged with explosive was fixed on a pneumatic lever. One movement of the hand was sufficient to fix the bomb firmly under the tank-car. A somewhat primitive clockwork attachment fixed the moment of detonation; it was worked by the rhythm of the train going over sleepers. Thus we could time the distance from Przemysl at which the explosion would take place. Germans never knew where the sabotage had originated, in Poland or Germany.

In the case of ore transport, the job was even simpler. A small container could easily be placed between the chunks of ore in the open trucks; the explosion usually occurred when the ore was going down the chutes into the furnaces, thereby damaging the furnace installations.

In all matters of sabotage and diversionary activity, the initiative and actual method of execution were usually left to those who were to carry out the job—the lower levels of the organisation. The correct procedure could only be decided upon and adopted with full knowledge of the circumstances on the spot, but the men who actually did the job were not in possession of the necessary means. For example, in the case of the sabotaging of the lubricating oil reserve, we were informed that it could be damaged by the workers at the supply point. But they were not in possession of the requisite chemicals. It was our job to make contact with the group of chemists who were working with us. After a month's concentrated work, 100 kilogrammes of the chemical required were concealed in a tender under some coal and smuggled to the destination, there to be unloaded by rail workers who were in the secret.

In this, as indeed in all our work, I depended on the co-operation of the whole population. Neither one individual nor a group of the best men could be efficient unless supported by the help of others. It was therefore of the utmost importance that our main political parties should reach complete agreement, which, for many reasons, was an intricate and complicated problem to solve.

It was a long time before this aim was definitely realised. Contact with the exiled Government was sometimes difficult (especially after the French collapse). Our main problem was whether, if an Underground civilian authority were created, it should act merely in an advisory capacity to the C.-in-C. of the Underground Army or as a civilian institution on an equal footing with the military command.

Rowecki reported to Paris (March 12th, 1940) that collaboration between the C.-in-C. Underground Army and a civilian Government delegate on equal terms was liable to produce friction which, in a country that was at the same time a battlefield, should be avoided at all cost. Yet the Polish Government decided that the Government delegate should not only have equal authority with the C.-in-C. Underground Home Army, so that two co-ordinated institutions were created, but that in certain questions he would even have powers overruling those of the C.-in-C. This decision was to weigh heavily on the development of the "Secret State" in the future.

In Warsaw work was hampered by the friction Rowecki had foreseen, till at last, in 1943, agreement was reached. As to myself, I must admit that my contacts with "the politicians" in Cracow were very good. We met regularly and always got on very well. The four parties were: National Democratic Party, Peasant Party, Socialist Party and Christian Democrats Party.

Through the political parties, I could reach every class and profession. I was henceforth assured of the co-operation of the trade unions grouped with the Socialist Party, of the masses of country people belonging to the Peasant Party, of the estate-owners, middle classes and artisans who formed the Nationalist and Christian Democrats Parties. For instance, the full co-operation of the Socialist Party brought with it the allegiance of the railway workers. With their help, it was possible to organise a network of railway intelligence covering the whole of Poland and reaching even into the heart of the Reich. In consequence, we were informed of every move and transfer of German forces and supplies, as well as of the current economic position of Germany.

At my suggestion, I met the Interparty Committee to present my plans and the methods by which I proposed to execute them. As a general rule, I never saw more than two or three people at a time; for once, however, the circumstances demanded that eight of us should be present at a meeting. It took place in a monastery in Carmelite Street in Cracow. While we conferred in one of the monks' cells, the monks kept watch inside and outside, ready to warn us of the slightest approaching danger.

I explained the principles which were to govern the co-operation between the Underground Army and the political parties. They were very simple. Each member of the military organisation had the right to belong to whatever party he chose; each had complete freedom to work for the future Poland of his own convictions. In the Underground Army, people of varied political opinions were united in a common aim: the expulsion of the Germans from Poland and the recovery of independence. Therefore, as regards military obligations, each soldier owed obedience to his superiors regardless of whether or not he agreed with their political opinions. This idea proved very successful, as experience was to show.

I stress all this because the Underground Army differed very much in character from the pre-war Polish Army. Then the backbone of the Army was formed of Regular officers, who were not allowed to take any part in political life. The Service had therefore been a self-contained professional group. The Underground Army, on the other hand, was a national one. To it belonged people of all walks of life and professions. Within its ranks were people who had never before handled a gun—often people who had taken a very active part in politics. That such an organisation succeeded was due to the fact that it had one common aim of paramount importance—independence.

The political committee at once took steps to communicate their plans and aims to the Polish Government in France. One of the first couriers was Jan Karski, who was known in Poland by the pseudonym of "Witold." He was chosen for the task because of his extraordinarily retentive memory. He had to meet all the representatives of the four parties and memorise their requests and opinions for transmission to their colleagues abroad. Karski's journey towards the frontier was arranged by one of my units specially trained for the job. A week after his departure from Cracow, I was in conference with Cichocki, Surzycki and Tempka, the leader of the Christian Democrats Party, when news arrived that Karski had been arrested. The situation was doubly serious, in view of Karski's retentive memory. If he gave way under examination, the consequences might well be catastrophic. He knew far too many names and people.

I immediately summoned the head of our organisation in Nowy Sącz, where Karski was being held prisoner. He told me that Karski, fearful of betraying his secrets, had cut the veins of both his wrists. His life had been saved and he had been moved to the prison hospital, from where he had managed to get word out that among other things he had been beaten behind both ears by the Gestapo. Torture had not forced him to reveal anything, but he did stress that, should the Gestapo methods be repeated, he could not guarantee his further silence. Consequently, he begged for poison or help. We could not explain why Karski had no poison on him. Perhaps the Gestapo had taken it from him. Perhaps he had trusted too much in his luck, which had once before held good on a previous journey to Paris and back.

In view of the fund of information in his possession, I took a very serious view of the case. A party was at once dispatched with explicit orders; Karski must under no circumstances be left alive in German hands. Every possible effort should be made to liberate him. Should this fail, suicide should be made possible.

A week later, I received a report that Karski had been successfully removed from the hospital. The story of his release has been told by him in his book, *Story of a Secret State*.

In May, 1940, a conference was held in Belgrade. Two Underground delegates went there from Poland—one from the German and one from the Soviet zone. Three officers were sent from Paris by Generals Sikorski and Sosnkowski. Some important decisions were taken at the conference. Among them was the authorisation for Rowecki, in his position as Commander of the Z.W.Z. (Union of Armed Warfare), to set up military courts with authority to sentence, in the name of the Republic, persons tried and found guilty of treason. It was thus that Underground courts were initiated; they became a State institution based on Polish law.

At the conference, the promotion of Rowecki and myself to the rank of General was announced. We had both previously received documents confirming the appointments we held. They were signed by Generals Sikorski and Sosnkowski and took the form of two slips of silk which were brought in by a courier, who carried them in his mouth enclosed in a rubber capsule.

The distribution of my time, at that stage, was strictly regulated. In the mornings there were Staff meetings. The Staff had talks with the leaders of the various sectors and other contacts from the region. In the afternoons, I had conferences with my Chief of Staff, Jaś, and, when necessary, with various Staff officers. It was then that orders were given.

The centre of the town had to be avoided, and I only moved about in the suburbs. My morning and evening meals were taken at my lodging, and consisted of a plate of gruel and *ersatz* tea with saccharine. Besides my work, I had a hobby to fill the long evenings, which had to be spent at home because of the curfew. It was the study of English. In Poland there was at that time a passion for learning English. The Germans opposed this study almost as fiercely as they attacked our Underground. To be caught selling English grammars or similar books meant at least deportation to a concentration camp. But the general enthusiasm for the language did not diminish. The price of an English book was something like 200 zlotys (about 40 dollars at the pre-war exchange).

A joke going round just then said that the pessimists were learning German, the optimists English, and the realists . . . Russian! Undoubtedly, the optimists were in an overwhelming majority. Indeed, optimism was the dominant note. Everyone expected a rapid German defeat. But I must confess I did not share this optimism, though throughout the five years of war I never doubted the certainty of an ultimate Allied victory.

The Germans too were diligent students of the English language. Only their aims were different. They were preparing for their "future jobs." A German post official in Cracow, boasting before his Polish subordinates about his own importance, produced to prove it a nomination to Postmaster-General—in London.

*   *   *

I had already begun to realise that our future hung on one big question: the real intentions of Soviet Russia and her attitude towards Germany. Her recent political moves seemed to be an answer to this. Russia was treating with Great Britain and France with the aim of stopping Hitler's further aggression. On August 23rd, 1939, to the astonishment of the whole world, the pact known as the Molotov-Ribbentrop Pact was signed. But what even then remained top secret was the additional clause, which only became known in March, 1946. The signatories had divided the booty among themselves. Russia got one-half of Poland, the Baltic States, Bukovina and Bessarabia.

As late as September 4th, 1939, the Soviet Ambassador in Warsaw, in a talk with our Foreign Minister, promised the delivery of oil, raw materials and arms to Poland. Not quite two weeks later, on September 17th, the Soviet armies marched into Poland and incorporated one-half of the country into the U.S.S.R. On October 31st, 1939, Molotov delivered a speech in the Supreme Council of the U.S.S.R. in which he said: "One decisive blow from the German and the Russian Armies against Poland and nothing remained from that ugly litter of the Versailles Treaty. Neither British nor French guarantees could help Poland."

In becoming Hitler's ally, Stalin had a deep political motive. By this agreement, he not only encouraged, but even helped Hitler to attack Poland and so launched the Second World War. He seemed decided then not to take any further part in the fight, but to wait fully armed until the adversaries had bled each other to death, which would give him the opportunity of a Communist conquest of Europe.

From the Soviet-occupied zone of Poland came news of mass deportations. All classes were involved, as well as a small number of Ukrainians and Jews. In February all eastern Poland saw mass deportations of Polish peasants. They were usually taken at night, after Soviet soldiers had surrounded the villages to prevent any escape. Sometimes they were taken out of their beds just as they were and kept standing outside in weather 36–45 degrees below freezing-point (−20–25° C.). In other cases they were treated more "humanely": an hour was left to them for dressing and packing a bundle of their most important belongings. Then they were put into trains, seventy-five to eighty in a freight car. The cars were tightly closed and well guarded. Sometimes, though not always, the deported were allowed to hand out the dead when the train halted on the long journey. In particular, many frozen children were left lying beside the railway tracks. When several of these trains were concentrated on a larger station, they moved slowly eastward, accompanied by the sound of patriotic and religious songs from the deported, *en route* to Siberia and Inner Asia for forced labour.

In the German-occupied zone the Communists refrained from activity, thereby showing that the Soviet were prepared to stand by their agreement with Germany. In March, 1940, my staff received information that a N.K.V.D. mission had come to Cracow to work out with the Gestapo the methods they were jointly to adopt against Polish military organisations. The N.K.V.D. was already aware that Polish military resistance was centralised and directed throughout Poland from one headquarters. The consultations in Cracow lasted for several weeks. I received reports of the discussions, the names of those present and their addresses. Apparently the N.K.V.D. methods for combating our Underground were greatly admired by the Gestapo, and it was suggested that they should be adopted in the German zone.

And indeed there was no doubt about the superiority of the

N.K.V.D. methods over those of the Gestapo. They were a hundred times more dangerous and efficient. In every country in the world, there are criminals and a greater or smaller number of opportunists prepared to co-operate with any government authority, regardless of its morality. During the whole five years the Germans seldom succeeded in persuading anyone to a flagrant act of treachery. In the Soviet zone, the situation was quite different. For there, the possibility of concealing opportunism by a change of political opinion existed. Using social slogans instead of national ones, the Russians were able to find quislings and to infiltrate deep into the life of the nation. Before the war, the number of Communists in Poland was very small. The opportunists who increased their ranks after the Russians had entered Poland were, I suppose, not very numerous either. They were, however, very cleverly and thoroughly exploited by the Russians. The mainspring of Soviet police tactics was their efforts to spread mutual distrust amongst the population. The result was that while the German methods unified and strengthened the nation, those of the Soviet weakened and split it. In the Russian zone, even old friends never revealed their political feelings to each other and everyone was the prey of suspicions.

In April, 1940, Karolina Lanckorońska, a lecturer at Lwów University, turned up in Cracow. She was a member of the Lwów Underground and had managed somehow to escape a mass arrest of her comrades. She reported on trials, deportations and executions of men who had been tried and condemned by Soviet courts according to Soviet law for deeds committed on Polish territory in free Poland between 1920 and 1939. A Polish judge, a Polish prosecutor or a Polish policeman would be tried and condemned for having sentenced, accused or arrested a Polish Communist in pre-war days. Their prosecution would be based on the Soviet laws on "activity against the interest of the U.S.S.R." She also gave a description of the situation at the University, which was still functioning. The professors were not imprisoned or killed and the University closed, as in Cracow. The Soviets were going at this job with special care. Many new professors from Kiev had been given chairs in Darwinism, Leninism, Stalinism, etc., and many of the pre-war chairs, especially in law and philosophy and history, had become vacant and had been suppressed.

Lanckorońska's report on the arrests in the Underground showed clearly how very much more difficult our work was under the Soviets. They had spies everywhere who penetrated into every corner of private life.

General Rowecki, who had also taken over command of the Underground movement in the Soviet occupation zone, had to cope with very great difficulties. One commander of the zone after the other fell into the hands of the N.K.V.D., and the ranks of the Underground were constantly decimated. The liaison kept up by couriers was interrupted incessantly and gave meagre results.

Some Poles, however, who had seen how things there really stood, were completely converted from their previous love of Communism.

In the early spring of 1940, we had definite information that the Germans were preparing for an offensive. Hitler was staking everything on this move and German garrisons were withdrawn from Poland and sent to the west. By the beginning of May, the eastern border of the Reich was left practically without defence. In Poland, the German-Soviet demarcation line was guarded only by a few divisions of second-grade German troops.

On May 10th the German invasion of Belgium, Holland and Luxembourg had started. Then the catastrophic events of June, 1940, followed rapidly one after another. Belgium capitulated on May 26th. The main part of the French Army was surrounded and the British Army was in retreat. Each day, the Allied defeat in the west became more evident. And so we turned expectant eyes to the east. At that precise moment, Russia had enormous possibilities in her hands. Knowing the weakness of the comparatively few German troops left in Poland, I had not the slightest doubt that a Soviet attack would encounter no serious opposition. I wondered whether Russia would repeat her manœuvre of September 17th, 1939, this time at Germany's expense. But the Soviet sphinx remained inscrutably silent. On June 14th Paris fell. Three days later, I left Cracow for Warsaw to discuss the situation with Rowecki. It was at Radom that I heard a German military band at the station playing their national anthem, "*Deutschland über alles*." Germans were discussing the news on the station:

"Ten minutes ago Berlin broadcast news of victory. The war's over. France has capitulated. England doesn't count at all. She has no Army. We'll finish her off in ten days. You see if we don't."

Next day I had a long talk with Rowecki. While the slightest spark of hope remained, our organisation would stay in being. We began to consider the new situation. He showed me the last dispatch sent by General Sosnkowski; it had left France after the capitulation. A closer study of the situation seemed to indicate that the defeat of France meant the end of our organisation. The liaison network, built up at the cost of enormous effort, the courier routes to and from France, the means for sending messages and instructions—all these had now collapsed with France. We should be without funds from abroad, probably for a very long time. All our plans were collapsing also. We had been preparing for a general rising. In April, we had received from Generals Sikorski and Sosnkowski detailed orders for this step, based on the assumption that sooner or later the German western front would crack, giving us a favourable opportunity for a successful insurrection. Now the chances of such an opportunity occurring seemed remote, to put it mildly. All logical basis for hopes of a German defeat had now gone. We wondered how the people would react. In less than one year they had had to bear two very heavy blows. We both realised that Underground fighting in our difficult circumstances and at the cost of such heavy losses as we were suffering could only be continued on the basis of faith in final victory. There was the danger that this faith might now waver and resistance end.

Discussing all this, we came to some fundamental conclusions. Our work must be switched over to a long-term policy. Our main task now would be intelligence work and Press and propaganda action. The turn of events had increased its importance considerably. Poland was now the only country with a resistance movement. A well-organised intelligence service in eastern Europe and on Reich territory could supply Great Britain with information of the utmost value. As regards our own people in Poland, we rated propaganda work as the most important task. We proposed to strengthen it by an Underground Press, with a view to maintaining the morale of the people through this critical stage.

At the time of the collapse of France, membership of the organisation, in my region alone, had reached a figure of about 40,000. The new situation necessitated going deeper underground. One of its consequences was a restriction in the recruiting of new members and a decrease in existing groups. An inevitable characteristic of conspiracy is that it cannot continue as such for a long period. After a time, its members unavoidably become known as conspirators to their immediate neighbours. Neither could a mass movement like ours continue to be kept secret.

My talk with Rowecki was prolonged. I wanted to return to Cracow that same day, but I was prevented because of a sudden ban on rail travel. All trains were being employed on the feverish transport of German troops from west to east. It was not yet a question of concentrating forces for an attack on Russia; only fifteen divisions were involved. But the German High Command had decided that they would be running too great a risk by leaving their eastern front unguarded any longer.

The ensuing six months were certainly the most critical period for the Polish Underground. True, the fears of Rowecki and myself were not confirmed by the facts. General Sikorski got safely to England with his Government and the greater part of his fighting forces. Even in this dark hour, no quisling government was formed in Poland. I think, as a nation, Poles have this positive quality, probably developed by the course of their history—they can keep up their endurance and spirit in the most sombre days, and they have survived many such through the centuries.

A new kind of moral support appeared. Prophecies of all kind passed from hand to hand, either handwritten or typed, and became immensely popular. As a matter of fact, we wrote quite a lot of them ourselves; it was our solution to the present dilemma, for we could hardly bolster up optimism with any logical arguments just then. Recourse to the imagination was considerably easier and had the desired effect.

One evening one of my messenger-girls came to me very excited:

"The English were over Cracow last night; they dropped leaflets. I've got one here."

With trembling hands, she took out a tiny wad of paper, which she unfolded and unfolded until it turned into a leaflet. It contained an appeal by British airmen to the Polish population not to weaken, and it promised an early beginning to a big air offensive against the Germans.

"But are you sure that this is really an English leaflet and not a fake," I asked, deliberately. "It might have been done by our own people to cheer us up."

The suggestion obviously shook her. Such a possibility had never entered her head. She thought hard for a bit and examined the leaflet closely. Then she said firmly:

"Quite impossible. The print is English."

The print was by no means English, as a matter of fact. Those leaflets were produced by the Underground Press and had certainly not been dropped by the R.A.F., which at that date had no means of operating as far afield as Poland. Bundles of leaflets had been launched into the air attached to specially constructed small balloons. At a given moment, the balloons released the leaflets, which scattered in the air and fluttered to earth. In the morning there they were, lying about as they had fallen. The result was a major sensation among Germans as well as Poles.

The second half of 1940 brought us a measure of failure and the arrest of several of my subordinates. One of the first victims was Surzycki, in September. A stenographer who used to copy documents stolen from a German administrative office for him was caught in the act and under torture she disclosed Surzycki's identity. His house was surrounded and careful search made. His mother, an old lady of seventy, who tried to conceal some documents, was discovered and severely beaten. Surzycki was removed to prison. His laundry, which was sent to his wife every fortnight, bore traces of blood and torture. He seemed a very weak man physically and he was in an advanced stage of tuberculosis, yet his powers of resistance were tremendous. After four weeks of imprisonment, he managed to get a message out of the prison; it ran as follows: "I have betrayed no one. Carry on with your work. Long live Poland." He was sent the same day to a concentration camp, where he died some months later. His friend, Tempka, leader of the Christian Democrats in Cracow, was to follow him soon.

Not long afterwards I was visited by a young officer from Silesia. When I had greeted him and asked him his news, I noticed his expression, and his torn and dirty clothes.

"Starosta is dead and the staff dispersed," he said. "I only got here by a sheer miracle."

The Gestapo, after twelve months of vain effort, had finally succeeded in discovering the hiding-place of our commander in Silesia. The house at Wisła was surrounded by police. Starosta barricaded the doors and windows to gain time to destroy all compromising papers and he tried to escape by the chimney. He was shot when jumping from the balcony to the street. Most of his men were arrested the same night, my informant being the only one who had managed to escape.

I asked him whether he was prepared to return to Silesia at once, and he nodded in silence. He left to hand over the command to the officer I had appointed. But Starosta's successor lived only three months. Five consecutive commanders of the Silesia sector were arrested in the space of two years. There was, nevertheless, never the slightest difficulty in finding a successor.

Moving about Cracow had by now become more dangerous. Accordingly I had to elect one place where I could remain in safety, talk to my subordinates when necessary and hold small meetings. My choice fell on a stationery shop belonging to a member of the Underground called Gedgowd. I was taken on as an assistant and officially registered with the German Labour Office under the name of Wolański. It provided excellent cover. I was in possession of real German documents and had no need to wander about the town. I spent the whole morning in the shop. My Chief of Staff, section leaders and liaison officers visited me as customers. No better camouflage could have been found. But it was here that I was to meet the greatest disaster suffered by the Underground in Cracow.

In the spring of 1941 one of the leaders of railway sabotage was arrested in Cracow. He was in close touch with my Chief of Staff, Jaś. Immediately after the arrest, I sent for Jaś and asked him whether the arrested man knew his address. Jaś said he did not. "He never came to my home," he assured me.

But Jaś was wrong. True, the arrested man had never called on him at home, but he had the address in his diary, having once sent coal there. During the night, the Gestapo arrived. They asked the doorman to which flat the coal had been delivered. The man said he did not know. They then resorted to their usual tactics of torture. After an hour the Germans were in Jaś's flat. They did not remove him, but stayed there with him, ambushing anyone who might call. Jaś was expected at a meeting at nine o'clock next morning. His failure to turn up caused acute anxiety. A liaison girl, sent to reconnoitre, fell into the hands of the Gestapo. When she did not return, an officer started out in the direction of the flat, observing every precaution. As he approached the street, he became aware that the road was full of spies, so he turned round and tried to walk away. At once someone shouted "Halt!" He did his best to make a dash for it, but was shot in the knee. It appeared that he was spotted by a Gestapo woman who was watching the street from a parked car.

I was as yet ignorant of what had happened. Usually Jaś came to see me about lunchtime. He did not turn up, of course, but it was not till the evening that I learned the truth. Orders were sent out at once. No meeting places or lodgings known to Jaś or the other arrested men were to be used again, and even the families of the prisoners were to leave their flats. I gave these instructions to the officer who brought the news of the arrests. He was to report to me the following morning, but he did not turn up at the appointed time. He had himself been arrested with sixteen others from our staff.

That morning, when I arrived at the shop, I found Gedgowd with a black eye and obvious traces of misadventure. I asked him what had happened.

"I was in a tram accident," he replied.

At the same moment I saw a man of typical German appearance in plain clothes. He said: "Yes, yes. We will examine the question."

Gedgowd gave me a quick, desperate look. Through the shop window I could see a civilian in the street who looked suspiciously like an agent. So the shop was observed as well. There was no hope of leaving by the street. A moment later a second Gestapo man appeared, and shortly afterwards all three went away. As they went, one of the Germans turned round and said to me: "Now you stay here and take care of everything. We'll soon be back."

I was left in the shop. The Gestapo man in plain clothes was still in the street. I could not leave. I wondered whether I had been spared by a miracle or whether I was just left there as a decoy. Suddenly my wife walked in; she had heard in town that Gedgowd had been arrested. I was furious when I saw her. It was perhaps an illogical reaction, but it was how I felt; I could be arrested at any moment, and to see her in the same danger was too much for me.

"Get out of here at once," I hissed at her.

"I'll go," she replied; "but you come with me."

"I won't. I am expecting people whom I have to warn, and I can't close the shop at eleven in the morning with the Gestapo in the street watching me. Go, I say."

She slipped a scrap of paper into my hand, gave me an imploring look, and went. The paper bore the address of K. Lanckorońska. She had moved into a new flat the day before, so the address was not known to those arrested during the last two days. Renia had thought of that because she knew that Gedgowd had got me my last flat, so that my address and *alias* were well known to him. From there she went to the Red Cross, where Lanckorońska was working, to warn her to expect me, and then she returned to me. I told her about more arrests I had heard of in the meantime, and sent her away again. She went, but hid in the gateway of a house not far off, and from there kept watch until she finally saw me lock up the shop and walk away, the Gestapo man having disappeared. I had to reach a flat to warn two of my officers.

At my new quarters, I at once contacted Rog, who had also escaped arrest, and together we made a list of the officers and women couriers who had been arrested. The list grew longer hour by hour. It was a fundamental principle of our security plan to assume that everybody arrested would, under torture, reveal what he or she knew. Naturally, they did not all do so, but we had to work on the assumption that they would.

The arrests had been made in almost every branch of the organisation, so that most of our key men who were still at large lived in a continual state of apprehension. The main object of the search was to find me. In the circumstances, I ordered that all our work should be suspended, except for the alarm system, which continued to warn members of further arrests and impending danger.

Rog and I kept the situation under review, but it soon became clear that I could no longer do any useful work in Cracow. All my ingenuity and energy would be used up in avoiding arrest. Messages reaching us from the prisons warned us that some of our arrested members had given way under continued torture and had betrayed the names of their colleagues. One of these was Gedgowd, who knew far too much about me. I could not hope to evade capture. Rog had some friends with an estate not far from the town, and he persuaded me to go there and live in concealment until the storm had passed. My future host was a major of the reserve called Kleszczynski who had succeeded in escaping from a group of prisoners of war in the first weeks of the war.

My wife brought a bag with my personal belongings to the city boundary. I parted from her with great anxiety, for I realised that she would be hunted as relentlessly as I had been. We arranged that she should leave Cracow shortly and take refuge in the Carpathians. Having worked out indirect methods of communication, we parted without any idea when we would meet again. Only a few days after I left Cracow the Gestapo raided my last lodging. To their intense annoyance, they discovered that I had gone. Soon after, the news trickled out of prison that my name and data were known to the Gestapo, who were even said to have my photograph.

On the way to my temporary refuge my host told me that nobody there suspected who I was. He had told them I was the agent of a friend's estate in western Poland and that I had been expelled by the Germans. His country house, like most others that the Germans, by chance, had not confiscated, had become a refuge for many families evicted from those parts of western Poland incorporated into the Reich. The Germans considered all private property belonging to the Poles in those areas as loot; they accordingly seized houses, furniture and land, even from peasant smallholders, and expelled the now destitute owners to the General Government. Thus this small country house was sheltering several scores of expelled families, who were all being fed and kept by my host. Life on the estate was a striking contrast to the conditions in which I had been living in Cracow. During my whole stay in the country I never saw a single German.

One meeting I had there was an immense and unexpected surprise for me. One of the Underground workers, Orzelski, a Socialist, had been arrested some time ago in Cracow. All we knew was that he had been tortured, but had not given in. Then he had been deported to Oswiecim concentration camp. Now one day, most unexpectedly, he turned up. It was mere chance, as he was on his way from one farm to another. At first I could not believe my eyes, but it *was* Orzelski, tired, ill, worn out, but dignified and in complete control of himself. I asked him how he had managed to get away.

"It's quite simple," he answered. "As you know, I was in Oswiecim, but suddenly, to my horror, I was sent back to Cracow for a new interrogation. I fell ill in prison, and was sent to the St. Lazarus Hospital. There I was well guarded by the police. But your Underground got me out. They brought me clothes and managed to open a locked side-door so that I walked out of the hospital. The authorities were looking for me dressed in my striped hospital pyjamas."

Orzelski told me many details about the things which were going on in prison. Some of my men had revealed my name under torture, and every detail about me was known to the Germans. But there was another thing in this encounter which was a great eye-opener for me. News and details about what was going on in Oswiecim had been leaking out for some time, but Orzelski was the first man I had met who had actually come back from there. His macabre description of horrors now well known to the world, was at that time something quite new and shocking, even after the experience of nearly two years of German occupation. It was Orzelski who first told me about standing to attention nearly naked for hours, working in water up to the chest for weeks, of the murder of every tenth man "as normal punishment," etc.

*　　　*　　　*

I went to Cracow from time to time to meet Rog and give my instructions, so I still had my work in hand. I travelled on a cart as a milkman. A regular meeting of district commanders was held in Warsaw at General Rowecki's headquarters on a fixed day. Up to now I had always attended. It was a point of honour for me to overcome all difficulties and get through to report to our chief on the appointed day. But it was not easy, as an intensive search for me was still going on, and all passenger traffic on the railways had been stopped so that German troops could be transported from west to east as quickly as possible. These troop movements were preparatory to the attack on Russia which was to take place a few months later.

I heard from Cracow that a car had been found for me. It had been hidden in a garage since 1939 to escape confiscation by the Germans, and considerable risk was attached to its use, as it had not got all the necessary documents or licences. But we were lucky and reached Warsaw in safety. We had seen a lot on our way. We had met big German units in battle order, mainly artillery, driving eastward in immense masses of well-trained men and beautiful modern arms. In Warsaw I reported to General Rowecki.

The period preceding Hitler's attack on Russia was a particularly critical time for us. All the countries occupied or threatened by the Nazis were concerned with the questions which were also of vital importance to the British General Staff: Where would Hitler's next blow fall? Who was to be the next victim? On the answer to these questions depended the outcome of the war.

We felt almost certain in the summer of 1940 that the next attack would be directed against the British Isles. Alternatively, the Germans might launch an attack in Africa and the Near East in order to cut British Empire communications. The third possibility, an attack on Russia, seemed to us, at the time, to be the least probable. But late in the autumn of 1940 our Intelligence Service reported that General Brauchitsch, Commander-in-Chief of the German forces, was at Spała. Later reports stated that Reichenau and Kesselring had joined him there. Spała had been a summer residence of the President of Poland. The Germans now used it as the headquarters of the commander of their troops in Poland. The arrival of the Commander-in-Chief of the German forces, followed by that of an army commander and a general of the Luftwaffe, indicated that the Germans were beginning to take a lively interest in eastern Europe. At the same time other messages reached us reporting frequent tours by German missions and staff officers along the whole Ribbentrop-Molotov Line. Fortifications on the Bug and San rivers were started.

All this activity might, of course, only mean that the Germans were taking steps to defend the rear of their main forces, which were to be engaged elsewhere. Nevertheless, we transmitted the information in detail to London by wireless. Meanwhile, nothing in either German or Soviet propaganda seemed to suggest the slightest discord in the perfect harmony between the two countries.

London replied immediately. We were asked to redouble our vigilance and concentrate on securing information. We began at once to comply with this request. Soon all Poland was covered by a close network of observation posts. Members of the Underground from various localities, well acquainted with local conditions, kept German railways, roads, airports, storehouses, dumps and camps under close observation. The work done by Polish railway employees was of incalculable value, as they were devotedly patriotic and knew every secret of the German transport system. Soon the work of our Intelligence branch began to show good results.

German preparations increased so swiftly in volume during the winter of 1940–1 that we could not keep pace with the decoding of reports. A mass of data, often given in great detail, flowed into our Warsaw headquarters. The Germans used all their skill and practical experience to mask their activities and an excuse was given for the construction of every new hospital, airport or store; often they were disguised in some other way. Only when all this information had been assembled and sorted out at our headquarters did the German intention to attack Russia clearly emerge. For instance, the number of hospital buildings and the amount of medical equipment on our territory could not be justified by fears of the most serious epidemics or even by the requirements of other German fronts. Considered in conjunction with the number of newly-built airfields, the great stocks of food, the requisitioning of billets for troops, to mention only a few factors, other conclusions had to be drawn.

Shortly before the beginning of 1941 these preparations were so far advanced that only the troops themselves were lacking for military operations on a scale never before attempted. The mass influx began in February, 1941. The railway employees and road observers sent us remarkably accurate reports of the number of regiments and divisions moving east. The names of generals commanding armies enabled us to identify larger units. We watched with fascination the plans unfolding themselves before our eyes like a drama on the screen.

The British were interested in warning the Russians of the danger of a surprise attack, and all the information we collected was transmitted by them to the Soviet Government. Our intelligence could, however, only be useful if it reached London quickly. This in turn depended on the speed with which reports from the provinces reached Warsaw. From Warsaw these were immediately transmitted by wireless to England. The difficulties were enormous. No civilians at all were allowed to travel by rail, as trains were reserved for the transport of troops. All Polish cars had long since been seized and their use was confined exclusively to Germans. Poles could therefore only travel by bicycle or on foot. We had to make use of every possible means of transmitting information, but we found that railway employees were the quickest and therefore the most satisfactory. Nevertheless, much valuable information was too late owing to the time it took to reach us in Warsaw.

The work at the Underground headquarters differed also considerably from the work of a normal army Staff. Here, too, liaison was the chief stumbling-block. Any headquarters staff work requires discussion on various subjects and the co-operation of different branches. In other words, headquarters should be able to reach out immediately to any point for further information and to call at once on any branch for its particular specialised work. But we could not make use of telephones, nor could we summon meetings of more than two or three people at once. Even detailed correspondence was denied to us.

Everything at headquarters was decentralised as far as possible. This entailed the daily distribution of many batches of correspondence to widely scattered points in Warsaw alone. Women carried out the bulk of this work. They were popularly known as "liaison girls." They came from all classes—rich and poor, young and old, ranging from schoolgirls to grand-mothers.

Every possible form of camouflage was used by the messengers. The Germans did not take long to get wind of these proceedings, and passers-by were often and thoroughly searched; the finding of any compromising material was inevitably followed by interrogation, torture, extortion of information about the origin of the material and usually a death sentence for the victim. In fulfilling this highly responsible and dangerous task, the Polish women gave proof of the utmost devotion and self-sacrifice.

Intermediary points in the distribution were known as "boxes." These were usually in shops or other places where a number of people circulated and detection was therefore more difficult. At the "boxes," the mail was sorted and collected by other messengers at fixed times. In this way, no messenger got to know the identity of his or her colleagues.

The messengers' routes had to be long enough for them to know whether or not they were being followed, thus giving them more chance of shaking off a "shadow," should the need arise.

Before a liaison girl was permitted to start work, she had to undergo a number of trials. She was informed that she would be shadowed by someone unknown to her and she had to shake him off before reaching her destination. She had several routes, and did not know on which of them she would be trailed. With practice, she soon became alert in detecting and observing anything abnormal and able, almost subconsciously, to sense the danger.

Nevertheless, these women were constantly exposed to danger and lived in a perpetual state of nervous strain. Theirs was, consequently, a most exhausting task. To be caught carrying mail was as grave an offence, in German eyes, as to be found in possession of a revolver, and several hundred liaison girls died soldiers' deaths.

In order to diminish the risk, centres were organised whose special task was to devise caches and gadgets which could serve to hide or disguise the objects carried by our messengers. Inventiveness had a wide field for exercise. Special handbags, pocket-books and dispatch cases with double sides and hidden partitions, mirrors, vanity cases, even kitchen utensils and children's toys were used to hide some particular object. Whenever one of them was discovered by the German police, all similar objects had to be withdrawn immediately from circulation and replaced by others. It was a constant battle of wits with the Gestapo and we always found that simplicity of ideas produced the best results.

Wherever we met or worked there had to be adequately disguised hiding-places under floor-boards, in furniture legs, table tops, etc. Thanks to these methods, the Gestapo, even after intensive search, tapping walls, stripping wallpapers, etc., were rarely successful in finding our files and archives.

In the organisation of our postal service, we had to achieve and maintain balance between speed and security. If the security measures were tightened up too much, delays in delivery were the result. On the other hand, added speed meant that less precautions could be taken. Security demanded that each girl should know as few of her colleagues as possible and this, in turn, required many intermediate points. We solved the difficulty by organising two liaison networks: a normal one which worked with relative slowness but greater caution and the other a rush service for such things as warnings of arrests or direct danger to a certain branch.

The service was not concerned only with the delivery of letters and messages, as in ordinary staff work. Other, more difficult material was carried, such as small arms and radio equipment.

A further difficulty was the transmission of such information as plans of fortifications, deployment of troops, prints of new German weapons or samples of German war materials. These had to be sent to London by special couriers.

Before France fell, a regular courier service had been organised between the two countries, the average time taken for a trip being between two and three weeks. And I must record here that the Hungarians helped us greatly in maintaining this service. The fall of France meant the collapse of our carefully prepared system. A journey right across the mainland of Europe and then over the Channel now became necessary.

The first task was to organise new routes and junction points for our couriers. The transmission of dispatches concealed in some object was naturally easier than getting a courier through. Indeed, we soon had a fortnightly through service for dispatches to London.

One of the courier routes ran straight across Europe, through Germany and France, over the Pyrenees and through Spain to Portugal—thence to England by ship or aircraft. Later in the war, British aircraft collected our dispatches from German-occupied French territory and even, on three occasions, from Poland itself. Another route lay through Sweden, and yet another through the Balkans and Turkey to the Middle East.

In the period leading up to the attack on Russia, the people who worked hardest and were in great danger were the wireless personnel. During the attack on Norway, the French campaign, and the fighting in Africa we had found ourselves far away from the theatres of war. But when Hitler decided to attack Russia, we were once more in the centre of events. We were operating at the junction between Russia and Germany and were certainly in a position to influence the course of military events. The Germans realised this also. They proceeded to do all in their power to cut us off completely from the outside world and to make it well-nigh impossible for us to transmit any information to the Allies. Their main attack was directed against our wireless stations.

Before the Germans started their preparations for the attack on Russia, we had sent weekly radio reports to London. Once the preparations were under way, it became necessary to transmit several reports a week, and when the flood of information reached its height several messages had to be sent daily—sometimes as many as twenty.

The Germans formed a special Gestapo department for the detection of transmission sets. Their methods were constantly being improved; mobile detector sets were installed in an increasing number of patrol cars, and they even employed aircraft on the job.

At the beginning, a radio set could function for ten hours in one place before being located. In the final phase, improved detection cut this period of safety down to a bare thirty minutes.

Radio transmission became highly dangerous and nerve-racking. It was a matter of fine calculation neither to stop too soon nor keep up too long. Minutes, often seconds, were of vital importance.

By March, 1941, Poland, west of the River Bug, was rapidly filling up with vast numbers of German troops. All roads were packed with columns of them, proceeding eastwards in an unending stream. The Wehrmacht was then at the peak of its triumph and efficiency. The troops which now crossed Poland were superbly equipped and armed with the most up-to-date weapons. The soldiers were intoxicated with their victories in Poland, Norway, France and Africa. Complete confidence and arrogance characterised them all, from the senior ranks down to the ordinary soldier.

Our Intelligence Corps identified five German armies in Poland at the time. We knew the names, strength and location of the divisions, as well as the numbers involved. If the Russians, through the British, knew the details of the German preparations as regards the strength and location of troops, it was undoubtedly due in great measure to the vast Intelligence machinery which the Polish Underground had put into motion.

The Russian forces concentrated on the River Bug were

only slightly inferior to those of the German. They had good artillery and were well equipped with armour. The greatest enigma was the Soviet soldier himself and the state of his morale. The experience of the war with Finland presaged little good, while the opinion current among the population under German occupation who knew something of the Soviet Army was that defeat and disaster would swiftly overtake the Red Army.

Towards the end of March certain factors emerged which seemed to indicate April 15th as the probable date for the German attack. All German leave had been cancelled from that date. All organisations working on the development of transport services and other military works had received orders to complete their tasks by the middle of April. Feverish German Staff meetings and orders issued to the German units to prepare for immediate action also supported this supposition. In due course, April 15th was reported to London as the presumed starting-date of the German offensive against Russia.

Then, however, the unexpected happened.

Since the autumn of 1940, little Greece had been maintaining a heroic resistance against a number of Italian divisions. Their resistance had great moral effect on the spirit of the Poles during the critical days of the war. Greek resistance forced Hitler to ensure the protection of his southern flank before he attacked Russia and obliged him to subjugate Bulgaria and Yugoslavia to achieve his plans. The decision of Yugoslavia to join the Allied camp came as a complete surprise. German preparations against Russia continued, by the very force of their impetus, for a few days. After that, whole divisions, already on their way to the east, were diverted and sent south against Yugoslavia and Greece.

Hitler's campaign in the Balkans was short and ended in victory. But indisputably it caused a delay in the attack on Russia—a delay of about two months. Personally, I feel not the slightest doubt that the resistance of these two small countries, Greece and Yugoslavia, contributed in a decisive manner to the salvation of the Russian capital and so perhaps of Russia herself.

Following as we did the German preparations in all their aspects, one fact did not escape our notice. German stores in Poland had provided plentifully for everything. There were vast dumps of food, equipment and material—everything, in short, except such things as fur or leather clothing, ear-protectors and skis, the essentials needed for a winter campaign in Russia. It was clear that they counted on their troops being billeted comfortably in towns and villages and not in snowy wastes by the time the winter came.

On the morning of June 22nd, 1941, I was awakened in my country hide-out at seven o'clock by the sound of distant artillery fire. I had no doubts as to its meaning. The detonations came from the east. Germany had attacked Russia.

*   *   *

A few days later I had an unexpected visit. In the early afternoon a young man appeared; he was the owner of an estate about thirty kilometres away and a friend of my host. He told me he had a book for me from a lady I knew, and asked me to read it. I glanced at it and understood that Renia had ciphered a message into the book. I decoded it at once. She had important news and was waiting for me down the road. She warned me that "Leon" (Gedgowd) had revealed in prison many vital details about me and others, including herself, and that she was only returning to Cracow to warn a friend before leaving under a new name. When we parted we had no idea when we should meet again.

As I learned later, she did go to Cracow to warn her friend. Then she wrote her a card and had it sent from a place she had never visited. She wrote that she did not know when she would be back in Cracow, as she had been given some painting commissions for landscapes and portraits.

On July 12th the Gestapo came to fetch her; they turned everything upside down, and arrested her friend. They had found the postcard and searched the whole surrounding countryside for a woman painter—in vain, of course. The friend got out after some months because she continued to repeat the answers which she had arranged with Renia. She told them she was quite sure that I was in England, because of the letter from the prisoner of war. The Gestapo men travelled to the place where the lady was living, saw the letter and released Renia's friend.

I myself was getting ready to leave for Warsaw, to where Rog also was transferred for safety's sake. I straightened out my affairs and handed over my command after eighteen months of work. My successors were less fortunate. In the next three years Cracow had four Underground commanders. Three of them, Colonels Spychalski and Godlewski, and General Rostworowski, were arrested and murdered, together with most of their staff. The fourth, Colonel Miłkowski, was arrested in 1944 and missing.

Cracow was a dangerous place, the capital of the General Government and also the Gestapo Headquarters.

The day I travelled to Warsaw again, in July, 1941, I certainly did not imagine that I was going for three years—and not easy ones.

CHAPTER II

DEPUTY COMMANDER OF THE HOME ARMY, WARSAW

THE ATTACK ON RUSSIA was very soon followed by political events which affected us directly. General Sikorski made a speech extending the hand of reconciliation to Russia. Poland and the U.S.S.R. were now faced by a common enemy, and the existence of both was being threatened. The moment had come for old conflicts to be abandoned; the harm which Russia had done us in 1939 was now put right.

On July 30th, with the co-operation of Great Britain, an agreement between the Polish Government and the Soviet Union was signed.[1] The relief with which it was greeted in Poland is easily understandable. Diplomatic relations, which the Russians had broken off on September 17th, 1939, were now resumed. Polish prisoners and deportees from our territories occupied by the Soviet authorities in the Soviet interior were to be freed from their prisons and concentration camps. Russia had ceased to be our enemy, and the British Government recognised no territorial changes effected in Poland since August, 1939; most important of all, a Polish army was being created in Russia under the command of General Anders.

In spite of all this, we continued to feel uneasy about the vital question of our eastern frontier. For the moment everything seemed to indicate that Russo-Polish relations had returned to pre-war status. In the German-occupied part of Poland hatred of the Germans was far stronger than the memory of the wrongs done to Poland by Russia. The news of every German victory was received with the greatest misgiving; that of each setback, with joy. Never in the history of

[1] "On the Motion for the Adjournment of the House of Commons to-day, Mr. Eden said:
" 'After the signature of the Agreement, I handed General Sikorski a Note in the following terms:
" ' "On the occasion of the signature of the Polish-Soviet Agreement of to-day, I desire to take the opportunity of informing you that, in conformity with the provisions of the Agreement of Mutual Assistance between the United Kingdom and Poland of August 25th, 1939, His Majesty's Government in the United Kingdom have entered into no undertaking towards the U.S.S.R. which affects the relation between that country and Poland. I also desire to assure you that His Majesty's Government do not recognise any territorial changes which have been effected in Poland since August, 1939."—The Times, July 31st, 1941.

Poland and Russia had the moment been more propitious for forgetting the past and establishing friendly relations. Eastern Poland naturally found it more difficult to forget. During the twenty-one months of Russian occupation about $1\frac{1}{2}$ million inhabitants of Eastern Poland had been deported, thousands of families being broken up in the course of a single night and hundreds of political prisoners had been murdered by retreating Russians. Many months were to pass before the people there began to understand that the German methods at least equalled the Russian in ferocity and inhumanity.

A few days after the conclusion of the agreement with Russia, Poland was flooded with leaflets dropped from Soviet aircraft which quoted the text of the agreement and called upon the people to help the Red Army and hinder the German advance. We fully understood our role. When Germany attacked Russia, the field of activity of the Polish Home Army became, overnight, the hinterland of the German front. All the most important lines of communication ran through Polish territory. In October and November, 1941, many successful sabotage operations were carried out, apart from over 10,000 minor acts, resulting in a fall of 30 per cent. in production in most factories.

Immediately behind the advancing German forces, our Intelligence Corps steadily moved eastwards. Their task was to secure information on the spot, and personnel had been trained during the German preparations for the attack. The information we supplied to London by radio or courier was communicated direct to the Russians by the Polish General Staff there.

The speed of the German advance surpassed anything in the former *Blitz* campaigns. Soviet prisoners of war came in from the east in an uninterrupted stream, and our attention was at once attracted by the treatment they received. The Germans confined them for weeks in closed lorries, into which eighty or more were crammed. Frequently they received neither water nor food, so that when the trains finally reached their destinations and the doors were opened hundreds of corpses were thrown out. Soviet prisoners of war in the many camps scattered throughout Poland met a similar fate. They were fed solely on rotten cabbage leaves. A few months of this diet reduced the prisoners to living skeletons and they soon died by hundreds. Cases of cannibalism occurred. When a

Soviet soldier had died of hunger, his comrades would eat pieces of his raw flesh.

We sent precise information to London about this, in addition to scores of photographs showing atrocities committed upon prisoners by the Germans. The pictures were almost all taken by Germans who witnessed or took part in these executions and atrocities. They delighted in photographing them, and sent prints to their sweethearts and wives in the Reich. The films were often given to Polish photographers to be developed, and it was in this way that we obtained prints which, to this day, remain a shameful proof of German barbarism. The habit of photographing mass shootings, hangings, etc., must have been very widespread, since, on the basis of these prints, the Polish Government in London was able to publish in 1942 "The Black Book of German Crimes" entitled *The New Order in Poland* (Hutchinson & Co., London). Over a hundred of the illustrations consist of photographs taken by Germans. After the book was published, Goebbels strictly prohibited German soldiers from having their films developed by Polish photographers.

It was almost at the same time that the Soviet military authorities issued an order that any Soviet soldier who was taken prisoner would be court-martialled for treason after the war. In the first weeks of the war Russian soldiers capitulated in masses, and it was only when they learnt of the treatment meted out to their comrades that their resistance began to stiffen. In the beginning, the Soviet soldier was ready to exchange his native régime for captivity in almost any circumstances, but as soon as he had irrefutable evidence of the reception awaiting him he fought to the end rather than fall into German hands. Had the Germans been less brutal the Soviet-German War might have taken a different course.

*　　　*　　　*

It was in those days of new work and adjustment that I settled in Warsaw. This was then very difficult, as the Germans had introduced stringent regulations about the registration of residents. It was very hard for "newly arrived persons" who had attracted the attention of the Gestapo in other places to move into the capital.

The Underground solved the problem in my case by giving me the authentic documents and identity papers of a man called George Korabski, who had died in Warsaw in 1939. I was also given every detail of his life which could be of any possible help to me. The house where he lived before the war had been destroyed during the siege of 1939. I was thus free to choose a lodging. Korabski would have been about three years older than I, and this also was an advantage, as the Germans were not so vigilant of men over fifty. It was the younger ones they combed out so assiduously for forced labour and for the still more simple reason—that the nation was to be exterminated.

At the end of July I was nominated Deputy Commander of the Home Army and Commander of the Western Area, with headquarters in Warsaw. Both districts of this province, Poznań and Toruń, were particularly exposed to the vigilance of the Gestapo. The liaison contacts were interrupted all the time by constant arrests, which undermined our work. It was then also that I was entrusted with other duties. As soon as I began to work in Warsaw, Rowecki put me in touch with the Government delegate who, supported by the agreement of the four principal parties (Socialist, Peasant, National Democrats, Christian Democrats), was to be in charge of a secret administrative organisation which would cover the entire area of the republic.

*   *   *

In 1941 the Z.W.Z. (Union of Armed Warfare) had about 100,000 soldiers all sworn in and organised in platoons intended to emerge only for the general rising. We created specially trained diversionary units. The Z.W.Z. had been renamed in February, 1942, "Armja Krajowa"—A.K. (the Home Army). The Commander with his staff formed the headquarters. Many different departments were subordinated to this headquarters, which had to deal with the very numerous and manifold tasks and duties which had fallen to the secret army. The commanders of the provinces and districts were directly subordinate to the C.-in-C. Two to four districts combined formed a province.

Our Intelligence system was built up quite separately from the bulk of the secret army. This part of our work developed into a machine whose activities extended to all countries occupied by the Germans. We could obtain information, not only from our own area, but from the lands lying behind the

German front in the east and from the Reich itself. The whole German war industry in Poland and in Germany was under our observation, as well as the harbours of the North and Baltic Seas.

*   *   *

Our main activity at that time had once more to be diversion and sabotage. Our diversionary work, of course, had as its aim the destruction of the German lines of communication. The means employed were the blowing up of bridges, destruction of the railway tunnels, mining of roads, attacks on transports and burning of German dumps and stores of equipment, arms and supplies.

At first we worked on our own territory—a relatively easy matter. Soon, however, the front moved beyond Polish territory. Diversion is necessarily most effective when carried out in the immediate rear of the enemy. We had to follow the German advance.

Accordingly, we made full use of the fact that the Germans were forcing Poles to work as labourers on the construction of airfields, barracks and so on, on Russian territory. We smuggled as many of our members as possible into the ranks of these forced labourers. They applied as carpenters, mechanics, etc. On arrival, they formed diversionary groups of five. Each member of a "five" worked in a different establishment. They combined only to carry out some major action, such as setting fire to a store or blowing up a bridge. Their task completed, they scattered once more to their various jobs. This was one method: the other consisted in guerrilla activity, which could only be carried out in large forest areas.

For organisational purposes, we divided the whole eastern front—from the Baltic to the Black Sea—into seven sectors; they spread out radially from Warsaw. It was in this way that the code-name of "Operation Fan" originated. Each of the seven sectors had its own separate organisation, with a common base for its countless "fives."

From the very nature of things, the "fives" had to establish some kind of understanding with the Soviet guerrillas, if only to co-ordinate the time and place of action. There had, for instance, been cases when, on one and the same night, a Polish group would blow up the arch of a bridge while a Soviet band did the same thing not ten miles away. In time, a kind of local co-operation grew up between the Polish and

Soviet guerrillas. Nevertheless, the relations between the central Communist Committee and our groups were bad from the outset; the attitude of the Communists was definitely unfriendly.

*   *   *

In the beginning, our only source of arms was the stores which had been buried by individuals and units after the September campaign of 1939. Some of these, in spite of precautions, had become badly damaged by rust. Moreover, the type of arms did not always suit the needs and methods of our kind of warfare.

Poland, lying at the extreme edge of British flight-range, was one of the Allied countries most distant from England. We seriously doubted if we could be supplied with arms by air.

The first attempt to drop a parachutist with a load of arms, explosives and money was scheduled for as early as December 20th, 1940. The crew were already at their stations in the aircraft when it was decided that the tanks could not hold the necessary amount of fuel for the flight to Poland and back. The second experimental flight to Poland was signalled for February 15th, 1941. Men and supplies were to be dropped in the Cracow district when I was in command there. A special detachment was to receive the aircraft at the appointed place and time.

On the evening of February 15th, I was advised that the flight would take place that night and that London had already sent out the first warning. Nothing happened. After some days the Germans posted up notices throughout the country offering substantial cash rewards for help in locating three very dangerous criminals.

A few days later still, the "dangerous criminals" reported to our organisation in Warsaw. They had jumped—but not over Polish territory. They landed in the Reich. They were, however, only about 100 kilometres from the Polish frontier, and fortunately at once found Poles to give them emergency assistance. They crossed the frontier and reached the capital in safety. The supply of arms they brought was, unhappily, lost to us.

In order to appreciate fully the enormous difficulties in these ventures, it must be remembered that we were separated from England by the full width of the Reich and the North Sea. Quite apart from anti-aircraft fire and German pursuit planes, the bombers bringing us men and arms had another indeterminate obstacle to overcome—the weather. Aircraft could take off in England only when the weather was favourable over England and the North Sea as well as the long 1,000-mile route to Poland. Taking this into consideration, we organised Underground meteorological stations and transmitted daily weather reports to London.

Another point requiring careful attention was the establishing of contact between the men landing and those awaiting them. It was essential that fresh signals should be arranged in advance for each landing. In our circumstances, the movement of arms from place to place presented considerable difficulties. The reception point had therefore to be selected with great care, taking into consideration both our immediate needs and those of future fighting. From time to time we would send to London by courier a precise map showing the exact spots selected for air descents, the signals to be used, specimens of the identity papers to be carried by the parachutists and detailed instructions for procedure after landing. In England, a special training centre had been established at which parachutists were instructed in the tasks awaiting them in enemy-occupied territory.

On the day when a plane was to take off for Poland, the B.B.C. concluded its broadcast in Polish with a prearranged tune. This served as a warning for a certain reception group to expect drops at a certain place that night. The reception unit would accordingly proceed to the spot arranged. They were fully armed. When the approaching plane was heard, lights were lit in such a way as to indicate the direction of the wind. At the same time, they flashed a torch from the ground signalling a given letter over and over again. The plane flashed the counter-signal, consisting of another letter, with the lights under the wings. Containers would then be dropped at a very low altitude and with great precision.

From that first supply operation on February 15th, 1941, 488 flights were made to Poland. In all sixty-four aircraft failed to return to base, and of these twenty-four were manned by Polish crews. Roughly a third of our arms and ammunition was derived from air supply, and about 353 specialists were parachuted into the country. At first, the supply planes were based in the United Kingdom, but the losses sustained over Denmark proved too costly, and after the capture of airfields on the Italian mainland the base was transferred to Brindisi. As the first flights were nearly always made by full moon, we called the parachutists "men from the moon." I well remember a talk I had with one who had landed that same night near Warsaw. To talk to a man who only the night before had been drinking a "nice cup of tea" in London seemed to me just as improbable as meeting the Man in the Moon in person! I remember feeling a strange, emotional excitement. These men brought with them the very breath of liberty.

In time, it became clear to us that the supplies and arms we received from the air would be insufficient to cover our needs. We therefore had to fall back upon our own efforts and ingenuity. Our Underground workshops finally came to be one of the chief sources of supply of arms and materials for diversionary action.

During our early days—from 1939 to the end of 1940—our production of arms and material was on a small scale, and consisted for the most part of transforming and adapting various materials seized from the Germans. However, towards the end of 1942 our sabotage operations grew in scope and intensity to such an extent that demands for arms could only be met by production on the spot.

As Deputy Commander-in-Chief, I was very closely connected with this branch of our work. Rowecki and I had to divide our duties as far as possible, and the production of war material fell to my charge.

It demanded the greatest ingenuity and presented considerable difficulties. Success depended on the solution of a number of problems. Our primary task was to procure raw materials and semi-manufactured materials or to replace them by substitutes. Specialists had to be found who combined exceptional courage with patriotism in the fullest sense of the term. Naturally, there were few men possessing all these qualifications, and of them many were quite irreplaceable. Sometimes the loss of a key man would put a stop to further production. The third problem was the elaboration of suitable methods and the classification of our actual needs, both for present and future operations. Finally, there was the question of how to transport and conceal the raw materials, semi-manufactured and finished products.

The production of war material had until now been carried on by several centres, working separately. Now it was centralised under the supervision of specialists. This supervision was entrusted by H.Q. to an engineer directly under my command. The whole operation was divided into two main parts: production of armaments for future use during the general rising, and production needed currently for diversionary action. Both centres were in close co-operation, and by their joint efforts very good results were achieved. (For instance, after a long period of study and experiment, they succeeded in producing automatic pistols and flame-throwers.) While the technicians prepared plans and methods of production, I ordered the preparation of a list of requirements for war material, with special consideration to current demand in connection with diversion. A group of scientists worked full-time on the discovery of suitable diversion material which would best serve each new situation.

Sometimes an invention which was the fruit of long, painstaking research and intensive effort would have to be withdrawn shortly after being used for the first time because the Germans had produced an effective counter-measure. This was the case with the altrimetric bomb. After prolonged research and experiment, it was produced in the form of an elongated cylinder, giving no external indication of its purpose. It was put into the tail of an aircraft and exploded as a result of the change in atmospheric pressure when the plane reached a certain height, thus damaging the whole steering gear. We succeeded in destroying eighteen Luftwaffe planes in this way. Soon, however, the Germans countered with such stringent precautionary measures among their ground staffs that it became impossible to use the device again.

The invention of a suitable means of destruction was often closely allied with the method employed. For example, an ordinary railway mine, which exploded when the first train passed over it, would cause an interruption in traffic for only about four hours. At one time we were anxious to interrupt traffic on one of the main trunk lines leading to the Warsaw-Malkinia sector of the eastern front for a minimum period of ten days. Our experts solved the problem, and the resulting interruption lasted as long as two weeks. It was done by specially devised mines which could be automatically blown up. A chain of these mines was laid across the tracks. The first, which was placed in the middle of the chain, went off as the first train was passing over it. Two more placed on the tracks on either side of the first exploded when the rescue train arrived from one side or the other. The remaining mines on both sides of the wrecked trains exploded successively when the repair trains arrived from both directions. Result: ten miles of track effectively mined. After the first train had been blown up, four repair and relief trains sent in to deal with it had been effectively destroyed. And that was the total number of this particular type of train which the Germans possessed in the district.

One factor which helped us in our arms production was the employment of Poles in German-controlled industrial plants in Poland. The number of Germans available was inadequate, and they had no choice but to employ Poles. It was therefore compulsory for Polish specialists and technicians to work in the factories, only the management being in German hands. In thirty-seven plants working for the German war machine the Polish workers were organised in secret groups, and they procured us raw materials, component parts and even finished products.

There was an unpleasant side to this part of the work. Anyone working in a German factory of this sort was immediately looked upon by his fellow countrymen as a collaborationist—quite apart from whether the worker in question was doing so under compulsion or voluntarily.

One of our greatest difficulties was to procure basic materials for explosives, such as saltpetre. It took some time before our technicians hit upon the plan of extracting it from artificial fertilisers. The two German-controlled factories for fertilisers at Chorzow and Moscice became our indirect principal suppliers. We bought up large quantities of their product through the agency of the big agricultural co-operatives and individual farmers.

The best explosive for our needs was cheddite. For this we had to have potassium chlorate, and to get it was no easy matter. There was only one German-controlled plant producing this chemical in Poland (Radocha). But the Germans fully realised how useful it could be to us, and both its production and its sale were under the strictest control. Attempts to seize or steal stocks from Radocha failed dismally. However, the contents of two railway wagons loaded with the chemical were seized by us while in transport. Also, an armed raid was made on the large chemical warehouses in Warsaw. But this only resulted in about $1\frac{1}{2}$ tons falling into our hands. The Germans countered by ordering their firms to reduce stocks of the chemical to a minimum level. In spite of this, Polish workers in the large match factory at Blonie succeeded in systematically filling the factory warehouse with surplus stocks of potassium chlorate, and the "theft" of the material duly followed. There was complete co-ordination with the factory workers down to the last detail. In another case, the Polish personnel in a German-controlled factory ordered a large quantity of this chemical to be imported from the Reich, and this likewise "disappeared." But all this proved quite inadequate, and our own laborious production of the chemical had to continue. In all, we seized or produced 70 tons of it.

For the production of another explosive, we secured 5,000 kilogrammes of urotropine with the help of large pharmaceutical manufacturers in Warsaw, Ludwig Spiess & Son, and S. Drozdowicz & Co., who were our best suppliers.

All this was made possible by the devotion to duty of the Polish staff; they would forge invoices and receipts which officially originated from German firms, but in actual fact represented "transactions" for our Underground Army. It was in this way that one of the largest foundries in the Reich supplied us with 16 tons of special iron sheeting essential to the production of flame-throwers. And it was thus, too, that in 1943 a consignment of steel wire was imported by air from Sweden as a rush order, ostensibly for the German Bruhn-Werke in Warsaw. We badly needed the wire for tommy-gun springs.

It sometimes happened that rather perplexing situations arose as a result of the enthusiasm of our people working in German-controlled factories. At one time, we needed steel of a specified diameter for our "Filipinka" grenades. Instructions were accordingly issued to all our groups in German-controlled works in central Poland to seize the largest possible quantity of it. Surprise was great when the amount stolen and hidden away was found to exceed our needs threefold.

In the production of hand-grenades, bombs, mines, and so on it was necessary to make use of varied substitute objects. For instance, 10,000 bakelite cups had to be bought up to be made into grenades of the "Filipinka" type. Another batch was made from the water-containers of acetylene lamps which were in general use at the time in Poland. A large consignment of key-rings came in very useful as the detonator rings on hand-grenades and bombs. And so it went on. It would take a large book to give a complete list.

While we got our raw material and semi-manufactured products from German-controlled works, for the most part our finished products came from small workshops operating under legal licences, but producing illegal objects. We found small metal-workers' workshops the most useful for the purpose. The work could then be more easily concealed behind the manufacture of some innocuous article for civilian use. Thus the production of tommy-guns was covered in great part by that of padlocks and ordinary locks. Hand-grenades—popularly known as "Sidolówki," since they bore a striking resemblance to the round cans of Sidol polish—were produced in the same place as the actual cans for the polish. Flame-throwers were made in a factory engaged in the production of fire-extinguishers. German inspectors and patrols were often deceived by this camouflage.

We also had establishments of a different category which were completely secret. False walls partitioned off parts of houses and cellars and concealed the actual quarters of the workshops. The work there was carried on under even more difficult conditions than those in the printing shops. Some chemical work could only be done at night; otherwise the special colours of the smoke from the chimneys would have betrayed them. In order to drown the clatter and hum of machines, workshops had to be installed near some place where legal goods were being produced with a good deal of noise. Thus one was installed in the vicinity of a mechanical mangle which made a tremendous clatter as it rolled. Another was on the floor above a welding shop.

Any operation connected with high explosive entailed grave personal risk and also the danger of an accident which would attract the Gestapo's attention. The work was therefore carried on under a great nervous strain. There was also a considerable number of women engaged in this work, from ordinary workers to the chemists in charge of sections of the factory.

Tests had to be made, and here again the risk was increased, especially if explosions or shots were entailed. We had to find adequate secret testing grounds. In this as in our other problems I met with the greatest co-operation from the peasants as well as from the owners of larger estates, who enabled us to organise a complete system of experimental camps and groups.

There was the case of a flame-thrower being tried out in the centre of Warsaw, on one of the blocks on Theatre Square. It had been decided to make the test in the ruins of some houses behind the Church of St. Anthony, the crypt and vaults of which formed one of our storehouses for arms and war material. Fire and smoke produced by the tests could be seen from the square. A large pile of wood was stacked up, with a number of chemical fire-extinguishers nearby. The object was to ascertain whether the flame-thrower was effective at a distance of nearly 35 yards—such was the stipulated requirement.

Before the test was made, the man in charge of flame-thrower production and of the test called at the fire station in the Town Hall building and also visited the police. He explained that he was the representative of the "Motor-Stock" German-controlled fire-extinguisher factory and warned them not to be alarmed if they saw flames and smoke, as he and his employees were about to try out a new type of extinguisher on the ground of this factory near Theatre Square.

The flame-thrower worked so effectively that the testing squad would willingly have made themselves scarce. The pile of wood burst into flames which rose to a height of some 20 feet and the whole of Theatre Square was wreathed in smoke. Luckily, neither the police nor the fire brigade turned out to investigate, and the fire was quickly controlled. The testing group then dispersed, well pleased with the results.

In spite of all this, the quantity of weapons at our disposal was always a small amount in comparison with the number of men to be armed; so we had to supplement armed action by attacks on the enemy's morale which would not require dynamite or guns.

One of them was what we called "Special Action N." German factories and workshops received orders from the respective German authorities that May 1st, 1942, was to be observed as Nazi Labour Day. All workers were to have twenty-four hours' leave on full pay. They were also to be informed of the significance of the day in the National Socialist order. After the outbreak of war with Russia, the Germans had reduced the number of holidays to the absolute minimum in order to step up their war effort. But this order was sent out on paper bearing the authentic letter-head of the German Labour Bureau and was couched in impeccable Nazi style. Every detail had been carefully worked out. The German works managers were completely taken in and had not the least doubt that the order was authentic.

We purposely sent the order out at the last moment, and consequently the German Labour Bureau discovered the trick too late to stop it through the normal channels. Public loud-speakers and telephones were hastily used to announce that the order had been "forged by criminal elements," and to instruct all workers to return to their factories at once. It was too late, however. Most industries throughout Poland remained idle for a whole day. Amongst others, the Ursus Tank Works and the enormous railway repair depots at Pruszkow, of vital importance to the German eastern front, were closed for the day. The German losses in production were comparable with those of a minor R.A.F. raid. The whole operation did not cost us a single man or a single round of ammunition.

On another occasion, all German residents in Warsaw received a communication on Nazi Party notepaper instructing each of them to deposit a food parcel for wounded German soldiers in the Warsaw hospitals. True to the German love of detail and precision, the items to be included in each parcel were minutely listed, even down to the number of eggs (and this at a time when eggs were well-nigh unobtainable, even by Germans). The German civilians all turned up on the appointed day at the office of the German Mayor in Warsaw. The office and its approaches were packed out.

Their astonishment was intense when they learnt that the authorities had no knowledge of the order. Officials stated that there, too, no one knew anything of the order. But the Gestapo at once ordered all the Germans who had turned up with parcels to be held and cross-examined. The investigation took a whole day, and the German housewives, exhausted and furious, finally returned home roundly cursing the chaos of their own authorities' offices. Our object had been to hamper the work of the authorities and, in fact, we succeeded in hamstringing it for a full twenty-four hours.

Hardly a week passed in which we did not send out forged communications of some sort: orders to register, announce-ments, invitations to non-existent party meetings and demon-strations and so on. The result was inevitable. German confidence in the orders of their own authorities was gravely shaken, and very often the German telephone system was jammed by inquirers checking up on the order that urgent business could not get through. Fischer, the Governor of Warsaw, was finally forced to send out a confidential circular to all his subordinates warning them against orders forged by Poles. This was what we had been waiting for. From then on, when a German official received an inconvenient order he would disregard it, on the plea that he considered it a forged one issued by our Underground. Frequent confusion resulted, and all without loss of life to us. Another effort on the part of "Special Action" had an even more acute effect on the German population. Our Intelligence discovered that the German stocks of gas masks were insufficient for their civilians in Poland. We decided to take advantage of this discovery. Accordingly, all German civilians received a confidential letter, signed by Boehme, who was Chief of the German Security Police at the time, which alleged that the Russians would very probably use poison gas in the near future and ordered every German civilian to procure a gas mask within the space of two weeks.

Masks were, of course, unprocurable in any shop in Warsaw, and the German administrative offices were therefore swamped with inquiries, both by telephone and in person, from the terror-stricken German civilians. The authorities were infuriated by the numerous and distracted requests. Boehme was forced to have a special proclamation posted up throughout the capital in order to cope with the panic. In it, he admitted that the original order had been forged by Poles and assured his countrymen that there was definitely no immediate danger of gas attacks. But the Germans did not react as he hoped.

"They've only just discovered that there aren't enough gas masks to go round," they complained to one another. "That's why they're trying to back out by throwing the blame on the Poles."

Another means of combating the Germans without the use of firearms was that of psychological warfare. It was both offensive and defensive. The Germans' first step in reducing the people of an occupied country to complete submission was to isolate them from all sources of news of the outside world. Their first act, after occupying Poland, was to confiscate all radio sets. Their next was to monopolise all organs of propaganda. The public was then subjected to that species of collective hypnotism known as "mass propaganda." The myth of German invincibility was drummed into our heads by slogans repeated over and over again by public loud-speakers, by the Press in Polish, by leaflets, posters, rumours and the whole bag of tricks. At Gestapo headquarters in Warsaw there was even a special department for the dissemination of false rumours among Poles. The whole campaign was designed to control the country's outlook and break its morale.

In order to counteract German propaganda, our own secret Press had to be efficiently organised, widely circulated and effectively distributed to every part of the country. This was the defensive aspect of our psychological warfare. Our offensive strove to spread defeatism amongst German soldiers. We had learnt from our own hard-won experience that propaganda, no matter how cunning and powerful, loses much of its effectiveness if it is known to come from an enemy source. Compared with the means at their disposal, the effect of German propaganda upon Poles was extremely feeble. Likewise, the influence of R.A.F. leaflets upon Germans was small, although the leaflets were well drafted. It became clear that concealment of the source of our propaganda would increase its effect considerably.

We acted accordingly. We collected a nucleus of people well acquainted with the mentality of the German troops, and set them to produce periodicals purporting to come from a German underground opposition in the Reich. The slightest trace of Polish origin was rigidly avoided. The publications expressed a variety of opinions and catered for every type, ranging from a non-existent organ of the German Socialist Catholic Party to the periodical of an imaginary opposition in the Nazi Party ranks advertised as "The Hess Movement." The very fact that there was no real German underground movement in Germany made our work more impressive.

Distribution had to be carefully thought out, since the periodicals and leaflets obviously could not be handed to Germans by Poles. In the larger Polish towns there were big wooden receptacles into which the Germans were encouraged to put books and periodicals for their front-line troops. Leaflets could be put into German magazines and dropped into the boxes. Ammunition cases and boxes of foodstuffs in troop transports going east provided us with another means of distribution. Another was the German Post Office system. We used this channel for sending tens of thousands of leaflets, though of course each had to be sent in an envelope of different colour and shape and addressed in different handwriting.

We obviously had to know the exact current psychological state of the Germans generally and the state of the morale of the German troops in particular, so that we could exploit these conditions to the full. An inexhaustible source of information in this respect was letters written by the Germans: letters written by soldiers, officers, officials and their families in Germany to their friends and relations on the eastern front, and vice versa.

All these letters had to pass through Poland, of course, and the postal officials were invariably Poles, owing to the lack of Germans for the work. We accordingly established a network of agents in the post offices. Letters were removed, opened and photographed, and sent on to their destinations with the shortest possible delay. Little did the Germans realise that a good cross-section of their correspondence was subject to the rigorous scrutiny of the Polish Underground.

As a matter of fact, our reports on German morale were considered of great importance. We used to transmit them to London, and some of them were brought to the attention of Mr. Churchill.

In 1942, we issued some tens of thousands of a particular pamphlet in German. On the cover was a caricature of Mr. Churchill and the caption: *"Churchill der groesste Lügner der Welt"* ("Churchill, the biggest liar in the world"). Any German could safely pick up the pamphlet on the assumption that it was another effort of Goebbels' office. But inside were extracts from Hitler's speeches and from *Mein Kampf*, showing how repeatedly and completely he was wont to contradict himself. Ten copies of the pamphlet were put into envelopes and posted to ten of the highest Nazi dignitaries, including Hitler, Goering and Goebbels. Another copy was taken to London by a courier, hidden behind the glass of his shaving mirror. This one bore a dedication to Mr. Churchill from the Polish Home Army, and General Sikorski handed it personally to the British Premier.

The appearance of even one copy of a publication of the Underground German-language Press at once alarmed the whole Gestapo in a district. We were even accorded the honour of being mentioned in secret orders of the German High Command, when German Army leaders were warned against publications purporting to come from German sources, but which were, in fact, products of enemy "kitchens." On no occasion, however, dared they admit that the "kitchens" were Polish or that a subjected nation had, in spite of everything, managed to deal an effective counter-blow in the field of their own speciality—propaganda. Some idea of the popularity which our publications enjoyed can be gained from the prices at which copies changed hands. Sometimes a single copy was sold by one German to another for as high a price as 50 marks.

There was nothing the Germans loved so much in those days as to exploit to the full their power over the weak, and there was nothing that infuriated them so much as a public joke at their expense—their sense of humour having always been poor, anyway. To reply to their terrorism with a joke was sufficient to drive them into a state of fury. Ridicule of the *Herrenvolk* played a large part in our psychological warfare. We even had a special branch in the Home Army to deal with the subject. It consisted for the most part of Boy Scouts and had the code name of "Wawer."

One of Wawer's most successful jokes originated during the winter of 1942. In the heart of Warsaw stood the statue of Copernicus, by the Danish sculptor, Thorwaldsen. On the base of the monument was the inscription: "To Copernicus. From His Countrymen." The Germans removed the inscription and replaced it by another: "To the Great German Astronomer." Just opposite the statue was a German police station. One day, a gang of working men in overalls and carrying tools, approached the statue. In a leisurely fashion they unscrewed the new plaque and took it away. The German sentry opposite did not intervene because he thought that such an open action must surely be legal, and that some alteration must have been decided upon by the authorities.

Three weeks passed before the German authorities noticed that the plate had been removed. Then a proclamation appeared, signed by the Governor himself. It was couched in the usual pompous German style and read as follows:

"Recently, criminal elements removed the tablet from the Copernicus monument for political reasons. As a reprisal, I order the removal of the Kilinski monument. At the same time, I give full warning that, should similar acts be perpetrated,

I shall order the suspension of all food rations for the Polish population of Warsaw for the term of one week.

"*(Signed)* FISCHER,
"*Governor of Warsaw.*"

Now, Kilinski had been a Warsaw bootmaker who had led the people during the siege of the city by the Russian invaders in 1794 and he has always been a popular hero with all Warsaw artisans. A few days later his statue was actually dragged from its pedestal and put temporarily into the vaults of the National Museum. The next morning, passers-by noticed a large inscription painted in tar on the light walls of the museum. It ran:

"People of Warsaw, I am here. *(Signed)* Jan Kilinski."

A week later, the hoardings carried a fresh poster, identical with Fischer's in format, colour and type. The text ran:

"Recently, criminal elements removed the Kilinski monument for political reasons. As a reprisal, I order the prolongation of winter on the eastern front for the term of two months.

"*(Signed)* NICHOLAS COPERNICUS."

Strangely enough the winter that year did last much longer than usual and caused a severe setback to the German plans for a spring offensive on the eastern front.

Wawer specialised in inscriptions on walls. A monogram like an anchor formed by the letters "p" and "w" made the initials of *Polska Walczaca* (Fighting Poland). It was a sign which came to mean as much for us as the fish-sign had meant to the early Christians. The symbol appeared everywhere. It was a point of honour with the Boy Scouts that the sign be chalked up under the very noses of the Germans. For white walls pitch was used. Once a small boy was caught red-handed with a pail of pitch. A tram-load of people watched in horror while the boy was led across the road by a German policeman. A very few seconds later the pitch was in the German's face, the pail was rolling down the street and the boy had disappeared among the passengers of the fast-moving tram.

A month after I was assigned to Warsaw I had news from my wife, Renia. After the arrest of her friend, she had gone to a country place, where no one except the host knew who she was. She asked me to let her come to Warsaw. I sent her new personal documents in a false name—Mme. Malinowska—the papers being conveyed to her inside the binding of a novel. She came to Warsaw at once. When we met I was rather taken aback—Renia was fair-haired! She had been dark ever since I had known her! The disguise was very effective and changed her a lot.

The billeting problem was not easy and I had to change flats frequently. For some time I lived in a worker's lodging near the Vistula. The room was not heated and when a sudden cold spell came my ears and fingers froze during the night. But it was convenient to have an independent room with a little gas-cooker. It was there that I began to study the art of cooking. I made breakfast and supper every day, and when Renia came on Sundays I prepared dinner for her. It was usually noodles with cauliflower, or eggs on tomatoes. My culinary ambitions did not reach higher.

Later on, it appeared that it was better to be a sub-tenant, as it attracted less attention. But then again we had to be very careful: by living with people who themselves worked in the Underground, one could fall into the hands of the Gestapo simply by bad luck should the landlords be arrested. At the beginning of the winter I had to leave my little flat, as my neighbours began to show interest in me. Later it came out that they were Gestapo agents. At another time, when I had a room which I liked, I was given notice after a few months and had to leave. I was sorry, but I certainly don't regret it now. Soon after I left, the Gestapo arrested everybody, landlords and tenants. The landlady had been working in the Underground without my knowing it.

As Renia wanted to take up work again, I put her in contact with Department No. 1 (Organisation), telling her future chief that she was my liaison girl from Cracow. No one knew she was my wife. She had charge of a group of code workers and could also continue her work for prisoners of war. Soon afterwards she took a post as interpreter in the legal Polish Relief Committee. This was necessary for her safety, as the Labour Office kept sending more and more people to Germany on forced labour. Now she could prove where and how she earned her livelihood, as she worked in her office from 8 a.m. to 3 p.m. (Her Underground hours were from 4 p.m. to curfew time.)

I also had plenty to do. Apart from my normal duties,

Rowecki consented to my making contact with the leader of the National Democratic Party, Stefan Sacha. I hoped I should induce him to subordinate his military organisation to Rowecki's command, as many other minor groups had already done, following the order from General Sikorski to unite all military organisations under the Commander-in-Chief, Underground Army. These talks were long and often tiresome for political reasons. After a few months we signed an agreement and the National Democratic Party transferred to the Home Army 70.000 Underground soldiers. Sacha was later arrested and executed like so many others.

In the course of the next two years other political parties and organisations gradually decided to make their soldiers join the Home Army. Among these the most numerous were from the Peasant Party, who transferred to us over 40,000 men. The Socialist Party, on the other hand, had been in closest collaboration with us from the very beginning and had already put her units at our disposal.

*   *   *

In the meantime, things went from bad to worse in the western area annexed outright to the Reich. The Germans feared the Polish element in this region might damage morale in the Reich itself, and the population was accordingly subjected to an even more severe terrorism than that applied in central Poland. The Germans had separated us from western Poland by a virtually impenetrable barrier. The boundary line was carefully manned by German frontier guards, with police dogs, snipers and so on. It was an extremely rare occurrence for a Pole to cross this barrier legally. Tales of what was happening on the western side filled us with horror.

While the Underground movement in central Poland was developing fast, striking its roots deeper and deeper, operations in western Poland were faced with difficulties and obstacles which increased as time went on. Commanders appointed and sent in by Rowecki to organise work there were invariably arrested and executed after a short tenure of office. Yet the western territories were of great importance to us. They formed the base for infiltration into the Reich proper, where the greatest harm could be done to the German war machine by diversion and sabotage activities, as well as by our Intelligence service. The lack of success on the part of our movement in the west made it clear that our method of work there would have to be different. For this reason, Rowecki sent me to study the situation on the spot.

I was to cross over on Christmas Day. It was a day when many German garrison troops were on leave; those not so lucky would most likely take to drink in an effort to drown their disappointment. In any case, they might be expected to be less observant just then. I took as guide with me a young officer who had been active in western Poland.

We set out on Christmas Eve and reached the boundary station of Glowno. Frontier guards usually patrolled the station and its approaches. My guide went on ahead towards it and then strolled into the waiting-room; after a moment he emerged with a newspaper in his hand, the signal that the coast was clear. The barmaid was a member of our organisation and had been warned of our coming. We exchanged passwords; mine was "Tea with rum." In a very short time we were both in her modest home adjoining the station. There we awaited a guide who knew all the frontier passages. He proved to be a young cadet officer who gained my full confidence at first sight. I asked him how often he had crossed the boundary.

"Since the war, thirty-odd times," he replied. "I've only fallen into German hands once, and then I was lucky enough to have a bottle of vodka with me which acted as an effective bribe."

His assurance was infectious, although the circumstances did not seem to favour us. It was a perfect moonlight night and the cold was intense, something like 36° below freezing point (−20° C.). The moonlight was reflected in the white sheet of snow which covered field and road as far as the eye could see. It was, in fact, the true Christmas night of tradition.

"It's out of the question to leave while the moon's so bright," said my young guide. "We'd be spotted like flies in this light."

So we decided to wait for the moon to set. We had to make some twenty-odd miles guarded by a double cordon of frontier guards. About midnight it began to grow darker and we set out. The snow reached to just short of our knees; it crunched in tell-tale fashion as we moved forward, stopping every now and then to look around us.

The first stage of the journey ended at a peasant cottage

right in the frontier zone. When we reached the hut it was
scarcely visible under its deep covering of snow. The guide
knocked on the window, a special signal which resulted in
the door being opened·to us immediately by the old peasant,
who admitted us without a word.

"How are things?" asked the guide.

The old man shook his head. "German patrol was here an
hour ago. There's a lot of them hereabouts."

This caused the guide obvious apprehension. I asked him
whether he was ready to chance it under these conditions.

"Yes," he replied promptly. "I don't like turning back
halfway. Let's risk it and try."

It was at this point that I changed my identity card for that
of a *Volksdeutsch*. These were Poles of German descent who
obtained privileges nearly equal to those of German citizens.
Many Polish citizens—men and women—were killed throughout all those years for refusing to become *Volksdeutsch*.

At last we set out. A vast, empty space lay before us. The
white plain was plunged in utter silence and the occasional
distant barking of a dog served only to intensify the stillness. It
seemed as though all humanity had taken refuge indoors. We ran
only about 100 yards before we fell flat on the ground. The
snow, which was as smooth and even as the surface of a mirror,
covered a ploughed field of frozen furrows. I had light, city
shoes, good for town wear, but quite useless for this sort of
thing. As I ran, I stumbled and fell again and again. A keen,
icy wind made breathing difficult, and I ran with a handkerchief pressed to my mouth. In this way, running across country
and dropping flat in the snow every now and then (we did
this to rest ourselves, even when the furrows ended), we at
length reached the boundary line. For a long time we lay
side by side, peering about and listening intently for sight or
sound of anything suspicious. The guide indicated something
dark in the snow on a hilltop to our right: it was a concealed
German observation post; luckily the guards on duty must
have been looking the other way.

In a whisper, my companion explained the situation. The
forest that lay ahead of us was full of surprises; patrols were
active there day and night. But it could not be avoided; there
was no way of by-passing it. Once it was crossed, the main
danger would lie behind us. All seemed quiet around us, so
we resumed our journey. That night we covered twenty miles

at cross-country speed from 1 a.m. until 7 a.m., under the greatest nervous and physical strain. By seven o'clock the greater part of the journey lay behind us and we drew near our next objective, the cottage in which my guide's parents lived.

Completely exhausted, we reached the tiny, one-roomed hut. My guide's sister prepared breakfast for us on a primitive iron stove. Day after day, night after night, these people were faced by new events, new adventures, new people and new dangers; living on that frontier was much like living on a battlefield. I listened to their endless stories, slipping further and further from reality. The warmth of the room stole over us like a drug and we were soon asleep. We had three hours' rest.

At noon we left the cottage. I now had to pass as a German. Poles, as I have already said, were not permitted to travel in these territories at all. We went by tram from Zgierz to Lodz, and from there we took the train. All the railway carriages bore notices: "*Nur fur Deutsche*" ("For Germans Only"). In the train to Poznań, we shared a compartment with a Gestapo man and his family. The atmosphere was festive and the Gestapo man started to talk to me, taking us for Germans. He was rather loquacious and obviously disposed to be friendly.

That same evening, we reached the small provincial town of Ostrow—the end of our journey. We went straight from the train to a secret meeting place known to my guide. Here, however, we met with an unexpected setback. Our intended host stated firmly that he could not take us in for the night. The German *Blokführer* was proving very inquisitive and keeping him under the closest observation. If any stranger was reported in the house, there would certainly be trouble with the police.

It was rather difficult; darkness was falling and to find shelter for the night in this town, where every Pole felt his home to be almost a prison cell, seemed to be a problem without solution. But our host had an aunt who lived nearby. The local Gestapo chief was quartered in her home. He had gone home on Christmas leave, and the good aunt agreed that I should occupy his bed for the night. This struck me as an excellent idea. I asked, however, if they were sure that he wouldn't turn up unexpectedly. It might have its amusing side, I thought, but it would hardly be pleasant if the chief of the Gestapo caught me in his bed. They assured me there was no fear of that.

An hour later, I was preparing for the night in the room of the Gestapo dignitary, over whose bed hung a portrait of Hitler. Never since 1939 had I fallen asleep with a greater feeling of security, although the room was not heated and the water was frozen in the basin. For once, I thought sleepily, I had every right to assume that no one would pay me an unexpected and unwelcome nocturnal visit.

The next day I talked for a long time with the local commander, who on his own initiative was re-establishing the organisation for the whole of Poznań after the last mass arrests. He was a reserve major in the Polish Army and now carried out the duties of local district commander. Compulsory employment made it quite impossible for him to leave the town. He maintained his liaison with the organisation through Franek Kaminski, his deputy, who had been an Army officer before the war and was now living under a different name and working as a labourer on the railway so that he could travel to and fro along the line in a way denied to others. Later both these men were arrested and murdered.

In their efforts to germanise western Poland, incorporated into the Reich, the Germans had brought in their own countrymen from deep in the Reich itself. In nearly every house was a German who supervised the neighbours carefully. Fear for their own safety and for the future made a police spy of every individual German civilian. The worst plague of all, of course, were the local Germans. They spoke Polish, knew the local conditions and relationships and quickly spotted every newcomer. All this combined to deprive the western Polish population of that cohesion which the people had in central Poland. There, the Germans and their Gestapo could shoot at us, it is true, but they had practically no access to our private lives. In the west, a German neighbour examined literally every Polish pot and pan. For instance, eggs were rationed to Germans only; any Polish housewife found to have an egg in her larder was punished by a spell in prison. Compulsory work was another difficulty. The only alternative for a Pole who did not work from morning to night was a concentration camp.

I soon realised that under these conditions it was out of the question to organise a large Underground staff. The work must be directed from outside—from Warsaw. It was only possible to act in the west through either the local population or such persons who had physical features and documents which would enable them to pass as Germans. Having arrived at these conclusions, I set out on my return journey for Warsaw on New Year's Day.

It was two o'clock in the morning when we safely reached the home of the barmaid from Glowno Station. Some railway workers were gathered there to celebrate the New Year. One of them patted my shoulder with great joviality, putting the most unexpected questions to me.

"Stockings or linen?" was his first.

I was completely taken aback and it took me a few seconds to realise that they took us for ordinary smugglers.

"Linen, of course," I replied as quickly as I could.

"What's your price?" he persisted.

This was quite beyond me. I had never expected to be faced with such a nice commercial poser. But my guide, alert as ever, came to my rescue at once.

"Forty zlotys a metre," he put in.

"Very reasonable," the railroad man mumbled, "you've been lucky. Do you want to sell any here?"

"No." It was again the guide who replied. "We prefer to get the stuff through to Warsaw. Prices are better there."

*   *   *

The next day I was in Warsaw reporting on my mission.

After my return I energetically began to reorganise the liaison connections with the western districts, Poznań and Toruń, which were under my command, and to rebuild their staffs once more. The difficulties were tremendous and seemed often to be insurmountable. Officers speaking fluent German were very scarce, and only these had a chance of surviving for any time in the west.

All this made a good deal of work, and more than once I could not spare the two or three hours to see Renia on Sundays. She was getting on well with her job, but in the beginning of September she was compelled to leave her office to preserve the good name of worthy Mme. Malinowska, the interpreter. She had told everybody that her husband had been deported to Russia—and now, in three months, she was expecting a child. She had to quit before her condition became too obvious. She continued to work in the Underground till three weeks before the child was born. She could not withdraw, partly because the field of her activities had been enlarged, partly because she had to train a responsible successor. At the same time she had to change flats twice.

One Saturday evening I had gone to the flat to help her get things straight before she moved in. It was only a few weeks before the arrival of the baby. I was in the act of putting up some black-out curtains when there came a violent knocking at the door. We looked at each other. We were not expecting anyone at that particular moment.

"Stay here," said Renia. "I will see who it is."

She took the acetylene lamp from the table and went into the passage. "Who's there?" she asked through the closed door.

"Police," answered a loud voice in Polish.

After a moment's hesitation, Renia opened the door slightly. It was roughly pushed wide open and two men in plain clothes burst into the flat. I watched the scene through the half-open door in the light of the lamp she was holding. I was still invisible in the dark.

One of the men pulled a card from his pocket and waved it before her eyes, saying:

"We're from the police. What are you doing here? Are you the owner of the apartment?"

"Not altogether," she replied. "I am moving in shortly."

"Your name?"

"Marynowska—Janina Marynowska," she answered, giving the name she was using just then.

"What are you doing here?"

"I told you. I've come here to fix things in my new flat."

"Anybody else here?"

Her reply did not come at once. I felt she must be very nervous. If she said there was no one and they found me, I should have been arrested without more ado. Then she answered:

"My brother is here. He came to help me put up the curtains."

"Where is he?" shouted the man.

"In there." She indicated the room.

The man dashed into the room and flashed his torch in my face. "Ah! Here he is," he called to his companion.

I had an identity card with me. It was made out in the name G. Korabski; with it was a work certificate which Renia had got for me through the Central Relief Board, where she had been working. The man glanced at my papers. None of us could doubt that they had me this time.

"Where do you work?"

Renia intervened because it occurred to her I might not yet have learned the address on my certificate.

"Don't interrupt," shouted the Gestapo man. "Is he your brother?"

"Of course he is. I've just told you so."

"What's your maiden name?"

Silence followed. Renia was very nervous by this time and in her distress had obviously forgotten this personal detail on her new identity card. In an effort to cover the pause and avert suspicion, I said, "Can't you see her condition?" as persuasively as I could.

The man showed signs of impatient anger. "Can't you hear what I said? What's your maiden name?" he shouted.

At that moment the tension was broken. I heard her answer calmly; she had remembered the name. "Oh, it's my maiden name you want—it's Tyszkowska."

"Then he is no brother of yours. Korabski is his name here. No doubt about that."

But she was a match for them. Calmly she pointed out that in Polish the word "brother" also means "cousin," and concluded:

"He is a cousin on my mother's side."

This explanation did not seem to satisfy the Gestapo men. They ordered me to go along with them.

"Will he be back soon?" she asked.

"Oh, he'll be back all right," jeered one of the men.

As we went downstairs, I wondered whether there would be a police car in the street. I wanted time. No; there was no van. There was a third man in the entrance. He flashed his torch in my face and said: "Yes. That's him."

"This is bad," I thought, "to be arrested merely by chance by a man who only knows me by sight from a photo. It's rotten luck."

I concealed my feelings because they were watching me closely, and I tried to see what they looked like. The one who professed to recognise me was dark, aged about thirty, with a long, lean face. I had never seen him before.

"If you recognise me," I said firmly, "let's go to the light and then maybe I'll be able to recognise you. There seems to be some misunderstanding." I asked, too, where he had known me, since I could not recall his face.

One of the others said: "You are suspected of being of Jewish origin."

My relief at this had to be stifled; it was enormous, although I was not yet out of the wood. I leaned up against the wall to get my breath and decided on a change of tactics. I let out a hearty laugh and demanded to be taken at once to Gestapo headquarters, where I proposed to prove that I had ten Aryan grandmothers and ten Aryan grandfathers on both sides and in all directions. If they did take me to Gestapo headquarters, they would certainly unearth more of my past than mere Aryan ancestors.

I took an insistent, mocking tone. Their assurance was shaken. The distance to the police station was a matter of a few hundred yards only. But it took us a good forty-five minutes to cover it. At every lamp-post we stopped to discuss the question, while my identity papers were examined over again. I continued to insist, with more assurance at each stop, that I be taken at once to the police station instead of being kept hanging around in the street like this.

Just before we reached the police station, they let me go. I dashed back to Renia in the flat and knocked at the door as I said, "It's me." I heard her cry of joy. She had not expected me to return. In fact, she had never expected to see me again.

In the evening of December 12th, 1942, I learned that I had a son. The child was registered in the way that illegitimate children always are: as a male descendant of Janina Marynowska. However, he was baptised soon after by a priest who not only knew that the boy was legitimate, but even knew his name. The Chaplain of our H.Q. performed the little ceremony secretly in a convent. Of course, there remains no trace of this is any public register. The Chaplain certified the birth and baptism on a tiny scrap of tissue paper, which he rolled up and put into a little wooden cross he had hollowed out.

Renia still had a few jewels to pay for the clinic and because of her needs I had accepted a monthly salary for officers since June, 1942, the amount of which did not depend on the functions we performed. Till then we had both been living on her heirlooms, because we thought monthly salaries for members of the Underground should be reserved for those who had no other source of income. All these personal troubles and worries, however, soon vanished completely from our minds, when in the beginning of the difficult year 1943 a new tragedy began to unfold.

The principle of collective responsibility imposed by the Germans upon the population for every act of resistance or sabotage which we carried out forced us to adopt methods of attack which would, so far as possible, avoid these German mass reprisals on the civilian population. We had, too, to establish a balance between our own losses and those we inflicted upon the enemy. But the end of 1942 marked a turning-point in the civilian state of mind. The change was not only due to the situation on the various war fronts; its immediate cause was in Poland proper: I refer to the massacres of the Jews.

From the very beginning, German policy had been moving steadily and systematically towards the extermination of the Jews in Poland—a community of about 3½ million souls. Immediately after the September, 1939, campaign all Jews were obliged to wear an armband showing the star of David. In December, 1939, they were ordered to settle in certain specified districts, thus reviving the idea of the mediæval Ghetto. On November 14th, 1940, the Warsaw Ghetto was closed. Any Jew found beyond its confines was shot on the spot. The Jewish districts had been surrounded by walls 8 feet high and German sentries were posted at the few entrances. Signs were erected, bearing the inscription: "Spotted Typhus. Entry and exit forbidden."

The next Nazi step was the liquidation of communities of Jews in the smaller towns and their transfer to the Ghettos of the larger towns. At the beginning of 1942, the Warsaw Ghetto, which was a very small area, held over 400,000 Jews. The houses were indescribably overcrowded, with as many as fifteen people to a room. The food rations allowed them by the Germans consisted of 4½ lb. of bread per month—nothing else. Thus the Jewish population was condemned to death by starvation. Human life, however, is stronger than the most heavily armed guards, and food trickled into the Ghetto by the most fantastic channels; through the cellars of adjoining houses, through the sewers, and through gaps which were torn in the Ghetto walls almost every night. But all this smuggling in of food was utterly insufficient, and appalling misery, want and hunger reigned within.

Trams which had to pass through the Ghetto were allowed to keep to their route at first, although they were not permitted to stop in the Ghetto region. This gave me an opportunity to see conditions for myself on several occasions. The general impression was one of swarming humanity. The appearance of a uniformed German among the seething mass produced indescribable panic. Driven by fear, the crowd would try to rush away and, almost miraculously, the street became deserted. The mortality rate was so high that I often saw corpses lying in the street, covered with newspapers. There they would remain till the municipal rubbish carts came and cleared them away the next morning. The area was completely blacked out at night as the electric current was cut off. Before the war, the Jewish districts in Poland had been inhabited by only the poorest Jews. The Germans had steadily increased their misery and want. And now to these districts were driven Jewish doctors, attorneys, industrialists and scholars.

In the course of months, the Ghetto in Warsaw became almost hermetically sealed from the outside world. Very occasionally, under the spur of starvation, an individual Jew would succeed in escaping when hunger overcame fear of death—for it was certain death for any Jew to fall into German hands outside the Ghetto. I never shall forget one isolated incident which I saw in the winter of 1941. I was going to a meeting in the centre of the city. At one of the busiest spots, I saw a Jewish boy of about fifteen or sixteen. He was crouched on the edge of the pavement, his legs doubled under him; his head had sunk on his chest and one arm was stretched out to the passers-by in mute prayer for help. He was emaciated—a living skeleton. Before him was an old cap into which people dropped coins and notes.

As I passed him, I dropped some coins into the cap and a passenger warned him: "Clear out as fast as you can; the German police may get you at any moment." He did not say a word, but slowly raised his eyes. In them I read the most dejected, hopeless sorrow. "Strange," I mused as I went on. "His cap's full of money—enough to buy him a few good meals and he looks more than hungry. And yet he doesn't budge."

A quarter of an hour later, I passed on my way back. There was a crowd around the boy, who was sitting in the same position. He still crouched with his head sunk, his arm outstretched, the cap before him, full of money. He was dead.

At that moment, two German security policemen appeared in the distance and the crowd quickly dispersed. The corpse sat there abandoned. The Germans approached with regular, unhurried pace. One of them seized the boy by the rags on his chest, lifted him up and shook him like a doll. Seeing the boy was dead, he flung the corpse down and gave it a violent kick.

Some hungry Jewish children, in fact quite a number, managed every day to slip out of the Ghetto and go to town, where the Polish population gave them food for themselves and their families. The Germans—not only the Gestapo and the police, but any German civilian who met such a child—would often shoot it on the spot with visible pleasure.

The first news about mass execution of Jews came from our eastern provinces where the Germans had taken them from the Russians. In the spring of 1942 we received the first fantastic rumours of the mass extermination of Jews in the smaller towns of the west which had been incorporated into the Reich. According to the first reports we received, a Gestapo man with a guileless, innocent face and engaging manner would visit these groups of Jews. He made a longish speech couched in a friendly tone. He promised an early end to their sufferings and said that they were to be transported to the east, where they would be settled. Work awaited them there; they would have housing accommodation and better and more plentiful food. His manner was exceptionally kind. He would pat the children's heads and distribute sweets amongst them. Completely unaccustomed to such treatment from the Germans, the Jews would be enraptured with joy and feel sure their troubles were ended.

They were then transported in trucks to the country estate of Chełmo, a few miles from Dąbie. There they were told to strip, as they were to have baths and be issued with working clothes. The naked Jews were then put into closed lorries, the exhaust fumes of which were piped into the inside. The journey to the forest took only half an hour, but by the time they arrived the Jews in the lorries had all been killed by carbon-monoxide poisoning. In the forest, mass graves were ready.

At first, this report seemed so fantastic, that I had doubt as to its truth; but towards the beginning of the summer of 1942 the Germans began to deport the Jews from the Lublin Ghetto. About 130,000 people disappeared behind the walls

D

of the concentration camp at Belzec. That camp was so effectively cut off from the rest of the world that we could not at first find out what was happening to the Jews inside. One thing, however, was obvious. The camp was not big enough to accommodate such a large number of people, and the conclusion that the Jews taken there were being murdered in some mysterious way had inevitably to be drawn.

On the night of July 21st, 1942, the eminent Polish surgeon, Professor Raszeya, was telephoned by some Jewish doctors to come to the Ghetto for a consultation about a patient, Mr. Abe Gutnajer, a wealthy antique dealer. As a pass was necessary to enter the Ghetto, Professor Raszeya doubted whether he would be permitted to answer the call, but, true to his professional sense of duty, he telephoned Gestapo headquarters and, to his surprise, was told that he would encounter no difficulty in either entering or leaving the Ghetto. An hour later, a pass in his pocket, Professor Raszeya was in the Ghetto at the patient's bedside. It was night-time. Scarcely half an hour had elapsed before the Gestapo broke into the room and shot the professor, two Jewish doctors and all the other inhabitants of the house. The only life they spared, whether by chance or intentionally it is not easy to say, was that of the patient, who was very seriously ill. The murder of Professor Raszeya was the signal for wild and continuous shooting which lasted all night. S.S. men shot at windows or dashed into apartments at random, firing at everyone they came across. Panic broke out in the Ghetto.

The next day I was awakened by distant bursts of machine-gun fire. The whole city was in a state of tension. It was widely known that something terrible was going on in the Ghetto. The walls had been surrounded by a double cordon of special units, composed of Latvians and Ukrainians who had been brought into Warsaw for the purpose the day before. We received reports of what was happening there from a Polish official who was employed as a specialist in one of the German factories in the Jewish district. He sent the information to our headquarters, and these data were later edited and published in pamphlet form as a testimony of one of the greatest acts of barbarism in our time.

"Whatever is told of the 'liquidation' of the Warsaw Ghetto," he wrote, "will always be inadequate to cover the sum of human suffering, humiliation and death—indescribable in its horror and scope. No one who has not himself passed through it can imagine the extent of it. Further, he will be quite incapable of believing that it all actually happened."

The "liquidation" of the Ghetto began with the appearance of official notices announcing that by order of the German authorities all Jews living in Warsaw, regardless of sex or age, "were to be transported to the east." Every person deported was permitted to take all valuables such as money, jewellery, gold, etc. This sounded suspicious—doubly so since, according to previous German orders, no Jew was allowed to be in possession of any gold. The wild and indiscriminate firing which had gone on all night was designed solely to terrorise the Jews into complete subjection. Towards noon, mass hunts began. Small groups, when rounded up, were driven to the square near Stawki Street, adjoining a railway siding. Hurried and jostled, the Jews were crowded into closed lorries, which were then secured by barbed wire. In this way, 5,000 people were taken away in one day. We were to learn that this was to be a daily event. In the Ghetto, the panic-stricken Jews fled from place to place, from street to street, seeking shelter in the cellars. Many thousands spent the night in the synagogues, wailing and praying.

The horror of it was increased because the Germans endeavoured to force the specially organised Jewish police force to assist in the work. The Chairman of the Jewish Council in the Ghetto, Czerniakow, who was also chief of the police force, was instructed by the Germans to assemble a certain number of his co-religionists in the so-called Umschlag Platz, near Stawki Street, every day. Unwilling to assist in the extermination of his fellow Jews, Czerniakow poisoned himself with potassium cyanide.

The names of concentration camps such as Belzec, Sobibor and so on, began to be mentioned. Rumours arose among the Jews that those who had already left had been given work, food and housing accommodation. These rumours were clearly started by the Germans in order to reduce their victims to docility. As early as July 29th we had learned from the reports of railroad workers that the transports were being sent to the concentration camp at Treblinka and that there the Jews disappeared without trace. There could be no further doubt this time that the deportations were but a prelude to extermination.

General Rowecki, swift in his decisions as always, made up his mind that we could not remain passive, and that at all costs we must help the Jews so far as it lay in our power. He called a conference, at which, however, some doubts were expressed. The argument ran: "If America and Great Britain, with powerful armies and air forces behind them and equipped with all the means of modern warfare, are not able to stop this crime and have to look on impotently while the Germans perpetrate every kind of horror in the occupied countries, how can we hope to stop them?" Rowecki's opinion was that failure to show active resistance would only encourage the Germans to further mass exterminations on the same lines.

We had a department in our organisation which arranged protection and help for escaped Jews and the distribution of money to them which had been sent to us from London for the purpose. A certain "Wacław" was the chief of the department, and he was now instructed by Rowecki to get through to the Ghetto and establish contact with the Jewish leaders. He was to tell them that the Home Army was ready to come to the assistance of the Jews with supplies of arms and ammunition and to co-ordinate their attacks outside with Jewish resistance from within.

The Jewish leaders, however, rejected the offer, arguing that if they behaved quietly the Germans might deport and murder 20,000 or 30,000, perhaps even 60,000 of them, but it was inconceivable that they should destroy the lot; while if they resisted, the Germans would certainly do so. When Waclaw reported this to Rowecki, the General decided to intensify the sabotaging of German lines of communication in such a way as to hamper and delay the deportations.

The Jewish leaders had handed to Waclaw an appeal addressed to the civilised world and to the Allied nations in particular. They demanded that the people of the Reich should be threatened with reprisals. The appeal was immediately transmitted to London, as we were already transmitting daily reports to there on the situation in the Ghetto. But the B.B.C. maintained complete silence. The tragedy of the Jews in the Ghetto was, as a result, intensified. They realised that the Germans had, for the time being at least, managed to conceal the enormity of their atrocities from the outside world.

If they had to die, the Jews at least wished to have the assurance that these crimes would one day be punished.

There seemed to be only one possible explanation for this silence on the part of London. The news was so incredible that it had failed to convince. We ourselves had, after all, been loath to believe the first reports we received of the exterminations. I was to learn later that this was, in fact, what had happened.

Meanwhile, fifty-eight trucks left the Ghetto every day with 100 persons in each. They were all bound for Treblinka. Around September 1st the daily quota was raised to about 10,000. Among other well-known Jews who were deported was Dr. Janusz Korczak. He had been running a model Jewish orphanage and was the author of children's books of high moral and literary value. We had offered to help smuggle him out and guaranteed him a safe refuge, but he refused. He preferred not to abandon his flock of waifs and strays, and he left the Ghetto with the children on their last journey.

I know of nothing more terrifying than the scenes described to me by eyewitnesses from the Ghetto. Two points in their stories struck me as being particularly typical. German railway men and Customs employees, who were not concerned with either the Gestapo or the extermination of the Jews, applied to the commanders of the extermination detachments to be allowed to assist in the work. And this without the slightest invitation, let alone pressure. It was evidently purely for the love of the thing that they took part in the man-hunts and shootings of human beings. Some of them would sit astride the walls surrounding the Ghetto and fire at the fleeing Jews below as though they were potting at rabbits.

The second point which struck me as so typical was also described by an eyewitness. Some numbers of Jews had succeeded, through subterranean passages and other means, in slipping out of the Ghetto and finding refuge with Poles. There were many children among them. A group of child refugees, exhausted and horribly emaciated, were resting in a roadside ditch just outside Warsaw when a large car came along carrying several German civilians, probably officials enjoying a week-end trip. The car passed the group in the ditch and then drew up. Sensing their danger, the children tried to make off across the fields, but they were too weak even to flee from death. The Germans got out of the car and pursued them, killing them one after another with revolver shots. Only two of the children survived: an eleven-year-old boy and a little girl.

By August 8th, 150,000 Jews had been deported from the Warsaw Ghetto. One month after the beginning of the massacre we knew all the details concerning their fate, despite the exceptional measures taken by the Germans to prevent any leakage of information from the concentration camp at Treblinka. At first we only received fragments of news, such as that passenger trains were no longer permitted to stop at Treblinka Station. Later, the whole story reached us. Train loads of Jews drew up at the camp situated in the forest where the Jews were driven from the wagons and ordered to deposit all their possessions—in particular, money and valuables. They were then made to strip and proceed to the "baths." An enormous sign board announced that clothing would be given out after the bath and that they would then be sent out in batches to their various places of work. As the world now knows the "baths" were poison gas chambers. The next stage was simply a communal grave, which was extended day and night by two mechanical excavators. Into the pit were flung row upon row of corpses of men, women and children.

After a time, trains from Treblinka began to pass through Warsaw. They were full of enormous stocks of clothes for transformation into raw materials for the German textile mills. So vanished the last trace of the victims. Polish railwaymen on the Warsaw junction noted three wagons loaded with human hair. We had a sample of this hair analysed and found that the Jews had been murdered by gas formed from some compound of cyanide hydrogen. It was later replaced by ordinary steam, so that the Jews were no longer poisoned, but suffocated.

September 10th was to be the last day of the extermination campaign. The Germans ordered all Jews still left in the Ghetto to assemble in a certain area. A crowd of them, resigned and apathetic, slowly marched towards the assembly point, some carrying bundles of food, although they now knew the fate that awaited them. A selection was then made by two directors of large factories employing Jews, Schultz and Tobbens. The Germans only retained those who seemed capable of manual labour. Terrible scenes ensued when parents and children were separated. One father whose wife had been deported earlier was chosen for life and work, but without his two children who went to their death. There were hundreds of such cases. Those whom Tobbens and Schultz had selected for labour were given *Lebensnummern* (life numbers) which they were obliged to wear stitched to the backs of their shirts. About 30,000 of these numbers were issued. The Ghetto seemed now quite deserted, but at least another 40,000 people were concealed in hide-outs so well camouflaged and so deep down that the Germans failed to discover them.

Naturally, the effect of all this on the Poles was profound. The Jewish population of Poland had, for the most part, spoken Yiddish, lived their own separate lives, dressed differently and kept to their own customs. They had undoubtedly been a foreign body within the Polish community. They thus differed very considerably from their brethren in western Europe and America. Xenophobia is an ancient trait and an unpleasant one, but it appears in every human society where a foreign community of any size lives alongside a native population. Xenophobia with regard to the Jews had appeared in some sections of the Polish nation, but it had nothing at all in common with German sadism and ferocity. The appeal to the nation to assist Jewish refugees, which appeared in our Underground Press, met with instant response in urban and rural areas alike. The Jews who managed to escape from the Ghetto and survive the German occupation owe their salvation to the Poles who gave them refuge. It should be borne in mind that all the members of any Polish family found harbouring a Jew had to answer with their lives.

Many Polish families went so far as to adopt a Jewish child to save it from death, although they knew that by doing this they risked being treated by the Germans as if they were Jews themselves. When the Jews were driven into the Ghetto, a Polish woman, mother of two children, took a Jewish baby and kept it with her own children. The parents, who had been living in the same house, had implored her to do so; they could not bring themselves to take the baby with them into the Ghetto. The Polish mother felt she could not refuse, and took the child, keeping its origin a close secret. But it did leak out, and one day two Gestapo men appeared in the flat and asked to see the children. The mother said there was only the little one at home, the two others were at school. The Germans answered quietly that they would wait for the children to return. In the meantime, they talked with the mother while the baby played on the floor. After about half an hour the older children, a boy of six and a girl of five, burst into the room. The Gestapo men took out their revolvers and shot both children on the spot. At the door they turned back and said to the mother, "Now you may bring up your Jewish brat," and walked out.

The events that had taken place made it quite clear, finally, that a passive attitude was of no use whatever. Our Staff came to a unanimous determination that defence measures must be adopted at all costs. The same conclusion was reached by the Jews still in the Ghetto hide-outs. It was in October, 1942, that the Underground Jewish Militant Organisation was founded amongst the young men working in the factories of Schultz and Tobbens. Members of all Jewish political groups were represented, the strongest being the Zionists, Jewish Communists and the Socialist *Bund*. As soon as the organisation was set up, two representatives were sent to establish contact with the Home Army.

Waclaw reported to us that the Jews planned to defend themselves should the Germans resume their liquidation of the survivors. This was just before Christmas, 1942. Rowecki instructed Colonel Chrusciel "Monter," Home Army Commander for Warsaw, to get into touch with the Jewish emissaries. They were a young Zionist of twenty-five who used the pseudonym "Antek" and his companion, who gave no name at all. The latter was so typically Jewish in feature that only to meet him, especially on the street, was fraught with the greatest danger. The Jewish envoys had their own ways of getting out of the Ghetto and back, and they emerged for meetings several times a week. During the first meeting they asked how far they could count on our help. They were promised a supply of revolvers, rifles, some machine-guns and about a thousand hand-grenades, as well as explosives for the production of mines. In addition, they were to have fuses and other necessary parts. It was not very much, but our own stocks were exceptionally low at the time. The Jews were well pleased with the offer.

Antek requested, in the name of his organisation, that our staff should prepare a strategic plan for the defence of the Ghetto. This was done. From then on arms and ammunition were smuggled into the Ghetto by the same channels as those formerly used for the supply of food. In addition to the weapons which we sent in to them, the Jews showed great initiative in procuring further supplies from other sources—in particular, by looting them from German railway transports.

Other assistance we were able to give them was instruction for making incendiary anti-tank grenades. A bottle was filled with a mixture of kerosene, petrol and sulphuric acid. The bottle was well corked and on the outside was stuck paper impregnated with an explosive solution. When the bottle was thrown and broken, the mixture of the contents with the explosive on the paper produced a fine detonation and fierce fire. We supplied the ingredients for the bottles, and they were later to play an important part in the defence of the Ghetto. The Jewish Militant Organisation, it is interesting to note, succeeded in purchasing arms from Germans also. They secured considerable funds for this purpose by forcing rich Jews in the Ghetto to make substantial contributions.

Preparations were made as far as possible, both inside and outside the Ghetto. We had not long to wait. The Germans resumed their extermination programme on January 18th, 1943. This time, however, they met with a surprise. In Zamenhof Street, a passing German column was greeted by a volley of shots and hand-grenades. A sharp battle ensued. The German police and Gestapo men fled in disorder. We learned from a telephone call which we tapped that a German detachment of sixty men lost half its strength, including twenty killed. The Germans now realised that they had to face a considerable armed Jewish force, and that this time they would have to fight. They therefore decided to adopt other tactics which would not entail danger to themselves.

Among the 80,000 Jews still in the Ghetto two schools of thought prevailed. The older generation continued to oppose the idea of fighting the Germans and favoured the bribery of high Gestapo officials and leaders to allow them a further lease of life. Long and bitter experience had, however, shown that these officials were only too willing to accept the bribes without keeping their part of the bargain. For this reason, the Jewish Militant Organisation refused to believe in German assurances and advocated that they should fight for their lives.

The Germans decided to profit by this divergence of opinion before applying force. Tobbens developed a propaganda campaign aimed at persuading the Jews that it would be in their best interests to accompany him to their new jobs. The J.M.O. replied with posters and notices declaring that this was merely one more German trick. It often happened that Jewish and German declarations were posted side by side on the same wall. Tobbens even went so far as personally to call meetings of Jews in the Ghetto, at which he argued publicly with members of the J.M.O. He offered inducements, such as a play-garden for Jewish children at Trawniki. But it was of little avail. The number of volunteers remained insignificant and the Germans decided to revert to their former methods. On March 29th, all American Jews were summoned to the Gestapo office. From there they were taken to the Jewish cemetery and executed.

At the beginning of April, 5,000 Jews were deported from the Ghetto, this time by force. Tobbens stated, at the same time, that these deportees had been sent to the labour camp at Trawniki, where they would receive humane treatment, be well fed and paid generously. Simultaneously, through intermediaries, the Germans let it be understood that they would stop further deportations if the Jews paid a suitable ransom in gold. The peace-at-any-price group were prepared to accept this offer, but the J.M.O. opposed the notion. A wholly unexpected occurrence, however, decided the further course of events.

Some fifteen or sixteen Jews had succeeded in escaping from the last group of deportees. They returned with news of the terrible truth. The 5,000 people who had allegedly been sent to work in factories had, in fact, been stopped at a place not far from Warsaw. They were then ordered to separate into groups and dig pits. Then they were mown down by machine-gun fire in groups as they stood on the edge. The next group had to spread quicklime over the last victims and then provided the next layer of corpses, and so on till none remained. As the news spread, the Ghetto seethed once more. The cry was raised: "Enough of ransoms. Not another man without a fight."

The Gestapo fixed April 19th for the final liquidation: the Jews in the Warsaw Ghetto were then to be exterminated to the very last man. As before, during the night the Germans entered the quarter and started to drag people from their homes. Heavy firing at once broke out and a hail of hand-grenades fell from houses which a moment before had seemed deserted. From windows and roofs the German detachments were subjected to a withering fire. An S.S. company entered the Ghetto in battle formation and equipment. It was greeted with machine-gun fire at point-blank range and forced to withdraw. Four armoured cars were hurriedly summoned and broke into the chief artery of the district, where they began wildly shelling houses. Two of them were put out of action and the other two forced to withdraw.

The Germans then instituted a regular siege of the Ghetto, at the same time avoiding as far as possible any losses to themselves. Batteries of German artillery were drawn up and began to shell the houses of the Ghetto at close range. It was Easter Monday evening at six o'clock when it began. The thunder of artillery shook the walls of Warsaw and window-panes rattled incessantly. In reply, the Jews set fire to the factories and workshops in the Ghetto, which were engaged in German war production. Establishments producing linen and uniforms, saddlery, mattresses, woodwork, etc., were burnt to the ground. The fighting was chaotic in the early stages, but gradually began to assume the character of an organised and co-ordinated struggle. Machine-guns, rifles, tommy-guns and hand-grenades were used on both sides. The Jews made several sallies, which resulted in the death of Germans even outside the Ghetto. Fighting lasted throughout Tuesday, Wednesday and Thursday. The German losses were about 100 killed. Then they again changed their tactics. They began to burn down one house after another, thus forcing the defenders back step by step.

Monter organised a series of attacks on the German rear-guard with the aim of diverting the attention of the enemy so as to enable the defenders either to escape or to improve their positions. Among other picked troops engaged were our diversionary Kedyw units under the direct orders of the Commander-in-Chief. The difficulty of their attacks was increased by the fact that their only access to the Ghetto was through narrow gaps in the walls. In one case, the Germans discovered one of the gaps which were being used by a Home Army unit. It was immediately blocked by the cross-fire of a number of machine-guns. A score of our men already on the Ghetto side were hit and the others were forced to withdraw.

It was on Saturday that organised defence finally broke down, leaving only isolated points of resistance. The heroic Antek fell at his post while operating a heavy machine-gun.

The Germans then began to concentrate the Jews in the Umschlag Platz in preparation for their deportation.

When it became clear that further defence was impossible, we decided to save the survivors of the fight. During the night Home Army units gained control of the manholes in the vicinity of the Jewish district. They were opened and surrounded by armed guards. A reception base had been prepared for the survivors in the forests near Otwock (about twenty miles south-east of Warsaw), where they were to rest, receive clothing and food and then proceed in small groups by night and under escort to further bases in the provinces. Our intention was to form partisan detachments in eastern Poland from these gallant survivors, which was indeed their only chance of safety. However, when our men got through the sewers to act as guides, they found that the remaining resistance groups were composed almost entirely of defenders in such an advanced state of nervous and physical exhaustion that there were quite unable to attempt the underground journey. Only about 100 people took advantage of this means of escape.

When organised resistance ceased the Germans continued systematically to fire house after house, often blowing them up, while cellars and shelters were flooded with water. They also used poison and tear gases to force the Jews from their hiding-places. Daily transports of Jews began once more to leave the city for the east. To the very end, the Germans used every precaution to avoid losses for themselves. I heard a story in this connection from one of our soldiers who had taken part in the fighting.

Isolated shots were coming from the attic of one of the houses. The Germans prudently remained in their hide-outs, carefully observing the house from 40 or 50 yards' distance. Finally, after a longer period of quiet, a Jewish boy of about sixteen appeared in the entrance of the house. His hands were raised above his head. "No. 5 Tlomackie Street surrenders," he shouted to the Germans. A well-aimed German bullet killed him on the spot. Only an hour later did the Germans enter the house with the same extreme caution and search it systematically from foundations to roof. It was empty. Not a single living soul remained. In the attic, they found a tommy-gun with empty cartridge cases lying around it.

In the last week of May, silence reigned over the entire Ghetto. The last house was destroyed; the last Jew killed.

In every Polish town, big or small, in every village, the extermination of the Jews proceeded. In Lwów and smaller towns of the east, events similar to those in Warsaw took place a little earlier. Generally it can be said that the action began in 1942 and that by 1943 the Ghettos had disappeared.

* * *

During the first phase of the German occupation, immediately after the campaign of 1939, the Germans executed ten Poles for every German killed. Soon the price for one German killed was raised to 100 Poles. These executions reached such proportions by 1942 that the whole nation came to the conclusion that there was but one way of reacting—to answer terror by terror.

Independent of this, our diversionary action, as has already been said, had been greatly intensified since the outbreak of the Russo-German War. General Sikorski sent this wireless message on April 27th, 1942: "The Home Army must make special efforts and inflict as great losses as possible on the enemy. Thus it will fulfil our duty towards our Allies." We knew that our principal task for the moment was sabotage, to hamper German activity at the front by disorganising the rear and by lowering German armament production. The following letter is quoted to show how the Allies valued this effort:

"MINISTRY OF ECONOMIC WARFARE,
"LONDON, W.I.
November 10th, 1942

"*Most Secret*
"F/57.5/125.
"MY DEAR GENERAL,—You may remember that at the instigation of the Chiefs of Staff I approached you some months ago and asked that instructions should be sent to the Commander of your Secret Army to intensify the sabotage of railway and other communications leading to the Russian front.

"According to information which we have now received from the Sixth Bureau, it appears that these attacks have recently been very successful. I should like to take this opportunity of congratulating you on the success achieved, and I should be grateful if you would send a telegram to the Commander of the Secret Army giving him our thanks and expressing our sympathy with the relatives of those who lost their lives in these operations and in the reprisals which followed them.

"Now that the United Nations have taken the offensive, the importance of the role of the Secret Army in Poland has greatly increased, and we look forward with confidence to the part which this force will play in the defeat of Germany.

"Yours sincerely,

(*Signed*) SELBORNE."

Our sabotage and diversion were increasing and actions of open resistance were becoming necessary. Special, well-armed units were then created on the whole territory of Poland. All minor diversionary groups were melted in. The new units were named Kedyw (Diversion Command). They waged war in the period of Underground conspiracy. From the beginning of open fighting in 1944, all major and minor acts of war were undertaken by the Kedyw. The Boy Scouts, especially the "Grey Files" (units of Boy Scouts organised in the Underground), supplied the Kedyw with many excellent young soldiers. The Kedyw had a great many units constantly ready. After every action they scattered again and disappeared. They were ready for action on three to five hours' notice.

A small staff, consisting of the C.-in-C., Home Army, his Chief of Staff, the Officer Commanding Kedyw, the Chief of Press and Propaganda Office and the Deputy of the Government Delegate, who directed the communal resistance action, gathered together. They planned the main outlines for all current activities in the sphere of diversion, sabotage, and general resistance throughout the whole country. The executive lay in the hands of the units of the Kedyw.

Among the diversion actions of major importance, we successfully blew up Army trains, destroyed the goods and machine-gunned trains, mostly as actions of revenge. In February, 1944, for example, we derailed seventeen freight trains and five fast trains; seventeen engines and seventy-eight railway cars were destroyed and the enemy lost 540 dead and 1,000 wounded.

All our actions of revenge were published in the Underground Press, of which we used to post a copy to the Gestapo. Each time we stated exactly those German cruelties for which revenge had been taken. This gave good results, because the Germans learned to know that atrocities committed on our

civilian population were becoming more and more costly to
them.

Apart from this, a good many special actions were carried
out. On January 18th, 1942, seven officers under the command
of "Ponury" (Gloomy) rescued a group of arrested comrades in
Pinsk. Gloomy had prepared the plan in every detail on the
spot since the beginning of January. On the 18th he and his
men, all in German uniforms, succeeded in rescuing by
an extremely bold and risky undertaking, all their comrades
and arranging their return to safe shelter, without the loss
of a single man. Gloomy—whose real name was Lieutenant
Jan Piwnik—was later on killed in action as a partisan leader
on the eastern border.

In spring, 1944, an extremely valuable associate, who had
been wounded, was arrested and taken to the St. John of God
Hospital in Warsaw, but the group Pegasus got him out.
The Gestapo kept their sick and wounded prisoners under
heavy guard. One day another wounded prisoner was brought
in with a strong escort of Gestapo men. The unsuspecting
guard at the gate let this Trojan horse in and the "wounded"
newcomer was carried upstairs. There he and his "stretcher-
bearers" succeeded in overpowering the interior garrison,
had the isolation cell opened and retired without difficulties
or losses with the man they had come to fetch. Such enterprises succeeded more than once with the help of Gestapo
motor cars, uniforms and personal documents belonging to
the killed Gestapo agents, who in 1943 numbered 1,246.

Towards the end of November, 1942, the Germans started
to remove the Polish population from the Zamość district and
brought in Germans from Rumania and Bessarabia to take
over the homes and farms thus forcibly evacuated. Their
plan was clear. After the extermination of the Polish population, the whole Zamość district was to be transformed into a
German settlement. The town of Zamość, a sixteenth-century
Polish city, was renamed Himmlerstadt.

In the course of 1942 and 1943 they deported 297 entire
villages from the four districts round Zamość, with over
100,000 inhabitants, including more than 30,000 children.
They used to surround the villages at night and gave ten to
twenty minutes for packing. Then they drove the people out,
using dogs to herd them to a transport spot. The old and those
unable to march were killed on the spot. The others had to

wait for twelve hours and more in the frost. When the cars appeared, they were squeezed in, sixty to eighty in a group, without food and often without water for a few days' journey in an unknown direction. The fate of the Polish children in this area was particularly terrible. All those of eleven and under were separated from their parents, packed into separate trucks and taken westwards towards Berlin, simply kidnapped to be brought up as Germans.

The inhabitants of the district reacted in spontaneous self-defence even before appropriate orders could be given. German reprisals followed, and in revenge our detachments were instructed to burn down the villages where Germans had been settled in the place of Poles. A number of other actions were undertaken at the same time. On New Year's Eve four railway bridges were blown up, two trains derailed, railway tracks torn up in three places and station and telecommunication equipment destroyed at several points. The systematic action spread fear among the German settlers, and they began to abandon their farms. The German plan was brought to naught.

In reply, the Germans decided to break Polish resistance by "pacifying" an even wider area. Accordingly, they brought in several divisions of Wehrmacht, field police, etc., with tanks and artillery. The operation was commanded by a staff of specialists who had conducted similar enterprises in other countries. Their objective was not our partisan detachments based in the forest, but the neighbouring rural population. Various villages were surrounded at dawn, the inhabitants packed into the local church or school building and burnt to death. In other cases, the people were driven to assembly points—open spaces surrounded by barbed wire—and thence some were taken to the Reich and others sent to concentration camps, where most of them met their death sooner or later.

These steps by no means had the effect the Germans desired, however. Rather did they strengthen the determination to fight in self-defence when the news spread throughout the country.

In view of the obvious necessity of protecting the civilian population, we began to organise partisan detachments. Their first major operation was our answer to the mass deportations around Zamość. Swift-moving and well-armed units, each from fifty to several hundred men strong, made their headquarters mostly in forests. It was from there that they attacked the enemy, usually at the most unexpected times and places. Their principal tasks were to carry out sabotage in open fighting and destroy the manpower and material goods of the enemy, as well as protect the civilian population from terror, perform acts of revenge, capture arms and munitions, protect parachutists, wireless stations, etc.

At the end of 1943 and in the beginning of 1944 our partisan units controlled large territories. The Germans did not dare to move about without strong cover, and they concentrated in towns and larger centres. They were fully aware of the rapidly increasing danger while they were fighting the Russians. All the Polish territory was filled with partisans, so they tried to liquidate them with the help of military operations on a large scale. Often they used several divisions of the Wehrmacht and the S.S., with armoured units and Luftwaffe. Their aim was to encircle our units and destroy them entirely. Our people had to attack the weakest point to break through the ring, often fighting hard and suffering great losses. But losses were also inflicted on the enemy. When we had broken through, the fighting continued in a different area.

German terror was one of the main reasons why partisan fighting was steadily on the increase in those years. Young people threatened with arrest, rescued prisoners, and terrorised peasants fled into the forests. Individuals who could not stand the nervous strain of continual terror and persecution and hoped to live a fuller life in open warfare or those who wished to revenge their next of kin, tortured and murdered—all these reinforced our partisan forces. This increase, in its turn, began to disturb the Germans.

In January, 1943, our Intelligence identified 247 battalions of German occupying forces; in November of the same year their number had gone up 180 per cent.; and in early spring, 1944, as many as 947 German battalions were stationed on Polish territory.

Our other weapon, the execution of Germans, was handled with the utmost caution. While the German methods of terror struck blindly at random, killing people regardless of guilt or innocence, our terrorism was never used against a single German who had not been selected with great care and for good reason. Our aim was always to paralyse the German extermination centres. We wished to convince every German

that if he perpetrated atrocities and crimes against the population, he would inevitably pay for it with his life. To this end,
we were obliged to strike at the men actually responsible for
the German terror and leave their pawns and subordinates
in peace for the time being.

On February 12th, 1943, seventy innocent Poles were
executed by German firing-squads in Warsaw. They were
merely passers-by who had been seized at random on the
street. Their names were listed on posters stuck up throughout
the city. The reason given for their execution was the alleged
"ceaseless armed attacks upon Germans." The posters were
signed by the Chief of Police and S.S. in Poland and Deputy
of Governor-General Frank, Krueger.

Sentence of death was at once passed by the Underground
upon Krueger. The sentence was carried out about two
months later, on April 20th, 1943, in Cracow, at 9.50 a.m.
The public was informed of the execution by our posters on
the walls and by the Underground Press. The Germans
tried to spread the rumour that the attack had failed and that
Krueger was still alive, but the fact remained that from the
moment when two bombs struck his car in the streets of
Cracow Krueger disappeared from the scene and was never
heard of again. From then onwards, we made it a matter of
principle that every German who signed an announcement
for the mass execution of Poles must at all costs be put out of
the way, in spite of any steps taken to protect him.

These executions were soon carried out on several officials
guilty of mass crimes. Among them was the infamous Hoffmann,
Director of the Labour Office, who had conducted large-scale
round-ups and deportations to the Reich. We also conducted
an acute war of nerves against smaller fry whom we wished
either to get rid of or to render harmless.

I think it was from Radomsk that we once received a report
about a troublesome district-farmer (*Kreis-Landwirt*) who
delighted in helping the Gestapo by not actively dangerous
but treacherous betrayals. Two of our men called on him and
told him they were Poles and had important details to give
him about the Underground, but for fear of their fellow
countrymen could only come on a longer visit when it was
dark. The German, delighted at the idea, told them to come
the next evening, when the office would be closed. He would
wait for them inside. They came and rang the bell. The

district-farmer, beaming, opened the door immediately. When they were certain that he really was quite alone in the office, they threatened him with revolvers and told him the Underground was now taking revenge on him for his behaviour. They made him undress from the waist downwards, kneel and put his head into the stove. When all this was done, they put a board on his backside, told him they were laying a hand-grenade on it, so that if he moved it would fall down and explode—and off they went. Two hours later the district farmer's mistress informed the German authorities that he had not come back from his office. His secretary investigated, found the man half-naked with his head still in the stove, and on the board—an egg. This incident made his further stay quite impossible; he had become ridiculous and was removed—which was all we had wanted.

We sent warnings to carefully selected Germans advising them either to stop their activities or to leave Poland. If they failed to accept this advice, they would be tried by the Underground courts of justice. After a lapse of some weeks, the same Germans received copies of the indictment. They were well printed, bore the seal of the court and a serial number. In appearance, they differed in no way from indictments received by accused persons in normal times, and since, during these weeks, sentences of death were actually being carried out upon other Germans, the recipients had no reason at all to doubt the mortal danger they faced if they refused to comply. In nearly every case, the German in question would demand a German police escort as protection, a special guard at his home and so on. As we sent out a considerable number of warnings, these requests were refused by the Gestapo, who had insufficient men to cope with the number of Nazis demanding protection. Then, at least a month later, we sent out the death sentences. Another month later, a reminder would be sent intimating that the sentence would be carried out on such and such a day.

It was rare that any one of them so treated was able to stand up to this nerve-racking procedure. In fact, they did all in their power to get out of Poland. Many of them completely changed their attitude to Poles and tried to gain their friendship—indeed, this method turned out to be the most effective we had yet tried. Poles noticed a marked change in the behaviour of many German officials. For instance, a certain German county-lieutenant at Mszana Dolna (south Poland), after receiving his indictment at once retired to bed and called in the local Polish doctor. He proposed to arrange for the immediate release of all Polish political prisoners in the county and offered to moderate greatly his policy towards Poles if the findings of the court investigation were quashed. The scrap of paper we had mailed to the county-lieutenant freed quite a number of Poles held in German gaols.

As the intensity of fear increased, the so-called man-hunts became a daily terror. The Germans went round capturing people for work in Germany, sending hundreds to concentration camps as retaliatory measures or merely in order to procure hostages. The man-hunts were usually undertaken by S.S. detachments or police units, though on certain major operations of this kind armed troops also took part; very often plain-clothes agents were employed in order to achieve maximum surprise.

The victims were men, women and even the youth of both sexes; the hunting grounds were streets, restaurants, cafés or railway waiting-rooms. People were dragged out of trains, trams, etc. Sometimes major operations were staged, when whole blocks of streets were cordoned off and the houses combed one by one. There was hardly a day in any larger town when one district or other did not suffer from some form of man-hunt. The captives were usually herded into closed lorries and taken off under escort to the nearest Gestapo depot for interrogation, after which all suspects were detained for further investigation. The remainder were either sent off to Germany to concentration camps or elsewhere, in accordance with the specific aims of the particular man-hunt. Only those who worked in German offices, industry or other employment under German authorisation, and were adequately reclaimed by their employers, could stand a chance of release after being caught in a man-hunt.

The warning was either the cry *"Lapanka!"* ("Man-hunt!") or *"Buda!"* (meaning the closed lorry in which prisoners were transported), and was usually spread by newspaper vendors or *ryksza*-drivers (a *ryksza*, the only type of wheeled transportation available for hire in towns, being a sort of one-seat vehicle attached to a bicycle). It was due to them that I escaped a man-hunt more than once. At one time, I was returning home on a dark evening not knowing that a man-hunt was on in the street where I was living. Some old woman who came from the opposite direction muttered "*Buda!*" as she passed me. I was able to slip away at the last moment.

From 1942 onwards the wave of mass arrests steadily grew in intensity. In January, 1943, during four days alone, over 35,000 people were caught in Warsaw, in which instance most of the men were sent off to concentration camps.

Every "professional" member of the Underground—particularly one holding a position of authority—was always warned of impending danger. It was one of the duties of our Counter-intelligence to do so. They revealed the names of the secret agents of the Gestapo and reported on what stage the searches for us had reached. I received many such warnings.

In order to secure descriptions and photographs of members of the Underground, the Germans frequently used agents disguised as beggars. One pair was notorious in Warsaw. A supposedly blind man used to play an accordion at street corners. His inseparable companion was a woman who sang to his accompaniment. Whenever they appeared, arrests would follow shortly after in the vicinity. Both were sentenced to death as Gestapo agents and executed.

In time one got experienced and noticed immediately the observer disguised as a beggar or fiddler, or the agent in plain clothes walking slowly up and down a small bit of the street or looking with interest into a shop window. By following the direction of his eyes, one could easily guess what he was interested in. A raid by the Gestapo on a house was in fact often preceded by a one- or two-day observation of the whole block.

I can still clearly remember the face and expression of an old bearded beggar who suddenly emerged before my house. I first noticed him when I was going out to a meeting. When I returned, he was still there. I did not like him, so I decided to pass the house. Late in the evening, when I went home, he was gone, and many of the tenants living in my house were gone too. They had been arrested. This was not an isolated case. More than once I escaped arrest or ambush because I had carefully observed everything going on around me.

Like every other senior officer, I had some places at my disposal for meetings and contacts. One of these was in the Grochów suburb. The tenant went out to her work every morning and I had a second latchkey and used her home for meetings several times a week. On one particular day, I was discussing the position of the Home Army in western Poland with two other officers. The table was strewn with maps.

The wife of the janitor heard men's voices coming from the flat at a time when she knew its tenant was absent in her office. We were deep in our work when a wild thundering started on the front door of the flat. Swiftly we removed the maps and papers and opened the door, only to be faced by the janitress, who, seeing three strangers, started to shout: "Holy Mother of God! Thieves." She turned quickly to dash down the stairs, alarm the whole house and summon the police. But, even more quickly, I grabbed her, drew her into the flat and slammed the door.

The situation was tense. All we could do was threaten her. I clutched her wrist firmly, gripping with all my strength, and with my face an inch from hers hissed: "We are not thieves. Anything but. If you don't shut up and we get arrested here, you will pay for it. Understand?" She did. We quickly left the apartment, leaving the poor woman trembling with fright. We never went near that flat again.

*   *   *

Quite apart from the specific problems presented by the struggle against the Germans and the question of uniting the national effort regardless of political opinions, the year 1942 brought to light obstacles of a new character.

During the first phase of the war in the east, the retreating Red Army left behind considerable forces which had been surrounded in numerous pockets, broken up and destroyed. The survivors found refuge in the large wooded areas to the east of our frontier and partly on our territory. When the Soviet command recovered from its first disasters, the organisation of Red partisan groups behind the German lines began.

As early as the autumn of 1941, the Russians had started to drop well-equipped paratroops in eastern Poland. One of them was a non-commissioned officer in the Polish Army who had been taken prisoner in 1939. On his return to Poland, he at once joined the Home Army, and it was from him we learned in August, 1941, not quite two months after the German attack on Russia started, that the Russians had organised a special training centre near Moscow for the instruction of Communist partisan commanders. The course lasted about three weeks and was attended by approximately 2,000 men from the age of eighteen, including Russians, Lithuanians, Byelorussians, Ukrainians, Estonians, Latvians and even Spaniards. Candidates were chosen, primarily on the strength of their political convictions and reliability, from the youths brought up in the Communist spirit who had passed through Communist youth organisations. On arrival behind the German lines, the Soviet paratroopers at once began to organise the larger groups of survivors and escaped prisoners in eastern Poland.

The Soviet partisans lived off the country and the population among whom they happened to be. That meant they had to requisition food and supplies of all sorts from the local peasants and farmers. This was quite understandable in emergencies, but very different from the behaviour of our partisans, who paid the current prices, a rule to which we scrupulously adhered. What was deeply resented was the brutal and ruthless manner in which it was done. It was really no different from ordinary pillage and theft. The activities of these Red partisans naturally brought reprisals from the Germans upon the local people, as in the case of our own actions. This was unavoidable. But whereas our men planned and acted with the greatest consideration, so that the minimum persecution should be inflicted upon the civilians, the Russian partisans were callous and showed themselves utterly indifferent to the fate of the local people. Altogether, their conduct was that of men fighting in an enemy country among enemies.

The behaviour of the Soviet partisans placed Rowecki in an embarrassing situation. Often the civilian population in the east would request the Home Army for protection against the violence and pillage of the Soviet guerrillas. Such help might very easily have led to fighting between Soviet and Polish partisans—that is to say, to a conflict between two groups of allied forces. This had to be avoided at all costs.

A more careful study of Soviet activities accentuated fears as to their real object. On the territory of Russia, the Ukraine and Byelorussia, Soviet partisan activity was of a purely military character, causing the Germans serious losses and inconvenience. But on Polish territory, it was very different. Here their attention appeared to be much less taken up with fighting the Germans than with political activity. Every Soviet partisan unit was commanded not only by an Army

officer, but also by a political officer, or *Politruk*, who represented the Communist Party. The larger units were, moreover,
equipped with field printing presses, and they conducted a
political propaganda campaign with the help of leaflets and
of meetings at which attendance by the local population was
compulsory. Reports also reached us that enlistment into the
Soviet guerrilla forces was being enforced on Poles or Polish
citizens. This political activity was being carried on within
the frontiers of the Polish Republic, which was fully covered
by our organisation.

Rowecki at once made clear the status of the Soviet partisans.
A Polish army was then being formed in the Soviet Union
under the command of General Anders. Politically, this army
was subordinated to the Polish Government in London.
Operationally, it was under the Soviet High Command.
This was quite understandable, since it was to fight on Soviet
territory on the eastern front. Rowecki maintained that he
had the right to demand the same from the Soviet partisan
forces operating in Poland. The Polish Home Army was surely
host on its own soil and the Soviet units guests and allies.

On this basis, Rowecki issued uniform instructions to all
the local Home Army commanders concerning their dealings
with the Soviets. They were to establish contact with the
Russians and arrange to define the respective zones of operation, the mutual exchange of information regarding the
enemy and the exchange of supplies. Primary conditions for
such co-operation were Soviet recognition that we were
Allied hosts on our own soil and a modification in the Soviet
guerrillas' line of action. Many local talks between the two
sides followed, including one with a large Soviet group known
as the Lenin Brigade which negotiated with the Polish command of the Nowogródek district, and another with Soviet
units in the Wilno area. Unfortunately none of these talks
yielded any results of lasting importance. More often than not
the Soviet commanders demanded that the local Home Army
forces be subordinated to them, although in nearly every
case the Polish forces were more numerous than the Russian.

Since the Soviet partisan forces had no central command
on Polish territory—the larger units being under the direct
command of Soviet headquarters on the other side of the
eastern front—Rowecki had perforce to look to the highest
level for a solution—that is to say, an understanding between

Moscow and the Polish Government in London. The dangers arising from the conduct of Soviet guerrillas in Poland were on many occasions the subject of conversations between the two. In November, 1942, the Polish Ambassador in London, Count Raczyński, filed a special note on the subject with the Soviet Ambassador, Bogomolov. This, however, also failed to produce a solution.

*   *   *

Every Underground group, even the smallest, began its activities by issuing its own Underground paper or periodical. By the time Germany started her attack on Russia, there were no less than 168 Underground periodicals being published in Poland. Among all these, however, there was not one single organ of the Communist Party. It was only in November, 1941, that a modest paper appeared under the title *Miecz i Młot (Sword and Hammer)*. And this was after twenty-six months of German occupation and five months after the beginning of the war between Russia and Germany. It was published by a group of Communists who had founded an organisation known as the League of Friends of the Soviet Union. As time went on, other similar small groups were formed.

The majority of the Polish Communist leaders had left the German zone to settle under the Russians in eastern Poland as soon as the occupation forces moved into Poland. They mostly went to either Wilno or Lwów, where high posts awaited them under the Soviet administration. But seven months after the outbreak of the Russo-German War, in January, 1942, the representatives of the Fourth Department of the Red Army Staff and the Comintern created a new branch in Poland under the name of the Polish Workers Party (Polska Partia Robotnicza, or P.P.R.). It was the Polish Communist Underground Organisation, which assembled the few Polish Communists living in Poland and those who had spent long years in Russia and now began to return from Moscow. All the leaders of this new P.P.R. group had been members of the Polish pre-war Communist Party, and it is they who now occupy the key positions in Poland.

At the same time, we noted the arrival of Soviet envoys in Warsaw. They at once contacted the P.P.R. and probably took over the administration of Communist political and military work. The presence of these envoys was shrouded in the greatest secrecy by the Communists. Only a very small ring of leaders was informed and received orders from them. We found out the name or *alias* of one of the envoys in the capital: Glebov, a colonel in the Red Army. He was the real founder of the People's Guard (Polish Communist partisan groups).

As long as diplomatic relations existed between Poland and the Soviet Union, and as long as these relations were more or less correct, the Communists in Poland acted with the greatest caution. They had long been looked upon in Poland as nothing but the agents of Russia. The general opinion was that a Communist was the exact opposite of a patriot. This was the result of many events. To begin with, the Polish Communists originated from a party which, along with the Russian Communists, had in Tsarist times aimed at a revolution in Russia and had rejected the idea of an independent Polish State. In 1920, when Polish independence was threatened at its very start by the invasion of the Red Army, the Polish Communists carried on diversionary activities against the Polish Army, while the Polish peasant and working-men's movements gave proof of the greatest patriotism. Later, during the period of Poland's regained and consolidated independence, Polish Communists were on some occasions sentenced by courts for treason and espionage directed and maintained on instructions and money from Moscow. As a result, the entire Polish nation, particularly workers and peasants, regarded the Communists with enmity and distrust. Before the Second World War the Polish Communist Party had something under 8,000 members. This was so negligible a number that even the Communists themselves had to admit their failure, and in 1938 the party was dissolved of its own accord.

Now, to take advantage of the confused situation and obtain power, the P.P.R. instructed its members to infiltrate into all Underground organisations, not excluding those of the extreme Right, in order to study them as well as to split them from inside. Looking back, it is clear to me that the beginning of our renewed difficulties with Russia coincided with the Soviet victory at Stalingrad.

In the early spring of 1942 we had received precise information regarding the number and position of the German divisions in the Ukraine. It was from there that the German offensive was later launched towards Stalingrad and the Caucasus. We transmitted this information to London, indicating at the same time the preparations being made by the Germans for the exploitation of the Caucasian oilfields. Behind their front the Germans were actually assembling, among other things, groups of specialists, and large stocks of drilling equipment. We advanced the theory that the German summer offensive would be directed southwards. All this information, together with its conclusion, was passed to the Soviet High Command via the Polish Military Mission then in Russia. The Soviet High Command, however, did not agree with our reports. They held that the German offensive would be directed against Moscow. Events were to justify our conclusions.

The disaster which overcame Hitler by the loss of Von Paulus's army seriously disturbed the balance of military power on the eastern front. The Germans lost their strategic reserves and it was clear that they would be forced into further retreat.

The battle of Stalingrad was one of the decisive turning-points of the war, and not only from the military point of view. Its political importance cannot be overrated. As the Red Army began its advance, which brought it from the Volga to the Elbe, Stalin simultaneously opened his great diplomatic and propaganda attack on Europe. Its first objective was Poland. All people who had been on Polish territory occupied by the Red Army in September, 1939, were claimed by Moscow as Russian citizens. This clearly meant that Russia was again putting forward her claim to the Polish territories which had been annexed by her on the basis of the Molotov-Ribbentrop Agreement, and that she considered the whole population as her subjects. Out of the $1\frac{1}{2}$ million deported whom the Russians had committed themselves to free, only 115,000 Polish citizens had regained their liberty. All the tremendous efforts of the Polish authorities to discover the whereabouts of the rest had failed.

In February, 1943, the Russian authorities began the formation of the first Polish detachments within the framework of the Red Army; these had nothing in common with General Anders's army. In March the Union of Polish Patriots was formed in Moscow under the leadership of Wanda Wasilewska, who had previously accepted Soviet citizenship and was a member of the Supreme Council of the U.S.S.R.

Concurrently with these events in Russia, Communist propaganda in Poland began more and more frequently to voice sentiments hostile to the Polish Underground Movement and to the Polish Government in London. The *Trybuna*

Wolnosci (Liberty Tribune), organ of the P.P.R., denying accusations made by the Polish people that it was dependent upon Russia, wrote: "Foreign agents are those who advocate British fighting methods based upon an attitude of waiting"; and in its attacks on the Polish Government in Exile and the Home Army, the P.P.R. now began to accuse them of following a policy of "waiting with arms at ease." At the same time, the Soviet wireless from the station Kościuszko and the Union of Patriots began a campaign of slander in Polish against the Polish Government and the leaders of the Underground, reproaching them for their "passive policy."

The P.P.R. made their co-operation with the Home Army dependent upon two rather strange conditions. They demanded that the Polish Underground State (which included both military and political organisations) should repudiate the Constitution of 1935. Secondly, they demanded that general open warfare against the Germans be initiated forthwith.

Now, the Polish Government in London owed its legality to the Polish Constitution of 1935. It was on the basis of this Constitution that the alliance with Britain had been concluded in May, 1939. Thus, practically speaking, the Communists demanded that we should break away from the Polish Government. The second demand was all the more strange, since the Polish Underground had been opposing the Germans continuously ever since they had occupied our country.

In reply, General Rowecki made further conversations dependent upon a straightforward recognition of the Polish Government in London and on subordination to the legal Polish authorities at home. He also required a clear statement from the P.P.R. that it was not subordinate to the Comintern and was not acting under instructions from a foreign power. His demands were immediately rejected by the Communists, and the P.P.R. continued to work outside the framework of the Polish Underground Movement.

Numerically speaking, the P.P.R. was a relatively small group, and little importance would have been attached to its announcements were it not for the fact that it was being backed by Russia. The whole of its activity and propaganda was synchronised with the policy followed by the radio stations broadcasting from the Soviet Union in Polish, which were, of course, under Soviet direction. It was therefore quite evident to us that all that the P.P.R. did should be looked upon as a feature of Russian policy towards Poland and the Polish Underground.

* * *

Nevertheless Rowecki wished to give some concrete proof to Russia that our policy was by no means one of inactivity. A careful study was therefore made by our Staff of the possibilities of large-scale diversion activities in the east in Russia's favour. Plans were drawn up and transmitted to General Sikorski in London. During the night of February 26–27th, 1943, Mr. Romer, the Polish Ambassador, had a conference with Marshal Stalin at the Kremlin lasting over three hours, in which he explained in detail the Home Army's entire activities and aims. He was able to inform Stalin of the Home Army's achievements and the recent destruction of enormous stocks of winter clothing destined for the Wehrmacht's next campaign on the eastern front. He also put forward the reason why the Polish Government opposed the idea of a general rising under conditions which could lead to nothing but disaster and a general massacre of the population.

At the same time, he transmitted to Stalin the proposition of the Polish Government for a plan of *simultaneous* interruption of *all* railway lines leading from Germany through Polish territory to the eastern front: 85 per cent. of German equipment and food was brought to the front by this route. The Polish Government was ready to execute this plan from March 1st onwards on one condition only. The moment would have to be co-ordinated with the Red Army H.Q., to assure the greatest possible military success, and justify the risk and the inevitable losses. Stalin rejected the offer, at the same time avoiding any answer to Romer's insistent question as to when the time and conditions would be favourable for carrying out the proposed plan.

While Stalin was rejecting organised co-operation with the Underground Army, the propaganda machine under his orders kept appealing violently to the Polish population for immediate, spontaneous, unorganised action against the occupier "with arms in hand or, should these be lacking, with whatsoever is at hand . . . a pitch-fork, a knife, an axe." It is clear that if these exhortations had evoked a desperate mass uprising, it would have been drowned in a sea of blood, and Poland would have sunk into complete anarchy without any real military gain for the Red Army.

Two months later, on April 25th, 1943, the Soviet Government broke off relations with the Polish Government. The occasion was the revelation of a mass execution of Polish officers in the Forest of Katyń.

In September, 1939, a large part of the Polish Army (about 250,000 men) retreating before the German onslaught had found itself in eastern Poland, where the men were taken prisoner by the Russians. True, no state of war existed between Poland and the Soviet Union, but Polish officers and other ranks were treated by the Russians as prisoners of war and placed in camps.

After some time, the families of these men began to receive censored letters from them. The postmarks revealed that the officers had been grouped in three large prisoner-of-war camps at Kozielsk (province of Smolensk), Starobielsk (Ukraine) and Ostashkov (north-west of Moscow). The last letters to be received from these three camps were dated April, 1940. All letters sent to them after that month were returned, stamped *"Retour-parti"* ("Return to sender: addressee gone away"). Grave anxiety reigned among the numerous families who had sons, husbands and brothers in the three camps. If they had been transferred to other camps, why had the letters not been sent on instead of being returned?

We had news from London that more than 8,000 Polish officers had been taken prisoner of war by the Russians. Of these, only about 400 men had been traced and found after the Russo-Polish Agreement. These were for the most part officers from the Griasoviets camp. All the others were missing.

We had to conduct a thorough search in the prisoner-of-war camps in Germany and in the areas under German occupation, as General Sikorski did not exclude the eventuality that they had been taken over by the Germans during their advance. But the intensive search yielded no results. Not a single Polish officer of the 8,000 was in a German prisoner-of-war camp. Not one was discovered on Soviet territory occupied by the Germans. There were, in this last area, a few civilians who, during the years 1939, 1940 and 1941, had been deported from Poland by the Russians. They said that in the spring of 1940 Polish prisoners from the camps at Kozielsk, Starobielsk and Ostashkov had been removed from these three camps and had probably been sent to forced-labour camps in northern Russia. We could learn nothing more through the channels of information at our disposal.

At the beginning of April, 1943, the chief of the German Propaganda Service for the Warsaw district summoned a number of Poles to the Bruhl Palace, headquarters of the Nazi Governor of Warsaw. They were received by a delegate of the German Ministry of Propaganda from Berlin. He rattled off the usual propaganda talk on how the war was being waged by the Germans against the danger of a communist flood—how they were defending European civilisation and so on. He then came to the point and announced the discovery of mass graves of victims of Soviet terrorism near Smolensk. The main theme of the address was "the bestiality of the Bolshevik régime."

Simultaneously, similar meetings were summoned in Cracow and Lublin. In all cases the Poles were told they were to be prepared for a journey; they were to be taken by plane to the actual scene of the graves, where they would see for themselves the truth of the German assertions. The Warsaw "delegation" of nine persons left by air on the morning of April 10th.

Rowecki unearthed information that the "delegation" had been received in Smolensk by a German officer, who described to the visitors the investigations which had already been made. His story was that in October, 1942, a group of Polish road-workers near Katyń had heard from the local population that in the forest nearby there were graves of Poles executed by the N.K.V.D. in the spring of 1940. The workers asked where the site was, and erected two birchwood crosses there. They used to gather there for evening prayers after their day's work was done. The wooden crosses attracted the interest of the German Intelligence Corps, and in February, 1943, the Germans opened up one of the graves and found that, in effect, it was a place of mass burial. They then examined the surrounding area in the forest and discovered other mass graves of civilians dating back at least ten years. One of the members of the delegation asked why the German authorities had announced their discovery only after a lapse of two months. The reply was that the local authorities had been fully engaged in active operations at the front and had failed to estimate the significance of their discovery. It was only when the report reached Berlin that higher officials had appreciated it.

The "delegates" were then taken to the burial ground at Katyń, where a terrible scene met their eyes. They saw opened graves in which lay rows of decomposing corpses dressed in Polish officers' uniform complete with insignia. In particular, they were shown the bodies of Generals Smorawinski and Bohatyrowicz. There was no doubt as to their identity, which was fully proved by the papers and letters found on the bodies.

On April 14th Rowecki sent the following radiogram to London: "The Germans have discovered the graves of several thousand of our officers from the camps at Kozielsk. Several Poles from Warsaw, Cracow and Lublin were specially taken to the place to inspect the graves. Their reports allow no doubt as to the authenticity of the mass murder." The message contained no reference to responsibility for the murders. On the same day, the entire German-controlled Press printed in Polish published accounts of the discoveries at Katyń.

The impression made upon the people was tremendous. No one asked who was responsible. Grief and sorrow plunged thousands of families into mourning. All other thoughts were swept away. The men had been the *élite* of the Polish nation and included many of our leading physicians and surgeons, attorneys and judges, university professors, artists and so on, who had all been mobilised as reserve officers in 1939. They also included many young Regular officers of great promise.

It was only when the nation recovered from its first shock that discussion began about Goebbel's communiqué. At that time the Poles knew nothing of the protracted and vain searches made by the Polish Embassy in Russia, of the repeated enquiries made by General Sikorski, Professor Kot and General Anders to Stalin, Vyshinsky and others and the failure of the Soviet leaders either to explain or to give other than evasive replies.

On April 15th Moscow broadcast a communiqué:

"In the past two or three days, Goebbels's slanderers have been spreading vile fabrications alleging that the Soviet authorities effected mass shootings of Polish officers in the spring of 1940 in the Smolensk area.

"The German Fascist reports on this subject leave no doubts as to the tragic fate of the former Polish prisoners of war, who in 1941 were engaged in construction work in areas west of Smolensk and who fell into the hands of German Fascist hangmen in the summer of 1941, after the withdrawal of Soviet troops from the Smolensk area. . . .

"In their clumsily concocted fabrication about the numerous graves which the Germans allegedly discovered near Smolensk, the Hitlerite liars mentioned the village of Gnezdovaya. But, like the swindlers they are, they are silent about the fact that it was near the village of Gnezdovaya that the archæological excavations of the historical *Gnezdovaya* (burial places) were located. . . ."

The Soviet communiqué thus brought us news for the first time—news for which the Polish Government had enquired of Moscow in vain. So far, the great mystery had been where the Polish prisoners of war had been located at the beginning of the Russo-German War in the spring of 1941. Now the communiqué revealed for the first time that they had then been occupied on road-construction west of Smoleńsk and that they had been taken over by the Germans.

A few days after the first visit of Poles to Katyń, the Germans sent further groups. I decided to send my own observer to ascertain how much truth there really was in the German assertions and to gather first-hand information. Before his departure, I had a long talk with him in which I told him what to look for.

April 17th brought a new development. In the afternoon, the Polish broadcast from London included a communiqué issued by the Polish Minister of National Defence, General Kukiel. After a brief summary of all the efforts previously made by the Polish Government to ascertain the whereabouts of the officers, the communiqué said: "Neither the Polish Government in London nor the Polish Ambassador in Kujbyszev had received any reply to their enquiries.

"We have grown accustomed to the lies of German propaganda and we can well understand the purpose behind its latest revelations. In view, however, of the abundant and detailed German information regarding the discovery of the bodies of many thousands of Polish officers near Smolensk . . . the necessity arises for the investigation of these graves and the verification of these allegations by a competent international body, such as the International Red Cross."

When he issued this statement, General Kukiel was undoubtedly actuated by our first message confirming the authenticity of the actual discovery. London radio announced that the Polish Government had applied to the International Red Cross, and shortly afterwards the Germans reported that they had made a similar application through the President of the German Red Cross.

Like a bolt from the blue came the news that the Russians

E

had refused permission for the examination of the Katyń graves by the International Red Cross. Their reply to the statement made by General Kukiel, Minister of National Defence, was to break off diplomatic relations with the Polish Government on April 25th. Just as disbelief in the German accusations against the Russians had before been universal, now public opinion became convinced that the Russians must be guilty. If they were not, surely they should have applied at once to some independent institution to confute the Germans' lies.

Russia's refusal caused consternation and embarrassment in Communist circles in Poland. Even they made no effort at this juncture to join issue in the discussion regarding responsibility. In P.P.R. circles, at secret meetings and conferences, the Communists openly admitted that "Polish reactionaries" had been liquidated. They also initiated a "whispering campaign" in Warsaw to the effect that a mutiny had broken out in one of the camps and that some of the officers had been executed. The Katyń massacre, having become the cause of the rupture in our diplomatic relations with Russia, had now assumed the highest political significance, quite apart from its moral aspect.

At last my observer from Katyń was back. His account began with a confirmation that the German figure of 10,000 corpses was exaggerated. "I can't say whether they didn't know the real figure because they hadn't opened up all the graves, or whether they purposely exaggerated the number," he went on, "but the fact remains that when I reached Katyń seven of the graves had been opened and they certainly don't contain very many more than 4,000 bodies in all. I kept closely to your instructions and worked among the exhumers for some days. I've seen and examined everything with my own eyes. I don't think anything can have escaped my attention. Here's the material evidence I was able to get."

He put on the table before me two revolver bullets, several cartridge cases, several lengths of cord and a parcel containing notebooks, diaries, letters and pre-war zloty banknotes.

"What does it all look like?" I asked.

"There are seven mass graves side by side in a small clearing on the slope of some rising ground known as Goat's Hill. Nearby is a house which, it is said, used to be a rest-house for the N.K.V.D. before the war. The place where the graves are has been planted with saplings. I'm not a forester, so I couldn't tell whether it was true or not, but the Germans say the age of the saplings indicates that they were transferred from the nursery some three years ago.

"The soil is sandy and therefore the bodies were in a good state of preservation, especially the upper layers. The bodies lay side by side in several layers. Some of them had overcoats wound round their heads. Nearly all of them had their hands tied with cord either before or behind them; I've brought you a sample of it. What struck me most was that all the shots had been fired in the same way; at the base of the skull where it joins the neck. The executioners must have been very expert at it. I also noticed in about fifteen or sixteen cases evidence of what they must have gone through just before death. I saw that some overcoats and tunics had been pierced by a four-edged weapon—perhaps some sort of bayonet. Some had had their jaw-bones broken. Perhaps these were the ones who fought in self-defence at the end. In some cases, the greatcoats wound round their heads were filled with sawdust. Probably this was another method applied to kill those fighting for their lives: when they breathed in the sawdust it would stifle them. Altogether, it's a sight I shall never forget as long as I live."

He had himself, he said, spoken with one peasant from the Gnezdovaya district. All that he could tell him was that in the spring of 1940 foreign officers were brought to the station in small groups and then taken in prison vans in the direction of Katyń. Access to the forest and even to its immediate vicinity had been strictly forbidden by the N.K.V.D. But he had heard the sound of shots from afar.

I sent the bullets, the cartridge cases and the lengths of cord he had brought to be examined by our experts. Examination showed that the cord used was made of a material unknown in central and western Europe. This, by itself, of course, proved nothing.

The ammunition, however, proved to be of German manufacture and bore the Geco trade-mark (used by Gustav Genschow Co. of Durlach, near Karlsruhe, in Baden). This important detail was transmitted to London. Later, however, it transpired that the Germans, far from denying this fact, had themselves published the information in their report. They explained that ammunition for pistols of this calibre had been exported in quantities from Germany to Poland and Russia, in addition to other countries. This was quite true. In 1939, Polish ammunition stores contained a good deal of ammunition made by this particular German firm.

The papers now remained as the last evidence to be sifted. The first object I picked up was a diary bearing the signature of Professor Pienkowski. First, there were only entries about events in the camp, followed by short, laconic notes on patients he had treated and a series of points which might well have been notes for some lectures he had given in the camp. The last entry was dated April 9th.

The next diary bore the name of Dr. Dobieslaw Jakubowicz. In short, disconnected sentences, Jakubowicz described the monotony of life in the Kozielsk camp. It took the form of a letter to his wife and little daughter:

"*October 17th, 1939:* Good morning, Mary and little Bozenna. How did you sleep? My night was bad—it was hard and I couldn't get my boots off. . . . Food's getting a little better and there's more order in camp now the officers have taken over the kitchen. . . . I love you, my love. Why are you so far away?"

The entries continued in this strain. The last ones, written in March and April, 1940, contain references to the transfer of officers to some unknown destination:

"*April 3rd, 1940:* Sixty-two were taken from the camp to-day. Wojciechowski went from our group. Oh, Marysienka. . . .

"*April 4th, 1940:* They're going on moving officers; we don't know where to. I love you, Marysienka.

"*April 5th, 1940:* They're still removing officers. Attorney went yesterday and Friga to-day. Mary, my little one, we don't know where they're taking us. Anyhow, every day brings us nearer to each other.

"*April 21st, 1940:* This afternoon I was taken away in a motor truck, after they'd searched my things, to a railway siding and to prison cars—fifteen men per compartment behind barred windows.

"*April 22nd, 1940:* Train moved off at 1.30 a.m. At noon, Smoleńsk."

Here the diary broke off.

I took up the next and saw it ended on April 12th, 1940. I looked through the remainder and ascertained that all of them, without exception, broke off either at the time of their departure from Kozielsk or on their arrival at the station of Gnezdovaya, near Katyń. The diary of Major Adam Solski brought his story to relatively the latest moment. His last entries were of particular significance. Here they are:

"*Sunday, April 7th, 1940, in the morning:* After yesterday, distribution of . . . [illegible]. Told to pack our things . . . by 11.40 to hall to be searched.

"After the search at 14.55 hours, we left the walls and barbed wire of Kozielsk Camp. At 16.55 hours, we were put into prison cars at the Kozielsk railroad siding. Never seen such cars in my life. They say 50 per cent. of the railway cars in the U.S.S.R., as far as passenger cars go, are prison cars. With me are Joseph Kutyba, Captain Paulszyfter and also a major, lieutenant-colonel and some captains—twelve of us. There's room for seven at the most.

"*April 8th, 3.30:* Departure from Kozielsk depot westwards; at Jelnia Station since 9.45.

"*April 8th:* We've been at a siding at Smoleñsk since twelve o'clock.

"*April 9th:* Morning. Some minutes before five, reveille in the cars and preparations to leave. We're going somewhere by automobile. What next?

"*April 9th:* Ever since dawn it's been a peculiar day. Departure in lorries fitted with cells (terrible). Taken to forest somewhere—something like a summer resort. Very thorough search of our belongings. They took my watch, which showed time as 6.30 [8.30], asked about my ring, which [was taken], roubles, belt, penknife."

These were the last words written by Major Solski.

The outstanding point of all these diaries was in their all breaking off short at the same point, either on leaving the camp at Kozielsk or on arrival at Katyñ in April, 1940.

One of the diaries had belonged to an officer who had been a close friend of a colonel from our Underground Staff ever since the days when they had been at the Higher Military Academy together. He was in possession of his friend's notes, which he had made when he was at college. Both the diary and the notes were handed to a handwriting expert, who confirmed beyond all doubt that both had been written by the same person. We could have no further doubts as to the authenticity of the material in our hands. Reading these documents found in the pockets of the murdered men, I could no longer have any doubt of the Russians' guilt. The problem of Katyń—of who had committed mass murder on defenceless prisoners—had ceased to be a mystery to me.

From the lists of names of the Polish officers murdered at Katyń, it was clear that they all came from one camp: Kozielsk. To this day we know nothing regarding the fate of the missing officers who had been in the other two camps at Starobielsk and Ostashkov.

*   *   *

The Russian objective began to be clear when the Soviets broke off diplomatic relations with Poland. A number of earlier moves, such as the formation of the Union of Polish Patriots in Moscow, the organisation of Polish units under Russian command (which was only officially announced by Moscow after the rupture) and so on—all now formed a logical sequence in a chain of events. We did not doubt that the Katyń discoveries and the consequent reactions of the Polish Government had merely served Russia as a pretext for breaking off diplomatic relations with our Government.

From the moment of the rupture, Soviet plans entered a new phase. Simultaneously with the creation of the army of Berling, who had deserted from General Anders and put himself at the disposal of the Union of Patriots in Moscow, the Polish Communists, obedient to the orders which they received from the Kremlin, began to prepare for the entry of the Red Army into Poland, as well as for the decisive phase of the political struggle between Moscow and the western Allies, where Poland was at stake. These preparations meant the high-speed formation of a Communist Underground, the nucleus of a political army and of a Communist secret State totally subservient to Moscow.

These efforts of the Polish Communists met with immense difficulties in the attitude of the Polish people. The Katyń affair, the rupture of diplomatic relations, Russia's intention to annex Wilno and Lwów, the incessant attacks on the Polish Government and its representatives in Poland, the hostile attitude of the Soviet partisans on Polish territory towards the Home Army—all this had opened the eyes of the nation to Moscow's real aim and the intentions of their agents in the P.P.R.

Misunderstanding and local frictions between the (very few) units of the Communist People's Guard and certain hot-headed elements of the National military organisation (not subordinated to the C.-in-C., Underground Army) were eagerly puffed up and skilfully used against Poland. The aim was to discredit the Polish Underground in the opinion of the western powers and make them believe we were fighting the Russians or the Polish Communist partisans under their protection. The aim of this deceitful Soviet propaganda was to deprive Poland of the moral, political and military support of the west. They went so far as to credit the Communist units with most of the success of the Underground Army. This compelled us to publish official communiqués and to mark every single action with our anchor-sign, the P.W. (⚓).

The political activity of the P.P.R. increased during the summer of 1943 with the arrival in Warsaw of the experienced Communist agent, Boleslaw Bierut. Intense efforts were made to gain the co-operation of all the Left groups, but for the moment this succeeded only with two members of the extreme Left Socialist Party, Osobka-Morawski and Hanemann.

In July, 1943, the name of the so-called People's Guard was altered to People's Army to give it more publicity weight and status. In the early autumn of the same year the P.P.R. began to work out a plan for creating civilian authorities of its own. The Krajowa Rada Narodowa (National Council of the Country) was designed to represent the nation. In fact, it only represented the P.P.R. and continued to try desperately to attract other collaborators.

We received confidential news, which we could not check, that on December 31st, 1943, this Council had its first session in Twarda Street, Warsaw. A manifesto, *The Democratic, Social, Political and Military Organisations in Poland*, was issued. It bore a long list of fictitious signatures—names of organisations and unions which had never seen the manifesto. It was a simple forgery, with the aim of confusing public opinion, and evoked a storm of protest from the free, independent organisations. At home, this manifesto did not deceive anybody, but public opinion abroad, unconscious of what was going on in Poland, was more easily influenced.

Also characteristic was the creation of the National Council at the very moment when the Red Army crossed the Polish border. On March 15th, 1944, a delegation left Warsaw for Moscow. It was composed of Osobka-Morawski, Spychalski, Hanemann and Sidor. With the help of a Soviet liaison group they crossed the Bug, where they were greeted by as many as 200 Soviet partisans. Then a Soviet plane picked them up behind the German front and took them to Moscow. We had detailed reports on all this from our partisans.

The rupture was a signal for an unusually violent propaganda campaign against the Polish Government. Our monitoring service covering the Soviet radio stations picked up such quotations from leading Soviet journals as: "The Polish Government has taken the treacherous step of an understanding with Hitler, foe of the Polish and Russian people, foe of all peace-loving people"; "the Sikorski Government has struck a treacherous blow at the common cause in the fight against Hitler," and "the Polish Government's aggressive lust has led it to agreement with the Hitlerite Government, which is tearing asunder the Polish nation."

These accusations roused indignation and fury in Poland. They were made at a moment when the whole nation was suffering exceptionally painful losses and sacrifices in a fierce and stubborn struggle under the direction of the Polish Government against the Germans. The loyalty enjoyed by this Government was the underlying reason why Poland had never produced a quisling.

At the time, Soviet policy towards our Underground movement seemed to be full of contradictions. To-day, however, with full knowledge of all the facts, this policy is revealed as a series of logical, consecutive moves, tending to one single aim. *This aim was to create a Polish Communist Government* and a Polish Communist Army. The Polish Underground was an obstacle in the way, and could be removed only if it broke with the Polish Government in London and became subservient to Communist leadership. Another obstacle was the collaboration of the Home Army with the western Allies in the war against Germany. The fact that Poland was an ally and not an enemy was a hindrance to Russian policy. So were the successes of the Home Army in their fight against the Germans, which could not be claimed as the work of the Communists. On international ground, they deprived Russia of valid arguments for attacking the Polish Government. Russia's whole diplomatic propaganda apparatus was working toward the removal of Poland from the Allied camp, toward breaking the links that connected the western Allies with their Polish partner, so as to finish with Poland when abandoned and alone. That is why Stalin, in February, 1943, rejected the proposal of the Polish Government for military collaboration with the Home

Army. He did not wish to help, but to liquidate the Home Army. That is why Soviet authorities purposely provoked hostile incidents with our units, so that they might accuse us afterwards, before an international forum, of passive, open or secret co-operation with the Germans, of preparing "massacres of Communists," etc.

In the sort of struggle we were carrying on in the Underground, the toll of human life was many times greater than that of a normal campaign between regular armies. For this reason, a leader of Underground resistance, even more than any other military commander, had to be morally convinced that the aims of his people would be achieved and the losses would not be suffered in vain. Ever since 1939 we had done all in our power to oppose the German invaders, and at the same time had done all we could to carry out our duty as an ally of the western powers and inflict as much harm as possible on the Germans. Our policy was a costly one, and therefore we felt the need to be assured that the policy we were following was the right one.

We got a message from General Sikorski (transmitted April 22nd), about his recent talk with Mr. Churchill. The British Prime Minister had reaffirmed his profound friendship for Poland and given his solemn assurance that the commitments undertaken by Britain with regard to Poland would be fulfilled at the appropriate time. This message was essential for us. After all, Britain was our most faithful ally, and democratic powers keep their pledges and respect their agreements. The message spoke of fulfilment at the appropriate time. This explained quite clearly why, as long as the Germans were not beaten, Britain did not take up the problem of Poland and eastern Europe. Quite apart from their commitments, Britain and the United States could not let down Poland—the keystone of eastern Europe.

Thus there was nothing else to do but continue our present policy: to tighten our bonds with the western democracies and redouble our efforts both in helping the Allies and opposing the Germans by increasing our work of diversion and sabotage. At the same time, it was decided to assume towards Russia the attitude that she was the "ally of our allies."

Some days later, our decisions were reinforced by details of the celebration of May 3rd, the Polish National Holiday, in London, which were broadcast by the B.B.C. The British

Government attached special significance to the occasion, and Mr. Churchill sent a message in which he emphasised that "Poles, both in Poland and abroad, are united in their determination to carry on the fight against the German oppressors of their country." Sir John Anderson, who officially represented His Majesty's Government at the celebration, pointed out that "Poland has been to us a loyal and faithful ally, and throughout the length and breadth of Poland not one quisling has been found." We interpreted these tributes as direct refutations of the Soviet charges that the Polish Government was collaborating with the Germans.

A few days later, Warsaw also received a message from Marshal Stalin, although in a strange form. On May 12th Warsaw was bombed by large formations of Soviet planes, which came in succession at intervals of a few minutes. Bombs were dropped on all the residential districts, scores of houses were destroyed and damaged and about 800 Poles were killed or wounded. Along with their bombs, the same aircraft dropped leaflets. On one side was the text of an interview Stalin had given to a *New York Times* reporter, Mr. Parker, on the occasion of the Polish National Holiday exercises in Moscow. It included Stalin's unequivocal statement that he desired "a strong, independent Poland." Overleaf was a call to the Polish nation to fight against the Germans, beginning with the stereotyped words: "Poles! The hour for action has struck. Pay back the enemy for the sea of blood and the river of tears which have been shed by the Polish nation!"

I do not know what military object was served by the bombing of Warsaw's residential districts, but the combination of the assurances on the leaflets and the bombs dropped on the population had a most adverse effect on the people's attitude towards Russia.

I remember that night well. I lived on the top floor and was standing in the open window looking at Warsaw illuminated by flares. A bomb exploded in the house opposite and I found myself lying in the middle of my room. When curfew time was over, I ran to see if the house where Renia and our son Adam were living had been bombed. The house was all right, but Renia was not at home. She had heard that the street in which I lived had been bombed and had gone to see if I was alive. We found each other away from home for the same reason!

CHAPTER III

COMMANDER-IN-CHIEF, HOME ARMY

THE LAST DAYS OF JUNE and the beginning of July, 1943, became known as "black week" in the history of the Polish Underground.

On June 30th I happened to meet one of the Underground politicians. Shortly before, he had met a friend who had just emerged from Gestapo headquarters, where his interrogation had been suddenly broken off. As he was descending the stairs, the whole building seemed to be in a buzz; officials, agents and even clerks were running down the passages and all seemed very pleased. He heard constant congratulations and also something about the "end of the whole conspiracy." A few minutes after 11 a.m. he saw a single man being led in under very strong police escort. He was handcuffed, but held his head up and walked with a firm step.

I heard this story with much anxiety. The description of the man and the way he was dressed seemed to fit "Grot" Rowecki.

In the afternoon I got a second report. At 10 a.m. some sixty Gestapo cars had arrived on Spiska Street with over 200 armed Gestapo men, who entered practically all the houses simultaneously. The whole area was cordoned off and even the roof-tops swarmed with soldiers. All those living in the houses were herded into one yard; it was evident that a very important man-hunt was in progress, so that everyone was extremely surprised when only one man was arrested, manacled and taken away. It took less than an hour.

Further news came through in the evening. I learned that Grot had not shown up at a meeting scheduled for ten o'clock that morning, and news had got round the city that Gestapo agents were openly boasting over the capture of the Commander of the Home Army. A conference of our special staff was due for next morning at nine o'clock. When we had all gathered, Grot was still missing.

We found out that on the morning of the 30th he had left for the scheduled meeting. On the way, one of his messenger girls handed him a small parcel of money wrapped in newspaper. Grot took the parcel and hurried off to one of his hiding-places. He had been there only a few minutes when the Gestapo arrived and sealed off the street. He must have been recognised by a Gestapo spotter. According to our counter-espionage, there was a special group of agents whose sole task was to track down Grot. They were provided with his photograph and kept watch in the main streets, railway stations and trams.

The loss of General Rowecki was our heaviest blow to date. We had, it is true, lost someone from our ranks nearly every month for three years. The war had already lasted much longer than the average life of a man engaged in Underground work. Quite a high percentage of those who had taken part in the foundation and building up of the Underground movement had been arrested; after varying degrees of torture, they had either been shot, or died in concentration camps. Their disappearance never broke the continuity of our fight or endangered the existence of the movement, because there were always newcomers to take their places. This loss was, however, of far greater significance than the others. General Rowecki was one of the founders of the Home Army and had been its Commander for three years. He had gained an enormous authority amongst his subordinates and indeed throughout the Polish nation. His pseudonym, Grot, was well known everywhere. To the public, Grot was a symbol, a mysterious person who, from the Underground, directed the fight of a nation. We, who knew him more intimately and were in immediate contact with him in the work, knew his great value as a leader, a strong personality, and an out-standing brain, directing and linking the complicated Underground machinery.

He created an organisation and methods of warfare without precedent. He united and centralised scores of military organisations which had arisen spontaneously, directed by the most varied parties and political groups. His personal tact and political talents (the latter hitherto unsuspected) in working with persons of various opinion were important here. He was a handsome man of engaging personality, and a good mixer; he found it relatively easy to influence people, even those of conflicting views sinking their differences under his persuasion. This charm and personality were never known to the public, but played a large part in smoothing out difficulties at the top level. His remarkably quick mind at once picked out the essential elements in every problem, and he could take decisions swiftly.

Grot's A.D.C. had been the only one to know about this flat in Spiska Street. A few places had been built in the furniture where documents of vital importance could be kept. I instructed a special group, previously trained and accustomed to clear endangered flats, to force their way into the lodging and retrieve all documents. This was done on the following day. Fortunately, the hiding places were well camouflaged and the Germans had missed them. When the Gestapo had left the flat, the group managed to get in, removing the seals on the doors. They had with them the carpenter who had originally worked out all the hiding places. With his help, they were all emptied; the parcel of 15,000 American dollars was discovered in one of them. They succeeded in leaving the flat safely with their dangerous load, and after replacing the seals escaped through the gardens, bringing us everything they had found.

Knowing Grot, I was quite certain that the most excruciating torture would not succeed in breaking him. In his possession were secrets on which depended our own fate and the very existence of our whole organisation. I was convinced that he would carry these secrets to his grave, and I was right. Nevertheless, security precautions of another kind had to be taken, as we could not know whether he had been watched for some time. All who had been in contact with him were warned and his various hide-outs were isolated as though infected. Nobody was allowed to visit them, and their inhabitants had to move elsewhere.

Our first idea was to free Grot from German hands. Various suggestions were made, but most of them were impracticable. Only one seemed acceptable, giving more chances of success than the others. In one of the workshops in the city there was a German tank, left there by the Germans for repair. The Polish workers had told us of it and had delayed their work, hoping that we could find some use for it. A volunteer reported that he was ready to drive the tank, filled with explosives, into the Gestapo H.Q., where Grot was imprisoned, and blow it up in a suicidal effort. At the same time, a Kedyw group would be standing by to force its way into the basement and get Grot out, alive or dead. Our Intelligence service was ordered to find out the exact place in the building where he was being held, what sort of arrangements there were for guarding him, the way to his cell and so on.

Unfortunately, the plan was never put to the test. The next day we received a reliable report that he had been taken to Berlin under strong escort. The same day the German news agency, Trans-Ocean, announced the arrest of General Rowecki, leader of the Polish partisans. There was then only one possible way of retrieving Grot: by exchanging him for another German prisoner. This was suggested to the Polish Government in London. The matter was put before Mr. Churchill, who promised help. In exchange, the Germans were then offered in turn several German generals in British hands. All these proposals were rejected. The Germans asked for Rudolf Hess in return for Rowecki, but Great Britain did not agree to this.

Three days after the arrest of Rowecki, another smashing blow fell upon us. General Sikorski died at Gibraltar. The Germans announced it triumphantly through loud-speakers posted at various points in the city. The population was in despair. Crowds gathered round the loud-speakers weeping. The General had been very popular in Poland, and the nation trusted his leadership. His prestige was one of the foundations on which the Polish nation had built its hopes for a better future. In the short time of "black week," Poland had lost two outstanding leaders. After General Sikorski's death, the hope of the Polish people was sustained by their faith and belief in Winston Churchill's "true friendship for Poland."

*　　　*　　　*

In July I received a message from London appointing me Commander of the Home Army. I at once issued an order of the day, which was published in the Underground Press and addressed to the soldiers of the Home Army. In it I announced that I had assumed command. On this order I signed my pseudonym "Bor" for the first time.

My Chief of Staff was General Tadeusz Pełczyński ("Grze-gorz"), who had also been Grot's Chief of Staff. After I took up command, he became Deputy Commander of the Home Army, which was at that time in a stage of rapid growth and numbered some 300,000 sworn members. In the next year, which culminated in the battle for Warsaw, our strength had risen to 380,000. The enrolled total did not include the hundreds of thousands of active sympathisers who collaborated with us, hid fugitives and soldiers on operations, fed and clothed them, sheltered partisans, supplied information and news, etc. It must be clear that a vast secret organisation like ours, with so many ramifications and tasks, could only have existed by the support of the whole community. The ties of solidarity between the Home Army and the community were so numerous that it was impossible to count all those helping hands, people who had not sworn the oath, did not know any of the secrets, and yet helped us so much, often at very grave peril to themselves. It might virtually be said that our auxiliary organisation was provided by the community as a whole. Exceptions to this rule, i.e. people who lived through those years of occupation and were in no way instrumental to our cause, were so few that one might almost disregard them.

The soldiers of the Home Army proper were divided into three categories. The first and largest group comprised people who led a double life. In ordinary, everyday existence, they differed in no way whatsoever from any other man in the street. They worked in offices and factories, on railways, in agriculture, etc.; every one of them was, nevertheless, in touch with his direct superior in the organisation, from whom he got orders and tasks to fulfil connected with espionage (Intelligence), sabotage or diversion, to be performed where he had access through his employment. Often a whole group was used as a team for some major task, in which case they had to be trained together. But the object in view was always the ultimate task, i.e. the general insurrection. After action, such a group was scheduled to return to "normal" life. In this way, practically the whole German economic and communication system was riddled and could be mined and blown up from within at short notice.

The second category of our members comprised what might be termed professional conspirators, i.e. people who worked full-time in the Underground or at least had to be available at any time of the day and night for work in our staff or its numerous branches, intelligence, liaison, etc. They therefore had no time for any occupation outside the conspiracy, nor any mode of life which would limit their availability; they had to live under false identity, with forged documents and labour permits. In addition, all our officers and senior executives had, by force of circumstance, to lead a completely underground existence, as the Germans had specific charges against them and orders were out for their arrest on sight.

The third group consisted of those who had broken with their former existence completely and set out to live a life of free men as soldiers of the partisan units. They lived mainly in the forests, wore uniforms and fought the Germans openly. The second group had first of all to be provided with forged papers, identity cards, labour certificates, movement orders and other documents issued by the German authorities without which one was in constant danger of arrest. To cope with this necessity, we organised teams of specialists who worked in secret laboratories. It was a task of immense responsibility, for the consequences of any slight mistake were disastrous. The Germans continually changed the look of the documents they issued and different documents were required in different regions so that the difficulties of the work were intensified. Document-forging establishments, however, existed not only in Warsaw but in every other district of the country.

Through their methods of torturing prisoners, the enemy had come to know a great deal of our organisation in three years. The only thing they did not know was the police-name given on our identity cards, and our address. The terrible nervous tension of people dogged by the Gestapo and awaiting arrest at any moment may be seen in the following example:

The Gestapo were going all out to get "Dzięcioł" (Woodpecker), the chief of our Intelligence Service, who was present at a meeting of five of us held in a house in the Vistula riverside district. Suddenly a violent knocking was heard at the front door. We looked at each other in silence as we waited for the door to be opened. Thoughts raced through our heads. Many of Woodpecker's men had been arrested, and one of them might have disclosed under torture the identity of his chief. The Gestapo were hot on his trail and it was to be expected that they would eventually track him. Many of our rendezvous had well-concealed hiding-places in case of trouble, but this had none. As we listened to the sounds coming from the entrance hall, we failed to notice that Woodpecker had slipped into the next room.

Finally, relief came. The smiling face of the lady of the house appeared round the door.

ORGANISATION OF THE HOME ARMY

Direction Commander of the Home Army (A.K.)

Executive organ: the Chief Command (K.G. Headquarters)

With the widening of the sphere of activities and tasks of the Home Army, its organisation developed progressively. The following table illustrates the organisation as a whole, after I had assumed command of the Home Army:

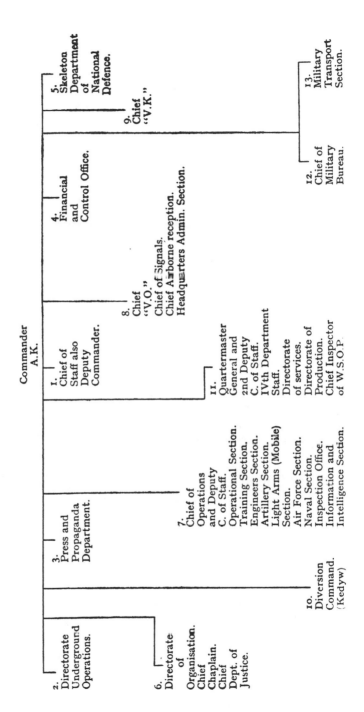

Commander A.K.

1. Chief of Staff also Deputy Commander.

2. Directorate Underground Operations.

3. Press and Propaganda Department.

4. Financial and Control Office.

5. Skeleton Department of National Defence.

6. Directorate of Organisation. Chief Chaplain. Chief Dept. of Justice.

7. Chief of Operations and Deputy C. of Staff. Operational Section. Training Section. Engineers Section. Artillery Section. Light Arms (Mobile) Section. Air Force Section. Naval Section. Inspection Office. Information and Intelligence Section.

8. Chief "V.O." Chief of Signals. Chief Airborne reception. Headquarters Admin. Section.

9. Chief "V.K."

10. Diversion Command. (Kedyw)

11. Quartermaster General and 2nd Deputy C. of Staff. IVth Department Staff. Directorate of services. Directorate of Production. Chief Inspector of W.S.O.P.

12. Chief of Military Bureau.

13. Military Transport Section.

"It's all right," she reassured us. "It was only the man to read the electric meter; he was rather impatient because I didn't answer the door at once."

We were turning back to our work when Woodpecker, hardly able to stand, staggered into the room.

"I've poisoned myself," he gasped, and pitched forward on to the floor.

Living, as he had, in constant danger of arrest, he had broken under the strain. He was so sure that it was the Gestapo at the door that he had acted without waiting for confirmation. It was with the greatest difficulty that his life was saved. It was touch and go for nearly two weeks. A few days after his discharge from hospital, he was arrested by the Gestapo. This time, he had no poison on him. . . . He was tortured, betrayed nothing, and was murdered.

More than once the Gestapo arrested my closest collaborators. Among these was my personal messenger, "Mrs. Maria." After interrogation under torture, when she revealed nothing, she was shot in the Pawiak Prison. She was stripped naked so that her clothes would not be spoiled by a bullet hole or blood and executed in a black paper slip. Her real name was Halina Stabrowska.

Departments Directly Subordinate to Commander Home Army

1. Chief of Staff, also Deputy Commander H.A. (A.K.).	
2. Directorate. Underground Operations.	The planning and direction of the general scheme of current resistance action, diversion, sabotage, communal resistance and relevant propaganda.
3. Press and Propaganda Department.	Welfare, political and social policy, Press, publications and general propaganda policy.
4. Financial and Control Office.	Budget, supply of necessary funds, hidden depots, premises and financial control.
5. Skeleton Department of National Defence.	Preparation for forming the Ministry of National Defence at the moment of liberation.

Departments Directly Subordinate to Chief of Staff

6. Directorate of Organisation.	General organisation, strengths, personnel policy, regrouping of para-military organisations, reconstruction of the armed forces, legislation, collaboration with prisoners-of-war camps and labour deportee centres in Germany, women's auxiliary services.
Also subordinate:	Chief Chaplain and Legal Office (Department of Justice).
7. Chief of Operations.	Planning and direction of preparation for insurrection.
Also subordinate:	(a) Operational Section.
	(b) Training Section.
	(c) Various Services Sections.
	(d) Office of inspection: senior commanders' reserve, control and inspection of districts at disposal of C.-in-C., regarding preparations for insurrection.
	(e) Information and Intelligence Section: all activities connected with intelligence and counter-espionage.
8. Chief "V.O." (Chief of Operational Liaison.)	Operational liaison organisation of radio liaison, production of radio equipment, direction of liaison sections (Units).
Also subordinate:	(a) Reception of airborne supplies, planning of airborne supply operations, organisation of reception and disposal of supplies.
	(b) Headquarters Administrative Section: Command Defence Units, organisation for period of insurrection, etc.
9. Chief "V.K." (Chief of Courier Liaison.)	Courier liaison between the Chief Command and London as well as between the respective districts. Chief Office of Commander A.K., radio-cypher and de-cypher, radio correspondence files. (Chief V.K. was a woman, Miss Karaś; pseudonym, Bronka.)

10. Kedyw (Diversion Command).	The direction of current diversion and sabotage action, disposal of special squads, sabotage training, production of battle equipment for sabotage, direction of district branches of the Kedyw.
11. Quartermaster-General.	General equipment and supply, both for current requirements and preparation for armed insurrection.
Also subordinate:	(a) Directorate of Production, organisation and manufacture of arms and explosives.
	(b) Chief Military Inspectorate. Insurrection defence services: territorial units for consolidation and security of areas captured by insurrection (liberated territories).
12. Chief of Military Offices.	Co-operation in matters regarding military requirements with Departments of Civil Administration (Government Delegate's Office).
13. Military Transport Section.	Road and rail transport.

B

The provincial organisation of the Home Army was based on the pre-war system of civilian administration, i.e. on voivodships and cantonal division.

In our terms, a "district" comprised the pre-war territory of a voivodship, and "area," that of a canton.

Commanders of provinces were directly subordinate to the Commander of the Home Army; a province comprised two to three districts and was only formed when it was found advisable to join several of the latter under one special command. Only seven districts were included in the provinces and ten were directly subordinated to the C.-in-C., Home Army.

A district commander and his staff were directly responsible for all matters pertaining to organisation in the given district.

A regional inspector was an indirect link of tactical liaison between a district commander and the commanders of two to three areas.

An area commander and his staff were responsible for all organisational matters on the territory of the area under his command.

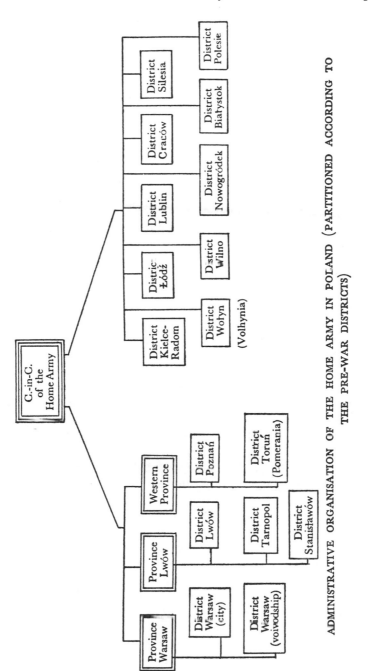

ADMINISTRATIVE ORGANISATION OF THE HOME ARMY IN POLAND (PARTITIONED ACCORDING TO THE PRE-WAR DISTRICTS)

Outpost commanders were at the head of squads (platoons) organised locally.

A platoon was the basic organisational and tactical unit. The usual strength of a platoon was approximately fifty men.

The tasks of our Intelligence, which had equally to supply the needs of the Chief Command of the Home Army and the Allies, could be divided into the following main branches:

The ascertaining of all economic and military problems relative to the German land forces or the Luftwaffe on the territories of Poland as well as in the rear of the German eastern front.

Economic intelligence inside Germany in the widest sense.

Intelligence regarding Germany's Baltic and North Sea ports.

Study of the morale of the German Forces and people.

Although two consecutive chiefs of this service—Lieut.-Colonel W. Berka "Wacław" and Lieut.-Colonel M. Drobik, (Dzieciol)—and their staffs fell into the hands of the Gestapo, the organisation continued to develop satisfactorily. Under the direction of its third chief, it achieved its best results in the years 1943-4 and rendered valuable service to the Allies.

All garrisons and every movement of the German forces throughout the General Government were under the closest observation of our local Intelligence network, which covered every district and area. The chief objectives on German territory were the industrial centres and the North Sea and Baltic ports; the latter being extremely difficult to cover because of the enemy's vigilance and extensive counter-espionage.

Members of our Intelligence and Information Service were recruited from every social sphere. We differed from most other intelligence systems by the fact that, on the whole, we did not depend on or employ paid agents. The commanding posts were mainly filled by Army officers, while economic problems were mostly handled by civil engineers. Much valuable service was rendered by Polish officers trained in Great Britain and parachuted into Poland.

Our intelligence reports were regularly dispatched by radio to London and in the years 1942-4 numbered 300 per month. They contained details concerning every aspect of the war. Apart from radio transmission, the essential facts of our Intelligence material were micro-filmed and sent every month to London by courier. We received from our Allies several official commendations of our work which expressed keen appreciation of the data we supplied. The Ministry of Aircraft Production wrote in 1944: "Reports from Polish sources are considered as the most valuable of all we received. They contain entirely trustworthy information. . . ." This excerpt is typical of the general tone of the acknowledgements we received.

*   *   *

One of the results of our Intelligence work was the delay in the perfecting of the German rocket-propelled weapons. In spring, 1943, we received information that the Germans were conducting experiments with mysterious weapons at Peenemünde, a fact which we immediately brought to the attention of London. Within a few weeks our agents obtained with much difficulty detailed plans of the experimental camp grounds, which we also dispatched to London. The Royal Air Force was thus able on August 15th, 1943, to raid the camp, turning it into a shambles and killing many of the staff. This delayed the use of the V1 for several months.

In 1944 the Germans transferred their experimental stations to Polish territory. One was built at a place called Blizna, near Mielec. A great patch of countryside was turned into an experimental camp and the Germans began practical trials with flying bombs. In the first stages of these experiments the difference of the fall of the missiles was very wide and ranged from a few to several hundred miles. As research progressed, it was found that the missiles landed most frequently in the region of the Bug River, near Wyszków. There was a certain number of casualties among the civilian population as well as destruction of property. Our special observers recorded the technicalities of every discharge, and a flying squad was detailed to gather the fragments after every explosion, having each time to win a race with special German motorised teams employed to obliterate all tell-tale debris. Although the Germans had motor-cars at their disposal, while our agents had only their legs to depend on, our patrols often got there ahead of the Germans. A special committee of technicians, set up in the Office of Research of our Intelligence organisation in Warsaw, then made research into the characteristics of the new weapon. All conclusions reached were immediately wired to London.

On one occasion when a missile landed without exploding,

our patrols managed to reach it before the Germans, remove it whole and dump it in a nearby stream. After a search lasting several days, the Germans finally gave it up and our men fished up the bomb and took it to a safe place, where our experts dismantled and examined it at leisure. The most vital parts were then taken to the Cracow district, where, together with the photographs of the bomb, all relevant technical specifications and the results of the studies, they were picked up by a Dakota plane which landed for that special purpose. In that way the Allies were fully informed about the "doodle-bug" well in advance.

*   *   *

In the scope of our anti-terrorist and revenge action, much effort was sacrificed in fighting the Gestapo and the German police, from whom the civilian population had so much to dread. Sentences were executed on the most obnoxious members of the Gestapo, usually in broad daylight, in streets or public places. In the course of the first six months of 1944 we "liquidated" 769 prominent agents of the Gestapo.

These activities went a long way towards lowering the morale of the Germans in Poland, and indirectly protected the civilians. They formed, in some respects, a method of self-defence. The diversion detachments also protected radio transmitters and convoyed transports of arms and equipment.

The transport of arms from the parachute drops to the hidden distribution depots was in most cases done by means of captured motor vehicles, the arms being disguised under various forms (oxygen bottles, etc.). Obviously, the best method was to have our men dressed up in either Wehrmacht or S.S. uniform, and more often than not transport took place under strong armed escort. Skirmishes with the German police and armed units often took place on these occasions, both in towns and out in the open; our troops, who always employed bold shock tactics, usually emerged victorious.

There is hardly space to describe all the sabotage and diversionary activities. The following list gives some idea of the results achieved:

Summary of Results of Sabotage and Diversion Action
in Poland from January 1st, 1941, to June 30th, 1944

Railway locomotives damaged	6,930
Locomotives further delayed during repairs . .	803

Rail transports derailed 732
Rail transports set on fire 443
Railway carriages damaged 19,058
Railway bridges blown up 38
Motor transport vehicles destroyed 4,326
Aircraft destroyed 28
Fuel tanks (cisterns) destroyed . . . 1,167
Tons of fuel destroyed 4,674
Petrol wells spiked 3
Rail-cars of wood destroyed (burnt) . . . 150
Military store depots set on fire 122
Breaches in electrical power in the Warsaw network
  alone 638
Major Army depots set on fire (destroyed) . . 8
Complete stoppage of factories 7
Faulty assemblies of aircraft engines . . . 1,710
Faulty casts of cannon barrels 203
Faulty manufacture of artillery missiles . . . 92,000
Faulty manufacture of aircraft radio transmitters . 107
Machines of major importance in war-production
  plants destroyed 2,872
Various acts of sabotage executed 25,145
Lethal bodily assaults on Germans 5,733

This summary gives only the more characteristic acts of
sabotage and is only half the picture of the scope of our
activities.

Our production of armaments reached its climax in 1943–4.
It is not possible to describe fully here its development and
operation in those five years of secret manufacture, which
strove to supply at any price the utmost possible needs.
Statistics hardly illustrate our efforts. In many districts production was organised under the control of and according to
instructions received from H.Q. At one period our equipment
included:

   5 mechanical workshops fitted with 44 machine-tools.
   2 machine carbine-barrel workshops.
   2 assembling workshops of machine carbine with complete
     equipment for serial assembling.
   4 hand-grenade filling workshops.
   3 firing test ranges.
   3 nitro high-explosive and cheddite plants.

1 pyrotechnic and chemical plant.
2 research and control laboratories.
1 flame-thrower assembling workshop.
2 flame-thrower experimental proof ranges.
1 design, drawing and blue-print office.

In the spring of 1944, our Underground production in Warsaw suffered a serious setback. The Germans discovered our methods of transporting materials. Within a short period, two of our larger arsenals were discovered by the Gestapo. They knew that the men within would be well armed, and they therefore avoided giving battle. They simply flooded the cellars from fire hydrants and drowned everybody inside.

In one arsenal, the Germans found 70,000 hand-grenades (there were then in all 320,000 in Warsaw) and in the other 450 flame-throwers, just half the total number in the possession of the Home Army in Warsaw. The Germans were astounded by this discovery after five years of ceaseless control by the Gestapo. How many might not be stored elsewhere? They redoubled their efforts and arrested many of our munitions production staff. The Gestapo tried to bribe one of the arrested men with the promise of a lovely villa and a large bank account in Switzerland if he would only reveal how we managed our production and transport and how we camouflaged the whole thing.

The man, "Jurek," one of the best technicians on machine-gun production, refused to give any information, and was executed. Before his death, he managed to smuggle the news of the Gestapo proposals out to us. It was interesting as being the first indication that the Germans, foreseeing possible defeat and war on their own territory, wished to prepare themselves for underground activity and to profit by our experience.

Compared with the war production of our allies, the figures of our Underground war industry are, of course, laughably small. But in our circumstances the volume which they represent was a remarkable feat of which we were justly proud. One-third of our armament was of our own production, including our whole stock of hand-grenades, mines, flame-throwers and a great part of our machine-guns, as well as many other arms and war material.

In the autumn of 1943 Himmler sent one of his most trusted

men, Major-General Kutschera of the S.S. and police to Warsaw. He was only thirty, but he had already made his mark by massacres of civilians in the other occupied countries of Europe. His relations with Himmler were of some intimacy, Himmler's sister being his mistress.

Kutschera's tasks had been clearly defined. As the Polish counter-measures had begun to yield results and the German officials were in many cases giving way to fear in their dealings with the Polish Underground, he was to destroy Polish resistance at all costs. In other words, he was to drown Warsaw in a sea of blood.

At first he succeeded. Public executions became a weekly occurrence. That was a return to the German methods of 1939, especially in our western provinces, then incorporated into the Reich. From time to time they had used this method, but Kutschera made public execution his daily weapon. In the course of one month in 1943 the death-roll for Warsaw alone was: October 16th, 20; 17th, 20; 19th, 20; 20th, 20; 22nd, 10; 23rd, 20; 25th, 20; 26th, 30; 30th, 10. In these two weeks 177 people were publicly shot in the streets of Warsaw, among them five women. In all German-occupied Poland approximately 15,000 people were executed during the winter of 1943-4. Public executions of this kind were also customary in Cracow, Lwów, Radom, Kielce, Przemyśl, Rozwadow, Jaslo, Debica, Jedrzejow and dozens of other towns. Apart from public executions, firing-squads were active inside the prisons and the number of people who were summarily executed in captivity was infinitely greater.

I fully realised that were we to break under this new pressure and Kutschera be convinced that his methods were effective, the more intensified and frequent would his method of terror become and the more numerous would be his victims.

His method was to round up chance pedestrians in the streets, seize several hundred of them and then have their names posted on the bill-boards and announced by loud-speakers. Single lists numbered as many as 200 at a time. The announcement of names would be accompanied by the information that if the families of the arrested people would disclose the names and whereabouts of members of the Underground, their relations would be released. In this way, he hoped to break our solidarity by forcing denunciations. His attempts, however, were unsuccessful.

Public executions would take place the next day, in broad daylight, in the streets of the capital. The victims were brought from the Pawiak Prison with plaster-of-paris gags in their mouths to prevent them from shouting patriotic calls as they died.

Once Renia, with her baby in the pram, passed Senatorska Street, where an execution had just taken place. The corpses had already been carried away, but blood was splashed all over the pavement and bits of brain were sticking to the walls. People were kneeling all around, and in a few seconds the whole place was covered with red and white flowers and burning candles. Flowers were put in every bullet-hole in the wall. Renia stopped to pray. German police appeared and she made off. When she looked back they were shooting and beating people up—all in vain, for after a moment the crowd was back again, and new flowers and new candles had appeared. Kutschera had 2,000 of these victims on his conscience, to say nothing of the secret executions which took place within the walls of the burnt-out Ghetto.

I decided that, cost what it might, Kutschera must be killed. The tactics of using terror to combat German terror seemed to be the only right solution. It was clear that, in view of his exceptional position, both in the senior ranks of the Gestapo and in his relations with Himmler, at least 200 Polish hostages would have to pay the price for his death. I calculated, however, that the removal of such a notorious criminal would convince his successor that nothing could save him from death if he followed the same tactics. In the long run, I argued, his death would save many human lives and go far to stop the intensified German terror, although the immediate price would be heavy. Before I made up my mind that Kutschera must die, a warning had been sent to him informing him that if he did not cease these atrocities he would be killed. A second warning was sent, far more categorical, adding that, though he had evaded death in Belgium and Czechoslovakia, he would not do so in Poland.

The date of Kutschera's death was entered on the list three months before it was to take place. It was the most difficult operation of its kind that the special Kedyw units had undertaken. Various items of information had to be gathered, despite the efforts made by the German authorities to conceal them. We had to know Kutschera's exact mode of life, his habits, his time-table for each day, the route he followed to his office and back and so on. It was not easy. He used a variety of cars. Sometimes his escort would be in civilian clothes, at others in military uniform, and occasionally in police uniform. He himself wore various uniforms, but never the insignia of his rank as major-general.

Three attempts were made: two of them failed. The third and successful attempt took place on February 1st, 1944, in the very heart of Warsaw. It lasted barely three minutes.

The officer in charge of the attack, Lieutenant Bronislaw Pietraszkiewicz, was chosen from among our ablest diversion soldiers. He went by the name of "Lot." He had previously been a Scoutmaster and was just twenty. He could preserve complete calm and self-control in situations demanding determination and coolness of action. Among his more striking earlier feats was the execution of a leading Gestapo official in the presence of his wife, who was unexpectedly accompanying him and was wheeling her child in a perambulator. To throw a hand-grenade at that distance would have killed the woman and child also. This was not included in Lot's orders and it was our principle that all our executions were on a judicial basis. Lot had to make a lightning decision in that split second. He took the added risk, drew a tommy-gun from the violin case he was carrying and shot the German dead at a distance of one yard.

The plans for the final attempt on Kutschera were worked out in detail. The scene was set just in front of S.S. and German police headquarters and only a few steps from Szucha Street and Gestapo headquarters. As a result of three previous attacks on Germans at this point, all the entries to the streets had been blocked by barbed wire and were guarded by S.S. patrols and concrete pill-boxes.

It was 9.55 a.m. when Kutschera's car appeared at the turning from a side street some distance away. As usual, his A.D.C. was at the wheel, and Kutschera was sitting next to him on the front seat. Behind them was a car with his escort of four Gestapo men.

An innocent-looking girl pulled her handkerchief out of her pocket. It was a signal to two of the attackers, standing on the other side of the street with tommy-guns under their coats. It was also a signal for a "German military car," driven by Lot with "Cichy" (Corporal Marian Zegier) as passenger.

Lot drove up to Kutschera's car, swerved left and blocked the way. Kutschera's A.D.C. jammed on the brake and stopped his car just as a collision seemed inevitable. A bare 2 yards separated the radiators of the two cars. Lot threw a filipinka; the explosion was so close that the door and part of the chassis of his own car were crushed. It took him and Cichy a few seconds to struggle out. Meanwhile, "Sokół" and "Juno" let fly two long bursts from their tommy-guns and wiped out the escort of four Gestapo men. Lot and Cichy were now clear of their car and rushed towards the general, who was still dazed by the explosion of the filipinka. Lot seized him by the lapels and dragged him out. He then fired a burst from his tommy-gun into Kutschera's head. Cichy finished off the A.D.C. in exactly the same way. Germans rushed up from all sides, firing at the "executioners." Firing came also from the windows of police headquarters and from the pill-boxes at the street corners. Lying on the ground, the Polish escort swept the street with short bursts from their tommy-guns.

While this was going on, Lot was busily searching Kutschera's pockets for his identity papers. But when Kutschera was dragged from the car, he had dropped his wallet under the car. Lot knew he had to get the papers—those were his orders—and it was his adherence to duty which proved fatal, since clearly every second was priceless. He was hit by a well-aimed shot in the stomach. Cichy had also been wounded. But both continued to search for the papers and finally found them. Then the four of them got into their car.

Sokół now took the wheel and Lot hunched beside him. They shot off at top speed along a prearranged route. Lot continued to give orders until they got about halfway, but then his strength gave out and he collapsed into unconsciousness. As they sped on, another bullet grazed the driver's head, but it was only a surface wound, and Sokół drove on. Their destination was the Hospital of the Transfiguration in Praga, across the river. It was one of the Red Cross headquarters of the Home Army. Many of the doctors belonged to our organisation, and we used to send there any of our soldiers who were wounded in and around Warsaw. They had been warned that their help might be needed that day. Both the wounded men, Lot and Cichy, were taken straight to the operating table on arrival.

Once their two wounded comrades were safely in the hospital,

Sokół and Juno decided to get back to the left bank of the river. If they had driven eastwards, out of the city, they might have got clear. Here again operations routine and the adherence to a precise plan proved fatal. They had reckoned that a car driving westwards would not be suspected, but in this they were mistaken. As they were crossing the Kierbedź Bridge, all the German patrols were notified. When they got halfway across they heard the wailing siren of the German emergency police squad. Just ahead, they saw a line of men in green uniforms barring the end of the bridge. That way was closed. Sokół decided to get back to Praga. He tried to turn sharply, but they were going too fast and the car hit an iron girder with terrific force. German police motor-cyclists now appeared at both ends of the bridge.

In a flash, Sokół and Juno leapt from the car, climbed the iron balustrade and jumped into the river 100 feet below. German rifles and machine-guns sprayed them from the banks and the bridge. They disappeared, came to the surface and started swimming rapidly downstream. Bullets splashed all around them. Sokół was the first to be killed. Juno continued to struggle on. Silent crowds watched with bated breath from the banks. Then the sound of a motor-boat was heard; the Germans had taken up the pursuit by water. But the swimmer refused to give in. The police boat gained on him swiftly. Shots fired at close range could now be heard. Once more the body of the mortally wounded young man appeared on the surface. Then it sank.

These events took place in the near vicinity of the Hospital of the Transfiguration. The arrest of the two wounded men might take place at any time. Their commander decided to act at once.

At 6 p.m. a police car drove up to the hospital. Sentries were stationed at every entrance and gate. The "Gestapo" rushed into the ward where the two men were lying after their operations. Doctors and nurses looked on with horror and despair as the "Germans" took them both away. But their faces cleared when, twenty minutes later, another batch of Gestapo men turned up to collect the Polish "bandits." They made a thorough search of the whole hospital, but failed to find their prey. Lot and Cichy were soon in a safe place. The same evening I received a detailed report of the day's events—the sentence had been carried out. Along with the report, a photo of Kutschera in smiling mood was put on my desk.

All four men were awarded the Virtuti Militari Cross, Poland's highest decoration for bravery to her soldiers. All the crosses were awarded posthumously. Both Lot's and Cichy's wounds proved fatal. Lot died the same day and Cichy the following morning.

Although the chief actors were dead, the final act of the tragedy had not yet been played. Two strange funerals now took place. A solemn requiem mass was said for Lot and Cichy in a tiny chapel at the cemetery. Lot's comrade in arms, "Wanda," sang his favourite *Ave Maria*. The two young men were buried side by side; the decorations were placed on their coffins. An hour later, in the same chapel, another funeral mass was celebrated, this time for another deceased person. In the middle of the ceremony the Gestapo suddenly rushed into the chapel and, to the terror of the congregation, tore off the lid of the coffin. An unexpected sight met their gaze—the face of an old woman, seamed with a close network of wrinkles.

*   *   *

It was in November, 1943, that I received a report which Karolina Lanckoronska, an Underground worker previously mentioned, had managed to send me out of the concentration camp of Ravensbrück near Berlin. This report gave details about the very special and refined persecutions Polish women had to undergo. It was then for the first time that I learnt of "guinea-pigs," seventy-four young Polish women political prisoners who had been repeatedly (up to five times) operated on for experimental purposes. From among all the women of all nations represented at Ravensbrück, only Poles were singled out as guinea-pigs and only Poles were executed. But the report also spoke of the proud and dignified attitude of the Polish women, none of whom expected to get out alive. I was to learn later on that the female detainees at Oswięcim had to suffer still worse and that they looked upon Ravensbrück as a "privileged" camp.

*   *   *

Our main source of war news was the wireless. The Germans declared merciless war on our transmitters. At first the sets worked in the city under the protection of special warning patrols, who announced the approach of German wireless-detection cars. Later on, the Germans realised that this was ineffectual, and they reorganised their attempts with the help of agents. Under hats pulled well down, they had minute earphones which helped them to detect transmitters without rousing our suspicions. The ruse was used on both sides, however. In reply, we organised attacks on German listening centres. In the spring of 1944 most of our radio sets worked in suburban areas, in large blocks of flats, changing their location with great frequency. The radio operators had their own jargon. The transmitting set was the "accordion," the operators "players" and the actual transmission the "concert." I once visited one of these concerts.

The two players first produced an enormous American Colt and put it on the table. Then one took up a position at the window while the second produced the set, literally from inside his shirt. It was about the size of a largish book and could thus be easily carried from place to place. He next produced six or seven yards of aerial, swearing as he did so, because the aerial had to lie at right angles to the direction of the trans-mission, and the size of the room was hardly adequate. It took him a good deal of time to solve his problem. Before he started work, we questioned him about the conditions under which he worked.

"What methods do the Germans use to locate you?" I asked.

"Their detectors work non-stop, night and day," he replied. "After a few minutes' concert, they have usually picked us up. Several of their sets usually pick up our wavelength at the same time, then give each other the angle of direction. The time it takes to pick us up varies, of course. Sometimes they manage it in fifteen minutes; if we are lucky, it takes them an hour or so. When they have fixed our approximate location, they give the signal to their mobile-car squads. Their task is far more difficult. They use magnetic instruments, worn on their wrists, and they have to get the exact spot where we are working. They must surprise us and reach us without warning. But we've got our own methods of avoiding a surprise visit."

"What are they?"

"Quite simple. We depend chiefly on hand-grenades and tommy-guns. Our escort always carries these. We never move without our escort, of course."

F

"Where is your escort now?"

The man smiled and pointed to the window. "Just try to locate them yourself," he said.

I went to the window and vainly tried to make out anyone who could have a tommy-gun or hand-grenades. Passers-by were moving quietly along the road outside. On the balcony of a nearby house a man was lounging in a deck-chair, his hat tilted over his eyes, reading a book. In the garden of our house several people were digging—obviously gardeners. Further away to the right, a girl was playing with a dog she was taking for a walk.

"These people digging in the garden are our escort," the player explained. "The man reading a book is our alarm post. There are other observation posts further down the road and in the woods. When the man reading takes off his hat, it means that danger is near."

He turned back into the room and continued: "At first they used to send out S.S. men as patrols. That was too easy. The sight of a uniform within a hundred yards' radius was the signal to break off the concert, and then it was impossible for them to continue their search. The only course remaining to them was to surround and search the whole area—and this required very large police forces.

"They soon got wise to this and sent out plain-clothes men. The only way of recognising them was by their frequent glances at the detectors on their wrists. It has now got very unhealthy for people to look at their watches too often in our vicinity; it may mean trouble for them," he concluded.

"Have you ever had to fight your way out?" I asked.

"Yes. Twice. Once some plain-clothes men succeeded in taking us by surprise, and the only thing left was hand-grenades. It was some months ago. The leader of our escort was killed and I was wounded in the leg. We managed to save the set, though. The second time we ambushed the Germans. We had been transmitting for a long time in the same spot and we strengthened our escort considerably. After we had been transmitting there for two days, a truck stopped opposite our house. The driver (he was dressed in civilian clothes) got out and started to tinker with the engine, cursing somewhat freely. No one would have suspected anything—it looked so natural—if he had not kept on looking at his 'wrist-watch.' We waited no longer; the escort shot him on the spot. About fifteen German police then leapt out of the lorry, armed to the teeth. A regular battle started. As this was the sort of thing we had got ready for, they had a warm reception, and after about twenty minutes of it they withdrew, leaving behind four killed, two wounded and . . . the truck.

"Another radio team of ours had a strange experience. They were transmitting in a forest when an old peasant woman came along, picking berries. It turned out later that she was wearing a magnetic 'wrist-watch' and a thin layer of berries in her basket concealed hand-grenades. Behind her, in the undergrowth, a long, scattered line of German police was advancing, so the fighting was much fiercer than in our case; but it turned out all right in the end. When we searched the body of the old 'woman,' we found miniature headphones under her kerchief. A cap pulled down over the ears is a warning to us now."

"You seem to have a pretty tough time."

The player smiled. "In town or in the suburbs where we have electric current, it's not so bad," he replied. "It's the devil of a job in country places where we have to run the set off a dynamo roaring its head off. Then it really is a concert. We have to see that a threshing machine or some other noise is going full blast at the same time to drown the beastly thing."

I asked a last question. "How do the men at the other end, in England, get on?"

"Well," he answered, "their position is not so good. Of course, they are working in perfect safety, but they know we may have to pay with our lives for the concert. When we interrupt our transmission without warning, they have no idea what is happening to us. They don't know whether we will come on the air next session or not. They must feel very worried about us. And we get to know each other. You can always tell a certain operator by the way he taps out his messages. Each of us has his own speed and style. We become great friends. If time and the Germans permit, we occasionally tap out a few words of greeting at the end. Naturally, they do all they can to help us. Sometimes they have to tap out their call sign for hours on end before they get any answer from us."

It was now time to start, and he sat down at the set with a sheet of paper covered with columns of figures before him.

Reception was weak and other stations were interfering badly. He had to repeat the message a second and third time in groups of twenty figures and time was short: they had only half an hour. The message was to be continued by a station working in the centre of Warsaw. This was part of the system; short periods of transmission and reception from each set in widely scattered places. In this way, continuity was maintained and the Germans had greater difficulty in detecting. Later on we were obliged to transfer the transmission sets deep into the forests, where they worked under the protection of Home Army detachments. The main problem then became to get the messages to the forests with reasonable speed.

The best form of defence is attack. Instead of waiting for the enemy to come and find our stations, we sought him out for ourselves, attacking and disabling his interception stations. In 1944 the Germans brought the most modern and technically perfect installations to Warsaw. They began to give considerable trouble to our whole wireless liaison system. Both the receiving and detecting apparatus was located at Gocławek, a suburb of the capital. A few days before the whole thing was due to be transferred to the Central Telegraph Office, where it would have been completely inaccessible, a strong Homy Army force attacked the station. The precision apparatus was destroyed, the station wrecked and the specialists killed.

*   *   *

The second source of information was the monitoring service, primarily from the B.B.C. and from Moscow, the latter transmitted either by the Soviet station or by the radio of the Union of Polish Patriots or another station called "Kościuszko." These three were the instruments of Soviet propaganda, and their broadcasts informed us on the attitude and methods of the Russian policy towards Poland. In secret studios, monitoring continued day and night. The most important programmes were taken down in shorthand and were published in a sort of daily digest. Besides this, we issued about thirty copies of the *Biuletyn Sztabowy* (*Staff Bulletin*) once a week, giving views and comments on the most important articles published in the Allied Press and referred to by Allied broadcasts.

Our printing presses had necessarily to be well organised and technically well equipped to cope with the large volume of work. In 1942, our Government in London issued postage stamps showing a secret printing press at work. The picture showed a primitive press at which the poor Underground printer was hard at work. This interpretation gave us all a hearty laugh when it reached us. Our countrymen in England had not quite visualised the true picture.

We had seven large printing shops in Warsaw and several reserve establishments. I inspected one of the large works, which was run in a private house.

It was in no way remarkable. An elderly, modestly-dressed woman opened the door. She was alone in the house. When I touched the walls, I could feel a light throbbing, due to the presses working below. We went into a large hall. There, the guide carefully swept a thick layer of dust from a small section of the flooring and revealed a faint square. He then pressed a rusty nail in the wall to indicate to those below that someone safe wished to come down and that they should open the entry. The outline of the square became clearer, and finally the slab of concrete was raised from its hole, revealing a narrow ladder. We went down and the slab closed behind us. We found ourselves in a small room where two soldiers were sitting, armed with grenades and revolvers. Should the printing shop be discovered by the enemy, the only course was to try to fight a way out. The presses stood in a fairly large hall. Around them four men were hard at work stripped to the waist, for it was very hot and stuffy. After only a few minutes, I became acutely conscious of the lack of air. The men worked in these conditions for twelve hours. They could not leave together at the end of their time, nor arrive together. Half an hour had to elapse between individual arrivals, and the same for departures, while all the time the greatest caution had to be observed.

One of the first things to attract my attention was a large shield bearing a white eagle—the heraldic symbol of Poland— hanging on the wall, the first I had seen during the whole occupation.

In one corner was a green light, a sign that everything overhead was in order. Near the front door of the villa was an electric button concealed in the wall. The old lady had only to press it with her shoulder for a red light to replace the green. The printers then had to stop the machines. While the red light was on, neither the printers nor their guard could leave, whether it remained on for two hours or two days. They had emergency stocks of food and water for such an eventuality. In many ways, it was rather as if these men were working in a submarine.

"Where do you get your electric current from?" I asked.

"We just connected up with the main power cable and so we get it at Hitler's expense," one of them replied.

They told me of the exhausting efforts that had to be made to excavate the subterranean workshop, and how cautiously the earth had had to be taken away in baskets; how much care had had to be used in the transport of the various pieces of machinery and in assembling them into complete presses. Once a press was anchored to its foundations, it could not be moved. Discovery meant that all the efforts which went to instal it were lost. They had to do all that work themselves too, so as not to initiate more people into the secret.

One of their gravest preoccupations was getting their publications away from the premises. Usually, empty beer barrels were used or wooden cases bearing the name of some manufacturer. They had to be so well and tightly closed that it was impossible to see the contents without taking the thing to bits. They were removed on ordinary push-carts, which were then in use in Warsaw for every kind of goods. Near the push-cart, among the passers-by, an armed escort would watch over the precious load. If anyone insisted on seeing the contents, a shot was the only way of finishing the argument.

*   *   *

From the very first days of the activities of the Polish Home Army, the propaganda factor was always considered to be one of the most powerful weapons of war.

One of the chief aims of propaganda was to bring about as nearly as possible complete harmony and comradeship between all ranks of our organisation, the members of which originated from very diverse social spheres and professed a multiplicity of political opinions. The idea was to stress the certainty of ultimate victory, to co-ordinate the attitude of resistance against the occupying enemy forces, to maintain public spirit and, finally, to counteract enemy propaganda.

In order to fulfil these aims, we were particularly careful always to present the truest possible picture of both the international war situation and the state of affairs on the home front, giving the reasons for measures ordered by the Underground. The main slogan of our propaganda was: the truth and true presentation of facts.

The principal channels of action were: whispering campaigns, the Underground press, periodicals and other publications, as well as all types of leaflets and pamphlets.

The number of items which went to press daily throughout the country exceeded 200,000 copies, an impressive number when one bears in mind that every one was printed, assembled and distributed by illegal and clandestine means.

The Press and Propaganda Office (B.I.P.) efforts can best be summed up by its publications, in the district of Warsaw alone. These included: the daily digest of radio news bulletins (monitored from B.B.C.); a daily digest of Reuter communiqués, a weekly general information bulletin, *Biuletyn Informacyjny*, which circulated 45,000 copies and was the most widely read of all the popular news digests; the *Wiadomosci Polskie*, a general political fortnightly which circulated 10,000 copies; *Insurekcja*, a scientific-military monthly (7,000 copies); *Żołnierz Polski* (*Polish Soldier*), a popular military monthly (12,000 copies). Besides these there were the *Agencja Prasowa*, a weekly, serving as basic bulletin for the Underground Press in the whole country, together with appropriate editorial comment and full review of the international situation; the *East and West Agency*, another weekly of a similar type, mostly concerned with border provinces of Poland; the *Głos Ojczyzny*, a monthly mainly intended for prisoners-of-war and labour camps in Germany; the *Głos Polski*, whose main object was to counter enemy propaganda and provide material for whispering campaigns, the *Staff Bulletin*, specially intended for internal circulation within the Home Army command.

Apart from general publications, each district and area had its own Underground Press and printing works, which catered for local needs.

Beside political and general news publications, the Underground Press of the Home Army issued a whole series of valuable books, leaflets, military and engineering manuals, circumstantial prints and many other items (e.g. a booklet of Home Army songs and marches, etc.). In Warsaw alone this category, aside from the periodicals, reached 120,000 items in the second half of 1944. Our secret military printing works in Warsaw comprised five working plants, capable of photo-chemigraphy, lithographic print, etc., with facilities for binding. Their output was sufficiently high to equal the output of all other Underground printing plants put together.

The educational influence of the Home Army Press was very strong and widespread, and produced the required effect of binding the whole community into solidarity with the Underground. Nor were partisan units hiding in the depths of the forests forgotten; special teams of war reporters were regularly sent to maintain contact with them.

Our propaganda specialised in playing spiteful tricks on the occupation authorities, which were immediately taken up by the whole community to some extent, providing it with a much-needed amusement factor.

One such trick played by the B.I.P. in 1943, which was rather successful, was the issue of a counterfeit special edition of the German-sponsored *Kurjer Warszawski* (*Warsaw Courier*). The form, print and every detail of the paper were identical with an original German issue. The contents, however, highly embarrassing to the Germans, were an exact statement of the military situation abroad and the Underground activity, derogatory items, and a verbatim report of a speech by Churchill. Warsaw had quite a lot of fun that day.

On May 3rd, the national holiday, the civilian authorities repeated the joke, this time issuing headlines, "The German Army enters Sweden," the contents being an appeal by the Government delegate for the holiday, Home Army communiqués, etc.

On the same day the wiring of the megaphones which the Germans installed in all the busiest spots for their own bulletins and propaganda was tapped in one part of Warsaw-Zoliborz and a patriotic Polish speech broadcast, together with a record of the national anthem. The effect of the Polish anthem being played in public can well be imagined. Pedestrians stopped and took off their hats and many of them wept. The whole proceeding only stopped when cars with the Gestapo and German police began to arrive. On the same date in 1944, the Polish national flag appeared on the Royal Palace tower. The Germans had to use the fire brigade to take it down.

The B.I.P. had a special department, the "N" Cell, whose task was the moral disarmament of Germans. This organisation supplied all sorts of leaflets and publications in German in such a form and by such methods as to indicate that they emanated from German secret anti-Nazi sources. Apart from these, which circulated widely in the German Army (and throughout Germany), the "N" organisation went in for a series of ingenious enterprises, all with the aim of harassing the Germans morally and bringing disorder and dissent into their ranks.

In September, 1943, large advertisements suddenly appeared all over the country with the title *"Fuehrer in Gefahr!"* ("The Fuehrer in danger!") and signed by Governor Frank, accompanied by fantastic news of the setting up of a dictatorship by a clique of high military officers. On February 24th, 1944, another counterfeit proclamation was stuck up, signed by General of the S.S. and Chief of Police Koppe, calling for the immediate evacuation from Poland of all German nationals.

*   *   *

All my major decisions, especially those concerning plans for further activities, were invariably taken in agreement with both the Commander-in-Chief of the Polish Armed Forces in London and the leading Underground authorities. This assured me of the support of the whole Polish nation, through its political organisations, for my work and the struggles of the Home Army. I was therefore in constant and close touch with the delegate of the Polish Government, S. Jankowski, and the Council of National Unity, in which were represented all the main political groups. Jankowski created the basis for a full and harmonious collaboration between civilian and military authorities. In time this collaboration grew closer, with great mutual profit.

The ranks of the Home Army represented all political and social elements, from the extreme Right to the extreme Left. Under my orders I had units of merely military character and others taken over from the political organisations. The commanders of the latter units and their men were subordinated to the operational command of the C.-in-C., Home Army, according to the normal regulations of military discipline. But each was permitted to form separate units, up to regiment or battalion strength, and keep its own traditions. When not engaged in operations, every individual or unit of the Home Army was free to carry on social and political activity and plan for a future Poland in accordance with its own ideology.

There were, however, two exceptions to the co-ordination

of all efforts under one command. One was the National Youth Organisation, which was called "N.S.Z." (National Armed Forces). As a result of my efforts to centralise our struggle under one command, part of this group accepted subordination to my orders at the end of 1943 and the beginning of the next year. The rest refused to do so and continued independent activity.

As the leaders of those who refused to co-operate were strongly anti-Russian, they maintained that as the German defeat was certain the German occupation of Poland was merely temporary and the real danger was presented by Russia. In consequence, they directed most of their real activity against Soviet partisans and Communists, regardless of the political results. Although dynamic, they were not numerous. Their bases were limited and in general their activities met with the disapproval of the whole of organised Poland.

The second exception was the "Polska Partia Robotnicza," the reconstituted Polish Communist Party, and their military arm, "Armja Ludowa," which took orders from Moscow.

Despite its numerical insignificance, its existence was a danger to us because of the anonymity of the Underground movement. The people saw no difference between this small group and the organisation to which the overwhelming majority of the fighters belonged. At the beginning, few people knew even the official name, Home Army. It was usually said in Poland that a man belonged to "The Organisation." In these circumstances, the deeds of P.P.R. units (which, of course, were also anonymous) were identified with those of the Home Army. This made things terribly difficult.

We had to make the Germans feel that they were dealing with a military organisation which permeated every section of national life and was directed by a centralised single command. They had to understand that they were not faced with gangs of bandits or several unco-ordinated groups. For instance, the sabotage of more than twenty German dairies working on supplies for the Army was carried out simultaneously in various districts of the Warsaw province. This brought a feeling of potential jeopardy to the Germans and taught them that they had to contend with a real though elusive strength which might strike at any moment. It was the most effective means of tying down important German forces, as it meant holding them in reserve for the protection of their lines of communication, of supplies and of other depots. This principle aimed also at the protection of the civilian population. We got practial results by such demonstrations as the execution of Kutschera, which stopped mass murders.

*   *   *

The tactics of the Communists were quite different. Two typical incidents were the bombing of a German column marching across the Aleje Ujazdowskie in Warsaw at the end of 1943, and when a hand-grenade was thrown through an open window into a German field hospital in Nowy Zjazd. In both cases about 100 hostages were arrested and shot. The Germans announced it by loud-speaker and, of course, public opinion laid the responsibility for both these incidents at the door of the Home Army, thus undermining the moral authority of its leaders. Everybody well understood that the casual death or injury of a handful or so of Germans did not make up for the subsequent shooting of 100 Poles. We had several cases of this sort of thing.

It soon became clear that among the Soviet partisans the political element was uppermost. It was recruited from the political secret service, N.K.V.D. In consequence, most of the Soviet partisans tried to avoid fighting the Germans, and confined their activities to infiltration into the country in an effort to gain control of it. From our point of view, the activities of the Soviet partisans and groups of the Armia Ludowa presented a specific danger, since they never took the safety of the Polish population into consideration.

When I took over the duties of Home Army Commander, the problem of the "forestmen" was one of my greatest troubles. The Germans were growing weak in the country. They maintained their authority by sporadic punitive expeditions, which were sometimes carried out by as much as a whole division. Such expeditions would surround several villages, killing all the male population and sometimes even women and children as well. Those left alive were sent to concentration camps. It was characteristic that the victims of these expeditions were harmless village folk, since the partisans remained in the forests, out of reach. Many people fled to the forests and had to live there by looting. This was how, besides Soviet and Polish partisan units, there grew up a new category of "forest folk." They were wild bands of all sorts of refugees living by robbery, and were a terrible plague to people in the neighbourhood, who were visited nearly every night by bandits, who gradually deprived them of their last belongings. The result was still another emigration to the forests of those who had been completely stripped of their belongings. Many of them joined our partisan units. We could not, however, accept everybody in our ranks. We could certainly not accept those who had looting and violence on their conscience. It would indeed have been tantamount to the Home Army's acceptance of responsibility for their deeds— a course which I had to avoid at all costs.

The activities of the forest gangs on the one hand and German "pacification" on the other faced the country with a threat of anarchy. Such conditions were, of course, extremely unfavourable to any organised Underground movement. The control of those opposing the occupying authorities from the Underground could only be possible if social discipline was observed. This was essential if I wanted to mobilise the help of the population wherever and whenever I considered the conditions most favourable to us and where it would most harm the enemy. If the mass of those in the ranks of the Home Army were to depart from the social framework and embark on a life of chaos and anarchy, I lost all means of pursuing organised military activity.

The state of disorder threatened both the carrying out of diversionary activity according to plan and the organisation of large-scale military activity later on, when events demanded it. That is why, in agreement with the Government delegate, I issued orders to the regional Home Army commanders to undertake the defence of the population against the violence of disturbing elements. When several of the gangs had been disposed of in the regions most affected, a substantial improvement was felt. But my order was immediately used by Communist and Soviet propaganda as a handle for an accusation against the Home Army, the Government in London and myself, for opposing Soviet partisans and armed groups of the Armia Ludowa, although they knew well that all my orders were forbidding clashes with Soviet or Communist partisans.

*   *   *

Our main aim was to prepare the Home Army for the final showdown, which would take the form of a general insurrection aiming at the liberation of the whole country.

It was to be in that final stage of operations that all the Underground forces which constituted the ranks of the Home Army were to emerge simultaneously into open battle. For that reason the general insurrection could not have a dress rehearsal or encore. The outbreak was envisaged in the case of a breakdown of the German armies on the front, also in the case of an internal collapse in Germany, provided that external help for the insurgents was available. Only then would the time be ripe for a full rising, supported by the whole community, with the ultimate aim of annihilating the whole occupational administrative machinery and driving out the occupier. Our main concern was to foresee such a moment.

Plans for the rising were elaborated in 1941, and were constantly modified to fit current needs.

One of the possibilities considered was that of a separate peace between Germany and Soviet Russia and a consequent transition of troops from the eastern front to the west, probably at a critical period of operations on the western front. The operation planned for such a circumstance bore the name *Bariera* (Barrier) and was intended to sever all transverse (east–west) lines of communications across Poland in a manner which would prove most destructive and difficult to repair.

*   *   *

The problems connected with the breach of diplomatic relations by Russia were getting more and more complicated. The Soviet propaganda campaign against Poland had by now been unleashed with full intensity. Radio transmissions in practically every language began to speak more and more about the "Union of Polish Patriots in Moscow" and the "Famous Polish Division, named after Kościuszko"—the newest name given to the so-called army of Colonel Berling, who, although himself a Pole, had nearly all commissioned posts under his command, from the rank of captain upwards, filled by Red Army officers. Inside Poland, these two bodies had appropriate counterparts in the form of the P.P.R., the Polish Workers' Party or the union of Communists, and the so-called Peoples' Army (A.L.) or Communist shock-units. As the front came nearer, the activities of these two bodies grew more pronounced.

A little earlier, the eastern front had seemed so far away

from our frontiers that no one ventured to foretell who would ultimately liberate Poland, nor at which point of our continent's wide perimeter the decisive Anglo-American blow would come. We had then lived under an optimistic delusion that it might be in the Balkans. Now, all was different. No one had any doubts left that the Russians would enter Poland, and on the breakdown of the German front on the lower Dnieper in the autumn of 1943 the only question left unanswered was *when*. . . . The theatre of operations up to now exclusive to the Home Army would then become part of the Red Army's sector, and it was clear that the latter would not hesitate to reap the best advantage from our sacrifices.

Inasmuch as the difficulties and friction with the Soviet partisans behind the German lines constituted a fairly grave problem, the question of liaison between the Homy Army staff and the Red Army command seemed to be a matter of the utmost importance, especially as the problems of sabotage and Army Intelligence, among others, were becoming vital. Therefore, in autumn, 1943, when we had become convinced that Poland would be subject to gradual occupation by the Red Army and that in such circumstances it might not be opportune to stage a general insurrection, I asked my Commander-in-Chief and the Polish Government in London what should be the attitude of the Home Army towards the Soviet Army in the wake of the retreating, though yet un-routed, German forces?

When my query reached London, discussions were already rife on precisely the same theme, the most topical for all Poles at that time. The result of these conferences between the Commander-in-Chief and the Government was the Government's instructions as to home policy, dated October 27th, 1943. These instructions, co-ordinated with the C.-in-C., envisaged two principal plans for action by the Home Army:

A

I. Possibility of an insurrection with the eastern front held outside the frontiers of Poland, at a time when the western allies (Anglo-Americans) would be able to advance deep into the European continent (from the west or south), and could guarantee effective aid, both direct and air cover, to our insurgents.

II. Intensified sabotage-diversion operations (for which action we chose the name of "Operation Burza" (Tempest), in the case of the German front breaking down without symptoms of internal disintegration, and the unfeasibility or refusal of direct support for the rising on the part of the Allies.

Owing to the possibility that Soviet armies would enter Poland before it was partly or wholly liberated by the Home Army, the Government envisaged the following situations:

B

I. In the case of re-establishment of Russo-Polish diplomatic relations, the Home Army was to undertake action in accordance with the Burza plan (intensified sabotage and diversion in the German rear), in collaboration and liaison with representatives of the Red Army.

II. Should diplomatic relations remain severed, the Home Army was to execute Burza none the less, with the one difference that the administrative authorities and the armed forces should remain underground and await further decisions from the Polish Government.

To emerge for battle with the retreating Germans and then crawl back into hiding at the advent of the Russians was in practice an entirely unfeasible proposition. I said so in my message of November 26th, 1943, to the C.-in-C.:

"On the basis of the Government's instructions for Home policy, I have issued an order to all provinces and districts, which I enclose. As can be seen from the order, I have given all commanders and units instructions to emerge into the open after taking part in operations against the retreating Germans. Their task at that moment will be to give evidence of the existence of the Republic of Poland.

"At that point, my order is at variance with the instructions of the Government.

"I can see no possibility of creating a vacuum on our territories through a lack of any *démarche* in front of the Russians on the part of the Army factor, which represents the Republic and her legal authorities. All our actions and achievements would be then immediately ascribed to elements standing at the disposal of the Soviets. My views are shared by the Government delegate and political representatives at home."

The Government delegate personally stated this view in London of his own accord, stressing the necessity of staying out in the open before the advancing Russians, in spite of the non-existence of diplomatic relations between them and the Polish administrative authorities. Otherwise, the Russians would find a basis for their accusations of an inimical attitude in Poland. With their highly developed intelligence system, they were perfectly well acquainted with the personal set-up of the Underground leadership in Poland.

It was not until February, 1944, that I received a reply from our Government (dated February 18th, 1944) with its decision on this question:

"The Home instruction, clause B.II, is hereby amended, as below:

"Your authorities and the armed forces in Poland are to issue instructions to local officials to approach, together with the local sector commandant or O.C., Home Army Unit, the staffs of the advancing Soviet formations with the following declaration: 'By order of the Government of the Polish Republic, we present ourselves as the representatives of the Polish administration (as commander of unit, district or area of the Home Army) with proposals to establish collaboration on these territories with the armed forces of the Soviet Union, for mutual action against our common enemy.'

"It should be declared that both the operating units of the Home Army, as well as those in the process of formation, are part of the Polish armed forces, and remain under the orders of the Polish Government, the Commander-in-Chief and the Commander of the Home Army."

Based on the Government's amendments to the Burza plan, as co-ordinated with the C.-in-C., I had already issued (on November 20th, 1943, under Ref. No. 1300/III) a detailed order to all province and district commanders clearly indicating that the main task of our battle preparations was action against the Germans. On no account should action of any sort be taken against the Russians entering our territories in pursuit of the retreating Germans, with the sole exception of self-defence, which is the right of every man.

The main points of the order can be summarised thus:

"Armed action against the Germans can assume the following

aspects: (*a*) a universal and simultaneous rising (insurrection), (*b*) intensified diversionary action (Operation Burza) on the whole of Polish territory.

"Instructions issued for the insurrection against the Germans, remain valid.

"The aim and task of the Burza action: to stress our will to fight the Germans, even under unfavourable conditions, i.e. not allowing a full-scale rising.

"Execution of Burza shall be based on intensive harassing of the retreating German rearguards, together with strong diversion over the whole area, particularly against rail and road communications.

"The order to begin Burza operations will be given by means of a special radio message (code). Receipt of this message by respective provinces and districts is tantamount to an order to prepare for action. District commanders may delegate powers to lower commanders; the principal intention should be to commence action at a moment when the German forces can be attacked with maximum effect.

"Attitude towards the Soviets: avoid friction with Soviet partisan detachments.

"In view of the entry of regular forces of the Red Army on to our territory, the local Polish commander should, on termination of operations against the Germans, declare his identity and present himself for an official reception in the given sector.

"With due consideration to every request by the Soviet commands, it must be remembered that the Polish authorities always remain the rightful ruler.

"Attempts to incorporate our units into the Soviet armies or Berling's unit should be opposed."

Subsequent to issuing these instructions, I talked with all province and district commanders in the course of the winter and spring of 1944, discussing the situation with them and giving them detailed orders concerning their future action in the expected operation. Only then was I certain that the provincial commanders were aware of the difficult situation and would find the right moment and place for bringing their detachments into action.

*   *   *

Meanwhile, diplomatic activities went into a new phase. In early October, 1943, when Mr. Eden was due to leave for

Moscow, Mikołajczyk had a talk with him. He told the British Foreign Secretary of the necessity of re-establishing diplomatic relations between Poland and Russia, especially in view of the Red Army's approach to the Polish frontiers. He asked Mr. Eden to act as mediator, pointing out that action by the Home Army on the German rear was being keyed-up for still greater intensity and was liable to be of great importance to all concerned. An agreement between both the staffs was essential, and such agreement must be preceded by adequate diplomatic liaison.

Mr. Eden was interested in the possibilities of aid for the Russians from the Home Army and promised to take up the matter in Moscow. At the end of October I received instructions from London to await the renewal of diplomatic relations with Russia and, in consequence, an operational liaison between our staffs. Then Mr. Eden received the following communication from Molotov in Moscow: "The Soviet Government would be willing to discuss the renewal of diplomatic relations, but only with such a Polish Government as would be favourably disposed towards the Soviet Union. Neither the Polish Government in London nor the Commander-in-Chief, General Sosnkowski, fulfils that condition."

To provide grounds for his assertions, Molotov again brought forward, among others, the statement about the "inactivity" and "passivity" of the Home Army in the face of the Germans. The same accusations were raised by Stalin two months later at Teheran with Roosevelt and Churchill. He said that General Sosnkowski and the London Government were deliberately withholding action by the Home Army against the Germans and directing all their efforts against Soviet partisans. Such assertions from the highest authorities of an Allied power were extremely liable to inspire doubts in the minds of British and American statesmen regarding the character of the Polish Home Army, especially in view of the circumstance that neither Britain nor the U.S.A. had any observers of their own on Polish territory at that time.

Of course, the Soviet radio and Press campaign, in every language, went much further than that. General Sosnkowski was openly accused of issuing a secret order to the Home Army forbidding action against the Germans. One official Soviet publication printed an article which said that the Polish Home Army was nothing more than pure bluff and that there was nothing there at all except a small group of Polish agents of the Gestapo. At the time this article appeared, the Polish Home Army was already 360,000 strong and its achievements in the struggle against the Germans were perfectly well known to the Russians.

In January, 1944, I received another message from London informing me that Stalin and Molotov continued to assert that the Home Army was doing nothing against the Germans and that its sole activity was the liquidation of Russian partisans. At the same time, the "Union of Polish Patriots" in Moscow broadcast fantastic news of a mass murder of Communists being planned by the Home Army in Poland. Thus it can be seen what a predicament we were in, and how difficult it was to decide a wise course. The Soviets were advancing their mistrust of the Home Army as their chief reason for not renewing diplomatic relations with Poland. On the other hand, any collaboration of the Home Army with the Red Army staff was impossible without prior diplomatic liaison.

Therefore, only two choices were open to us:

(1) To make all our further battle activities dependent on the renewal of diplomatic relations with Russia and to refrain from all action until such time.

(2) To continue to fight the Germans regardless of Russia's political and military attitude.

It was clear that the adoption of the first alternative was liable to corroborate Russian assertions about the hostility of the Home Army. Bringing our efforts against the Germans to a close at that particular moment would undoubtedly cancel—and not only in the eyes of the Russians—the enormous sacrifices which Poland had made for the Allied cause.

We ourselves should then be giving Russia evidence to "prove" to the world the very thing that she was trying to prove by lies—that Poland was in the enemy camp and was not one of the Allied nations. We should have lost the support of the western Allies, whom we still trusted to defend our cause with Russia; we thought nevertheless that the only chance of gaining anything was a constant demonstration of our will to fight Germany to the last, sparing no effort, in the teeth of every adversity. We had to show our goodwill towards those whom the Western Powers called their "great friends and allies in the east." To-day we know only too well that our trust in the western powers was too optimistic; nevertheless, it was deeply rooted in the hearts of the whole Polish people at the time, quite as deeply as our determination to stage a final showdown with the Germans, despite terrible sacrifices. Public opinion would never have understood an order to stop the fight; it would have been taken as tantamount to capitulation and quite unacceptable to the soul of the Polish community.

In reality, therefore, there was no option at all between the two alternatives. We had to run the great risk of undertaking open action without any co-ordination with the Red Army command, without even an indication of what would be the attitude of the new occupant towards the open formations of the Polish Army who had emerged from the Underground. We had to take up battle—it was a matter of principle; once again we faced the question of freedom and independence.

In London there appeared at this critical hour a split among the highest Polish authorities over the conflict of opinion between General Sosnkowski and Premier Mikołajczyk. The General maintained that the Soviet Government's ultimate aim was to deprive us of national independence, possibly even to turn us into a seventeenth republic of the Soviet Union, and that for this reason all our sacrifices and losses would turn out to be completely fruitless, in default of sufficient guarantees from the Russians that the independence of Poland would be duly honoured. For that reason, General Sosnkowski saw an absolute necessity to base any further action on our part, as well as the emergence of the Home Army into the open, upon the resumption of diplomatic relations with Russia. Mikołajczyk, on the other hand, seemed to believe in the possibilities of a compromise, in this question holding a similar opinion to that of the British.

To me, the aims of Soviet policy had become only too clear. The old Tsarist imperialism had merely put on a new dress, and even become much more dangerous under its mask of cynical fraud. The new methods brought about the subjugation of conquered nations and states by means of anarchy and corruption from within. Moreover, I was only too well acquainted with their methods of secret action, methods which have neither moral boundary nor scruple. I had no illusions whatsoever as far as Soviet Russia was concerned.

We believed, however, in the support of our interests by the western powers, realising neither the reasons for the policy of appeasement nor the universality of the spirit of submission to Russian demands as far as Poland and our vital interests in general were concerned. By taking part in fighting the common enemy, we were proving the right of our nation to free and independent existence. By our own actions on the field of battle and the aid which we were thus able to afford the advancing Russians, a suitable foundation for reaching agreement could have been created had the Russians shown any goodwill. We believed that the western powers would acknowledge our goodwill and our share in the battle and victory, and that they would exert the necessary influence on the Soviets in bringing to bear at least part of the principles of the Atlantic Charter.

From our point of view, we had good grounds for such reasoning. We were an integral part of the Polish armed forces who were fighting in the distant free world at the side of the Allies, and those same Allies were constantly supplying us, the Home Army, with airborne arms and equipment. As Commander of the Home Army at that crucial moment, I was clearly aware that I was holding in my hands perhaps the last trump card we had in that game in which the stake was the independence of our country.

The whole community, with the exception of an insignificant group of Communists, associated the future return of our Government from London, after national liberation, with their hopes for independence. For them, that Government was a symbol of freedom and of the legal continuity of our State. As such, it enjoyed the loyal support of an enormous majority of the people. This support was given to the London Government as an institution independent of alien influence and authority, not to any particular member or members of it. The people knew quite well that on the return of that Government they would be able to change or substitute at leisure any of its members. They also realised that Moscow wanted to impose another body, "favourably disposed towards the Soviet Union" and that this body might shortly arrive, backed by Red Army bayonets; no one had any doubts as to the possibilities of changing or substituting any members of *that* Government.

These considerations led us to the final decision—*to fight*. We took up the gauntlet once again, this time for open battle. Together with the Army, our civil authorities were to emerge into the open in order to manifest thereby our rights to be masters in our own land.

On November 20th, 1943, I issued an order to the whole Army which contained a series of preparatory measures for the execution of the Burza operations.

I had, for instance, to reckon with pressure from the Soviets to incorporate our units into the Berling army, which served Russia, and not Poland. I had therefore to instruct district commanders to oppose any such proposals. Our position was now quite clear: if the Soviets were to accept our co-operation in the eastern districts, on the various sites of the Burza action, it seemed likely that full operational collaboration between our units and the Soviet forces would become possible on other territories of Poland. Every commander of a major group was in possession of a short-wave transmitter and his own cipher code and could therefore remain in constant contact with me. Thus, through the intermediary of our units on the Russian side of the advancing front, the Soviet Army staff could, if they wished, establish radio contact with my headquarters.

Preparations for Burza action were started at the end of 1943. Partisan groups were assembled into larger units and directed to districts which lay across the German lines of retreat. In the eastern provinces, which were the first to start Burza operations, all soldiers of the Home Army were being mobilised. Regiments, battalions and divisions received names and numbers as in 1939. Arms and ammunition, radio and other equipment, stores, warm clothing (short uniform overcoats, caps and boots), hospital equipment, etc.—all these things manufactured at home in secret workshops— were being gradually smuggled to the forests. The Polish partisan groups in the east grew into substantial regular forces long before the Red Army front reached them.

I issued once again an order to all units to avoid trouble or friction with Soviet partisan detachments, in reply to which I received several alarming dispatches from Volhynia. On November 7th, 1943, "Bomba," one of my bravest partisan commanders, who led a unit of 640 men, had been asked to come and meet the commander of a Soviet partisan unit, one General Neumann. The aim of the meeting was the co-ordination of mutual action against the retreating Germans, who, according to the Soviet sources, were preparing for major operations in the vicinity. Bomba set out to the proposed meeting with fourteen men. None of them was ever seen again. The leader of another Soviet partisan detachment, a Colonel Bohun (assumed name), invited the commander of one of our units, Captain "Drzazga," and his adjutant for a talk in order to "co-ordinate mutual action against the Germans." They also never returned, but their bodies were later discovered on the spot where the Soviet camp had stood.

The first encounter of the Home Army with regular Red Army units took place in Polish Volhynia (eastern Poland). In this sector, on the night of January 3rd, 1944, the Russians first crossed the Polish frontier, driving a deep wedge into the German lines. At that time, when some of the Red Army spearheads had reached our territory, other sectors were still held on the line of the Dnieper; that is, north and south of Krzeminczuk. A violent counter-attack from the Germans at Zhitomier stopped this wedge and delayed the further Russian occupation of Poland for some time.

*   *   *

In the meantime, the Russians dealt our country another blow from a different and unexpected quarter. Our Government in London was not informing the people at home properly about the international situation; for that reason, our political leaders and myself were astounded by a radio message which reached us in February, 1944, calling on the Council of National Unity to express its opinion regarding proposals given to the Polish Government by Mr. Churchill for reaching an agreement with the Soviet Government. Briefly, these proposals were:

(1) An agreement by the Polish Government to accept the so-called Curzon Line, leaving our ancient cities of Lwów and Wilno on the Soviet side, as the basis for the Polish eastern frontier.

(2) An agreement by the Polish Government to the dismissal of the Commander-in-Chief, General Sosnkowski, and of General Kukiel from his post in the Cabinet.

(3) A Russian acknowledgement of complete independence in the future area of Poland, augmented by part of East Prussia, Dantzig, Upper Silesia and territories up to the Oder River.

In answer to these proposals, the Home delegate sent the following resolution of the Council of National Unity in his dispatch dated February 15th, 1944:

"(1) We agree to the western boundaries proposed and the promise to expel the Germans.

"(2) We do not agree to a *Junctim*, joining the problem of the western boundaries with the eastern. The western territories cannot be considered as an equivalent, since they are restored lands formerly taken away from Poland.

"(3) We hope for the resumption of diplomatic relations with the Soviets, with the aid of our allies, upon condition that our full sovereign rights will be respected, with no meddling in our internal affairs.

"(4) We categorically oppose the taking up of any discussions with the Soviets as far as our eastern frontiers are concerned. We stand by the principle of inviolability of the boundaries determined by the Treaty of Riga, which was also signed by the Ukrainian Republic, as the Soviets are in no way concerned with frontier adjustments, any more than the Germans were concerned with the Corridor of Dantzig; our independence is the stake in question.

"(5) Nobody here would understand why Poland should pay for the Soviet war effort by her territories or her freedom; they would not understand why Poland went into war at all and is now in her fifth year of strife against the Germans. Poland was the first to fight the Germans, not only for her own freedom, but for that of Europe; she was named 'the inspiration of the world' by Roosevelt. And now, notwithstanding our terrible sacrifices, the Polish nation is determined to fight the new Soviet aggression for its own and Europe's freedom. The Polish nation believes that the Allies and the world will understand its attitude and actively support it.

"(6) If violence and brute force should win instead of right and justice, there will be no peace in Europe, and the Polish nation will never submit to force. We believe, nevertheless, in an honest fulfilment of treaties and trust that, in the interests of all peace-loving nations, the principles contained in the Atlantic Charter will prevail. For that reason we hold the opinion that the settlement of matters of principle should be delayed until a more favourable moment.

"(7) We shall not give in or bend; on the contrary, there will be a breakdown and anarchy in the Polish nation if there should be submission to Soviet demands.

"(8) Knowing the true aims and methods employed by our eastern neighbour, we do not attach much importance to agreements regarding future authority of our representatives on the territories occupied by the Russians; we have no confidence that they will be loyally observed.

"(9) Understanding of the seriousness of this moment is preponderant in the Polish community, whose unanimity of opinion in its unflinching will to fight for the freedom, integrity and independence of Poland is complete.

"COUNCIL OF NATIONAL UNITY.
"HOME DELEGATE."

The resolution of the K.R.N. was an absolutely true rendering of the views and opinions at home. How much truth and foresight it contained, viewed with the perspective of even a few years!

*   *   *

Operations on the eastern front continued. During the spring of 1944 a long bitter fight developed in Polish Volhynia around Kovel and Wlodimier (Wlodzimierz). The Polish Home Army's 27th Division took part in this battle, fighting a whole series of major and minor actions against the Germans, mostly in the rear of the German lines, and capturing and holding several localities.

On March 20th there took place the first instances of concerted action by Polish and Red Army units in two separate sectors. Co-operating with regular Red Army units, Home Army detachments captured Turzysk; others took part in the battle for Kovel on that same day. As a result, direct contact was established with the Russians by "Oliwa" (Lt.-Colonel Kiwerski), O.C., 27th Infantry Division. He sent me the following message on April 4th:

"On March 26th I spoke to the commander of the Soviet Army Group, operating on the Kovel sector—General Sergeyev—and Colonel Charytonov. After reference to their higher authorities, the Soviet Command wants to co-operate with our division and stipulates the following:

"(1) Complete operational subordination to Soviets, here and across the Bug River.

"(2) They acknowledge that we are a Polish division which has its authority from Warsaw and London.

"(3) The division can maintain full contact with its authorities.

"(4) We are to reorganise from a partisan unit into a normal Army division.

"(5) The Soviet command precludes the leaving of any partisans in its rear.

"(6) We shall receive, in return, full equipment for one division, arms, ammunition, artillery, M.T. transport and supplies."

I immediately radioed back my agreement in principle. I demanded that the division be treated as a reconstituted unit of the Polish armed forces, remaining under the authority of the Home Army (mine), the C.-in-C., and the Government in London. While operating against the Germans, it was to be temporarily subordinated, in a tactical sense, to Soviet command. My message stated further: "In giving your answer to the Soviet commander, you are to explain that your group is the first which they have encountered on Polish territory. As they progress, they will reach other Polish detachments fighting against the Germans, all belonging to the Home Army, as you do. In these circumstances there arises the necessity of regulating in principle the relations between the Soviet Government and our Government in London, rendering possible a concerted action on Polish territories—respectively by the Soviet Union and by Poland in the war against the Germans."

From that moment onwards, operational liaison with the Soviets consisted, as far as they were concerned, of constant requests for the execution of specific tactical tasks. The attitude adopted towards our men by the Russians in the front lines was on the whole satisfactory. This lasted till April 9th, 1944. At that time, very heavy fighting had been in progress, and the Russians were finally thrown back eastwards, but as they had at the last moment left Home Army units to hold the positions at all costs, the latter could not withdraw in time. As a result, our 27th Infantry Division and the 56th Soviet Cavalry Regiment had both flanks turned during fighting on the Turia River and found themselves encircled. The main Red Army forces were retreating further and further east. Colonel Oliwa was killed and his deputy, Major "Zegota," radioed me for orders as to whether to break out eastwards or in our direction. As the latter course seemed more feasible, Zegota was advised to push through into the German rear. After five days of bitter fighting the 27th Division cracked the German ring and was able to retreat to the Pripet Marshes.

Contact with the Soviet Command was maintained through a liaison unit hidden in a thickly wooded area and guarded by both a Home Army and a Soviet partisan detachment. There Major Zegota had a long talk with the commander of N.K.V.D. partisan detachments for special operations, who was at least candid. He stated clearly that he represented the N.K.V.D. and was in close contact with Moscow. He proposed that Zegota join the Berling army, holding out as bait the prospects of rapid promotion. Zegota refused and asked that co-operation be in accordance with my instructions. He also expressed his fear lest other units of the Home Army who found themselves behind the Russian lines might be forced to join the Berling unit. He received the promise that this would not happen. All the same, reports which I was getting from the other side did not bear out this promise. A message received on March 23rd told of the disarming of our smaller detachments after they had openly approached the Russians. On March 15th the Russians had disarmed our unit at Przebraze, arrested some of the men and shot the commander; at Rozyszcze the commander and three men were shot, a few were hanged and some twenty were arrested and taken to Russia. A radio message of April 6th, also from Volhynia, stated that "the Russians are cutting off our contacts east of the front line where they are putting into effect their own conscription . . . age limits seventeen to thirty-five. . . . The mobilisation of men is taking place on the whole area from the frontier to the rivers Styr and Stochod, immediately after the occupation of each locality."

Our experience from Volhynia seemed to indicate that the Russians were applying alternate lines of policy in respect of the Home Army. In the front lines they took advantage of our aid in the fighting, recognising the character of our units as part of the Polish armed forces. On complete occupation of a given district, however, they executed the commanders and enrolled the men by force into the Berling army.

Our 27th Division inflicted severe losses on the enemy in the course of the fighting in Volhynia; it took hundreds of prisoners and captured a mass of arms and equipment. The aid which it gave the Red Army was substantial, but its achievements were never given the slightest mention in the Press or radio news in the west.

This was by no means an isolated case. Apart from attempts

to break us from within by the aid of the P.P.R., reinforced by Communist agents well-trained in Russia, as well as armed action repeatedly undertaken by Communist shock-troops of the so-called Peoples' Army against our partisans, the official authorities and Soviet propaganda never relaxed their efforts to minimise our part in the battle and undermine any vestige of confidence in us felt by the people of the west.

A good illustration of that fact is a message from the Commander-in-Chief (No. 2027) in March, 1944, in answer to a dispatch from the Commander of the Home Army, listing the results of sabotage action for the past month:

"Reference 350. Very important information, difficult to make use of in its existing form. The Allies, under influence of unfavourable propaganda, suspect that neither the central H.Q. nor the Home Army Command are really in control of the Underground as a whole. The dates and events of battle and sabotage are taken as accidental and unintentional from our side."

In order to disclose the Soviet machinations and show the Allies the full potentialities of the Home Army, the Commander-in-Chief advised the Home Army of the necessity of executing Operation "Jula," which was the disruption of rail communications on several lines at the same time; or even of the major diversion coded as Bariera.

In his next message (March 12th), General Sosnkowski ordered:

"Ref. No. 2020. . . . The Allies have approached us suggesting preparations for action against communications. The political situation may render such action necessary from our point of view, to demonstrate our goodwill in respect of the 'Friends.' These aims should nevertheless not be realised at exorbitant expense owing to the inimical attitude of the Soviets towards our cause. We consider that a stoppage of traffic on railways for twenty-four hours will give the required effect. On my part, I suggest the region Rzeszow-Sanok-Przemysl-Sambor. We are ensuring secrecy at our end to prevent the Soviets from taking propaganda advantage for themselves or placing any obstacles in your way. . . ."

Operation Jula took place three days after the order was given, i.e. on the 6th.

(a) A span of over 150 feet of the railway bridge over the Wisloka, on the Przeworsk-Rozwadow sector, was blown up. Traffic was stopped for forty-eight hours.

(b) A steel conduit, 25 feet long, at Rogozno, was exploded under a passing munitions train. Rescue transports were derailed by automatic mines. Traffic was resumed after thirty-four hours on one track only.

(c) A steel conduit over 20 feet long was blown up under a passing munitions train on the Jaslo-Sanok line, near Nowosielce: thirty-three hours' stoppage.

Our own losses—three men wounded in skirmish at the bridge.

The Commander-in-Chief radioed the following (Ref. 3323) on April 27th: "I have received full accounts of Jula and admire the brave men of the Home Army. Many thanks to you."

The execution of Jula proved the flexibility of the Home Army to the British Imperial Staff, as shown by a letter from the Minister of Economic Warfare, Lord Selborne, to General Sosnkowski:

"MINISTRY OF ECONOMIC WARFARE.

May 3rd, 1944.

"*Top Secret.*

"F.1582/125.

"MY DEAR GENERAL,—Thank you very much for your letter of the 28th April and for the accompanying report from G.O.C. Secret Army in Poland on Operation Jula. I have read this report with very great interest and admiration for the Polish officers and men who, after four years of tyrannical oppression and in the face of overwhelming difficulties, are still able on your orders to carry out an operation of this importance with such precision and effect. I am well aware that this success is only one of many similar achievements to which, for security reasons, you have felt unable to give wide publicity. Nevertheless, now that units of the Polish Secret Army have made contact and are co-operating with the Red Army in their advance, I feel strongly that the Polish cause will best be served in the eyes of the world by publicising as widely as possible, within the limits demanded by security, the unreserved support which the Soviet troops are receiving from the Polish Secret Army, and I am doing and will continue to do everything in my power to ensure that they receive the open recognition which is their due.

"I am very grateful to you for your reiterated assurance of readiness to carry out further operations of this kind in accord with the general plan of the Allies, and I have no hesitation in affirming the high value which the Allied military commanders place on this offer.

"The close co-operation existing between the British military authorities and the Polish authorities gives me great satisfaction, and I hope you will always regard the British military staff as a loyal friend who is willing and eager to help Poland and from whom you will feel no need to withhold any information regarding the Polish Secret Army which may help us to help you.

"Yours sincerely,

"SELBORNE."

*   *   *

In spite of mounting difficulties from within and abroad, the Polish Underground continued to grow, gaining also in political importance. In that respect, big changes took place in spring, 1944. The delegate of the Government until that time, Mr. Jan Stanislaw Jankowski, was appointed by Presidential decree of April 26th, 1944, Deputy Prime Minister or Vice-Premier for Poland. By virtue of this appointment, he named on May 3rd a Council of Ministers for Poland, which included, apart from the Vice-Premier, three representatives, one from each of the main political parties—the Socialist, National and Peasants parties. These Ministers supervised the activities of the respective departments of the Government delegate's office, corresponding to the principal branches of State administration, excluding military affairs. The network of their organisation spread over the whole country.

A juris-competent and advisory body previously aiding the delegate was the Council of National Unity, formed in January, 1944, without whose assent no political decisions of any kind were made. Thus, this Council of National Unity became a virtual Parliament for Underground Poland; it was composed of three representatives from each of the four main parties and one from minor parties, as well as representatives of the Church and the co-operatives, altogether seventeen deputies. Owing to the difficulties of assembling a plenum, an execution committee of the Council was chosen which was given the powers of a plenum session. This committee was composed of one delegate from each of the major parties and one from the remainder, attending alternately; five members altogether. The Chairman of the Council of National Unity, as well as of the Committee, was a very popular Socialist, Mr. Kazimierz Puzak.

My own relations with both the Vice-Premier and the members of the "big four" were extremely close and marked with mutual confidence. I had meetings every week with the Vice-Premier, at which we discussed and co-ordinated practically every current topic and problem. I was usually invited once a month to attend the sessions of the Committee, at which the Vice-Premier was always present. At these sessions I informed the party representatives of the military angle of the situation, and Army matters in general, and submitted suggestions which came into the Army's sphere of interests. The only opposition which the Council of National Unity had to reckon with was the Communists (P.P.R.). By these means the nation stayed together and fought, in spite of the political pessimism which was harassing everyone.

In May of that year there was brighter news. The great experience that never fell to the Home Army—namely, to be victorious in open battle in co-operation with our allies— was enjoyed vicariously through the achievements of another part of the Polish armed forces. The news that General Anders with the Second Polish Corps had captured Monte Cassino in the Italian campaign, thus opening the road to Rome for the Allied advance, not only filled us with joy and pride, but also with hope for our country's future.

Shortly afterwards, however, battle operations on our own territory and, with them, further difficulties with the Red Army, entered a new phase. In July, 1944, a successful push brought the Russians up to the town of Wilno. Units of the Home Army, mobilised for Burza operations, had been, for some time past, waiting in the Rudnicka Forest, south of the city. As in Volhynia, these troops, three brigades in strength, were conducting intense partisan action against the Germans, at first mainly concentrated on railway sabotage. Later, the Wilno District Commander had the Nowogrodek district subordinated to him for tactical purposes in connection with the execution of Burza, and reported to me that practically all the provincial areas of Wilno, Oszmiana, Lida and others were completely under control of our units, now over 10,000 men strong, excepting only major towns and railway junctions.

The latter were strongly held by the Germans, who were comparatively passive and mainly concerned with holding these points of military importance. The Soviet partisans, who were built up strongly in these regions, were inimically disposed both to the local populations and to our units. Our commander in the Wilno District, Colonel "Wilk," did all he could to improve conditions and ventured on several meetings, both in person and through envoys, with the Soviet partisan leaders. Modes of co-operation were constantly devised and agreed to, only to be broken immediately by the Russians. Moreover, the Soviet partisans badly mistreated the civilian population.

About that time the Home Army managed to intercept an order to Soviet partisan detachments to fight and endeavour to liquidate our units by force. In such a state of affairs, the only solution was to get into contact with regular Red Army units. We had already learned that co-operation was only possible when our units were sufficiently strong, on which occasions the Red Army felt that they had something to gain by tagging us on. But after a battle it was the N.K.V.D. who had the last word. We had to hope that the situation would clarify.

There was no indication of that, however. The hostile attitude of the Soviet Union to our head authorities continued, together with their demand for the incorporation of half of the pre-war Polish lands into the U.S.S.R. This, combined with efforts to undermine us from within by means of special agents and Moscow-trained *provocateurs*, the hostile actions of Soviet partisans and the openly hostile attitude taken by the Communist units of the People's Army, combined to evoke feelings of dislike and mistrust towards the Soviet Union among the rank and file of the Home Army. In spite of strict orders issued beforehand to avoid all strife with both Soviet partisans and the Soviet-sponsored and reinforced "People's Army," I found it essential, in view of the imminent Soviet invasion, to put the matter clearly before all officers and men under my command, as seen from my final order (July, 1944).

In summary, this order stated that the Soviet had to be treated as a co-combatant in our struggle with the Germans; nevertheless, they were questioning our right to our eastern territories and considered all lands east of the so-called Curzon Line as theirs. They had broken off diplomatic relations with our Government and denied the legality of our chief authorities, endeavouring in that way to force a solution of the Polish

G

problem solely in accordance with the interests and political aims of the U.S.S.R., under pretence of co-operation. Consequently, the Soviets were on the one hand a mighty co-combatant in our struggle with the Germans, and on the other they remained a threat to our independent existence.

While it was necessary to co-operate wherever possible, we had always to make clear that the whole country and the Home Army recognised the supreme authority of our Government and the Commander-in-Chief; that battle operations against the Germans should be conducted independently, so far as possible, and liaison with Soviet staffs be established only in the case of acute tactical necessity; that information regarding Germans should be given to the Soviet staff, on request; that battle co-operation should take place only within the bounds of specific aims set out by the Home Army Commander and in specified localities; that the attitude of Home Army soldiers toward the Russians must be dignified; they should on no account embark on political discussions with Russian soldiers, and should stress the fact that we were fighting for Polish independence and an internal rule which would be decided by the free will of the nation; finally, attempts to incorporate Polish units into the Red Army or the Berling unit must be rejected.

*   *   *

In the first days of July, 1944, the battle for Wilno began! On July 7th two brigades of the Home Army made an attack on the city from the south. Next day at 4 p.m. regular Soviet forces, approaching from the north, joined in; simultaneously, units of the Home Army hidden in the city started operations from within. Wilno was thus taken from two sides by frontal attack, combined with effective action from the Underground; our units in the south were the first to storm their way into the town and the mopping-up of isolated German resistance points lasted till July 13th. Our forces captured the most heavily fortified area in the city. Wilk contacted the Russians immediately; they sent a liaison officer to his headquarters on July 12th. On the 15th Wilk sent me the following message: "As commander of Home Army group, I was asked to confer with General Cherniakhovsky, commanding 3rd Byelorussian Front. Talks held in good spirit. No mention of politics nor of joining Berling units. Our proposal to form one infantry division and one cavalry brigade for immediate dispatch to front approved without restrictions. Please confirm." I sent my approval by return.

On July 14th I had news that the officer commanding one of our groups, composed of four battalions, received the following acknowledgement from General Cherniakhovsky: "I thank you and your men for co-operation in fulfilling military tasks which were my objective." It was not the only acknowledgement which the Soviets gave our units. There was a whole series of them.

On July 17th Wilk was again asked to attend, together with his Staff of some thirty officers, a Staff conference with General Cherniakhovsky. None of them came back from that conference. They were all arrested and taken away. When this outrage became known, the Home Army units withdrew into the Rudnicka Forest, near Wilno. They were immediately sent an ultimatum to disarm and enrol in the Berling army. I received further news from the Wilno district during the Warsaw rising, on August 22nd, from which I learned that some 5,000 Home Army troops had been disarmed and put into a concentration camp in Miedniki, whence they were later transported east into the depths of Russia, probably to the Kaluga region. The remainder were conscripted into Berling's forces.

In the Lwów region, it seemed at first as if co-operation were to succeed at last. The Soviet commanders maintained close liaison with our officers. We were able to supply them with much valuable data regarding German concentrations. Owing to the fact that the Red Army was feeding on the land, an agreement was reached as to the regions and methods for requisitioning foodstuffs, aimed to prevent undue hardships (in fact, rank robbery) for the population. Our men were often used as patrol guides and rendered many other valuable services. District commanders of the Home Army informed the Soviet staffs of the disposition of German forces. As the front advanced, our units openly participated in operations. In that way some 7,000 of our troops turned out in this region.

*   *   *

The battle for Lwów began on July 17th. As the Russians advanced on the city, more and more Home Army units emerged and took part in the fighting. On July 27th street fighting was in full swing, and two days later the Germans were driven out completely. The local Home Army

Commander, Colonel "Janka" and his Staff disclosed their full identity to the Russians and set up their headquarters at 17 Kochanowski Street; relations seemed excellent. The Soviet General Command made arrangements for an official visit on the 29th, in the afternoon. The visitors were General Gruczko, Chief of N.K.V.D. of the 1st Ukrainian Front and General Ivanov, representing Marshal Koniev. The talks took place in the presence of the Chief of Staff of the Home Army units. The Soviet generals stated that they could under no circumstances tolerate the presence of units of the Polish armed forces, even totally subordinated to Soviet command. They demanded the disbandment of formations and enlistment into Berling's army. Janka, seeing no way out, accepted the Soviet demands, upon which he was invited to the Soviet headquarters for further talks. After a meeting, with photographs taken by Tass camera-men, Janka and his Chief of Staff were sent back to Kochanowski Street in a General's car. They immediately informed their officers of the results of the conference. Compulsory enrolment into Berling's army evoked bitter feelings among the officers and men. On July 31st Janka and five members of the staff were flown by special plane to Zhitomier for further talks. They never returned. . . .

On the same date, the Soviet Command ordered an urgent meeting of the whole Home Army Staff at the H.Q. in Kochanowski Street in order to co-ordinate instructions. The whole Staff gathered; the N.K.V.D. surrounded the building and arrested everyone, including the sentries. They were all imprisoned in a building on Łącki Street, where they were later joined by the regional Government delegate, Professor Ostrowski, and many more soldiers of the Home Army.

Later, when Warsaw's fight was drawing to a close, I got news by radio from Lwów: "The prison at Łącki Street is packed full of men from the Home Army. There are rumours that they will soon be transported into Russia. The Commander and two colonels abducted after Lwów's liberation are interned in Moscow. Many of the small units are hiding in the forests; they see no other way of avoiding prison and deportation to Russia. This presages a growth of those units with consequent fighting against the Russians." I immediately radioed the following order:

"Forbid forming any conspiracies (partisan units) under Russian occupation. Disband all existing detachments."

At that time I also received a radio message from the Lwów political representatives: "We beg for an inter-allied commission; we implore intervention on behalf of imprisoned members of the Home Army and Delegation, suffering terrible mistreatment. *We are ready to bear every sacrifice, even the greatest, to open the lid of our coffin.* We trust that measures will be taken worthy of the sacrifices which Poland has made in this war." That was the last message I ever received from Lwów.

* * *

About July 20th, the Russians were approaching Lublin. The Lublin District had begun Burza operations in three divisional groups. The district commander, Colonel Tumidajski, also had at his disposal Underground units ready to fight inside the towns. Serious battles with larger German units had been in progress since the beginning of June.

Nine days after starting Burza action, units of the Lublin Home Army district had captured seven towns on their own. Aided by Red Army units, they captured eleven more, including Lublin. They destroyed a number of heavy *panzers* and enemy armour, and captured considerable booty. It even happened sometimes that during the battle Home Army officers took over command and led Red Army units engaged in action.

Although in the Lublin region Communist units forming the so-called People's Army were maintaining an openly hostile attitude towards the Home Army and trying to undermine the Polish community with the help of trained agitators, the organised Soviet partisans and regular Red Army troops were at that time behaving much better. They were glad to make use of the operational prowess of Home Army units, and even laid stress on their practical value.

Unfortunately, immediately battle operations were successfully ended in that region, "Marcin" (Tumidajski) was arrested (July 27th), freed, then re-arrested. The commander of the Fourth Soviet Army, General Kolpachev, gave him an ultimatum. Either all Home Army troops would join the Berling army or disband and give up their arms. Marcin chose the second alternative. In the course of their talk, General Kolpachev asked him whether he had received instructions to fight the Germans and co-operate with the Red Army; Marcin gave him the gist of my orders. When asked whether he had ever received orders to fight the Russians,

Marcin denied it vehemently. Both he and the local Government delegate were arrested shortly afterwards. We now know that Marcin died in 1947, somewhere in Asiatic Russia. Similarly, within a fairly short period, other members of the Home Army found themselves in the notorious concentration camp (set up by the Germans) in Majdanek, near Lublin. They were all rounded up when they tried to reach Warsaw to aid the rising, which had now started.

The Home Army's achievements during the execution of Burza throughout the country were considerable and by no means limited to the few spectacular actions described above. Throughout the areas that lay between the former Polish eastern boundaries and the Vistula, not only organised major units (infantry divisions and cavalry brigades), but also a plurality of smaller local and partisan detachments fought hundreds of bitter encounters with the Germans, inflicting severe damage and casualties. The Russians were generous with their praise while the fighting was still on. Whenever a given operation came to an end, however, this attitude abruptly changed; submission to Berling was invariably demanded, failing which all opponents were arrested; units were surrounded as they stood and forcibly disarmed.

News of this procedure was reaching me very gradually. It was only during the Warsaw battle that I got the whole picture. By then I had no longer any doubts that favourable treatment of our troops in individual instances was only due to opportunist reasons and that their liquidation was simply a matter of time. As I have mentioned, some of our units were jeopardised only when they set out to help the Warsaw rising; many of them were allowed by senior Soviet officers to start on a forced march in the direction of Warsaw, only to be surrounded and liquidated without warning *en route*. Polish radio operators were making superhuman efforts to let us know, in Warsaw, the fate which was befalling their units at the hands of the Red Army. . . .

Thus, when on the one hand Anglo-American aid was reaching us in the form of moral support and airborne supplies, which was generally understood as an act of encouragement in our stand against the Germans, on the other their Soviet ally was rounding up our best soldiers into concentration camps and deporting them into the depths of Asia.

PART TWO

CHAPTER IV

THE WARSAW RISING

AT THE END OF June, 1944, the Russian offensive had started. In its first impetus it broke the German Forces known as *Heeresgruppe Mitte*, composed of four armies. Two of these, the 4th and the 9th in the Orsza-Mohilew sector, were dispersed and mopped up. The 3rd Panzer Army, after heavy losses, withdrew from the fighting area along the River Dvina towards Riga. Only the 2nd Army avoided massacre by a hasty retreat in the direction of Brześć on the Bug River.

The way towards the west was opened by the Red Army, which in just three weeks covered about 250 miles and, none the worse for it, was ready for new victories. Soon a terrific attack was launched by the 1st Bielorussian Army Group from the Kovel sector under the command of Marshal Rokossovsky. It was directed towards Warsaw, occupied Lublin, crossed the Vistula near Deblin, Puławy and Magnuszew in the course of July, and the Soviet attack moved straight towards the capital.

Almost simultaneously a second offensive had begun, led by the 1st Ukrainian Army Group in the region of Wołyń and south-east Poland. Swift successes marked it from the very start. Encircling Lwów from the north with a broad swing, it cut the retreat of the 8th German Army, thrusting it against the Carpathian Mountains. Lwów was taken on July 26th, then Przemyśl and Jaroslaw, and finally the River Vistula was reached, where the Soviet forces formed a deep bridgehead on the western bank near Baranów, to the south of the town of Sandomierz. The north wing of the offensive marched on Zamość and wiped out the 4th German Panzer Army, which tried to bar the way to the middle Vistula.

During July we witnessed a complete German defeat. Its extent was measured, not only by the advance of the Soviet forces, but also and above all by the German losses. Out of six armies, three were completely annihilated, two pushed

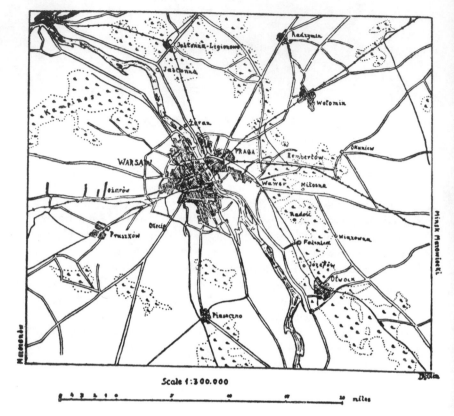

Scale 1 : 300.000

ENVIRONS OF WARSAW

aside and only one—the 2nd Army—survived, though also incompletely.

The situation of the Germans was all the more precarious because they had no adequate reserves in their immediate rear on the western bank of the Vistula.

In these circumstances, I reported to the Commander-in-Chief on July 14th:

"Although diplomatic relations with Russia have not been re-established, the Home Army cannot stand idle in the face of the German retreat and the Soviet advance, nor in the case of an internal collapse of the German forces and the threat of Soviet occupation. The Home Army must fight the final battle against the Germans, either in the form of Burza or insurrection, even both forms together. Should German disintegration occur in the eastern territories of Poland, we should stage the insurrection in the remainder.

"The guiding thought of our final encounter is:

"(a) To show the world our undaunted attitude against the Germans and our will to fight them till the end.

"(b) To deprive the Soviets of the spiteful propaganda argument for putting us into the category of silent allies of the Germans or into that of neutrals.

"(c) To take under our auspices that part of the community which does not form part of the Home Army, but nevertheless wishes to vindicate its wrongs at German hands—in order to draw it into mutual action towards independence and not let it fall under Soviet influence.

"Inaction on the part of the Home Army at the moment of the Soviet entry is not likely to mean general passivity on the home front. The initiative for fighting the Germans is liable then to be taken by the P.P.R. (Communist) and a considerable fraction of the less-informed citizens might join them. In that case the country is liable to move in the direction of collaboration with the Soviets and no one will be able to stop it. Also in that case the Soviets would not be received by the Home Army, loyal to the Government and the Commander-in-Chief, but by their own adherents —with open arms. No obstacle would then remain to challenge a fraudulent claim that the nation wanted to become the Seventeenth Republic.

"The Home Army expresses the will of the nation to gain

independence. This forces the Soviets to have to break us by
force and hinders their working against us from within.

"I agree that coming out into the open involves the grave
danger of annihilation of our most spirited elements. Nevertheless, the Soviets will not be given the opportunity of doing it
in secret, and they will have to resort to open acts of violence;
that on the other hand may evoke the protest of well-wishing
allies."

Originally, the Burza plan was calculated to avoid fighting
in major towns in order to spare the defenceless population
and safeguard historical buildings. With this object in mind,
we did not at first plan any action inside Warsaw. Instead,
according to the Burza plan, the Home Army units from
Warsaw were to be concentrated outside the city, from where
they should attack the rearguard of the German forces withdrawing from the capital.

However, in the middle of July the Command of the Home
Army decided a modification of the Burza plan with regard
to Warsaw, preparing the capture of the capital just before
the Russians would enter it. The attack was to be made from
within by the Home Army units stationed in Warsaw. The plan
for this action had been prepared in detail years ago and
constantly modernised; it was well known to all those responsible, as it had formed part of the plan for an eventual general
insurrection in the whole country.

From observation of the progress of fighting on the eastern
front we found that most towns passed into the hands of the
Red Army only after bitter and prolonged fighting and
consequent destruction. The Germans used to defend stub-
bornly all important communication centres, and particularly
larger towns situated on major rivers. We were aware that
Warsaw would not be spared, and by a battle inside the city
we hoped to shorten the struggle and to save the capital from
the fate of Stalingrad, which later was to befall also Budapest
and Dantzig.

We were convinced that the Soviet attack, still in full swing,
would not only be able to cross the Vistula, but would form
a deep bridgehead as basis for the future offensive towards
Germany. Furthermore, the overwhelming superiority of
Russian forces over the Germans, who in this sector did not
dispose of any troops still capable of facing an attack, except
the 2nd Army, weakened by losses, made us certain that the

struggle for Warsaw, with the help of an organised fight within, would be of short duration.

Finally, the participation of the Home Army in the battle for Warsaw would definitely silence the lies of Soviet propaganda about the passivity of our country and our sympathies towards the Germans, and the liberation of the capital by our own soldiers should testify with unquestionable strength the nation's will to safeguard the sovereignty of the Polish State. We hoped that in our precarious situation, the Home Army battle for Warsaw would raise an echo all over the world, though the most successful and costly actions in other regions had seemed to pass almost unnoticed.

General Sosnkowski was against a general insurrection, on account of the patent lack of goodwill on the part of the Russians, but he agreed with our own views about the necessity to continue the Burza operations. On July 7th he sent a message as follows:

". . . 4. Taking into consideration the contents of the preceding points, execute your instructions No. 1300/111 dated November 20th, 1943, by a gradual deployment of the Burza plan. Regulate the speed of action at your own discretion, as the situation demands. For political reasons, the Government would like to give the Burza action the character of an insurrection. My opinion is decidedly against representing it as such, so as not to misguide the lower commanders and local leaders.

"5. If by a lucky course of events you should be able to gain even for a short time control of such cities as Lwów or Wilno, or even of parts of the countryside, however small, following the retreat of the Germans and before general occupation by the Red Army, you should do so, assuming fully the part of host."

In his subsequent dispatches during the course of July which, in connection with his presence with the 2nd Polish Corps on the Italian front, reached us only with considerable delay, he warned us against starting a general insurrection, but ordered the continuation of the fight according to the Burza plan. This also agreed with our own point of view.

Our Government in London, however, admitted the possibility of a general rising. By a resolution of July 25th, the Government gave full power to its delegate in Poland to take

every decision necessitated by the Russian advance, in case
of emergency, even without formerly contacting the Government itself. This decision was passed on to the Government
delegate by order of Prime Minister Mikołajczyk on July 26th.
I quote the message:

"At a session of the Government [Cabinet] of the Republic,
it was unanimously decided to empower you to proclaim the
insurrection at a moment which you will decide as most
opportune. If possible, let us know beforehand. Copy, through
Army, to the Home Army Commander.

"STEM,
"Minister of the Interior."

Besides these divergent opinions of our authorities abroad,
we at home had to deal with another factor: the attitude of
the country and the capital itself. Warsaw by now was fully
aware that the battle would not pass it by. The hope that it
would be fought for the dignity, freedom, and sovereignty of
the Polish nation gave the inhabitants a strength of spirit
capable of the greatest valour and sacrifice. The general lust
of revenge for the years of tragedy and humiliation suffered
under the Germans was overwhelming and practically impossible to check. The whole town was waiting breathlessly for a
call to arms, and the vast majority of the population would
have considered a passive attitude as a betrayal of the Polish
cause. In an atmosphere of such intensity there was grave
danger of an outbreak of less disciplined elements, whether
through deliberate provocation or merely some accidental
circumstance, leading to the unleashing of an unplanned
rising.

In this attitude there was some logical reasoning as well as
idealistic emotion. The threat to our independence was
generally recognised from the growing aggressiveness of the
Russians. Since it was impossible to avert tragic developments
the people felt the necessity of maintaining a clear line of
political action and full participation in the events sweeping
over our country. And in this final open and unflinching fight
with the German occupant they saw the best way to safeguard
the national rights of Poland.

With the decision to introduce fighting in Warsaw into the
Burza plan, we were well aware that the battle in the capital
should not take place too late, when the fate of the city had

already been decided by military developments from without. It should occur early enough to allow us to influence the course of events. On the other hand, we were well aware from the beginning what tremendous danger a premature rising would invite. Our reserves of ammunition and food were only adequate for seven to ten days' fighting. But the principal difficulty lay in our inability to co-ordinate our activities with the Soviet Command.

Previously I had expected that military co-operation between the Red Army and the Home Army in eastern Poland would have enabled me to make wireless contact with the Russians before they reached Warsaw. Bad will on the Russian side, independent of the rapidity with which their offensive developed, made this impossible. Therefore, for the time being, I had to act by myself and to rely on my own estimate of the situation.

Nevertheless, I was in continual contact with the Government delegate, whom I kept closely informed. I also asked him to fix a meeting with the representatives of the Council of National Unity (Underground Parliament). At this conference I asked if they thought it absolutely necessary that Warsaw should be liberated by the Home Army before the Russians should capture the city, and received a unanimous affirmative. My second query as to what period of time they thought should elapse between our gaining control of the city and the entry of Soviet troops received the answer that at least twelve hours would be desirable in order to enable the administrative organs to get together and come out in their full part of host to receive the entering Soviet armies.

These opinions were essential for me. I had now only to select the most opportune moment to emerge from the Underground into open battle for the capital.

I was in touch with the whole country by radio and constantly received reports. They would come from our units fighting in the east on the development of Burza; information and reports also came from the parts of the country still under German occupation. We also got quite a lot of intelligence and information on the movements of the Soviet and German armies. All this was achieved by our radio stations dispersed throughout the country, some of which were mobile: patrols on bicycles and a wide network of observers carefully watching every German transport at crossings, bridges and railway stations submitted their observations immediately to us.

To keep the increasingly tense situation well in hand, daily conferences became an absolute necessity and I had to see regularly my Staff and the Government delegate. As many more people than usual took part in our meetings, the risk of arrest was also much greater. My associates were warned not to arrive together. Each had his time fixed exactly at intervals of between ten and fifteen minutes. But for the people who met and a few messengers, no one knew the addresses of our meeting places, which were changed daily. Even the guards had no idea whom they were guarding. A few streets away there was a "letter box." Girl messengers and couriers brought telegrams, reports and information there; they were collected every hour and handed to me personally.

The Germans were evacuating Warsaw at high speed. Railway installations and industrial plants were dismantled and removed. The rapid Soviet advance caused a high pitch of nervous excitement amongst Germans and Poles alike. On July 20th came the attempt against Hitler's life. This coincided with news of the swift success of the Soviet armies on the beginning of the Allied offensive in the west from their beach-head in Normandy. German morale fell visibly. Retreat and evacuation turned to panic. All the German offices in the city, including the Post Office, closed down. Newspapers published by the Germans ceased. The Gestapo burned documents in the greatest haste and prepared to decamp. The German Governor, Fischer, and the German Mayor, Leist, departed. German civilians besieged the railway stations. On account of the inadequate number of trains, they fled by all possible means of transport, offering sky-high prices for the hire of a horse and cart. When, after one of our Staff conferences, I went through the city, I saw scenes which confirmed the reports. Across the Vistula bridges an endless flow of German transport fled from the east. This retreat bore no signs of being an organised move. It was chaotic rout. That afternoon I purposely walked through the city and under the bridges. I wanted to see for myself the retreat of the Germans and the state of their units. Tanks were moving along both sides of the streets; they were covered with soldiers and interspersed with horse-carts and soldiers afoot. Troops mingled with civilians. Often a German soldier or civilian led a stolen cow along, and even a herd of cattle was being driven by a crowd of fugitives.

The sight of fleeing Germans roused joyful excitement amongst the population. In an overcrowded tram I saw a conductor who, in an effort to gain a living, used to sell, in addition to his tickets, cigarettes, soap and cosmetics. To-day he encouraged the passengers with the words: "Please, ladies and gentlemen, please hurry up, because the firm is departing, the firm is closing down and going into liquidation!"

The passengers reacted with laughter and applause. The people now lived in the certainty that these were the last days of German rule in the capital.

Far more important than the flight of the Germans or the reaction of the people was the news which reached us from the front. About July 22nd, our monitoring service intercepted a call from the commander of the 4th German Panzer Army issuing uncoded wireless orders to his units. The army was completely routed in the Zamość sector. The dispersed and beaten units were ordered to withdraw to the west on the other side of the Vistula. It was significant that such orders should be given *en clair*. It proved how complete was the rout of the 4th Panzer Army. The German command obviously wanted to be sure that this order would reach even the smallest units, who were not provided with cipher. We received the news that the Russians had reached the Vistula and crossed it. I was struck by the fact that the Russians crossed the river on the very same day that they reached its eastern bank. It proved clearly that they had met with no serious enemy opposition and that the Vistula was no longer an obstacle to their further advance. Soviet patrols were pushing deep into the country from this bridgehead without meeting any opposition.

In my dispatch to the Commander-in-Chief on July 21st I expressed my conviction that the Germans were facing a major disaster in the east. They had neither sufficient strength nor reserves to stem the Soviet advance. The Russian offensive had opened wide the gate for further moves to the west. I accordingly considered that if the Germans did not bring up fresh forces, they would never succeed in stopping the Russians. That this assessment was accurate was later confirmed by official documents. It is quite clear that at the time the Russians had an overwhelming preponderance.

The situation was summarised by General Guderian in his testimony at the Nuremberg Trial. In a book entitled *The Destruction of Warsaw* (Edition-Awir-Katowice, 1946), there is a verbatim quotation from General Guderian as follows: "On July 21st, 1944, I received a new appointment as Chief of Staff of the German forces on the eastern front. After my appointment the whole front—if it can be called a 'front'— was hardly more than an agglomeration of the remains of our armies which were endeavouring to withdraw to the line of the Vistula; twenty-five divisions were completely annihilated."

On July 25th I ordered the stand-by for every eventuality, at the same time informing London of my action. Later on I sent a message in which I requested a warning to be sent to the Germans that the shooting of Home Army soldiers when taken prisoners in open fighting, either singly or in units, would be a breach of international regulations on the rights of combatants. On the 26th I radioed: "We are ready to fight for Warsaw at any moment. I will report the date and hour of the beginning of the fight." In the same message, I asked that the Polish parachute brigade should be used in the fight for Warsaw, and requested air attack against the German airfields near Warsaw.

The dispatch in answer to my message was dated August 2nd and so reached us when the fighting had already started in Warsaw. Minister Kwapiński, who deputised for Prime Minister Mikołajczyk during his absence, directed:

"In connection with the suggestions of the Commander-in-Chief as to avoiding open sortie and full action in accordance with the plans you have set out, the Polish Government does not see it possible to change its previous instruction and your decision. The question of armed action and going out into the open is entirely in your own competence. This includes insurrection.

"For Chairman of the Council of Ministers,
"Kwapiński."

Having decided to fight, we faced a situation without precedent in the carrying out of full mobilisation in a town occupied by an enemy. For the first time a revolution was worked out as a military operation, according to a prearranged plan. Our strength amounted to nearly 40,000 Underground soldiers and about 4,200 women. The majority were workers, railwaymen, artisans, students and clerks in factories, railways and offices. These men had to be informed verbally of the place, date and hour to muster. It was only after many rehearsals and thanks to a continuously improved system of warning that we achieved the rate at which an order given by me reached the lower ranks in two hours. This enabled us to decide the rising no more than twenty-four hours before it was to start. But the task of informing 40,000 men, of giving them the code word and fixing hours and places of assembly was not the whole work. There was also liaison between the fighting groups to be established. Commanders of all ranks had to be constantly furnished with information and orders, and thousands of instructions had to be distributed throughout the city. All these tasks were carried out by girl messengers. From dawn till dusk they covered the length and breadth of the city, climbed numberless stairs and repeated orders and reports, mostly by word of mouth. Every Underground soldier was then faced with his own difficulties, which he had to overcome personally. Since the mobilisation had to be conducted secretly, every worker had to have an explanation ready which would satisfy his colleagues and his family.

The most difficult task was the distribution of arms. A few months earlier, the job of carrying a rifle across the street under the observation of the Gestapo was a manœuvre requiring carefully laid plans. Now, however, the task confronting us was that of removing Underground stores from their hiding places, and sometimes even of digging up thousands of rifles, revolvers and grenades. These arms had to be cleaned and distributed throughout the city among the waiting men. They were transported through the town hidden in barrels, in oxygen cylinders, in coal carts, or covered by the most fantastic sorts of goods. Warsaw resembled a powder magazine. Any spark could have provoked an explosion. In these circumstances, I forbade the disarming of individual Germans in the streets, because it led to the exchange of shots and to street skirmishes which could so easily have developed into a general battle.

The situation on the front undoubtedly distracted German attention to a certain extent. They had not, however, neglected some security precautions. All the buildings occupied by Germans—railway stations, installations of public use, barracks and stores—had been protected from outside by pillboxes and barbed-wire barricades. The garrisons of these buildings were strengthened by the addition of S.S. units, military police and Gestapo. German sentries with arms at the ready could be seen everywhere. On the roofs of German buildings appeared sentinels with field-glasses who watched the street day and night. Heavy machine-guns were mounted on public squares and cross-roads. In addition to foot patrols, German armed cars with heavy machine-guns moved through the streets.

On July 27th Governor Fischer returned to Warsaw, probably as a result of a reprimand from his superiors, after his hurried departure of a few days before. On July 28th his appeal to the population was posted up. It ordered 100,000 men to assemble on the following day in public squares. The population was to be used for the construction of defences—the first preventive preparation aimed at the danger of insurrection within the city. I ordered Fischer's appeal to be completely ignored, but I was fully aware that the Germans would start other preventive actions. If the Russians did not occupy the city within a few days, the Germans would certainly start evacuating the population. In the Staff discussion on the morning of July 26th, the first suggestion that the rising should begin on July 28th was made to me. I decided, however, to wait for further indications.

It was then that we learned that the Russians had formed a "Committee of National Liberation" in Chełm. The great majority of the committee were members of the Union of Polish Patriots from Moscow and members of the former Polish Communist Party. In their announcement, the Russians declared that the administration of all Polish territory would be transferred to this Committee. There was no doubt that this was aiming at the formation of a Government completely dependent on Russia.

On July 29th a courier arrived from London. He told me of Mikołajczyk's last attempts to renew relations with the Russians. It appeared that he had suggested that he should reorganise his Government in such a way as to guarantee a friendly attitude towards the Soviet Union. From our point of view, the most important item in this proposition was the suggestion for renewal of diplomatic relations and the addition of a clause on military co-operation to the Polish-Soviet Agreement of July, 1941. After several talks, Lebiediev, the

Soviet Ambassador, imposed conditions which Mikołajczyk did not feel able to accept. They included the repudiation of the Constitution on which the legality of the Polish Government was based, a stipulation that the Polish President be changed, and the immediate acceptance of the Curzon Line as Poland's definite eastern frontier without waiting for the peace conference. The Russians also demanded that the Polish Government should publicly declare its appeal to the International Red Cross to investigate the Katyń Forest murders to be a calumnious insinuation against the Soviets. Despite all this, Mikołajczyk had not lost hope that, with the assistance of the western powers, he would reach a compromise.

After July 25th we heard the sound of the Russian guns across the Vistula grow nearer, and for several evenings Soviet bombers had been attacking military objectives in Warsaw. These attacks were a very important sign for us; we knew that the Soviet Air Force was only used in the immediate rear of the enemy. At the end of July Warsaw was included in the operational area of Soviet bombers and fighters, the Soviets having captured at least six airfields with permanent installations between the Bug and the Vistula, within a radius of 125 miles of Warsaw. The closest was at Dęblin, not more than twenty minutes' flight from the capital.

On July 29th there appeared on the walls of Warsaw the appeal of the P.A.L., an Underground military organisation under Communist control. The appeal, signed by "Czarny," the political leader of the organisation, and Skokowski, the military chief, stated that the Government delegate and myself had fled from Warsaw. Czarny called on the population to fight the Germans and to accept his leadership.

The Communist forces in Warsaw were not large. We estimated them at a few hundred men in all. They developed a very strong propaganda by newspapers and leaflets, appealing for an immediate rising and accusing the Home Army of holding up the fight against the Germans. In the course of July this propaganda had increased in intensity. On July 30th our monitoring service picked up a call from Moscow in Polish, addressed to the people of Warsaw. This call was broadcast for the first time in the evening transmission at 20.15 on July 29th and was repeated later on by the wireless station, Union of the Polish Patriots. The appeal ran as follows:

"No doubt Warsaw already hears the guns óf the battle which is soon to bring her liberation. Those who have never bowed their heads to the Hitlerite power will again, as in 1939, join in battle against the Germans, this time for the decisive action. The Polish Army, now entering Polish territory, trained in the U.S.S.R., is now joined to the People's Army to form the Corps of the Polish Armed Forces, the armed core of our nation in its struggle for independence. Its ranks will be joined to-morrow by the sons of Warsaw. They will, together with the Allied Army, pursue the enemy westward, drive the Hitlerite vermin from the Polish land, and strike a mortal blow at the last of Prussian imperialism. For Warsaw, which did not yield, but fought on, the hour of action has already arrived. The Germans will no doubt try to defend themselves in Warsaw and add new destruction and more thousands of victims. Our houses and parks, our bridges and railway stations, our factories and our public buildings will be turned into defence positions. They will expose the city to ruin, and its inhabitants to death. They will try to take away all the most precious possessions and turn into dust all that they have to leave behind. It is therefore a hundred times more necessary than ever to remember that in the flood of Hitlerite destruction all is lost that is not saved by active effort, that by direct, active struggle in the streets of Warsaw, in its houses, factories and stores, we not only hasten the moment of final liberation, but also save the nation's property and the lives of our brethren."

This appeal was not the only one to be made. The next day similar ones were picked up from the Soviet-controlled station, Kościuszko.

In principle, these calls were nothing new. Soviet propaganda had continually appealed to the Polish nation for a general rising against the Germans. They had been addressed to Poles even when the Red Army was not on the bank of the Vistula, but on the Dnieper, and were usually accompanied by accusations that the Home Army had no wish to fight, and sometimes even that they had collaborated with the Germans. These accusations were often directed personally against me or against the Polish Government in London and General Sosnkowski.

A Soviet manifesto was also published, signed by Molotov

and Osóbka-Morawski, then just appointed head of the Committee of National Liberation. The manifesto started with the words:

"Poles! The time of liberation is at hand! Poles, to arms! . . . Every Polish homestead must become a stronghold in the struggle against the invader. . . . There is not a moment to lose."

These appeals and calls were also printed in leaflets and dropped by Soviet planes over the city and its environs.

The appeal of July 29th was repeated several times, and worded in a very explicit and emphatic way; it seemed to indicate that the Russians judged the situation ripe for the beginning of our fight. This was of special significance, in view of our inability to co-ordinate the time of the rising with the Russians.

* * *

According to the reports I received, the German defence lines were broken on July 28th and Soviet forces occupied Otwock, Falenica, and Józefów, on the outskirts of Warsaw. We heard also that Panzer units, which had crashed through the southern sector of the German bridgehead, penetrated as far as Anin and Wołomin. Soviet patrols, after crossing the Vistula to the south of Warsaw, were approaching Mszczonów (thirty miles south-west of Warsaw) and operating in the deep rear of the German lines in the Warsaw sector. On July 30th, at Radość, within ten miles of Warsaw, one of our intelligence officers met a Soviet tank column which was probably a strong patrol. He talked with some of the men in the column, and all of them were extremely optimistic that the Russians would occupy Warsaw in the next few days. Later the tanks withdrew unhindered to the east. Our information posts across the Vistula, dispersed over the eastern periphery of the city on the border of the suburb, Praga, sent in continuous reports of the appearance of Soviet patrols in the vicinity or even on the outskirts of Praga. One of these patrols of about thirty men, wearing German greatcoats over their Soviet uniforms, succeeded on July 30th in reaching the centre of the suburb, Zerań. The defence of the bridgehead was in the hands of the 73rd German Division, supported by small units of infantry, S.S., police and airmen, assembled in haste. On July 30th, however, the Hermann Goering Panzer Division, withdrawn from the Italian front, started to march through the city from the west.

On July 31st we received information of further advances by the Soviet wedge which was operating deep inside the enemy positions. The presence of Soviet units in Radość, Wiązowna, Wołomin and Radzymin was reported, all between eight and ten miles from Warsaw. A panic started among German units at Legionowo and, led by its commander, the garrison left the barracks. In broad daylight, quite a substantial group of Home Army soldiers marched to the abandoned buildings and armed themselves with the weapons left by the enemy. In Warsaw, engineers mined the bridges over the Vistula. The German communiqué O.K.W.,[1] published in the early afternoon, announced: "To-day the Russians started a general attack on Warsaw from the south-east." A Soviet communiqué announced the capture of the Commander of the 73rd German Division. This proved that the Russians were not only in the vicinity, but actually inside the German Warsaw bridgehead. That same day we learned from the wireless that Prime Minister Mikołajczyk had left for Moscow.

On July 31st, Monter, our Commander of the Warsaw district, was due at Staff H.Q. at 6 p.m. He arrived unexpectedly at 5 p.m. with the news that Soviet armoured units which had broken into the German bridgehead had disorganised its defence, and that Radość, Miłosna, Okuniew, Wołomin and Radzymin were already in Soviet hands.

After a short consultation, I decided that the moment had come to begin the fight for the liberation of Warsaw. I expected the Soviet attack to be launched hourly. Although all decisions about fighting within the Burza plan were left entirely to me, in this exceptional instance, with the fate of the capital at stake, I wished to submit my decision for the approval of the Government delegate.

I immediately sent my A.D.C. to him, asking him to come and see me. He was with me in half an hour. Briefly, I put the situation before him. In my opinion, it was the right time to begin the fight.

He heard me out and then put questions to various members of the Staff. Having completed his picture of the situation, he turned to me with the words: "Very well, then. Begin."

I turned to Monter, who, as Commander of the Warsaw

[1] *Oberkommando der Wehrmacht.*

city district, had been entrusted with the Burza preparations
as well as with command of the fighting:

"To-morrow, at seventeen hours precisely, you will start
operations in Warsaw."

The button had been pressed. Thousands of orders spread
through the city that same evening.

After a good deal of deliberation, I had fixed zero hour for
five o'clock. Hitherto all our activities had been timed for
dawn or dusk, so this, I decided, was the best way of taking
the enemy by surprise. At five o'clock the traffic in the city
was at its heaviest, with people returning home from work.
It would then be less difficult to conceal units moving to their
appointed places in the hurrying crowd of workers coming
out of offices and factories. Also, if we began then, we should
have a few hours of daylight in which to take over German
positions in the city before dusk, according to plan.

The next day I again met the Staff to issue final instructions
and orders. This was our last meeting in hiding. On my way
I walked through streets full of thousands of young men and
women hurrying to their appointed posts. Many of them
wore soldiers' top-boots and wind-breakers and carried ruck-
sacks. Nearly everyone had a bag or a dispatch case; some had
parcels. All this roused my anxiety and I feared for the secrecy
of our zero hour. Every few paces there were German patrols,
while armoured cars moved ceaselessly through the streets.
Throughout the morning a fine rain fell. The insistent sound
of gunfire reached us from across the Vistula. All that night
and the following day the deep note of detonations was
heard; it was the Germans dynamiting railway equipment
near Praga.

I left Staff H.Q. at 2 p.m. My A.D.C. put the pistols which
we had always kept there into a portable gramophone-case,
frequently used for this purpose. He took them to the Kammler
Factory in the suburb of Wola, which was to be my headquarters during the rising. The factory buildings were to
accommodate my immediate staff. With us were to be the
Government delegate with his secretary and the Chairman of
the Council of National Unity, to enable us to be in constant
contact. Also on the spot was to be the radio station for transmission and reception to ensure communications with the
city, the country and the world. The remainder of the Staff
were to be housed in neighbouring streets. The meeting time

for the staff on August 1st was fixed for between three and four o'clock.

The Home Army soldiers were still normal passers-by, mixing with the crowd of civilians and entering their assigned houses in small groups. The buildings had been chosen with care, according to a definite plan. For the most part they were corner houses, commanding important cross-roads or facing railway stations, German barracks, stores or public works departments. Briefly, they were close to all the points which were to be attacked and taken in the first impetus. The men rang the bell of the flat indicated and handed to the occupants orders for requisition, signed by the authorities of the rising. The inmates showed excitement, but never the slightest resentment. On the contrary, they invariably did their best to help in every way and offered the soldiers their best food. The men took up their positions at windows, in attics and on chimneys. The entrances to the blocks were then closed and barricaded from within. A sentry in the courtyard forbade all inmates any access to the street for fear that the final preparations might be revealed to the enemy. Thirty minutes before zero hour, all preparations were completed. The soldiers brought out their arms and put on white-and-red arm-bands, the first open sign of a Polish army on Polish soil since the occupation. For five years they had all awaited this moment. Now the last seconds seemed an eternity. At five o'clock they would cease to be an underground resistance movement and would become once more Regular soldiers fighting in the open.

At exactly five o'clock thousands of windows flashed as they were flung open. From all sides a hail of bullets struck passing Germans, riddling their buildings and their marching formations. In the twinkling of an eye, the remaining civilians disappeared from the streets. From the entrances of houses, our men streamed out and rushed to the attack. In fifteen minutes an entire city of a million inhabitants was engulfed in the fight. Every kind of traffic ceased. As a big communications centre where roads from north, south, east and west converged, in the immediate rear of the German front, Warsaw ceased to exist. The battle for the city was on.

It so happened that just before the action started my Staff and I found ourselves involved in a fight which might well have proved fatal for us. I went to my headquarters in the Kammler Factory just before four. It was situated in a part of the city which was completely unknown to me. The buildings faced two narrow, parallel roads, Dzielna and Pawia Streets. Both were dead-ends closed by a wall surrounding the Ghetto. On the other side of this wall was a large area of charred ruins. Our headquarters adjoined another factory on the Ghetto side, which belonged to the tobacco monopoly. It was occupied by a German garrison and, like all such buildings, was guarded by two pillboxes. Each of the two streets was covered by one of these pillboxes, because this factory looked out both ways. Altogether it was an unhealthy neighbourhood. At five o'clock the whole surrounding sector was to be occupied by the Kedyw Battalion, one of the crack units of the Home Army. It had been tried out in many street fights and partisan actions, and there was no doubt that it would ably accomplish its task. Its commander had been there before us, had taken his bearings and formed a detailed plan. His unit was to smoke out the Germans from our immediate vicinity. But events did not go quite according to plan.

I walked towards the Kammler Factory, and approached to within 15 yards of one of the pillboxes. Through the slit I could see the barrel of a machine-gun trained on the street; the pillbox was occupied by alert German soldiers. I reached the building which was to be G.H.Q. and, with the utmost caution, was allowed to enter. Inside the factory, the guard platoon had assembled with its commander, Lieutenant Kammler, owner of the factory, who reported to me at the gate. His men were all workers from the factory. On the day of the rising the whole organisation was transformed into a fighting unit. The men had an excellent appearance; I eyed them with approval. When I asked Lieutenant Kammler how things were in the vicinity of the factory, he said: "Not too good. During the night the Germans increased their garrison in the tobacco factory to fifty men. They have two machine-guns."

"How many men are here with you?" I asked.

"Thirty-three actually on the spot," he replied.

"And what arms?"

"Fifteen rifles, maybe forty grenades and a few filipinki."

Filipinki, as mentioned earlier, were grenades of our own production. They had been used with great success in sabotage and street clashes with the Germans and had great explosive power.

I told Kammler to remain quietly with his platoon and not to reveal his presence until the expected Kedyw Battalion had arrived and occupied the tobacco factory at five o'clock, as planned. I then went up to the second floor, where the General Staff, the Government delegate and the Chairman of the Council of National Unity had already assembled. Engineers in one of the neighbouring factory sheds had begun to instal radio equipment.

Suddenly, from the empty street overlooked by our windows, came the sound of an approaching lorry. I went to the window and saw a heavy lorry carrying a few German railway police. It passed the first factory entrance and turned into the second, which probably had now been opened. A thought immediately flashed through my head: our sentry at the gate would have a rifle in his hands. A clash was inevitable.

At the same instant, two rifle shots rang out in quick succession. The lorry suddenly reappeared in reverse and simultaneously, through the other gate, emerged Lieutenant Kammler, revolver in hand, with two other soldiers. Kammler killed the driver on the spot, as well as two other Germans standing in the lorry. The nearby German pillbox immediately opened fire and machine-gun bullets sprayed the street. Kammler, with his two companions, leapt for the gate. From the tobacco factory we could hear signals and warning shouts. Together with the Chief of Staff, I hurried down to see what the actual situation was. It appeared that in the same building there was a German store of railway uniforms which they had been removing for the last few days, and the lorry had come to pick up another load. At the sight of an armed Pole, the German next to the driver seized his weapon. He was too late, however; the Polish sentry beat him to it.

At any moment we could expect Germans from the nearby garrison to arrive on the scene. Brief orders were shouted and our platoon was swiftly posted at windows and gates. When I returned upstairs, I could see German soldiers in full equipment occupying the house opposite. Machine-guns from the two pillboxes sprayed both streets constantly. One burst crackled through our room, spattering a line of holes across walls and ceiling. Glass flew and dust and plaster filled the air. The Germans in the windows of the house opposite were within a grenade's-throw of us; high factory windows were no protection. I proposed that the Government delegate, other civilian officials and a few of the women with us should go to the back of the building, but the women refused. I was relieved to see that, with the exception of the secretary of the Government delegate, no one was showing any sign of nervousness. All unarmed persons were put to work barricading the gates below. In little more than a minute, both gates had been reinforced with barrels, handcarts, tables, planks and furniture, of which there were mercifully plenty about. Everything movable was pushed against the windows of the ground floor to provide cover as far as possible. The buildings formed a fairly large group provided with several exits and a number of places where an intruder could easily enter unobserved. Our thirty soldiers were completely lost in all these buildings. I looked at my watch. It was half-past four. The incident had started fifteen minutes before and we had to defend ourselves unaided for half an hour at least before help would reach us. The soldiers watching the Germans through a small crack in the gate reported that they were obviously preparing for an attack under cover of the machine-gun. It was firing insistently at our window at 15 yards' range.

"For God's sake," said the Chief of Staff, "we can't let them force their way into the building. Once in, we'll never get them out again with the arms we've got." Then, turning to the men, he said quickly, "Which of you is the best grenade-thrower?"

Two came forward at once. Grzegorz told them to get two filipinki each and come with him to the second floor. There they met with another difficulty. The big heavy window was closed. They had to get it open to throw a bomb, and to show themselves in the window would have caused an immediate reaction on the enemy's part. However, they managed to smash the window with a length of iron piping. At once the whole German fire was directed on it. They succeeded, all the same, in throwing a fiilipinka in the direction of the machine gun. An explosion followed and the machine-gun was silenced. After a while we saw two dead soldiers being pulled away from the gun by the legs. This discouraged them for a time from attacking us, but they retaliated with hand-grenades. One grenade severely wounded two of our soldiers. A little later on I was informed that the wireless station had been damaged. Meanwhile, the German police, whose barracks were in Leszno Street, 300 to 400 yards away, hurried in to help their comrades. In our narrow street another heavy German lorry appeared, filled with police armed with tommy-guns and grenades. Obviously, however, they did not realise the exact location of the fight. The Germans already on the scene gave warning signs and shouted to them to stop, but the men in the lorry did not grasp what was happening and drove on under our window. This was just what our men had been waiting for. From a window, another filipinka landed plumb in the middle of the lorry. It swerved suddenly, hit the wall opposite and burst into flames. In a few seconds, thirty-five enemy dead and the wreck of the lorry were all that remained in the road.

Then Lieutenant Kammler reported a new danger. I followed him to the other side of the factory, overlooking the Ghetto. From a window he pointed out a large circle of police closing in on our factory across the ruins of the Ghetto. Kammler was worried. With the small force and arms at our disposal, this new attack was beyond our control. Instinctively, I looked at my watch again. It was already five o'clock. All over the city the fight had begun. The expected Kedyw Battalion should now be starting their attack on our district, but I could see no possibility of their reaching us. Both streets were by now so well covered by machine-guns that even a mouse would have had difficulty in slipping past.

Minutes passed. We were still covered by fire on all sides. Our shots were rare, but well aimed. Now the sound of firing in the city reached us and the line of advancing German police was stopped by an attack on their rear.

At six we had another alarm. Our spotter on the roof started shouting desperately for help. Six soldiers at once dashed upstairs. It appeared that the Germans had attempted to reach us through the roof and our sentry in the chimney had been badly wounded in the head. The Germans had managed to reach the attic, and it was only there that they started a fierce exchange of fire with the men who had rushed to help. It took fifteen minutes to wipe out the Germans, but we had our losses too. The wounded spotter was replaced by two others, with orders to report to us every few minutes. It was now clear that the insurrection had already engulfed the centre of the city and our district, but we could still see no sign of relief, and its chances of reaching us looked slender. The Germans too had their worries. They were perturbed by the noise of fighting behind them, and their attempts to force our factory ceased.

It was just after seven when, to my astonishment, two soldiers from the Kedyw Battalion reported to me. I asked them how they had managed to get through to us when every route was under enemy fire. They replied cheerfully that they belonged to an advance patrol and that the rest were following them. They had got through from Okopowa Street by blasting their way through the walls of attics, which enabled them to travel partly on the roofs and partly through the attics. Their tough journey had started several hours earlier—in fact, as soon as they had been warned by the sound of the first shots from the factory. Half an hour later, the main part of the battalion began to come in. Soon the situation had changed to our advantage. The Germans were on the defensive, and we went over to vigorous attack.

About eight o'clock I heard more shouting from the attic. This time it did not signify alarm, but joy. One of the soldiers came down and asked me in great excitement to follow him at once to the chimney stack. There we were greeted by the spotter on duty. "The flag! The Polish flag!" he shouted, pointing. "Our flag—right in the middle of the city!" From the roof a wide view of the capital enabled us to see the blaze of the fires. From the tower of the highest building in Warsaw, the sixteen-story Prudential Building, which dominated the whole centre of the city, flew a large flag. I concentrated my gaze. No; it was not a Nazi flag. Now I could see the white and red. After five years, the Polish colours were once more floating defiantly over the city. Looking more closely, I saw that similar flags were already flying from the cupola of the Post Office Savings Bank, from the tower of the Town Hall and other buildings. This was the first sign, the first report on the course of the fighting that I received. I tried to make out where the fires were located. Over to the west something was burning close to the Western Station. The clouds of smoke were black and dense and might be from burning petrol. Probably we had fired a German fuel dump. Several buildings in the centre were on fire, one of which must be the Central Station or perhaps the wooden huts the Germans had put up in its vicinity. The glare over the city, the smoke rising from burning houses and perhaps even the flag on the Prudential Building—all these should be visible to the forward Soviet troops on the Warsaw bridgehead. We could clearly hear their continuous artillery fire. The German heavy guns were replying to the Russians from this side of the Vistula now—from the west, beyond Powązki. I went down to speed the sending of two messages to London, which, however, did not go off until August 2nd owing to the damage to our transmitter.

I

"WARSAW.
"*August 1st, 1944.*

"To the Prime Minister and the Commander-in-Chief:
"The date for the beginning of a struggle to capture Warsaw was jointly fixed by us for August 1st at 17.00 hours.
"The struggle has begun.

"*Home Delegate and Vice-Premier of the Polish Government.*
"*Commander-in-Chief, Home Army.*"

2

"WARSAW.
"*August 1st, 1944.*

"We began the fight for Warsaw on August 1st at 17.00 hours; arrange immediately for ammunition and arms to be dropped at the lights (specified) and also in the squares giving on to the city. . . .
"As the fight to capture Warsaw has begun, we ask for Soviet help to be supplied by an immediate attack from outside.

"*Home Delegate and Vice-Premier of the Polish Government.*
"*Commander-in-Chief, Home Army.*"

My first message to the soldiers fighting in the capital read:

"Soldiers of the capital!
"I have to-day issued the order which you desire, for open warfare against Poland's age-old enemy, the German invader. After nearly five years of ceaseless and determined struggle, carried on in secret, you stand to-day openly with arms in hand, to restore freedom to our country and to mete out fitting punishment to the German criminals for the terror and crimes committed by them on Polish soil.

"BOR.
"*Commander-in-Chief, Home Army.*"

The wireless station was unfortunately still out of commission. Technicians had been hard at work on repairs all night, and the messages had to wait. As yet the world knew nothing of the beginning of the Warsaw rising.

*   *   *

In the night a heavy rain damped down the intensity of the fires which burned fiercely in the city and suburbs. At 3 a.m., while it was still dark, our men broke into the tobacco factory. Part of the German garrison was killed and the rest taken prisoner. The pillboxes presented the greatest difficulty, but they were finally destroyed by filipinki at 5 a.m. The wireless expert reported that spare parts were essential for the repair of the damaged sets. They pointed out that one of our underground stores of signals equipment was a few streets away, about 500 yards off. The necessary parts could be got there, but to reach the store was a difficult and dangerous undertaking. Two men were sent over. By morning neither had returned. Later I learned that both had been killed on the way. At dawn, another volunteer offered to make the effort. The fact that no one outside Warsaw knew what was going on made people at G.H.Q. feel uneasy. Half an hour later, the soldier returned in triumph, bringing the necessary parts. Before noon on August 2nd we finally managed to contact London and to send the first messages. That morning, in the early hours, the first report from the city reached me.

On the whole, the Germans had been caught off guard. In some parts operations had started ahead of schedule, due to the difficulty of concealing concentrations of units. Fortunately, the official German authorities treated these local skirmishes as "merely stupid shooting," to quote a German report which we found on a prisoner a few days later. Thanks to this estimate, our plan to take the Germans by surprise with our zero hour was successful. It was not till about a quarter-past five that the Germans sent out a general alarm to all troops. Formations of German tanks and armoured cars had been standing by for this call at several points on the outskirts of Warsaw. At 5.15 eighteen of their heaviest tanks were seen crossing Unia Lubelska Square, moving towards the centre of the fighting. It looked as though the Germans attached great importance to the use of Panzer units; they probably expected to overcome the rising in a few hours by the mass use of tanks; instead of which the Panzer monsters, heavily armed, appeared to be helpless when in a street where they were attacked from doors and windows on all sides. The most effective weapon used against them was a bottle of petrol corked with explosive. Sometimes a bottle would be wrapped in a rag soaked in an incendiary solution. Filipinki were also effective, as sometimes were just rags dipped in petrol, ignited at the last moment and thrown at a tank from an upper floor. In twenty minutes the whole population of the city had fully grasped what was going on; people ran out on all sides to help us. From that moment onwards it became almost impossible to distinguish soldiers from civilians. Whether a man was armed or not was no indication, because in every group or unit rushing to attack there were several soldiers carrying only a bottle; some were even empty-handed, hoping they might be lucky enough to pick up booty in the form of a coveted rifle, tommy-gun or grenade. In the battle it was indeed almost a rule that soldiers without arms should either take them from Germans or recover them from our own dead.

For the first few hours the fighting was isolated into countless small independent episodes. It was, of course, quite impossible to draw any front line dividing the two sides. Polish and German positions formed something very like a chessboard. Germans barricaded inside their buildings were supported by tanks from outside. Heavy fire made the movement of messengers almost impossible in many parts. In the first hours, each Home Army unit fought on its own, and consequently there was considerable difficulty in getting from one street to another. The inhabitants accordingly began blasting holes in the walls of cellars between adjoining houses. It was thus that parallel with the streets a huge labyrinth of underground passages was opened up for communication purposes; it ran through adjoining cellars and sometimes across the back courtyards of the houses. By such underground communication lines our forces were moved, our wounded transported, ammunition supplied and personal liaison assured. An immediate and voluntary traffic control through cellars and courtyards was organised which enabled people to find their way in this fantastic subterranean maze.

In the suburb of Stawki, our men captured a big store of German uniforms and immediately appeared in S.S. uniforms, which were the best the Germans had. Only their white-and-red armbands distinguished them from German soldiers. However, in some cases the Germans were taken in by this fancy dress, and it was thanks to it that we captured our first armoured cars.

The impetus of the opening onslaughts was so strong that it cannot be compared with the attack of any regular army. It had all the drive and enthusiasm of a revolutionary uprising which was at the same time directed as an organised military operation. We attributed our success of the first few days to the impetuous fervour of this first onslaught. It more than made up for the poor quality of our arms on the one hand, and the enemy's superiority in equipment and training on the other. But this enthusiasm had its disadvantages also. It was impossible to impose strict discipline in the use of ammunition; one solitary German would attract a hail of bullets and grenades. The reports which began to come in on the second day would announce the capture of this or that position and at the same time stress the great expenditure of ammunition. For the time being, however, I consoled myself that booty would cover this in part.

During August 2nd most of the reports which reached me came from the central sector. At a quarter to four, the main Post Office had been occupied despite tough enemy defence. The relief from outside which was to have been furnished by German tanks was unsuccessful. Shortly afterwards, I was informed of the capture of the main Post Office Station, the gas-works, the filters and the Central Railway Station which, however, was later retaken by the enemy. On the same day the main electric plant fell to us. The occupation of the latter was a characteristic episode. Its Polish garrison had been formed from technicians and engineers working there in the Underground days, at which time they had themselves evolved plans for seizing the plant. A few months before the rising the Germans had increased their defence, using a special unit called *Werkschutz*. Numerous pillboxes were built and machine-gun trenches dug; the fire from these guns was directed both outside and inside the building. The plant had already assumed the appearance of a front-line defence position with barbed-wire barricades within and around the premises. A few days before the rising the Germans further increased the garrison and armed them to the teeth. We expected the electrical plant would be a hard nut to crack; at the same time, it was naturally an extremely important key-position for us, since it was the

H

only source of current in the city. The signal for the fight was given by the explosion of a mine laid under one of the pillboxes. The ensuing struggle lasted nineteen hours. Tasks were divided between the workers. Some of them kept the plant going, while others joined in the fight. The German garrison, attacked from within, defended themselves with incredible fierceness. In the end they were obliged to capitulate, and most of them were wiped out. Immediately after we had captured this objective, the Germans proceeded to shell it with their 88-mm. guns, despite which the plant continued to furnish us with current. The cranes which transported the coal to the furnaces were damaged by artillery fire, and this work was promptly taken over by hand-carts, which involved additional manpower and heavy work. As workers were gradually absorbed into the defence of the plant, the task of keeping it running was undertaken by men from the neighbouring district. After thirty-five days of continued service, the whole plant was completely destroyed by artillery and air attacks, and ceased functioning on September 4th.

As early as the evening of August 1st I had discovered with satisfaction that the electricity was working. This was of the greatest importance to us, since it meant that such things as the wireless transmitters and the workshops producing ammunition could continue functioning. Equally important, it went far towards maintaining the high morale of the people. The supply of current also enabled a printing machine to start work by August 2nd, and this was how my message was printed. The machine also produced the first issues of the Home Army Press, headed by our *Biuletyn Informacyjny*, and on August 3rd the manifesto issued by the Home authorities, which ran:

"WARSAW.

"*August 3rd, 1944.*

"Poles!

"The armed struggle for the liberation of the capital has begun.

"On August 1st, the Home delegate, Vice-Premier of the Polish Government, and the Chairman of the Council of National Unity, in agreement with the Commander of the Home Army, decided to resort to arms.

"Three days of battle with the occupying forces have brought us great tactical and moral successes. The forces of the Home Army have conquered the larger part of the capital, broken the enemy's resistance, and at the same time set free in every Polish heart enthusiasm for the struggle and faith in its success.

"The entire Polish community, and above all the whole people of Warsaw, are coming generously and unselfishly to the aid of the fighters. All have put themselves under the orders and at the disposal of the leaders of the rising, lending all their strength and showing excellent moral discipline as well as great devotion in action.

"We shall meet more than one obstacle yet on the road to complete liberation, but the united forces of the whole Polish nation, under the Polish Government in London, the Home Council of Ministers and the Commander of the Home Army, will overcome them, just as to-day they are breaking the resistance of the enemy in the streets of Warsaw.

"All workers, peasants, labourers and the intelligentsia alike are fighting together for a democratic Poland, a Poland of social justice; a Poland of the people.

"Long live Independent Poland!

> "*Home Delegate and Vice-Premier of the Polish Government.*
> "*Commander-in-Chief, Home Army.*
> "*Chairman of the Council of National Unity.*"

Throughout August 2nd heavy rain fell. This in no way diminished the fighting. Wola was a district of working-class houses. Its capture was completed in the early hours of August 2nd, thanks to the very effective co-operation of the Polish Socialist Party militia. Both in the Underground days and during the rising, these units fought in the Home Army under my command. At 5.45 the B.B.C., in its Polish broadcast from London, announced for the first time the news of the outbreak of the rising in Warsaw. This news was later repeated in broadcasts in other languages, and during the night of August 2nd it was also announced by neutral stations. I ordered systematic monitoring of the Soviet radio stations. For the moment, however, Moscow was silent. From the reports which had already reached me, I was able by August 2nd to send a message to London indicating Napoleon Square and the Jewish cemetery as places where munitions and anti-tank weapons should be dropped. In the same message I requested that the Polish Parachute Brigade should be dropped in the Wola district.

Reports telling me of the occupation of single German positions were now followed by news of the occupation of whole districts. In our hands were: the centre of the city; the Old Town (Stare Miasto); two districts on the banks of the Vistula, Powiśle and Czerniaków; and, of course, Wola. All these sectors were linked up. In some places, subterranean communication lines had to be used for movement from one district to another. We were completely cut off from Praga, the suburb across the Vistula, and did not know what was happening there. Later I learned that the Germans had sent in strong Panzer units which crushed the rising there in five hours. The western end of the bridge leading to it changed hands continually. A large part of the southern district was completely in our hands, but we had no contact with it. In the residential district of Kolonia Lubeckiego the fighting had taken an unfavourable turn, but for the time being it continued unabated. To the north, Zoliborz was cut off. The Germans forestalled the insurrection when they saw units assembling, and they were the first to open fire from their tanks at three o'clock in the afternoon. In consequence, our units there withdrew to the nearby Forest of Kampinos at first, but later they attacked from their new positions and took a large part of the suburb. My estimate was that about two-thirds of the city on the western bank of the river was in our hands, although in some cases this included isolated patches. Our units were everywhere on the offensive. In the first twenty-four hours our main achievement was to keep the initiative in our hands. In the centre of the city the Germans still held nests of resistance, such as the Gestapo headquarters, the Sejm (Parliament), the Bruhl Palace (seat of the German Governor) and the Bank of National Economy. But all these points were surrounded and isolated by our forces. The danger of Panzer units, which looked so formidable at the beginning, was partly overcome, at least on this side of the Vistula. By the evening of August 2nd I had received news of the destruction of more than twelve heavy German tanks. I hoped that this would discourage the enemy from using their Panzers on a large scale.

I was soon to have experience of them at close quarters. At eleven o'clock on August 3rd I was in my room looking through the reports still coming in from all parts of the city. Through the open window I heard the noise of fighting coming closer and closer. Since morning, the whole district of Wola had been the scene of heavy fighting with German units which had been moved to our sector, in particular to the cemeteries in our district. These cemeteries were of special importance, because I had indicated them as the place where supplies could be dropped by the Allies. For a few minutes I could clearly distinguish a new sound in the enemy fire; it was the sound of gunfire from heavy German tanks. The noise drew nearer and nearer. Troops of enemy tanks had taken up positions on Kcrcclego Square, a few hundred yards to the south; they were preparing for an attack along Okopowa Street. Their tactics were to advance between 200 and 300 yards, firing their machine-guns, and then stop and fire their guns. A few minutes later I saw a troop of Tigers drive through Okopowa Street not more than 200 yards from our factory. Their clear intention was to cut off our units which were being attacked at the same time from the west in the region of the Protestant cemetery. If they discovered G.H.Q., we could expect a direct attack on the factory.

We were in immediate danger, and I accordingly ordered a partial evacuation of G.H.Q. I learned the day before that Okopowa Street was occupied by the Kedyw Battalions, their Commander, Colonel "Radosław," being quartered no more than 300 yards away from us. During the two days of fighting our soldiers had already gained a good deal of useful experience in fighting tanks. Things were not serious if only the soldiers were not overcome by the sight of 40 tons of steel clanking along a street accompanied by the non-stop fire of machine-guns, and if they would allow the tanks to come within close range. These heavily-armoured monsters were not vulnerable to our grenades when thrown singly. A few filipinki had to be tied in a bunch and then thrown under the caterpillar tracks with the pin of one of the filipinki drawn out. The first time I actually saw the result of a direct hit by one of these bunches was when this troop of tanks returned a few minutes later and was attacked near Radosław's quarters. One of them got away, still firing, in the direction of Kercelego Square. The other two were left behind. One had a splintered track. It was swung round at right-angles by the impact and tore a gaping hole in the nearest house. The other appeared undamaged. Radosław immediately produced crews for both tanks. There happened to be a tank lieutenant in the nearest **unit who had been instructor in our Underground cadet** school. Here was his opportunity to put theory into practice. The damaged track could not be repaired in the present circumstances, and the lieutenant had to give up all thought of putting the Tiger into service; it would therefore have to be used as a gun. He changed its direction of fire by 180° and began without delay to shell the neighbouring German military police barracks. That Thursday was a lucky one for units in Wola. Radosław got a report from the Protestant cemetery that German infantry had been repulsed in a counter-attack. Our men had captured a grenade-thrower, three heavy machine-guns and three lorries of ammunition for Tiger tanks.

So we had a decent reserve of ammunition in addition to our two tanks. Unfortunately, the other tank, which seemed undamaged, was also out of order. They could not get it going. The German tank crew, who very willingly gave full information about how the complicated Tiger worked, were unable to diagnose the trouble. From a nearby building emerged an elderly workman. The rising had probably caught him there unaware, because he was wearing an oily old boiler-suit.

"Sir," he addressed the senior officer, "I know something about this sort of thing. Let me have a go at it. Up till last Saturday I was working at the *Heereskraftfahrpark* (Military Vehicle Maintenance Park). Up to now, I have repaired nothing but German tanks, but maybe I'll manage to deal with this one of ours!"

I must confess I was doubtful whether he could. There were no tools except the set in the tank, and working conditions were far from healthy. The whole job would have to be done under enemy fire. Bullets were showering over and the German tanks would most likely counter-attack to re-take the abandoned Tigers. I walked further on towards the Protestant cemetery. There overturned crosses and ploughed-up graves proved the effectiveness of the enemy grenade-throwers. The indescribable desolation was filled with the sharp sound of battle. Our units had entrenched themselves and strengthened their position. From the reports made to me on the spot, I found out how strange the names of our units sounded when introduced into the military orders. The west wall of the cemetery was held by the "Parasol" (Umbrella) battalion; close to it was the "Pięść" (Fist), to the east were the "Kedyw" battalions, along with the "Rudy" (Rusty) and "Zośka" (Little Sophie). These were not only Underground code names; they were often titles chosen in tribute to a commander killed in action or to the memory of some friend. Rudy, for instance, was the pseudonym of one of the platoon commanders who gave his life in 1943 in Długa Street. Zośka was the nickname given to the commander of the group who accomplished one of the most daring diversionary actions, liberating a transport of prisoners being taken to the concentration camp at Oświecim.

Everywhere I noted the excellent morale of the troops and their increasing military experience. An hour later, as I returned to my quarters, I passed the two captured tanks. On one of them a pennant with Polish colours was flying, and I could already see at a distance the Underground emblem painted on it—the anchor formed by the letters PW, which had hitherto, through five years of Underground, appeared only on the walls. Now for the first time perhaps the same men were painting it on a tank which had so recently been German. The crew were loading up the ammunition captured in the other sector. I went along to see how the repairs were progressing. I was in civilian clothes with only the normal armband. The officer who had taken charge of the tank was looking after it as though it were his firstborn child; he was obviously jealous of his charge and refused to allow me near it. "What the hell do you want here?" he snapped. Radosław, who was standing near, informed him and, thanks to his timely intervention, the testy lieutenant finally allowed me to have a look at his prize and even relented so far as to permit me to board it. They were all in high spirits because they expected to get it working at any moment. I saw the volunteer workman, his sleeves rolled up and assisted by two Kedyw soldiers, busy with some mysterious job on the engines.

He did not seem unduly impressed by the German machine-gun fire and continued his job unperturbed. And then, a little later, the engines really did start up. The master-craftsman had certainly every right to be proud. With oily hands, he wiped the sweat from his smiling face and turned towards me: "For two days, sir, I have been asking them to take me on. They refused and said I was too old to fight. And now, look! The old fellow has his uses, hasn't he?"

He certainly had—very much so, showing a real soldier's

courage. And there, beside the tank he had repaired under enemy fire, I awarded him the Silver Cross of Merit with Swords. Jan Lumeński, the workshop mechanic, thanks to whom the first tank went forward to action under Polish colours, was the first civilian of the rising to be decorated.

At Radosław's quarters, I listened to the reports from the front line and talked to soldiers coming in. The reports were serious. Corporal "Spokojny," the sighter of a heavy machine-gun crew, was still upset when he talked to me:

"Our first company went in to counter-attack at the cemetery. At the beginning the going was hard, but finally we managed to advance to within grenade distance. The Germans started to withdraw. With my machine-gun, I was covering the crossing of Powązkowska Street; I was right on the target at 600 yards' range. I knew, sir, that few Boches would manage to get across. The first two dashed out: my aim was too high, but the next three were in my sights. Down they went. I let Andrzej know that he had that spot well covered. I waited for more Germans; they would have to cross that street as our chaps were speeding up. Suddenly Andrzej, lying close beside me, sweeping the streets with binoculars, shouted into my ear: 'Stop, don't shoot! Civilians.'

"We looked more attentively. It was true. They were standing side by side across the street. I thought, sir, that they were crazy. Did they really want a close-up, or what? I sent a burst into the air. No one moved. We peered again. At last I understood. Those people were bound to a long ladder, which the Germans had pushed across the street to use as cover. Beyond the screen, I could see the green uniforms of the military police. I had them all in my sights at 600 yards. It was well within the gun's range, but how could we fire through the bodies of our own people? I consulted Andrzej. We could wait no longer. If we hadn't fired, to-morrow every German would advance behind Polish hostages. It was difficult, sir, but it couldn't be helped. It was soon over. After a couple of bursts they and the ladder were flat. Six hundred yards is a good range for a machine-gun, and ours was a beauty."

I knew that Spokojny was not the only one to be faced with such a decision. Similar reports were now pouring in from all sides. On Poniatowski Bridge the Germans attacked our barricade, forcing civilians ahead of them. In another place, German tanks, not trusting their heavy armour, took cover behind a crowd of civilians herded before them. This was the pattern of total war, German fashion, Warsaw, August, 1944. I cabled to London requesting that the German command in Warsaw be informed that I was prepared to adopt serious reprisals against German prisoners of the Home Army.

I did not continue my inspection of the fighting line, but instead went into the region we had liberated. The streets of Wola, which had been deserted in the first hours of the fight, were filled with civilians who had emerged now that the Germans had been cleared out. At last, after five years, they could breathe the air of liberty. Everywhere indescribable enthusiasm reigned. Every inhabitant of Warsaw, man, woman or child, tried to help in some way and to take part in all that was going on. All commanding officers were bombarded by incessant requests for arms. There were cases where boys of twelve and men of seventy begged for a pistol or at least one grenade. They supported their demands by pointing to the posters, which, in staring headlines, made the call: "To Arms!" By the second day's fighting this poster had appeared all over the city. Unfortunately, we had not enough weapons to arm all our soldiers, let alone the civilians. So they tried to help us in other ways. Everywhere I could see people rushing in different directions with bottles of petrol, with bread, with spades or picks. The soldiers with white-and-red armlets were frequently stopped by passers-by who plied them with questions: "Is there anything you need? Perhaps some petrol or blankets? Perhaps a torch would be useful, or dressings, bandages, food?"

In some cases this help proved of decisive importance to the success of our action. For instance, on August 2nd and 3rd, without any specific orders and on their own initiative, civilians put up hundreds of barricades to hamper the movement of German tanks towards our positions, at least two or three on every street. They sprang up before our eyes in a couple of hours. It was quite simple. The inhabitants of neighbouring houses threw out from their windows tables, divans, cupboards, chests—in fact, everything movable they possessed. They tore up pavements and used the blocks of cement, and then, in front of this barrier of miscellaneous objects, they dug a deep trench. I passed one group occupied in this way. Among the furniture taken from a German lodging I even saw a pram! So great was the enthusiasm for this work that the Government delegate had to appeal to the people not to use such objects as pictures, antiques, type-writers or other things of value. Houses on both sides of the street were covered with national flags. The Polish colours, white and red, caught the eye everywhere. I could not help wondering what sort of hiding-places had concealed so many Polish flags through five years of occupation. A closer look at one of them showed me that it was made from a red cushion cover and a piece of white tablecloth.

Every trace of Hitler's domination disappeared—even before I could issue any directive on the subject. I saw people busy taking down German shop signs and street names. Portraits and photos of Hitler and other prominent Nazis were dragged from German offices and hung on the outside of barricades forming the front line. The Germans firing at the barricades willingly or unwillingly hit the face of their Fuehrer and his aides. Every hit was greeted by bursts of laughter and applause from the Warsaw crowds.

Suddenly, I heard shouts from one of our look-out posts: "Don't fire! We are bringing in a captured armoured car!" One of the many taken in the vicinity was pushed to an assembly point. People in the streets reacted with shouts and applause at the sight of the Polish eagle or the uniform which they had not seen for five years and when they saw German prisoners or captured arms. In this case, a window was flung open and a loud-speaker started up the song "Warszawianka," the Polish revolutionary song composed 114 years before. Everyone in the street, whether passing by or busy at the barricades, stood to attention and joined in the song. I was deeply affected by the fervour of the crowd. I think those moments were my happiest of the whole war. Unfortunately, they were short-lived.

On my return to the Kammler Factory, I found reports awaiting me on the incredible bestialities being practised by the Germans on civilians. This cruelty affected all the civilians in districts and buildings still in German hands. At the begin-ning, the Germans had set fire to most of the houses in these districts. The city was covered by a smoky glow. In many cases the inhabitants were not allowed to leave their houses or else not given sufficient time to do so. Thousands of people were burned alive. In Kolonia Lubeckiego the inhabitants were forced to go to the cellars, regardless of age or sex,

and were murdered there by hand-grenades thrown through
the cellar windows from the street. Others were assembled
behind wire in open places and kept there for days. Women
were raped; young men were immediately shot. For the
perpetration of these atrocities, the Germans used soldiers
from the so-called "Kaminski" Brigade, which consisted of
Soviet prisoners who had been freed and enlisted in units
serving the Germans. They were completely savage and
lacking in any kind of human instinct. Later on I learned
that amongst the many victims of these atrocities was M.
Maszynski, a well-known actor, very popular in Warsaw.
He, his wife and his two sisters had their throats cut in their
flat.

Local commanders, reporting these atrocities, asked for
authority to adopt measures of reprisal against the Germans
in their hands. We had already taken over 1,000 prisoners,
in addition to an even greater number of civilians. Even
before the insurrection I had issued orders on the treatment
of prisoners. I forbade lynching and any unauthorised application of justice, stipulating severe punishment for infringement
of these orders. A German prisoner was to be treated in
accordance with international law. I condemned the torturing,
beating or killing of any prisoner without trial. I based my
attitude on the following principles: first and foremost I
wanted the Germans to know that they were dealing with a
regular army and not with a mere crowd of guerrillas. Having
requested combatant status for my own units, I considered
that I should respect the same rights when dealing with the
enemy, even if he did not do so. Also I wished the Polish
soldier to develop a method of fighting completely different
from that of Germans.

From the first day of the fighting, Polish special courts
functioned throughout the city. If a prisoner proved to be a
member of the S.S. or Gestapo, this was sufficient to have
him court-martialled, as it could be expected that almost
every one of them was a war criminal. German civilians were
also subject to investigation before these courts, which were
competent to judge them. In spite of the incredible fierceness
which characterised the fight from its very first moment, I
can vouch for the fact that cases of lynching and individual
persecution were extremely rare on our side. In spite of the
German atrocities, I decided to keep to the principles already

fixed, and I accordingly answered all requests with the statement that my previous orders still held. It was explained to the soldiers that the fight was being waged, not against the Germans only, but against their methods.

Germans who fell into Polish hands were quite convinced that they would be killed. Their behaviour was always marked by complete submission and a desire to buy back their lives by grovelling. It is no exaggeration to say that they competed with one another in the expression of their hatred of Hitler and the Nazis. I had on my Staff a senior officer who a few months earlier had come to Poland from Italy. There he had had opportunity to observe the operations of the 8th Army, including the 2nd Polish Corps under General Anders. He was struck by the difference in the behaviour of the German prisoners. In the hands of American, British or Polish troops on the Italian front, where they knew that they ran no risk, they were very assured and arrogant, flaunting all their fanaticism. Here, in our hands, they were servile and grovelling. Among the prisoners taken in the first week there was a German fireman who belonged to the *Feuerschutz* in Koepenick, near Berlin. A few days before the rising, the Germans had withdrawn all Polish firemen and engines from Warsaw. This had filled us with apprehension, and we concluded that they were going to set fire to the capital. I was struck, therefore, by the presence of a German fireman from near Berlin. The explanation was unexpected. From the prisoner's statement it appeared that Himmler had personally ordered a large unit of the Koepenick Fire Brigade to be sent to Warsaw on the second day of the rising, not, however, to extinguish fire, but as specialists to organise the firing of the city proper and large built-up sections.

On August 3rd we achieved further successes and managed to consolidate our positions in the conquered areas. The main part of the northern district of Zoliborz, which we had lost in the first hours, was once more in our hands. We could still hear artillery on the Russian side of the Vistula and we expected the Red Army in the next few days. It was true that the Russian bombing of German objectives in the city had ceased on August 1st and their night raids had stopped as well, but we argued that bad weather conditions must be responsible. After all, the Luftwaffe was not active over the city either. More difficult to explain was *the complete silence of the*

Soviet wireless on the subject of the Warsaw rising, although it was actually taking place before their eyes—the fires burning in the capital must have been clearly visible to advanced Soviet units within ten miles of our position. It was not till the following day that the situation took a definite turn for the worse.

August 4th. After midnight I turned in for a few hours' rest. After four hours' sleep, I awoke suddenly with a vague feeling of apprehension which I could not at first analyse. In the last three days we had grown accustomed to the noise of the fighting in the city and to the incessant thudding of Soviet and German heavy artillery in the battle outside the city. I had grown to distinguish automatically the noise of tanks attacking our position from that of the explosion of filipinki and the distant but equally clear artillery barrage across the river. I leaned over the balcony, from where I could usually hear the artillery in the east. After listening for a couple of minutes, I realised the cause of my apprehension. The sounds across the Vistula had ceased. In their place, complete silence reigned. In the streets on this side, the battle had in no way abated. Somewhere very close a tank fired from time to time, and the glass of the windows rattled in reply. I woke Grzegorz and the Home delegate, who was sleeping with us. They too were struck by the ominous silence from across the river. We tried to explain it away as a normal lull in the fire which could happen on any front, even at the most tense moments. But the silence continued throughout the day, making more of an impression. None of us could have predicted that it was to last for over five weeks.

*   *   *

Everyone began to feel uncertain about the duration of the fight. When it started, we did not expect it to last for more than seven to ten days and we hoped it would be a matter of only three or four. Once it had begun we were consequently cut off from the outside world and deprived of the means of collecting such information as would give us a true appreciation of the military situation outside Warsaw. Indeed, our only source of information now was our monitoring service and our wireless contacts with various points throughout the country. These sources were unanimous on one point—the fierce fighting going on between the Russians and the 2nd German

Army on a line running from Warsaw through Minsk Mazo-
wiecki and Siedlce. We attached great importance to the
presence of our Prime Minister, M. Mikołajczyk, in Moscow.
We knew that he was in constant wireless contact with London,
and that he was now receiving daily news about the situation
in the capital. For the time being, however, no information
about his talks was given on the wireless. Of his actual moves
all I knew was that on July 31st (i.e. forty-eight hours before
he could have received our message announcing the start of
the fight) he had had his first talk with Molotov and that a
few days later he had had a talk with Stalin. I presumed that
in these talks the question of co-operation between the Soviet
Command and the rising in Warsaw must certainly have
been discussed, as well as the problem of help for the capital.
Impatiently I awaited news from Moscow.

On the morning of August 4th the Germans dropped
leaflets over the city. These took the form of an appeal bearing
my signature, in which I informed soldiers and people that
Mikołajczyk's talks in Russia had ended unsuccessfully, that
the Russians had adopted a threatening attitude towards
him and, as a result, I called on everyone to cease fighting,
lay down his arms and return home. I was one of the first
to learn of my "appeal": the factory next door was
smothered in them and soldiers brought them in to G.H.Q.
at once.

But five years of occupation had developed shrewd instincts
in the people and they were not easily misled. Neither this
nor similar steps subsequently adopted by the Germans
caused the least dissension. German forgeries were guileless
and not difficult to see through.

In the early afternoon German fighters appeared, flying
low, and strafing soldiers and civilians in the streets. Bombers
followed in their wake. Two o'clock saw the first Luftwaffe
raid on Warsaw since 1939. Twenty-four Junkers, flying in
close formation, dropped incendiaries and explosives on Wola
and the centre of the city. For the present, the bombers kept
to a considerable height and had only a small fighter cover.
At four o'clock the raid was repeated.

Another thing which was beginning to impress us was the
sudden and complete cessation of Soviet air activity over the
city. For some days before the rising, Warsaw had been raided
every night by the Soviet air forces. On August 1st, however,

activity ceased. In view of the clear skies, we could no longer attribute this to the weather.

We still held the initiative and we were still on the offensive; the fierceness of the fight and the soldiers' enthusiasm were no less intense, but the cost in ammunition was heavy and we found it was not being balanced by the supplies we took from the Germans. It was the opinion of many district commanders that if the fight continued at its present intensity our ammunition would last no more than another four or five days. In these circumstances, Monter asked me to give him a general directive for future action. This presented me with a very difficult decision. I could not count on an end of the fight in four or five days' time, nor could I be certain that sufficient help would be dropped to us from outside within this period. I attributed our superiority over the enemy tanks to one element: the spirit of the soldiers and the general co-operation of the entire population. I was fully aware that the army under my command was a revolutionary one. Its successes were due to the drive which enabled its soldiers to charge and take a strongly fortified enemy position, often without the help of even a heavy machine-gun. Any order limiting the use of munitions would deprive them of their greatest source of strength, hamper their drive, destroy their initiative and force them to adopt a defensive attitude. Consequently, their morale would have to undergo a severe trial. How would the units then react? Would enthusiasm give place to discouragement? With a heavy heart, I decided to give the order that all commanding officers should enforce rigid economy in the use of ammunition. Henceforth, offensive action should only be undertaken in cases of tactical necessity. Our offensive was accordingly slowed down.

At the same time, I radioed to London, urgently requesting supplies of ammunition and anti-tank weapons. This message was to be sent top priority and repeated on the following days. We were faced with a fight for several more days and we had to be supplied for its duration. I stressed that we would risk everything to keep our hold on the capital and that a correspondingly great effort must be made to help us.

Signal lights, marks and tunes for supply operations to Warsaw had been agreed upon before the rising. Since the second night, special units had been watching in the squares, cemeteries and parks which were in our hands, waiting for the Allied planes. One prearranged tune meant that arms would be dropped the same night, while a second one signified that no operation was scheduled for that night. To-day we had heard a tune announcing a supply operation, but to a point in the country, not to Warsaw. In spite of this, an observer's crew waited that night of August 4th in the neighbouring cemetery of Powązki and the sound of aircraft—different from the throb of German engines—was picked up; after midnight, I myself heard the drone of a plane that was very different from the familiar noise of the Stuka engine. I stepped on to the balcony and saw the signal lights ready. At 2 a.m. a liaison messenger reported to me. He had a tommy-gun hanging from the white nylon cord of a parachute. Apparently two lone Halifaxes had reached Warsaw. Twelve containers were collected, which was, of course, a drop in the ocean in comparison with our needs, but the appearance of the two planes had a great effect on everyone's spirits. As the drops had not been announced that night for Warsaw, I supposed that the Polish air crews had left their course and dropped supplies direct to their capital on their own initiative.

For the time being, food was not so short as ammunition. In the Underground days we had assembled large reserves, sufficient to feed our soldiers for ten days. Since then we had captured large German food stores at Stawki.

It was on August 4th that the Germans first attempted to take the offensive. Their lines of communication across the city were still cut by our troops. True, the bridges across the Vistula had been re-taken by the Germans, but the roads leading to these bridges were all either still in our hands or covered by our fire. Wola blocked their way to the west. Stare Miasto and Mokotów cut their routes north, west and south. Our position in the Post Office Station, which was built across the main Warsaw railway, controlled the main railway from east to west. In the tunnel which ran under the station building our troops had derailed a train evacuating armed German railway guards. Soon afterwards, they destroyed a considerable length of rail. This blocked the line so effectively that throughout the whole rising not one train got through. Prior to the rising, an average of 200 trains had passed through every twenty-four hours. Of the four bridges across the Vistula the Germans could now use only one: the railway bridge north of the city. But even there no train was able to get across. The enemy had replaced the others by two pontoons: one at Siekierki, south of the city, and the other to the north, at Bielany. All German traffic, both Army and supply, was forced to take these two circuitous routes round the city.

It was clear to me that the first German effort would be directed towards opening the main arteries traversing the city proper and cutting a passage to the river across our positions. For the time being, they were still using their tanks, armoured cars and guns for this purpose, suffering heavy losses in the process. Up to the evening of August 4th reports put the figure of tanks destroyed at fifty. All inhabitants, regardless of age and sex, lent a hand. A record was established by a twelve-year-old boy who attacked a Tiger tank when it was on the point of advancing against a barricade, throwing a bottle of petrol at five yards' range. Flattened against the wall, the boy waited for the precise moment. The tank burst into flames. The crew leapt out, their hands up, and were taken prisoner. The small boy was carried shoulder high by his comrades and had definite ideas about a reward. He asked for a soldier's tin hat. His request was at once granted and he was duly presented with an old French helmet of the last war which, funnily enough, happened to be handy. The boy was promptly nicknamed "Tiger." They armed him with filipinki and he managed to knock out and destroy two more tanks. Tiger finally managed to reach the rank of sergeant. And his was not an isolated case. On the same day, in Polna Street, the thirteen-year-old son of a well-known judge, Semadeni, destroyed another German tank, but lost his life in the act. Two hours later, his father fell dead in similar circumstances.

Another method against tanks was minelaying at important cross-roads. But we had very few mines, so we often had recourse to a ruse. Lengths of pavement were painted white and boards on sticks bore the following warning in Polish: "Beware of mines!" Such places were always studiously avoided by the tanks. I was told of a case where a German tank turned back in one central street at the sight of a beer bottle attached with two white strings to the windows of opposite houses. Probably the crew feared a booby trap and thought it was just one more new way of attacking tanks.

On one of the steep streets running down to the Vistula

a garrison of Polish soldiers, defending a house against attacking panzers, rolled wooden barrels covered with aluminium paint down the slope. The barrels bumped and drummed their way over the paving stones. Two tanks at once opened fire on the barrels, making every effort to avoid contact with such doubtful objects.

Besides the Home Army there were the fighting groups belonging to the Communist organisation and the two others affiliated to them. On the fourth day of the rising, the Communist Party (P.P.R.) posted up a declaration in which it called on all its members to take part in the fight and to accept tactical orders from our sector commanders. The same applied to the two other groups, which accordingly occupied the sectors we allotted them. The insurrection revealed their numerical weakness. The Communists mobilised about 400 men, and they fought in the sectors of Stare Miasto, Zoliborz and the city. The Security Corps put up one battalion, which took part in the defence of a central sector. No units of the Polish People's Army (P.A.L.) appeared. At the time the Home Army numbered more than 600 platoons—that is to say, about 40,000 men. The fact that these groups accepted my command was clear proof of the unbroken unity which bound the whole population. They had certain practices peculiar to them, such as the wearing of red scarves. They started to print their own news-sheets, which were posted on the walls beside our newspapers and proclamations. Our mutual relations were at that time correct. The Communists' attitude towards the rising was then positive.

The wireless was still our main source of information and our means of contact with Poland and the outside world. Thanks to it, I was kept informed of the activities of all Home Army units outside the capital. On August 4th I received the news of the following events: diversionary activity in the German rear in Podlasie; the liberation of political prisoners evacuated by the Germans from Rzeszów; the capture at Krosno of four heavy German guns and six A.A. guns. The situation on the Russo-German front in the Warsaw sector remained confused both in German and in Soviet communiqués. To-day, for the first time, the Germans announced the start of the rising. Colonel Hammer, war commentator in the German Information Service, discussing the situation on the eastern front, said: "The attack on Warsaw is being made from three directions, and at the same time partisan units are fighting against forces of German police inside the battle area." Soviet wireless stations still maintained complete silence of the subject of the rising. The announcement in the Soviet war communiqué about their advance on the western bank of the Vistula, close to Sandomierz, was my only information of Russian moves affecting the position of Warsaw.

In the city, the fires were far more numerous now, as a result of the Luftwaffe raids.

August 5th. From early morning, the Luftwaffe attacked Wola. This time the bombers operated without any fighter cover, dropping their bombs at low altitudes, sometimes as low as within 100 feet of the roofs. Where the bombing was near their own positions, they dropped bombs lashed together with cords, to avoid scattering. The whole district was covered with a pall of dense smoke. The people left the burning houses in masses, carrying with them the remainder of their belongings, and went in search of places of less danger. In the early hours of the afternoon a German armoured train started to shell Wola. In the immediate vicinity of my quarters, columns of smoke were flung skywards at short intervals. This smoke soon settled into heavy clouds which filled the sky over the capital. At the same time, tank attacks and infantry onslaughts on our district increased. Across the Vistula the same silence reigned and still no Soviet planes appeared. In the afternoon, German planes again dropped leaflets with my faked signature. This time they announced that the Home Army was parleying with the Germans on the question of common action against Russia.

That day, something happened which looked like the first sign of establishing liaison with the Russians. In the centre of the city our soldiers held up a man who was enquiring insistently as to the whereabouts of the Polish Commander. He was at once taken to Monter. He was a foreigner and was immediately interrogated by the Intelligence Service. When asked whence he came and what he wanted, he replied: "I am a Russian officer under the orders of Marshal Rokossovsky. My name is Captain Konstanty Kaługin."

The Intelligence officer asked whether he had any authorisation or identity papers. Then Kaługin took a miniature identity card 1 inch square from a knot in a red handkerchief. A magnifying glass showed it to be that of Konstanty Kaługin,

officer of the Intelligence Service in the rear from the Czarny
group. He carried no authorisation with him. According to
his story, he was dropped with one companion by parachute
on July 15th in the Lublin district, 150 miles south-east of
Warsaw. His task was to reach Warsaw and make contact
with the Underground. Soviet partisans had helped him to
make his way to Warsaw. He reached the city just before the
rising. The rising itself, and the street fighting, cut him off
from his companion, who carried a radio transmitter and
ciphers. He had failed to find him again and was thus left
without means of liaison. Now he asked Monter for permission
to use our wireless to contact Marshal Rokossovsky's H.Q.
He also asked to be briefed on the situation. This request was
granted and Kaługin received full information both on the
German positions and on our situation. He swiftly noted all
he was told and took it down in code. When asked about the
Soviet position, Kaługin said with great assurance that the
occupation of the city was to be expected within the next few
days and that the Russians, having wiped out three German
armies in the first phase of the offensive, now had an overwhelming superiority in divisions.

Conversation was conducted in Russian and German.
Kaługin spoke perfect German. He was short, athletic in
build, aged about thirty. When questioned about his personal
data, he answered that he was born in, and came from,
Stalingrad. As to his Service record, he stated that he had
done the six years' course at the Academy of Panzer Armies.
He also said that in his previous mission he had been sent into
German territory, where he worked as a Soviet Intelligence
agent. Warsaw was his second war task. Everyone who talked
to him was struck by his mastery of the political situation in
Europe and his knowledge of the history of Poland, Germany
and Russia.

When he met Monter, he suggested that he should send a
signal to Marshal Stalin informing him of the exact position
in Warsaw and requesting help. Monter contacted me at
once. I presumed that the Russians must have been fully
informed by Mikołajczyk about the course of the fighting in
Warsaw. On the other hand, I realised the added value of
information supported by a Soviet officer. I therefore agreed
to send the message. It was transmitted by us to London in
Kaługin's exact words, requesting arms and liaison facilities

with Marshal Rokossovsky. Kaługin's message was supported by a similar radio message from Monter on the following day.

Both were acknowledged by the Chief of the Polish General Staff, London: "Proposals of both Kaługin and the O.C., Warsaw Sector, Home Army, immediately transmitted to Moscow through British channels, as were your previous requests for Soviet attacks from outside. No Soviet answer yet received." No answer, indeed, was ever received from the Soviet Union.

Kaługin offered to help us in any way he could. The Germans were using many units composed of Soviet liberated prisoners to fight against us. Monter's staff suggested that Kaługin should draft a propaganda leaflet to them in the name of the Red Army. He did so at once. It was couched in the best Soviet propaganda style and revealed that Kaługin, in addition to his tank course, must also have undergone a thorough training in political affairs. He stayed with Monter's staff until the day the Russians occupied the suburb of Praga, on the eastern bank of the Vistula. All that time he enjoyed complete freedom of movement and visited all the sectors we held, getting from one position to another through the sewers. It was by this route that he visited my H.Q. in Stare Miasto. When the Russians reached the opposite bank, he crossed the river with our help and joined them. To this day the aim of Kaługin's mission is still a mystery to me.

The two German tanks which we had captured on the previous day were now used in our attack on enemy positions in the old Ghetto, which included a concentration camp of Jews from different parts of Europe. The Germans hardly expected Polish crews to be manning German tanks and at the sight of the approaching Panzers the guards started to cheer in the certainty that relief was reaching them. The camp was overrun. The guards were shot on the spot in retribution for their treatment of the prisoners. Three hundred and fifty Jews were liberated.

In the afternoon, a delegation called on the H.Q. of one of our staffs with a request for arms. This time it was the deaf-mutes from the Institute on Trzech Krzyży (Three Crosses) Square, in the centre of the city. There were twenty-two inmates, men and women, on the first day of the rising; even before then they had belonged to the Underground movement and had worked for us, producing on the institute printing press forged documents and identity cards for members of the Underground. During the rising theirs was to have been an auxiliary task. It was planned that they should sew uniforms for our soldiers and serve in the hospital to be installed in their institute, but in fact these projects were never realised. In the very first hours of the fight the Deaf and Dumb Institute became one of our advance fighting posts, where numerous enemy counter-attacks had to be repulsed. The deaf-mutes were in possession of a few arms which they had themselves collected and concealed. They took up their position near a regular unit and fought as the garrison of the building, serving under the command of their chaplain, a very old priest, who acted at the same time as their interpreter with the soldiers. The deaf-mutes felt the same hunger for news as the rest of the people of Warsaw. Every day, their chaplain gave it out from our Press in sign language, so that they were kept regularly informed. Their only complaint was that they had not enough arms. The delegates tried to explain in their own language to the officers that they should be provided with more arms. It was a truly pathetic sight. These men had already been deprived of so much in life and yet they were ready to sacrifice what still remained to them. In spite of the general shortage, the officers managed to spare them a few tommy-guns and a little ammunition. They certainly deserved it, both on account of the importance of the position they were defending and by the courage they showed in the fight. Later on I awarded decorations to several of them, including a woman.

In spite of every kind of misfortune that befell the civilian population, I continued to receive constant proof that they were meeting all trials with magnificent fortitude and that their morale was high. This applied not only to the people in the liberated areas, but also to those in districts still in German hands; fugitives would slip through the barricades whenever possible and bring in first-hand news. One woman managed to escape from the National Museum, one of the great assembly centres established by the Germans for the Poles who had been expelled from their dwellings. She had already had one escape—when her house was set on fire by incendiary bombs in the cellar. When she emerged alive she was rounded up, along with a crowd of other people from the same street, and sent to the National Museum. In the basement, over 2,000 had already been assembled—most of them had been there for four days. They were left without food or water. Most of them lay motionless on the cement floor, in a state of complete exhaustion. From time to time the German guards would thrust their way through the basement shouting to everyone to get up, ready for a journey. When, with the greatest difficulty, they had all got to their feet and gathered their belongings, they were told to wait again. They had as many as ten to twenty of these false alarms a day. The Germans also constantly threatened them with mass execution. One day, a German military police officer arrived at the Museum. He offered everyone life and freedom if they would persuade the Poles to relinquish their arms and pull down the barricades which were no more than a couple of hundred yards from the building. He proposed that fifteen people should be chosen as intermediaries and gave them half an hour in which to consider the proposal. When he left the basement, a buzz of talk broke out, sounding like bees swarming, and then a man wearing a Gas Company cap stepped forward. Silence fell, and he spoke in a calm, strong voice: "No Pole could ever agree to persuade his countrymen to surrender to Germans. Far better to be shot here with our wives and children than to contribute in the slightest degree to the failure of the rising. We will choose no delegates whatsoever." The last words were taken up by the vast crowd. Any fears were drowned in the general acclaim. Ten minutes later, the German officer received a negative answer. Next day, all the people rounded up in the National Museum were taken out and removed to an unknown destination. Our informant managed to escape on the way; the others were in all probability sent to the concentration camp at Pruszków, near Warsaw.

The situation in Wola grew worse. That the district was the main objective of enemy attacks was clear both from reports and the actual proximity of the attacks. After their unco-ordinated fighting of the first days, the Germans had now organised themselves in this sector. As I had foreseen, their primary aim was to force a line of communication from east to west; this was of vital importance to them if they were to maintain their bridgehead on the Vistula. Wola was the western gate of this line and therefore had at all costs to be cleared as soon as possible. After the first few days, the method of German attack was stabilised. It appeared simple and effective. Before attacking a street, they dropped explosive and incendiary bombs; the bombing was then supported by the fire of their land forces. The German infantry made free use of their flame-throwers, incendiary grenades or simply petrol. The fires, synchronised with further air attack, forced our troops from the barricades and surrounding houses, thus rendering the task of the attacking tanks and infantry easier. In this way the enemy succeeded, in the first days, in driving wedges into our positions.

It appeared, however, that the Germans' lust for destruction was shortsighted. The fire of the burning houses spread swiftly. Our units had time to return to their barricades and take up their former positions, this time between ruins; at least they had no other fire to fear. The fight for a barricade would sometimes last several days. Wola was, nevertheless, exceptionally difficult to defend, surrounded as it was by open spaces like the waste area of the Ghetto and the Jewish and Christian cemeteries. On August 6th enemy tanks had reached Kercelego Square in strength, within 500 yards of my H.Q., and our units were forced out of the cemeteries in heavy fighting. To our rear was the area of the Ghetto and Pawiak, the famous political prison, transformed during the rising into a German fortress which we were unable to overcome. This placed G.H.Q. in the front line of battle, making its work very difficult to carry on. As I have already said, the direction of operations had been left in the hands of Monter. I had at G.H.Q. only a small team to help me in my task of directing the whole Burza operation. The High Command was divided into three separate groups. The first was with me, and so were the Government delegate and the Chairman of the Council of National Unity. In spite of every effort to reduce this team to the minimum, we still numbered more than twenty people, defended only by the 1112 Platoon. Our staff work required constant wireless and messenger liaison with the city, for the exchange of reports. These were numerous and the considerable movement entailed might have revealed the position of G.H.Q. Therefore, we had installed a central liaison point a few hundred yards from the factory. The second command group took no part in actual operations; its departments were ordnance, supply and production. It was stationed elsewhere in the city, but maintained close contact with me. The third group formed a reserve pool of Staff officers, ready to undertake any work in any emergency. We had adapted the work of the Command to the conditions which obtained on the first day of the rising. I personally had full opportunity to observe the psychological reactions of my immediate colleagues. What I saw confirmed my previous Underground experience. Then it had often happened that I was in personal touch with those who were leading partisan groups into action. Some of them, in measure with their own courage, would often take useless risks and show unnecessary bravado. They would, for instance, lead their men in an attack on an armoured train or tank with only a stick in their hands, but if I summoned them for discussions to Warsaw, where they had to observe all the Underground rules of security, some of them would be unable to control their nervousness. Now, during the rising, I observed a contrary reaction. For instance, one of my Staff officers had for years in the Underground era, shown great powers of self-control and outstanding personal courage, but now he was unable to adapt himself to the new conditions. Had I not known him thoroughly, I should have said that he was frightened. This was a direct result of five years of conspiracy and prolonged nervous tension. For some of them, the change-over from a state of continuous potential danger to the open and immediate danger of enemy fire was too swift, but after a short time they returned to normal and could be entrusted with the most exacting tasks in the front line or elsewhere.

The Government delegate, the Chairman of the Council of National Unity, the Chief of Staff and myself all shared one room. We had a luxurious billet. Part of the floor was covered with a thin layer of wadding, discovered in a neighbouring factory, over which were spread curtains. This formed our sleeping quarters—though all we did was to lie down there for a couple of hours or so a day, fully dressed, ready for any emergency. Quite apart from danger, there was always the arrival of important reports or signals from London to be dealt with. Although we were only a few hundred yards from the enemy, my room companions were always cheerful, a fact which greatly helped our work together. I had known the Chief of Staff, General Pełczyński, for a very long time, certainly long enough to know that I could count on him in any situation. The two "civilians" never lost their calm or sense of proportion either. When things got bad, the Government delegate used to insist, with a smile, that he should not be treated as a civilian. "After all," he would say, "I did serve in the 1st Uhlan Regiment thirty years ago!"

Dysentery was beginning to spread. I fell victim to it at this point. It was quite impossible to diet, of course, but the messenger girls were untiring in their efforts to help me and to find a little suitable food. As there was no time for being ill, I was all right again after a week.

On the evening of the 6th, the situation on our sector grew steadily worse. Our factory was under continuous enemy machine-gun fire. Several neighbouring houses had already been destroyed. Liaison was becoming more and more difficult —nearly impossible. I accordingly decided to transfer my quarters to another part of the city in order to have more freedom for the work of G.H.Q. and to avoid complicating the situation for the commanding officer of the local sector. Our only way of withdrawal from Wola was by now through the ruins of the Ghetto, leading to Stare Miasto. The route had been reconnoitred and on August 7th at about three o'clock our Staff was divided into three groups and we decided to move to Stare Miasto. Indeed, this was the only possible decision, since we were completely cut off from the centre of the city. We left the factory soon after three, and for the first time I walked through the Ghetto. Hitherto, I had only seen this mysterious, dead wilderness from a distance, over the high walls which separated it from the rest of the city. Only three points were still occupied by living people, and they were prisons: the military detention prison, the Pawiak and the concentration camp in Gęsia. We had managed to take two of these. But the Pawiak, with its stout walls, barred windows and guard towers, had proved so far to be an unconquerable German fortress, the fire from which covered a wide area of the Ghetto.

As late as the previous day, it would have been quite impossible to walk across in daylight. The Germans had posted machine-guns on the high tower of the prison church, and they covered all routes through the ruins; but now our captured tank had dealt with them. I had watched the incident from the factory windows. The tank knocked down the wall of the Ghetto and took up a good position; its third shot got home, and the church tower was no longer any danger to us. I walked through the Ghetto ruins with the first group of my staff. One hundred yards ahead was our security patrol. We went forward by dashing from one bit of cover to another to avoid the machine-guns of the Pawiak proper. It took us two hours to walk through Stawki. We dashed along the last stretch in single file and finally reached Krasinski Park. There I awaited the return of the first group, who had now gone on ahead to select our new quarters. Jankowski and Pużak had gone with them.

In Stare Miasto, my new quarters were part of a school in Barokowa Street which the Germans had transformed into a hospital. The back of the building touched on Krasinski Square, which we had already named as one of the spots where air supplies for Stare Miasto should be dropped. The school had several stories and from its roof there was an excellent view of the whole of Warsaw's battlefield. Stare Miasto, or Old Town, was a district of high, narrow, ancient houses, characteristic of central European towns in the Middle Ages. Houses and churches, compressed into a small area, huddled together, flanking the narrow streets. The defence of the district was maintained by strongholds, like the Treasury Printing Building on the Vistula side, the Town Hall towards the city centre and the Bank of Poland, among others, on the flanks. We found the situation very different from that in Wola. Stare Miasto was as yet untouched by fire or bombing. True, the air-raids had caused the whole population to take shelter in the cellars; medieval subterranean passages, deep cellars below the old houses, arched courtyards, communicating doors between buildings—all were filled with people. Moving from place to place was an exhausting and difficult procedure, for in the second week of August there were about 170,000 people crowded into the district—something like twice the normal population.

Every day, new waves of refugees from other parts of the city poured in to find refuge and help. The appearance of the actual streets was also considerably altered; pavements had been torn up to provide stones and cement blocks for barricades. The overturned tramcars, carts and miscellaneous furniture of the first days, thrown together in haste by the people, were now being replaced by more suitable material, this time under the supervision of engineers. When the paving stones were taken up the fine Vistula sand was uncovered; one walked ankle-deep in it in the streets. When I watched the defenders of Stare Miasto marching along singly or in groups, I could not help thinking what an extraordinary force this Home Army was, probably the oddest in the world. First of all, there was the incredible mixture of uniforms. The majority were wearing German S.S. uniforms, either taken from captured stores or "leased" from prisoners; at first sight, they looked like the *élite* German troops except for their white-and-red armbands. Mixed with them were Polish pre-1939 uniforms, carefully preserved as relics in hiding for five long years. Tin hats varied too: they were German, Polish, French or Russian—some of them from the last war. Others wore firemen's helmets. Finally, there were blouses or tunics and forage caps of every colour and design, made either in the years of occupation or now during the rising. Another peculiarity was that one-seventh of the force were women. Used chiefly as messengers to maintain liaison with isolated posts and distribute news-sheets amongst soldiers and civilians, they also worked in the medical services and attended to the welfare and feeding of the soldiers.

Women were not allowed to carry arms, since there were not enough for the men, but there were special women's patrols trained in mine-laying and the blasting of holes and passages through walls in the buildings engulfed in the fight. In those hard days I realised that, psychologically speaking, the women had far greater resistance than the men. In my immediate entourage was a girl with the pseudonym of "Basia" who had been Rowecki's and later my messenger right through the long Underground years. In the occupation during this war, nearly all her family had been murdered by the Gestapo, leaving her almost entirely alone in the world, and she devoted herself heart and soul to the Underground movement. Her calm and cheerfulness, even in the grimmest moments, were a tonic to everyone on the Staff.

The first officer to report to me after I had moved in to my new H.Q. in Stare Miasto was Colonel "Wachnowski" (K. Ziemski), who a few days previously had been dispatched to the district by Monter to study the situation. Wachnowski considered it was extremely serious. In addition to everything else, there was the state of chaos produced by the arrival of large numbers of civilian refugees, to say nothing of the influx of units of every type which had been withdrawn from other sectors. Monter appointed Wachnowski commander of the sector and he at once set about organising the defence. In two days he succeeded in restoring order by dividing the sector into four parts. On our eastern flank flowed the Vistula. The enemy on the eastern bank was kept under constant observation from the tall Treasury Printing Press Building. Wachnowski divided responsibilities and tasks and organised medical help and supplies. He used to come every evening and report in detail on the day's operation.

The character of the fighting changed very much after we lost Wola. Fighting with extreme fierceness, helped by aircraft, tanks and artillery, and burning houses systematically one by one, the Germans succeeded on August 9th in breaking through our positions and opening a route to the Vistula at the Kierbedź Bridge. The route was blasted across streets, buildings and gardens. The monument to the Unknown Soldier, which was in the Germans' path, was wiped out. Tanks and German cars rolled over it. Houses on either side of the route were thoroughly burned out; windows and every breach in the charred walls were filled in with bricks to prevent us from flank sniping. About twenty heavy tanks maintained a constant patrol, to and fro, the whole length of the way.

This German wedge completely cut us off from all contact with the centre of city. The fight for Warsaw had now split up into a series of isolated actions. We were cut off from Żoliborz by railway tracks along which patrolled two armoured trains. On the other hand, Żoliborz and Stare Miasto still covered and controlled the main highway towards Modlin, the big fortress to the north of Warsaw. To the south, Mokotów still blocked the southern route from the city. The other three areas left to us, the centre Powiśle and Czerniaków, blocked the way to two of the four bridges and the central railway line respectively. We also held the commercial quays on the Vistula at Czerniaków.

Inside each of these isolated districts, the Home Army was itself surrounding various German points of resistance. They were mostly massive public buildings which the Germans had previously prepared for defence and the capture of which, without heavy guns, required the fiercest and most exacting fighting. We cut off water, gas and electricity from the Germans isolated in these points. Constant efforts were made with tanks to supply them with food and ammunition. These attempts cost the enemy their heaviest losses in armoured cars and tanks, so they changed their tactics and supplied their encircled units from the air, dropping containers from altitudes of between thirty and fifty feet. It was an operation requiring great precision, and often bags of food destined for the enemy fell into our hands. Despite our lack of ammunition and flexibility in our methods of fighting, the battle continued unabated. After the fall of Wola, we managed to hold our positions in the other sectors. Perhaps this was due to the heavy losses in men which the Germans suffered in the first ten days. A prisoner taken on August 10th revealed that his unit, the 494th Infantry Battalion from Zegrze (a garrison town near Warsaw), had lost 50 per cent. of its men in Warsaw between August 3rd and 10th. At the same time, the protracted length of the fight and the slackening of the Soviet offensive enabled the Germans to bring in fresh forces and introduce new methods of destruction. We now had air-raids at regular forty-five-minute intervals. It took just that long for planes to take off from one of the nearest airfields, drop their bombs, return to base, refuel, reload and take off again.

A few days after the first air-raid, the Germans started to use *Nebel Werfer*. These consisted of two mine-throwers joined together, and they proceeded to rain phosphorus bombs and blast projectiles on the city. Large blocks of houses were set on fire by the first, while the second would blast whole storeys away. When in action, the *Nebel Werfer* made an unmistakable recurring sound rather like the lowing of a cow. Consequently, the people nicknamed them "moo-cows." Their sound preceded their actual explosion by a few seconds. At first they caused a certain amount of panic among civilians. Later on, however, as they grew accustomed to it, the noise served to warn people to take what shelter they could in the few remaining seconds. Artillery fire increased daily in intensity. The two armoured trains created havoc in the city. Nearly every day the Germans installed new railway guns and mortars of the heaviest calibre around the city. They also started to use Goliaths, as they were called. These were miniature tanks, filled with explosives and controlled by electricity; they were used to destroy barricades. A normal tank usually controlled the movements of a Goliath. Our soldiers very soon discovered that by destroying or damaging the control wires with a grenade they could immobilise a Goliath, and its 500 kilos of explosives was a very valuable prize. If a Goliath managed to hit a barricade or any other obstacle, it blew up with a tremendous explosion. One tank, often of the Tiger type, controlled three or four of these robots.

Sniping was used by both sides. The snipers usually tried to cross the enemy lines, conceal themselves in the attics of houses in the rear and from there pick off the enemy with accurate fire. We found numerous snipers in our rear and called them "pigeons" on account of the odd little holes in buildings which they used. We used to get bricklayers, well acquainted with the construction of the roofs, to discover their hide-outs. "Pigeons" carried supplies of bread and water for several days, because it was naturally extremely dangerous for them to leave their posts. They were always first-class shots and used telescopic sights. Owing to their activity, streets in our hands often came under their fire and gradually the traffic disappeared, moving through the cellars or along the back of the houses. At many points, notices warned passers-by of danger from snipers.

In spite of their enormous superiority in men and material, the Germans often had recourse to ruses. At the beginning of my sojourn in Stare Miasto, I saw one example at noon in our new H.Q. in the Ministry of Justice. I heard a tank clattering along the street to the accompaniment of shouts and cheers. I leaned from the second-floor window to see a German tank flying a Polish flag and manned by a Polish crew.

"Another tank captured," I thought with satisfaction, noticing the skill with which the driver negotiated the barricade. Men, women and children crowded round, shouting gaily and cheering the crew. Suddenly there was a terrific explosion and the scene was blotted out by clouds of smoke and dust. The force of the blast flung me back from the window as if I had been a feather. Glass and plaster rained down. After a few minutes of complete confusion and stupefaction, I got up and went back to the window—or, rather, the gaping hole where the window had been a few minutes before. When the dust had settled, I could see the results of the explosion. Of the tank crew not the slightest trace remained. The explosion killed about eighty people, among them many children who had joined the cheering crowd. Human bodies were flung as high as the roofs of nearby houses. Limbs were scattered within a wide radius of the explosion. Two corner houses were completely destroyed and part of our building was severely damaged. It was our first encounter with a German booby-trap. The tank had been loaded with explosive, fitted to a delayed-action fuse and left within tempting reach of our positions. I immediately sent out warning instructions to all units. As a result of the blast, I was affected with acute sinus trouble. Every day at a regular hour I was attacked by intense pain which made thinking impossible. My head was swathed in bandages, and this lasted until I left Stare Miasto.

Shortly after my arrival in the Stare Miasto, I got my first news of Renia. A woman with the pseudonym "Anka" told me that she had spoken to her across the street and tried to persuade her to get to the Stare Miasto, because Foch Street, in which she lived, was adjacent to the German positions and consequently not only under constant fire, but also in danger of being overrun by the Germans. Next day we learned that the whole street had in fact been occupied by the Germans, who set fire to the buildings and drove the inhabitants out on to the barricades on Theatre Square (Teatralny), and later in the direction of the Wola quarter, along the freshly-pierced communication artery across the town. Our posts, seeing the civilian convoy, withheld their fire to let it pass. I did not hear anything more till the very last days of the fighting. Renia was at that time awaiting her second baby. At that time most of us were without news from our wives and children; all our families were facing the same peril.

People from the surrounding country used to send us frequent warnings of the arrival of fresh German forces. The same units which a few days before the rising had fled through Warsaw in panic, chaos and disorder had been reorganised and were now being sent back to the capital. Most of them were S.S., police and Luftwaffe ground staff, but we also discovered amongst them tanks from the Hermann Goering, Viking and Totenkopf Panzer divisions. The 73rd Infantry Division was also in action in Warsaw. It had previously defended the bridgehead against the Russians. The slackening of the Soviet offensive had clearly freed considerable German forces, which were then used against us.

From the news which we received from sources outside the city, it appeared that at the beginning a certain general had been responsible for the German forces fighting in Warsaw. His H.Q. was near the capital, at Wilanów (a famous summer residence of the Polish kings, built by Sobieski). About August 8th this general was replaced by S.S. General von dem Bach, whose name was familiar to me. He was an expert in putting down risings in the rear of the front line. Wherever revolts broke out, he was at once sent with his staff. His first step in Warsaw was to drop thousands of leaflets headed "Ultimatum" on his objective. The routine formula was an appeal to the population to come out with white handkerchiefs on their arms; they were warned that the town was about to be completely destroyed and that the same fate awaited anyone who remained. In the case of Warsaw, his leaflets promised all who left the city the chance of settling in western Poland and of finding work there. On this occasion, however, von dem Bach met with no success. After five years of experience, and especially after the mass executions of the Jews, the people of Warsaw suspected that gas chambers awaited them behind these assurances.

August 10th. Using the wireless communiqués and radio reports coming in from our posts outside Warsaw, I was able to piece together what had been happening between the Russians and Germans on the Warsaw front since August 1st. It seemed that the Soviet attack which was progressing on a wide front, had been halted between August 1st and 4th. By counter-attacking, the Germans had managed to recapture Siedlce and Minsk. While this was going on, the sector of the Soviet front nearest to Warsaw maintained its position within ten to fifteen miles of the city. Outlying suburban places like Radość, Miłosna and Sulejówek were still in Russian hands. Nothing in the German communiqués gave any indication that the Russians had suffered a decisive defeat. The Russians still held airfields between fifty and 150 miles of the capital. The Germans had not disposed of the Soviet bridgeheads on the western bank of the Vistula. On the contrary, in some cases they had been widened and strengthened by the Russians. Further south, the Soviet offensive was going very well and had reached places thirty miles west of the Vistula in the hills of Święty Krzyż. Conditions were, therefore, still favourable for a Soviet advance from the south.

The attitude of the Russians in the first days of August did not then destroy our hopes and from day to day we still expected a big Soviet attack toward Warsaw. The main cause of our anxiety was the unbroken and inexplicable silence of

I

Soviet radio stations on the subject of the rising. The silence was in strange contradiction to the oft-repeated appeal for an armed rising broadcast before August 1st. There was also another element. On August 6th, in a broadcast of the Union of Polish Patriots from Moscow, an article from the Red Army newspaper, *Red Star*, was quoted. Its title was "The Black Gang of General Sosnkowski," and it insulted the Home Army, insinuating that it was collaborating with the Germans. This broadcast disturbed us because it seemed to show that our deeds in Warsaw had in no way changed the Russian attitude to the Polish Underground Movement or to its leaders. Radio reports on the course of Burza operations in the country, which came in about the same time, also dashed our expectations, in particular the hope that we would be able to contact the Red Army by our military activities. For it was then that I received the news of the numerous arrests. Without exception, all commanding officers of Home Army units who had led diversionary actions in the German rear east of the Vistula, and had reported at the end of their operations to Soviet military authorities, had been seized. Radio operators also suffered the same fate.

On August 9th I received the following message from the commanding officer of the Home Army units operating in the Radom sector: "Soviet armies supported by the Home Army occupied following places: Szydłów, Stopnica, Bogoria and Pacany. Soviet forces clearly slowing down their advance, despite the absence of any serious German opposition."

The news of the outbreak of fighting in Warsaw, broadcast by the B.B.C. (London) on August 2nd, was relayed by all transmitters of the Allied and neutral nations with the exception of Moscow. On August 7th, the London Communist *Daily Worker* repeated the view of the Soviet Press that the battle in Warsaw was a product of the imagination of Polish *émigré* circles in London.

It was only on August 8th that Moscow gave, at 3.15 p.m., the following radio communiqué:

"The People's Army has staked its young life, its souls and its hearts, to show the world that it can afford a heroic deed of such magnitude, to which other nations can only listen!

"The *provocateur* wireless station Swit, at the service of the Home Army, pretends that it is the Home Army which has risen to action and that it is fighting for the freedom of Warsaw and Poland, and that at this moment all operations by the Soviet Army outside Warsaw have ceased—that from the time they started, the Soviet artillery, formerly so closely audible, has become silent. Do not believe it, citizens of Warsaw! Do not heed it, Heroes! Hundreds of thousands of your friends, the Soviet troops, and with them 120 thousand of General Berling's army, are fighting at the gates of Warsaw and your liberation is only a matter of days. General Sosnkowski and General Bor, the *provocateurs*, are merely evoking derisive laughter by their pretence that the freedom of Warsaw is being bought with the blood of the Home Army!"

This proclamation proved that Moscow was trying to create the impression that the Warsaw rising was being fought by units of the Communist People's Army (an organisation which was capable of putting out only five platoons, as compared with over 600 platoons of the Home Army) and that Communist-sponsored elements were the only real patriotic force in Poland.

We still waited with increasing impatience for results of Mr. Mikołajczyk's visit to Moscow. On August 10th I received a telegram from the Prime Minister, informing me via London of his last talk with Stalin on August 9th. He stated that Stalin had shown a far greater understanding of the problem of the fight in Warsaw in this talk. Stalin explained that he had originally expected the Soviet forces to enter Warsaw about August 6th, but that they had been halted by the German counter-attack. In spite of this, Stalin had no doubts regarding the final issue of the fight and had promised the full support of the Soviet Air Force within the limits of its possibilities.

It was only in the middle of 1945, when I came to London, that I found out the following details of the talks in Moscow, which throw a certain light on Russia's attitude towards the Warsaw rising. Directly after his arrival, Mikołajczyk, in his talk with Molotov on July 31st, forecast a rising inside the city at any moment. Molotov's answer to that announcement was that the Soviet armies were only some six to seven miles from the outskirts of Warsaw, and never even gave the slightest indication that he considered the rising as premature or aimless. In his next talk—this time with Stalin on August 3rd—Mikołajczyk was able to announce the rising in full

progress in Warsaw, and requested facilities for transport
there without delay, immediately after Warsaw's liberation,
in order to set up a friendly government, based on the four
main parties and the Communists. Evidently the proposal
did not meet with Stalin's approval, as the only comment it
evoked was that the Germans were still in Warsaw.

On the other hand, on Mikołajczyk's direct appeal for aid
for the fighting city in the form of airborne supplies, Stalin
replied (according to the protocol of the Stalin-Mikołajczyk-
Romer talk, August 3rd, 1944): "What sort of an army is this
Home Army of yours, without artillery, tanks or air force?
It has not even enough light arms to fight properly. In terms
of modern warfare, it is just nothing. Those are small partisan
units and not a regular armed force. I hear that the Polish
Government has ordered these units to drive the Germans
out of Warsaw. I do not understand how they can possibly
do it; they have not enough force. Besides, these people are,
on the whole, not fighting the Germans; they are only hiding
in forests. They are not capable of doing much more than that."

This was Stalin's attitude on August 3rd.

On August 6th, Mikołajczyk, Grabski and Romer held a
conference with representatives of the so-called Lublin Committee, in the persons of Wasilewska, Osóbka-Morawski, Andre
Witos and Zymierski (the latter had left Warsaw only shortly
beforehand and suddenly reappeared on the Soviet side).
On Mikołajczyk's demand for adequate aid for the Warsaw
insurgents, Wasilewska answered: "I think that there must
be some misunderstanding. You gentlemen must be badly
informed about the situation in Poland. As far as Warsaw is
concerned, people who left the capital on the 4th and arrived
in Lublin yesterday unanimously confirm that, apart from a
bomb-attack on a motor car on the corner of Koszykowa
Street, there has been complete quiet in the city for the last
four months. Also we made sure in the Soviet Information
[Intelligence] Bureau that, until that date at least, there has
been no fighting in Warsaw at all."

When Mikołajczyk tried to quote the German radio regarding
the progress of the rising, the only answer he received was
constant reference to eyewitness accounts that there was no
fighting in progress in Warsaw.

Mikołajczyk's second and last interview with Stalin took
place on August 9th. Stalin's only reply to his repeated requests

for immediate aid for the insurgents was that he had reckoned initially with the liberation of the capital on the 6th, but that a German counter-attack had upset his plans. He also spoke of four to five German Panzer divisions operating in the vicinity of Warsaw, when, in fact, there were only three (the Hermann Goering, the Viking and Totenkopf Standarte). After prolonged argument, in the course of which Stalin kept on coming back to the great difficulties of bringing aid to Warsaw, he finally agreed to the parachuting of a Soviet liaison officer into the capital, together with a radio-transmitter and equipment for establishing a link, on condition that the Polish side would submit detailed proposals as to the place and method devised to receive him.

I then received the following signal from the Commander-in-Chief, General Sosnkowski:

"Stalin has promised Mikołajczyk to give early assistance to Warsaw and particularly to parachute arms. To contact the commander of the Warsaw garrison, a Soviet liaison officer, with ciphers, will be parachuted. In order not to delay this help, I sent, without contacting you, the following message to Moscow through the British Embassy: 'Parachuting a Soviet officer to the city is not safe owing to technical reasons. Our troops are ready to receive him at any time in Kampinos Forest, whence he will be directed to the commander of the Warsaw garrison. Location: 22° 46′ Greenwich longitude and 25° 18′ latitude [one kilometre south of Truskaw]. Alternative point: 20° 40′ longitude, and 52° 19′ latitude [seven kilometres east of Truskaw and fourteen kilometres north of Blonie Station].'

"During night, ground will light signal of six lights in arrow formation, indicating wind direction. Fly over arrow. Approaching plane will signal, flashing letter D. Ground answer: letter K. At both points jumps can be made by day or night. During day, points may not be marked. Parachuted officer, on landing, will shout '*Janek*' and ground personnel will reply '*Kazik.*'

"Help required most urgently centre of the city. Warsaw requests supply of automatic and anti-tank weapons and German ammunition: 7·92 mm. and 9 mm. in area of Napoleon Square (direction of flight, Swietokrzyska Street) and area of Krasinski Square (direction of flight, Długa and Nowolipie Streets).

"Posts in Kampinos Forest request arms for 3,000 men.

"Warsaw requests air bombing of following objectives:
"Okęcie and Bielany airfields, Citadel fortress, Central
Institute of Physical Training, and Bema fort. Precision
bombing is required, as Polish units are in the proximity.

"*(Signed)* SOSNKOWSKI."

This dispatch was never answered, either, and Stalin's word
was broken once more.

From our viewpoint, it was clear that all our efforts and
plans, all our tactics and actions, had to aim at one thing: to
hold out until the Russians renewed their offensive on a large
scale. We could only do this if we received an immediate
supply of arms and ammunition from outside. Our situation
did not permit of delay for international discussions. Up to
August 11th, we had seen in all five Allied planes over Warsaw
—two on the night of August 4th and three on the night of
August 8th. We had consequently received no more than five
air supplies, which was hopelessly inadequate. I was fully
aware of the technical difficulties which British planes had to
face, starting as they did from bases 1,000 miles from Warsaw.
There was something ridiculous about the situation, when
Soviet bases were no more than fifty miles away. But neither
soldiers nor civilians could understand the Allied difficulties.
Everyone in Warsaw knew that in eastern Poland there were
American bases for shuttle-bombing operations. Everyone
knew, too, about the bombing of Bucharest, Ploesti and
Koenigsberg, all of which were further from English bases
than was Warsaw. Finally, everyone knew of the existence of
the Polish Air Force. It had taken part in the Battle of Britain
and later in all operations over Germany. In all, this Air
Force had suffered over 2,000 casualties. Everybody had
heard the B.B.C. praise Polish operational achievements on
land, sea and in the air—in Norway, at Tobruk and Monte
Cassino, and just now in the Falaise Gap. That was why the
population of Warsaw and the defenders of the city were
unable to understand the argument that air operations over
the capital from British bases were impossible on account of
the heavy losses. According to our calculations, the supply of
5 tons of ammunition every night would have been sufficient
to enable us to hold our positions and prolong the fight.
Supply on this scale could have been furnished by a regular

flight of five planes daily. In view of the fact that 1,000,000 people were being threatened with massacre by the Germans, the argument that the operations would prove too costly in air-crews failed to convince anybody.

Therefore, in addition to the messages requesting help which I radioed to the Polish Government in London, we decided—Jankowski, Puzak and I—to send one direct to President Roosevelt and Mr. Churchill:

"In this desperate struggle, strength of spirit without weapons will not suffice. In the name of the principles that right and justice shall overcome might, in the name of the Atlantic Charter and of the Four Freedoms, confident of having fulfilled our duty to defend the independence of our country, confident of the just part we have played in the war effort of the Anglo-Americans, we have the full right to address to you, Mr. President and Mr. Prime Minister, this ardent appeal for immediate help to be sent to wounded Warsaw.

"These words spring from the deep conviction that help will come from you, the leaders of the great nations of the United States and Great Britain."

Independently of the military and civilian authorities, appeals had also been sent, on their own initiative, by the trade unions and the P.P.S. to the British Labour Party, by the women's associations, and so on.

At the beginning of the rising, the Germans had few anti-aircraft guns in the city. I was, however, afraid that the discussion which had developed in the Press and on the wireless all over the world about supplying Warsaw by air would attract German attention and result in the strengthening of anti-aircraft measures.

Consequently, the announcement, made by the Polish Vice-Premier in London, Mr. Kwapiński, and given out by wireless on August 10th, that help would be given to Warsaw in such quantity as to be sufficient, raised indescribable joy in the capital. Several newspapers printed in Warsaw published an extra edition. People gathered in the streets and cheered the Polish Government, the United States and Great Britain. Everybody awaited the coming night in the greatest tension. But that night, just as on the previous ones, the long-awaited British planes did not appear over the city. The next day, however, the B.B.C., at the end of the Polish audition, broadcast the tune "Red Belt," which at that time was the signal announcing air supply over Warsaw that night.

All the squares, parks and cemeteries which had been indicated as dropping points were surrounded by cordons of sentries. Entrance was permitted only to the personnel dealing with the reception of containers. At nightfall, I climbed to the roof of our building with two or three officers to watch the operation. By nine o'clock the enemy fire had slackened and only intermittently could we hear tanks shelling somewhere in the vicinity. Whenever I watched the battle from the roofs of Stare Miasto, I always strained my ears for sounds of fighting outside the city; as usual, there was nothing now but silence from the Soviet lines. In the city, fires raged everywhere; each night anything from twenty to fifty more houses would be burning. Special observers were watching on the roofs round the square ready to give warning of the first sign of the planes.

Down on the square I could see shadowy forms moving towards the middle. Fifteen women from the P.P.S. militia advanced in single file; each one had a hurricane lamp. They formed a large cross in the centre of the square and lay down, watching the starry sky. Near the square were special shock platoons, ready to fight should any containers land in no-man's-land between our positions and those of the enemy. We waited till midnight. Suddenly, a soldier standing near me pointed straight ahead and shouted, "Here they come! Look! Over there! The lights!" And indeed the beam of a searchlight south of the city swept the sky, giving us the first signal. Then another flashed on—and another— and still more. For a time, they wove about and then merged on one point which they led towards us. Immediately after, we heard the sound of guns. We could see tracer shells of four colours exploding against the dark sky—red, green, blue and yellow. And then we heard the unmistakable throb of Allied engines. Now we could clearly see a plane approaching from the south-west. The A.A. increased every minute, filling the sky with flashes, and the Germans opened fire with heavy machine-guns. In the beams of searchlights, we could now easily make out the red, white and blue circles on the wings. The lights still led the plane. The impression was of a gigantic moth flying towards the light. The observers on the roofs gave

the signal: planes were nearing the target. Down in the square
a huge cross appeared in lights; it was the women with their
hurricane lamps. They only lit them at the last moment in
order not to reveal the dropping places or to attract German
mortar fire. The plane came down almost to roof height and
its enormous shadow slid over houses and streets. As it flew
over the square, it left behind six long white wraiths which
opened and slowly floated down to earth. Then more planes.
We counted them by the searchlights which trailed them across
the sky. There were seven. They flew in low. The night, which
had relapsed once again into stillness, was now rent with a
thousand chaotic noises. The A.A. started up again; from
houses, cellars, basements—crowds of people poured into
courtyards and streets shouting, cheering, waving handkerchiefs
and laughing with joy. At last help had come!

Then we were helpless witnesses of a dramatic sight. A
plane coming towards us had been hit and one of its engines
was on fire; from the distance we could see the trail of flame
in its wake. The burning plane came lower. It looked as though
it must crash on the houses at any moment but that very same
second it dropped its load just clear of the ground, near
Napoleon Square. It flew on, crossed the Vistula and only
there, on our horizon, I saw a vast spurt of flame and smoke
rising to the sky. . . .

All the planes had gone now, but throughout the city the
battle raged with new intensity. The Germans lit up the
whole city with searchlights—it was like broad daylight. On
the roofs of the houses we could see the shadows of soldiers
searching for containers. Some had fallen between Polish and
German positions. Our shock platoons, standing by for this
eventuality, rushed in to collect them. One container had
fallen on the sports ground called "Swiss Valley," where the
Polish positions were within 50 yards of the Germans. Fighting
flared up on the whole sector. The Germans tried to stop our
soldiers from reaching the container with a heavy machine-
gun barrage. Three times our attack was repulsed. It was not
till morning that our men succeeded in securing it.

On Three Crosses Square, a container landed on the cupola
of St. Alexander Church, within 200 yards of the Bank of
National Economy, a German stronghold. Four brave men
climbed to the cupola to collect it. A machine-gun burst
killed them all. Others then climbed on the inside, grasping

the cornices, tore open the roof of the cupola and the container fell into their hands through the hole.

Another fell between the electric plant, a Polish position, and the University buildings, still held by the enemy. All our efforts were vain. In the morning, the Germans in their turn tried to collect it, but our tommy-gun fire kept them at a distance from the prize. Germans and Poles prevented each other from approaching it; during the following night the enemy kept it in the beam of a searchlight. Approach seemed quite impossible, and a deadlock ensued, and yet, a few days later, a young man of twenty reported to the Commandant of the electric plant, who recognised him. A week before he had dismissed him from the unit and relieved him of his Home Army armband because the young man was proved to have worked in the German Todt organisation. When the Commandant asked him coldly what he wanted, he volunteered to fetch the container.

The Commandant agreed that he might try, and that same night he made his first attempt. It was not successful; the Germans at once opened fire, barring his way. But on the following night he met with complete success. A faked attack was arranged at another point to distract enemy attention for a brief moment. Under this cover, the volunteer managed, in a series of very slow crawls, to move the container out of sight of the Germans. The rest was easy. He was reinstated immediately in his old unit.

For two more nights supplies were dropped. Each time between ten and fifteen British planes, with South African, English and Polish crews, flew over the city and, from low altitudes, carried out their task with a courage and skill that filled us with the deepest admiration. One Liberator, shot down by enemy machine-gun fire, crashed on the street within 50 yards of my quarters. The crew was killed, but the fire of the plane was immediately put out by people from the neighbourhood. They dismounted the rear gunner's heavy machine-gun and it was used against the enemy that same night from our position at Stare Miasto.

In the city these supply operations resulted in an immediate improvement in the morale of soldiers and civilians alike. We managed to collect 80 per cent. of the containers, which enabled us to continue the fight and even undertake local counter-attacks and the liquidation of isolated German pockets. The soldier, who for days past had had to fight in permanent fear that he would at any moment come to his last bullet, now experienced tremendous relief. He knew that for the next week at least there was no danger of having to cease fighting for lack of ammunition. Besides ammunition, we were supplied with tommy-guns and piats—anti-tank weapons for close-range work—which proved of priceless value to us.

Unfortuntely, our joy over these supplies was brief. On August 13th Moscow broke its two weeks' official silence on the Warsaw rising. That day, Moscow, as well as the B.B.C. from London, broadcast the following announcement on the official Soviet Press Agency, Tass:

"Information from Polish sources on the rising which began in Warsaw on August 1st by order of the Polish *émigrés* in London has recently appeared in various newspapers abroad. The Polish Press and wireless of the *émigré* Government in London have asserted that the Warsaw insurgents were in contact with the Soviet High Command and that this Command had sent them help.

"The Soviet Agency, Tass, is authorised to state that this announcement by the foreign Press is either a misunderstanding or a libel against the Soviet High Command. Tass is in possession of information which shows that the Polish circles in London responsible for the Warsaw rising made no attempt to co-ordinate this action with the Soviet High Command. In these circumstances, the only people responsible for the results of the events in Warsaw are the Polish *émigré* circles in London."

We had listened intently to all the announcements regarding the Warsaw rising, and I never heard that the Polish Government had ever stated that we were in contact with the Soviet Command. The only B.B.C. item which could possibly have caused any misunderstanding in that respect was immediately corrected by a special message to London.

This announcement was the start of a campaign of accusation conducted against the Polish Government and myself by the Soviet wireless. I was represented as the chief cause of all the misfortunes which had befallen the population and of a rising alleged to have been started for political motives.

The Soviet communiqué gave rise to a wave of resentment

and suspicion towards the Russians on the part of the population, as well as the people with me. Two things were still
fresh in our memory: the appeals of the Soviet radio for the
rising to commence and their accusations of inactivity on the
part of the Polish Government and the Underground authorities. Had the Russians announced at the time that they were
not able to liberate Warsaw because of a local reverse which
led to a miscalculation, it would have been understood and
their explanation accepted. Even more difficult to explain
was the Soviet accusation of lack of co-ordination, when the
Home Army units actually fighting side by side with the
Russians and trying to make the appropriate contacts were
disarmed, and their commanders and wireless operators
arrested or killed by the Russian secret police.

The Tass communiqué coincided with the news of Mr.
Mikołajczyk's return to London from Moscow. His talks there
had clearly led to no agreement between the two governments.

From this I concluded that for the moment I could not
count on Soviet air supply or the bombing of German strongholds or airfields. It was then that Monter sent out a messenger
girl with a letter from Captain Kaługin. The contents were
identical with that of his dispatch to Stalin of August 5th,
which had never been answered. The courier was to get
through the German lines and reach Otwock, which was in
Russian hands. There she was to report to the Soviet military
authorities and deliver the letter from Kaługin, together with
a request from Monter for help. We never found out whether
she reached her objective, but the appeal remained unanswered.
If we were to hold on, we had only our own strength to rely
upon now.

It had been decided to start producing arms and ammunition
in the workshops and factories in our areas. We were obliged
to do so even in the present difficult situation because the
prolongation of the fight had used up our reserves. The
Germans had now begun bombarding Warsaw with shells of
the heaviest calibre, the type normally used against reinforced
concrete fortifications. The impact of these shells on the
relatively thin walls of the houses seldom resulted in their
explosion. Special bomb disposal units of sappers were organised whose task it was to remove the fuses from unexploded
shells. The heaviest of these provided us with about 300 kilos
of high quality explosive. Goliaths served us in much the

same way: each one captured gave us 500 kilos of T.N.T. The explosives thus obtained were used for the production of hand-grenades made from empty food cans. We also produced mines, which were our chief weapon in fighting inside buildings. Besides this, we made some primitive but very efficient weapons for street-fighting. For instance, grenade-throwers were made from lengths of water pipe; motor tyres were made into a sort of catapult which projected bottles of petrol from longer range; flame-throwers made from water-pipes of fire-engine hydrants were of great help.

Intensive search was going on for the arms which had been hidden in previous years. Search was sometimes made through strange channels. For instance, one day a man came to tell us that he knew a small farm near the city at Zaborówek where arms and ammunition were buried in 1939. He gave a password, the name of the person on the spot who had charge of them and an exact description of the place. A message was sent to London for transmission to the Home Army commander in whose area Zaborówek was situated, telling him that a certain woman knew of buried arms and ammunition on her farm. A messenger was to be sent to the woman to tell her that he had come from "Limping Joseph to fetch the barley straw." She would then answer that she had "only oat straw." Only then should the messenger ask for the arms. Thus news sometimes had even to go through London to reach the right quarters in Poland. In this case the arms were successfully dug up and, in spite of endless difficulties, they were smuggled through the German lines and finally delivered inside the city.

The question of food supply for the capital was becoming a whole problem of its own. The food reserves which had been collected and prepared for the army before the rising, in the expectation of our fight lasting no more than seven or ten days at the most, were by now exhausted. The basis of our food supply was provided by captured German stores or the requisitioning of shops which had been protected against looting from the very first. Now the civilian authorities, acting on the Home delegate's instructions, introduced rationing and organised distribution among the civilians. People burned out from their houses and refugees from other districts were fed in communal kitchens, where a standard meal was provided for everyone. The civilian attitude was extremely helpful; they willingly shared their private food reserves with each other. The great difficulty was to get stocks through to isolated districts. For instance, the centre of the city had a number of food shops well stocked with such things as flour, barley, dried peas and so on, but completely lacked any sort of fresh vegetables. The suburbs, on the other hand, with all their vegetable gardens, were very short of most other types of food. Interchange between districts was necessary. Horse or motor transport was obviously out of the question on account of the barricades and enemy fire, and the transfer of food became of vital necessity. Other means of transport had to be found. The civilian authorities put out an appeal to all those who wished to take part in the fight, but for whom no arms could be provided. They were asked to report to the authorities and subsequently organised into transport columns. Every night single files of strong, able-bodied men and women could be seen, weighed down by sacks of food, medical supplies and sometimes even ammunition. Through subterranean passages, tunnels, sewers and streets covered by enemy fire, they carried food to the points where it was most needed. Loss of life in the ranks of these transport columns was as heavy as in front-line units. It was, indeed, organisations of this kind which made it possible for Warsaw to carry on the fight for sixty-three days.

Transport columns were not the only means of combating hunger. As soon as it was clear to me that the fight was likely to last far longer than we had anticipated, I instructed our commanders near Warsaw to order farmers living in the country immediately surrounding the city to refrain from fighting and to direct all their efforts towards supplying the capital with food and ammunition. I considered that their help with supplies would outweigh their fighting value.

The farmers' organisations were of great assistance. They co-operated with the local commanders and started secretly to collect foodstuffs for delivery to trustworthy people in villages such as Wilanów, Piaseczno, Rzeszno and Pruszków. Peasants who were in the secret then carried the food to selected people, handing it over with the prearranged formula: "For Monter from Censorship." These people, in their turn, took it to Kampinos Forest and sometimes, when possible, they smuggled small quantities directly into the city with the help of local peasants. The plan began to work, and in this way some districts in Warsaw were able to supplement their food reserves. The scheme continued until the evacuation of the population from suburban villages by the Germans.

In spite of the hell which Warsaw became, the life of the people followed a general pattern evolved after two weeks of fighting. There was a front line on the barricades and in the strongpoints where firing went on and attack succeeded counter-attack. This front line made a fantastic pattern. Where it crossed courtyards or ran between the storeys of buildings, it often happened that the Germans held the basement and ground floor, while the Poles occupied the upper floors—or vice versa. As close as 20 yards behind the actual fighting there were hospitals, medical points, social welfare centres, the Press and the civil authorities. All these services were trying to organise life in the inferno as far as possible. Actually, there was not a single place in Warsaw which was out of range of artillery fire, incendiaries and mines, or grenades and bombs. Raid followed raid in such quick succession that from dawn to dusk the whole city lived in a state of continual alert. Every day, in nearly every street, more houses fell victim to the Luftwaffe. These were the circumstances in which the civilian and military authorities had to work in their efforts to prevent panic and anarchy developing.

Valuable help in the problem was provided by the Home Army Press. In the second half of August, there were at least fifteen newspapers in Warsaw. To overcome the difficulty of distribution, each district had its own issue. For instance, Stare Miasto had the *Warszawianka*, Mokotów the *Baszta* (Bastion), and Powiśle the *Barykada Powiśla* (Barricade). In addition, all the political parties published their own papers. The popularity of all these issues showed a thirst for news and proved the desire of the people to express their political views freely or to discuss plans for Poland's future. For five years such practices had been rigidly suppressed. During that time the Army had had to control the underground news-sheet, *Biuletyn Informacyjny*. It had appeared every Wednesday with unfailing regularity; and every Thursday the new issue had appeared on the desk of the Gestapo chief with equal promptitude. Every week it had been sent to him by post, completely fooling the German authorities.

During the rising this *Biuletyn Informacyjny* appeared daily

right up to the final day of the fight. Twice its printing press
was completely destroyed by air attack. Twice the printing
staff suffered heavy losses, but not once did the paper fail to
appear. A few newspapers even had illustrated supplements in
which appeared photographs of the street-fighting, sketches
and cartoons. To meet a rapidly developing need, information
centres were formed. The situation in the city naturally
tended to encourage rumours which spread like wildfire and
might well have resulted in panic. As a counter-measure to
this danger, we issued a communiqué every evening which
included an exact account of the day's fighting, precise figures
of our booty, losses on both sides and so on. To anyone who
was not in Warsaw during those grim days, these daily
communiqués would doubtless have seemed boring and
monotonous. They usually told of the occupation or destruction of some building, factory or park. But every detail of this
sort was news of the deepest interest for every man and woman
in the district in question. It was as important to them as
the taking of, say, Paris, was to the outside world during
invasion days. Positions changing hands in the immediate
vicinity of their houses could have direct influence on their
immediate future. Their lives and fate depended very much,
for instance, on the result of the fight for the Post Office
Station, the Borman Factory, the Town Hall or the Siemens
Arcade. It was for this reason that those communiqués were
read with breathless interest, and news of the destruction of
two German tanks in Warsaw raised far more enthusiasm
than the destruction of whole Panzer divisions in Normandy.
One was distant, the other close and urgent. Similar communiqués were issued by Monter in the centre of the city and by
other commanders about the fighting in their own sectors.

I did not introduce censorship. I considered that the security
of every individual was so deeply involved and the feeling of
responsibility so widespread that no control was necessary.
Censorship was accordingly replaced by regular Press conferences, which were held daily, even during the fiercest battles.
Editors sometimes had to travel a long way to these meetings,
at which Communist papers were also represented. Paper was
allotted from a central distributing centre. At the conferences
we gave editors confidential information off the record, as
well as the news for publication. Nothing of a confidential
nature was ever divulged.

In spite of the number of papers published, the supply was still inadequate in some cases. Frequently, papers failed to reach points very distant from the printing press because people often relieved the girls who distributed them of all their copies before the rounds were completed.

So we had to find additional means of getting news to the people. For this we started special loud-speaker patrols which broadcast on public squares several times a day. At the same time they took the opportunity to supply Germans with the news. They would approach to within a short distance of the enemy positions and speeches in German were delivered, asking them to surrender. The usual immediate result was a furious outburst of fire in the direction of the loudspeaker. To avoid this danger, sham loud-speakers of cardboard were set up in obvious positions. They attracted the fire while the real instruments went on working in concealment. The ingenuity shown by these wireless patrols tickled our sense of humour even in the most tragic days. For instance, at one point they threatened Germans surrounded in a strongpoint with the use of a new weapon, the V6. It was described as a crawling mine which would climb the walls of buildings and explode only when it reached the floor occupied by the enemy.

A State security corps (P.K.B.) was instituted by the Government delegate to maintain order in the city. Its main tasks were to ensure discipline among civilians, to prevent lynching and looting and to oppose the German fifth column. To prevent German snipers from infiltrating into our positions in disguise, two measures were adopted: special identity cards for soldiers of the Home Army and control points for the checking of passers-by. It was forbidden for people to move about the city after dusk unless they were in possession of the password, which was the same for the whole of Warsaw, even the isolated districts, which were informed of it each evening by coded radio message. The doors of houses were barricaded from within with bricks and earth. For purposes of circulation, narrow passages were left open, allowing one person to squeeze through with difficulty. Even these were closed at dusk and closely guarded during the night by sentries who consisted for the most part of the inmates of each house concerned. Nearly every house in Warsaw became, in effect, a strongpoint ready to defend itself against enemy attack from without. The inmates lived a life of their own. They usually had

communal meals together in one kitchen, shared the same
shelter and in many cases all lost their lives at the same
moment. Every courtyard had its altar; I do not remember
seeing a single one without. A life spent in constant touch
with danger had the effect of deepening religious feeling to a
degree I had never seen before. At countless altars in the
courtyards, priests celebrated mass for the people. One priest
would often say as many as three masses a day. I remember
once, during an inspection, I passed through a courtyard
which had been hit a few hours previously by a heavy shell.
In the centre the inmates were saying their evening prayers
together, kneeling before a small heap of shattered plaster
which was all that remained of a statue of Christ.

On August 17th the German radio announced for the first
time that they had wiped out the "Warsaw Revolt." They
chose to do so at a moment when the greater part of the city
was still in our hands and we were blocking the communication
lines which crossed Warsaw. That same day, the Germans
adopted new tactics. They started to shell the city with heavy
railway guns which they had previously used in the siege of
Sevastopol. News reached me from outside the capital that
one of these heavy guns had been mounted near Płochocin,
fifteen miles from Warsaw. The shells were 600 mm. in diameter and nearly 2 metres long. They weighed $1\frac{1}{2}$ tons, and
the blast of their explosion could destroy whole blocks from
top floor to basement. The Germans showed great precision in
the use of these guns, directing their fire on definite points of
strategic importance. For instance, they aimed at district
commands, wireless positions, stores and dumps. The first
shell fell in the immediate vicinity of Monter's H.Q. but
luckily failed to explode.

On the same day, German envoys for the first time approached
our positions in Saxony Park under cover of a white flag.
They handed the Polish officer who met them a letter addressed
to Monter and signed by General von dem Bach, who was
commanding the German forces in Warsaw. The letter called
for surrender, promising the insurgents combatant rights.
Should this proposal be rejected, General von dem Bach
threatened the city and its inhabitants with complete annihilation.

The German letter caused not the slightest doubt or hesitation either amongst Monter's staff or my own. To begin with,

all my hopes and expectations were still based on the certainty of an early renewal of the Russian offensive, which would result in the occupation of the capital. It was the only solution to our present difficulties that any of us could foresee. I could not believe that the military situation which had recently developed could last unchanged for more than one or two weeks. In our opinion, based on past experience, capitulation would only mean the massacre of soldiers and civilians alike. The Germans had broken their word too often to inspire us with any confidence now. They had always called our Home Army soldiers *banditen*. If taken prisoner, our men were shot or hanged. Civilian men, although they had taken no part in the actual rising, for the most part met with the same fate. Other civilian prisoners were evacuated to the west with brutality and confined in a camp at Pruszków. We knew nothing of their ultimate fate. In these circumstances, it was difficult to have any doubt that our only course was to hold out and continue the fight.

I ordered Monter to leave General von dem Bach's letter unanswered. Instead, we had an opportunity to give the enemy an explicit answer in another way. We intended it as a reply to two of their efforts: their call for capitulation and their announcement that the rising had failed. For the purpose, we used the wireless station Błyskawica, which broadcast in Polish, English and German and was picked up in England for the first time that day. This very fact clearly proved to the world that Warsaw had by no means relinquished the fight. Our failure to surrender was further emphasised by an offensive which had now begun on isolated German positions.

This offensive was made possible by the arms and ammunition which had been brought in by Allied planes and by our own arms production, especially of flame-throwers, and in the course of three days it brought us a series of successes. One of the main German bases in the centre of the city, Cedegren, the massive concrete building of the Telephone Company, was captured. Cedegren was one of the highest buildings in the capital. The surrounding streets had been under constant and direct fire from its well-armed garrison, and the life of the whole district had been paralysed. Ever since the first day of the rising our troops had tried to overcome it by every means at their disposal, but all attacks had been repulsed. It looked as though we should never be able to

force a way into the fortress without artillery. Monter therefore
maintained a tight blockade. Water, gas and electricity were
cut. The nearest enemy position, in Saxony Park, was not
more than 100 yards away, and the Germans made several
attempts to send supplies of food and ammunition from there
in tanks. Two tanks did manage to reach the building, but all
further attempts were successfully frustrated by our troops.
All subsequent tanks and armoured cars sent from Saxony
Park were burned or destroyed. When the Germans had lost
seven of these vehicles through mines or piats, they refrained
from further attempts.

The main credit for the capture of the building went to a
worker of over sixty. He had been a technician working for
the telephone company and knew the building inside out.
He reported to one of our units at the very beginning of the
rising, asking to be enlisted and given some sort of arms.
His request was refused. He was told that there were not
enough arms for men far younger than himself, that he was
too old and unfit for active service. They advised him to join
some working party.

But the old man was undismayed and went on in his own
way. Adjoining the telephone building on its western flank
were the ruins of houses destroyed in 1939. Working at night,
he dug a passage under the ruins, utilising some of the cellars
of the destroyed houses. Through this passage, which, when
finished, was about 100 yards long, he succeeded in reaching
the actual building and in getting into its cellar through a
small window. The work took him over two weeks of hard
effort. Having achieved his aim, he reported to the local
commander and informed him of the existence of the secret
passage into the building. At 2 a.m. the following night a
patrol of engineers went along the passage, laid mines and
blasted a wider opening through which the main attack was
then led. The Germans were taken completely by surprise.
A battle of fierce intensity developed inside, as every floor and
every corridor was barricaded. Our troops used mines for the
most part, blowing passages through walls from one part of
the building to the other. Particularly efficient was a women's
patrol called "Minerki" (Mine-laying Women), which before
the rising had specialised in the mining of railway tracks and
bridges. Good use was also made of flame-throwers. The battle
raged in clouds of acrid smoke which took away the men's

breath. The Germans obviously thought they had nothing to lose. They withdrew from one floor to another, fighting viciously. When, after eight hours of this, our men reached the tenth story in the tower oi the building, which was already on fire, they realised with astonishment that the Germans ahead of them had disappeared. On reaching the top floor, they had all swooped back to the cellars down a huge fireproof tube which carried the telephone cables from top to bottom of the building. Thus the battle which started in the cellars and was fiercely contested floor by floor to the roof returned ten hours later to the cellars, where the enemy was finally wiped out with flame-throwers. Only 116 Germans were taken prisoner; the rest lost their lives in the flames, but the building itself was saved from destruction.

A few hours before the reduction of the German garrison, a yellow flag was flown from one of the upper stories. This was an S.O.S. to the enemy units in Saxony Park and to the Luftwaffe. But the blockade proved to be thorough and effective. From a distance of 100 yards, helpless Germans were obliged to look on while one of their main strongholds was overpowered. The workman who initiated the forcing of the building was lightly wounded when a bomb exploded. His service was rewarded with a revolver and ten cartridges.

On one of the prisoners, our men found a diary which was later brought to me by messenger through the sewers. It was a pocket diary belonging to a certain Kurt Heller from Munich. Daily entries illustrated clearly both the feelings of the Germans and the dramatic aspects of the fight which had now been going on for three weeks.

I quote a few extracts, taken verbatim from a copy of *Biuletyn Informacyjny*, subsequently brought to London:

"1.8. This afternoon beginning of street fighting in Warsaw.

"2.8. We are still surrounded.

"3.8. Ulrich killed. S.S. Sturmfuehrer killed and many others.

"4.8. Still cut off. No help from outside. We expect relief to-day or to-morrow. No food. Water very short.

"5.8. Rudolf killed. Others with him. Can't keep going much longer. Luttewitz killed. Hollweg badly wounded.

"6.8. At noon shelled by own artillery; no losses. Attempt at sortie failed, one killed, four badly wounded, of which one died. Fourteen of us now killed. Buried at eight this morning in the courtyard. Bad air from the dead; they smell.

"8.8. Our men 100 yards away, but opposition of bandits too strong.

"9.8. Food very scarce.

"11.8. All remainders taken by police, even our cigarettes. Situation no good for resistance.

"12.8. Hunger acute. Every day only a drop of soup and six cigarettes. Police have taken everything from us. Was not even allowed to keep a bit of jam. When will these sufferings stop?

"13.8. Heavy fire from tanks on bandits' positions. Our tower often hit, but no losses. Tank brought food for five days. When shall we be freed?

"16.8. Terrible hunger. At night we are terrified. When first stars appear, think of home, wife, and my boy, who is buried somewhere near Stettin. Can't take it all in. Now am in same position.

"17.8. Poles tried to smoke us out by fire and bottles of petrol. More men lost their nerve and committed suicide. Frightful smell from corpses in the street.

"18.8. Completely cut off from outside world.

"19.8. No hope of relief. Surrounded by Poles. Who will be next for the mass grave down in the courtyard?"

A characteristic note in the diary is the mention of the German police. In nearly every German unit were a few S.S. men and military police, who controlled the others, and forced them to fight, sometimes by terror methods.

In the next few days, the units in the centre of the city were able to make further advances. The result was the liquidation of more German strongholds and the capture of priceless ammunition. The fight for German police head-quarters was exceptionally fierce. The actual battle took place in the adjoining Church of the Holy Cross. Inside this house of prayer a fierce struggle raged in which both sides fired and threw grenades at 10 yards range. The heart of Frederick Chopin, walled up in one of the pillars, was witness of the battle. Just before the end, the Germans set fire to the church. Roof and towers were burned through, but the heart of Chopin was untouched. The flames did not reach the pillar where the urn was immured.

Most of the prisoners taken at Police H.Q. had served in Warsaw for the last four years and had distinguished themselves by their bestiality towards the people. Our special courts had a clear case for establishing their guilt as war criminals.

Air supply by the R.A.F. on an adequate scale lasted only three days: August 12th, 13th and 14th. Then it stopped almost entirely. From time to time single planes still appeared over the city, but the help they brought was too small to be of practical value. The Soviet attitude towards the rising did not allow us to hope that help by air would reach us from that quarter, although clearly this would have been the easiest way. I based my calculations on the hypothesis that the Russians would ultimately start an offensive on the Warsaw sector and that our policy meanwhile must be to hold on until such time as they did. At the same time, replenishment of our dwindling stocks of food and ammunition was a vital necessity for the continuation of the fight—a point which was thoroughly appreciated by the leaders of the political parties as well. I received a visit from two representatives of the Peasant Party (P.S.L.) at my H.Q. in Stare Miasto. They suggested that I should order all the units of the Home Army in the country to march on Warsaw for the relief of the capital. They considered that this would mobilise the peasant element in the Home Army and that effective diversion in the enemy rear could be carried out. This, they thought, might force the enemy to divert part of his forces and to some degree relieve the city. My opinion was that the scheme would not alter the situation to any great extent. The German blockade of the city, already effective, was daily growing in strength. The possibility of units breaking through into the capital could not be seriously entertained. The only advantage which might result was a rise in the defenders' morale. I thought, too, that units approaching us from all over the country could bring stocks of arms which might subsequently be smuggled into the capital. Bearing this in mind, and hoping that an increase in partisan activity in the enemy rear would hinder his lines of communication and force him to disperse his units, I accepted the suggestion of the Peasant Party leaders and sent the following message to London:

"Repeat following order *in extenso* through B.B.C.: 'Home Army Command, August 14th, 1944. 10.30 hours. The struggle for Warsaw is prolonged. It is faced with an overwhelming enemy superiority. The situation demands an immediate march to help the capital. All available, well-armed units should proceed at once by the swiftest possible means towards Warsaw. They will attack enemy strength on the perimeter and in the suburbs of the capital and subsequently break into the city to help the defenders.

" 'Bor,
" '*Commander, Home Army.*' "

Realising that the result of this plan would be limited, I decided to adopt another scheme for the help of the capital from outside. North of Warsaw, within five miles of the outskirts, is the vast Forest of Kampinos, about thirty miles long and ten wide, lying along the western bank of the Vistula. For eighteen months it had been an assembly area for our partisans attacking German lines of communication. Just before the rising, the strength of the Home Army in the Kampinos area was increased by the arrival of further units which had been harassing the German rear in the east and had now reached the forest, after covering a distance of some 400 miles. My appeal, broadcast by the B.B.C., had provided further strength in the form of the newly mobilised peasant units. I appointed Captain "Szymon," who had previously commanded the Palmiry-Młociny sector across the Vistula, to the command of the whole Kampinos force. When he took up his new appointment in mid-August, he had 4,000 men. Later, in September, the figure rose to 7,000.

I received a reply to my daily-repeated requests to London for help. In view of the strength of the A.A. artillery in Warsaw, air supply over the city was not possible; the losses involved were too great. I therefore asked that the supplies destined for Warsaw should be dropped in the Kampinos area; both dropping and collecting would be possible in the forest and the supplies could subsequently be smuggled into the capital. At the same time, I gave Szymon the relevant orders. The Forest of Kampinos was now to be the supply depot for food and arms for Warsaw. It was there that agricultural supplies should be concentrated; it was there, too, that supplies of arms would henceforth be dropped. Home Army units throughout the country could be expected to concentrate in the area. From them should be collected all available arms and ammunition which must be given to fighting Warsaw.

The Forest of Kampinos is separated from the northern suburb of Zoliborz (which was still in our hands) by an open, treeless strip one and a half or two miles in width. In this stretch is situated the airfield of Bielany and across it runs the main road from Warsaw to Modlin, a vital communication line for the German front. Szymon decided to use 90 per cent. of his forces in an attempt to overrun the airfield and open up a permanent way through to Zoliborz. He instructed his cavalry simultaneously to aim at the cutting of the main road. In the initial stages he met with success: the airfield was taken and the main road cut. Unfortunately, however, his cavalry were unable to keep up a protracted defence against the tanks and armoured cars which now attacked from the direction of Modlin. The Panzers succeeded in recapturing the airfield. Our Home Army units were obliged to withdraw to the forest, having lost over 100 in killed and wounded. Szymon was among the latter. The failure of the action forced the forest units to adopt other tactics. One of the battalions was reorganised into carrier platoons which smuggled food and the supplies dropped by the R.A.F. by night through to Zoliborz. Each man carried between 60 and 100 lb. on his back. Other units from the forest organised a series of diversionary attacks to distract German attention and enable the transport platoons to get through.

The Germans tried to stop the activity of the forest units by setting fire to the woods from the air, but at each attempt the partisans succeeded in mastering the flames. The forest had now become a supply depot of great importance because the R.A.F., after they had found the losses incurred over Warsaw too heavy, had, in accordance with my request, directed all their supply operations to the forest, and they kept this up to the end.

Our units in Kampinos continued their allotted work to nearly the end of the rising. Almost daily battles were fought against the Germans, inflicting substantial losses upon them. Although the enemy ring separating the forest from Zoliborz was drawn tighter and tighter, our men never relaxed their efforts to get supplies through to the capital. It was not until the end of the rising, when the whole forest area was surrounded by the enemy, that Major "Okoń" and his men cut through the German lines and tried to force their way further south to larger forested regions. On their way they were surrounded by considerably superior forces and these, with the help of two armoured trains, finally liquidated them.

Zoliborz, as the nearest point to Kampinos, derived the greatest profit from the supplies. One of my intentions therefore was to open up a communication between Zoliborz and Stare Miasto, which was completely surrounded by the enemy. I concluded that the next big enemy attack would be directed against Stare Miasto because of the important communication line on which it lay. The two districts were separated by a strip 800 yards wide in which were situated old forts built in the nineteenth century. A railway which circled Warsaw also ran through the strip. Two armoured trains constantly patrolled there, and from them the enemy shelled both districts persistently. Before the rising, it had been quite a pleasant walk of ten minutes from Stare Miasto to Zoliborz. It had then been covered with allotments and was frequented by courting couples; now, after only two weeks' fighting, it had become an impassable obstacle. Among the rows of vegetables which had been so carefully tended were machine-gun positions and across them were barbed-wire entanglements and deep trenches. Anti-aircraft and anti-tank batteries had taken up their positions on a neighbouring sports ground; they kept up constant fire on our district. I ordered Wachnowski, who commanded the Stare Miasto sector, to use every effort to establish direct contact with Zoliborz, in order to get supplies through. The first person who managed to reach Zoliborz was a ten-year-old boy, Wacek. He asked the commander to allow him to try because he was certain of getting through. Very shyly he explained his plan:

"When do you want to go?"

"Now; at once."

"How?"

"Straight across the gardens. We used to go there often and they always let us pass."

"Who do you mean by 'we'?"

"Basia and I, sir."

"And who is Basia?"

"Basia is my goat. Didn't you know, sir?"

His eyes sparkled in anticipation of the trick he was about to play on the Germans. His idea seemed to have chances of success. Indeed, some sectors of the front were less noisy at certain hours. During these lulls Wacek had been pasturing his goat in the no-man's-land between the two districts. The Germans apparently never thought he had any connection with the fight and they did not fire at him. The sector commander reported the incident to Wachnowski and he decided to try out the plan. Next day, during a lull, Wacek set out towards the German artillery, leading his Basia by a rope. Neither the boy nor the goat betrayed any nervousness, although in Basia's halter was hidden a message informing Zoliborz of our intentions and how to organise contacts. The calm of both and the excellent appetite shown by Basia at the patches of grass between the allotments prevented any suspicion in the enemy's mind. In the evening Wacek breathlessly reported to the sector commander that he had just returned from the other side, having completed his mission. The next day, the pair set out again, but this time they did not return—and so the attempt to maintain liaison with Zoliborz broke down. Under cover of night, some volunteer patrols left Stare Miasto for Zoliborz. They were informed as far as possible by our forward units on the position in no-man's-land and where German concentrations might be expected. After a tense period of waiting, we heard shots and saw streams of tracer bullets concentrated on one spot. One patrol came back carrying their wounded commander. Of the other patrols we heard no more for the time being. I therefore ordered that the subterranean possibilities through the sewers should be reconnoitred. Two patrols went down a manhole and tried to get under the German lines. The patrol leader reported the following day that they had managed to go a few hundred yards with the greatest difficulty when a flood of water broke the safety rope and the guide was drowned.

Meanwhile, the need for contact with Zoliborz and Kampinos grew steadily more vital, as I was receiving constant reports that the Germans were preparing a general attack on our district and were concentrating large forces for the purpose. Kampinos informed me by radio that they were still receiving supplies by air, and so I continued to hope that we would get help from them. Our efforts to establish a means of doing so did not relax.

On the evening of August 16th the duty officer reported the arrival of two officers from Zoliborz. I asked them to come in at once. The elder entered. I did not need to ask him how he had come. He was covered in stinking slime to the waist which dripped to form black puddles on the floor. With wet hands he undid a package which was tied round his neck. It contained a revolver, a spare clip of ammunition and a message from the commander of Zoliborz. The man was "Agaton," the leader of one of the patrols which, two days before, had voluntarily made the attempt to contact Wachnowski at Zoliborz, and of whom we had since heard nothing. After crawling through barbed wire for very many hours, the patrol had managed to cross no-man's-land and reach the railway. Water from a broken sewer pipe then made further crawling impossible, and they had to make a dash across a street. They were at once detected and flares were sent up. Luckily, however, the Germans were reluctant to leave their positions at night and contented themselves with machine-gun fire, which was not very accurate in the darkness. The patrol reached Zoliborz without loss. They reported to "Zywiciel," commander of this sector. Agaton handed him the orders he had brought, as well as pieces of quartz which were needed to establish radio liaison with Stare Miasto. The same night, the patrol went on to Kampinos and delivered my orders to Szymon. Agaton told me that one infantry battalion had succeeded in reaching Zoliborz from Kampinos, but that a further attempt to follow this up to Stare Miasto had been unsuccessful.

This pioneer effort to use the sewers for communication with Zoliborz resulted in the establishment of continuous messenger contact between the two districts. On the night of August 17th my Chief of Staff, Grzegorz, went by this route to Zoliborz. He was to organise the passage of an ammunition column to Stare Miasto. The transport was to have a forest battalion as cover for the journey; they would make the necessary attack. Another attack, led by Wachnowski, would support it from our side.

Two days later I received a report, by the same route, that the projected attack would take place that night at 1 a.m. I awaited zero hour with some anxiety. After dusk, a profound silence covered the Zoliborz sector. Only the strip between us was lit up every fifteen minutes by German flares. Our units at the Stare Miasto end had taken up their positions for the attack. Hours passed. On the stroke of one, a column of flares leapt skywards from the Gdansk railway station. We could hear the blasts of filipinki and machine-gun bursts on all sides. The Stare Miasto troops returned the fire. Soon the night was lit like daylight, the Germans sending up white flares to light the battle and red to request artillery support. One of the armoured trains answered the appeal at once; its quick-firing artillery was easy to recognise. Our units attacking from the other side could now be seen all along the line; they had set fire to warehouses and reached the railway. They had now only a few hundred yards left, but were covered by machine-gun nests and hampered by the barbed wire. The machine-guns did not spare their ammunition; they fired non-stop, their tracers flashing fantastic patterns over the battle scene. Then suddenly enemy artillery from the neighbouring citadel started up also. The attempt to take them by surprise had failed. The enormous German superiority in fire made the break-through impossible. The attack from Stare Miasto did occupy some enemy forces, it is true, but the main attack broke down under the artillery fire.

It was on August 19th, at nine o'clock in the morning, that the Germans started the concentrated attack on Stare Miasto which I had been expecting. It was to be the climax of the rising. During the nineteen days' fighting, the Germans had managed to collect forces from various regiments and battalions, from the ground staff of the Luftwaffe, from police and S.S. units and from the Russian Kaminski Brigade, a total of about 40,000 men. Our forces in Stare Miasto amounted to 5,000 men, armed with machine-guns, tommy-guns, grenades, a few piats, grenade-throwers, bottles of petrol and other primitive means for fighting tanks.

An order found a few days later on a dead German officer gave the exact figures of the enemy strength attacking Stare Miasto. They were commanded by an S.S. general. The concentrated attack was made in a semicircle stretching from the citadel in the north round to Teatralny Square and Karowa Street in the south. The tangent of the semicircle was formed by the Vistula at our backs. The main blow came from the west, where an infantry attack of ten battalions was supported by two battalions of engineers, one company of Tiger tanks, twenty field guns, fifty Goliaths, two batteries of 75-mm., one battery of 280-mm., and one battery of 380-mm. (the same type as the Germans used to shell Dover across the

Channel), a platoon of mine-throwers and one armoured train. From the Vistula side the attack was supported by two gunboats and artillery in unknown quantities from the suburb of Praga across the river. Air support was given by Stukas diving in formations of anything from three to twelve machines. At first the planes attacked every hour, but later the intervals between raids were reduced to fifteen minutes.

In order fully to understand the concentration of fire produced by these forces on that day, it must be recalled that the area under attack was no more than a half-mile square. Countless refugees had flocked into the district and the population of the confined space had been increased to about 200,000 by August 19th. The refugees were sheltering in all the available subterranean passages and cellars of the historic medieval houses which, in times gone by, had been the homes of wealthy burghers. They were no protection against the shells of heavy siege artillery. The old buildings collapsed like houses of cards, burying those who had sought shelter in their cellars. They soon became the communal graves of thousands of people who were buried alive.

The heavy artillery fire, the shelling from the armoured train, the fire from the gunboats on the Vistula, the explosion of land-mines and the dive-bombing had, even during the first hours of the attack, started fires throughout the district. The carved oak beams in the old houses burned like matchwood. Simultaneously, the infantry attacked the main insurrection strongpoints, such as the Town Hall, the Bank of Poland, the Old Arsenal, the Treasury Printing Building, the Royal Palace and the John of God Hospital.

The Royal Palace lay on the German path to the Kierbedź Bridge. This drew upon it an attack of special intensity. The Palace had been destroyed by the Germans in 1939, largely after the siege. The clock had stopped then at half-past twelve and remained thus for four years. On August 19th the Polish flag was still flying from the clock tower, where it had been hoisted on August 1st. Now the fighting reached the interior of the building. The audience chambers, the ballroom and the throne room—where, a few years before, receptions for diplomats and heads of states had been held—were now the scene of a battle of incredible fierceness. Both sides used flame-throwers, mines and grenade-throwers. The Germans also employed tear-gas bombs. Our troops had two opponents to fight—the attacking Germans and the fire. It was several days before the Germans finally succeeded in overrunning the Palace. The buildings which formed part of the Palace group were connected with the Gothic Cathedral of St. John by a passage which crossed the street as a covered bridge. In the old days it was used by the King to reach the royal stall in the Cathedral. For three days this 8-yard-long bridge divided Polish from German troops. From our side, near the Cathedral, German voices could be heard. The defenders of the Cathedral learned to recognise the different German orders and knew when to expect the fire of grenade-throwers or a burst from a machine-gun. Occasionally a hand grasping an automatic revolver would appear from behind a bit of Gothic carving and fire blindly towards our barricade.

Finally the fight reached the Cathedral proper. Across the centre of the nave ran a barricade which defended the Polish position in the apse and sacristy. The centre of the Cathedral was littered with fragments of the vaulted roof and piles of rubble. It was only on August 29th that the spreading flames finally put an end to the battle for the Cathedral. The remaining walls collapsed inwards.

After a few days of hell, the fight for Stare Miasto settled into a rough routine. This was due to a certain regularity in the activity of both sides. At eight o'clock in the morning the Stukas attacked, flying in at about 300 feet in varying formations. They circled widely and then made precision attacks. Often they used time-bombs which exploded only after they pierced several floors; at the same time, the artillery would start up. The two armoured trains were especially deadly. They stood within 300 yards of Stare Miasto, occasionally changing their positions for different targets. The main devastation was caused by "moo-cows." Normally, the artillery fire went on non-stop until the afternoon; then the Germans would start their tank and infantry attacks against our buildings and barricades.

The Goliaths were the first to attack. Their object was to blow up barricades and heavy concrete structures. They were opposed by our forward soldiers, who watched for them on the far side of barricades, hidden in ruins or in the angles of walls. They would try to cut the control wires with precision grenade-throwing. The Goliaths were followed by heavy Tigers which attacked while firing at short range. Only then did the infantry begin—by that time they were usually faced with ruins. The enemy was allowed to advance unchallenged, sometimes to within a grenade's-throw, sometimes into a building. Only then did our men open fire and a fierce struggle would begin. It was often hand-to-hand. The fighting would frequently go from the ground floor to the cellars, where enemy sappers would get below our positions through deep tunnels and blow them up. We used these tactics also, but on a much smaller scale, owing to our shortage of explosives.

Lack of ammunition was our constant nightmare. It was felt by everyone, from Wachnowski to the commander of every barricade and down to every soldier, who from his window or behind his sandbag could only rarely return the enemy fire. My discussions on the subject with Wachnowski were endless. We never stopped searching for a way to fill the gap which was threatening our ability to go on fighting. Lack of ammunition necessitated special tactics which imposed the greatest self-control on everyone. The soldier well understood he must only shoot at close range and at certain targets. It meant that he must allow the enemy to approach as closely as possible and not withdraw under his opponent's fire.

After dark, artillery fire ceased. The proximity of their positions made night-shelling a danger for the Germans. It was then our turn, and our units would start to attack under cover of darkness. What we had lost in daylight we often retook at night. Thus buildings frequently changed hands. We lost and retook the ruins of the Town Hall, St. John's Cathedral, the Bank of Poland and the John of God Hospital.

In theory, the soldiers had twenty-four hours in the line and twenty-four hours' rest. But the idea of rest was as theoretical as that of front line or rear. In the whole district no point was more than 500 yards from the firing-line. Also, the "dangerous" front line was surrounded by burnt-out ruins and therefore ran no risk of further fire. After twenty-four hours in the line, a unit would withdraw for "rest," which meant it would fall back 200 yards and immediately settle into deep sleep.

When inspecting the sectors, I would see these young boys sleeping on pavements, amid rubble, on half-demolished stairs—wherever they could find a space. Artillery barrages and the noise of collapsing houses had no power to disturb the soldier's exhausted sleep. He kept his rifle slung over his shoulder, as experience had taught him never to part with his arms or lay them aside. His only comfort was to release his belt and slip his tin hat to the back of his head. At any moment he might be wakened by the men next to him with the call: "Fire to be put out." Fires were a curse in comparison with which the strongest infantry attack faded into insignificance. In fact, Stare Miasto burned without pause. The only redeeming element was that not all the houses were attacked by flames at the same time. Soldiers and civilians had constantly to transfer wounded, ammunition and food to cellars which had already been burnt out. We had, of course, no adequate fire-fighting equipment and very little chance of quelling the flames. All we could do was to try to stop the flames from spreading to key positions or to control them long enough to get people and supplies clear.

In the beginning, people from burning houses moved to buildings as yet undamaged. Later on, they learned that the safest places were those already burnt out. Rarely did the flames reach basements, and therefore under the ruins there were always shelters where crowds took refuge.

Every unit which left the firing line for "rest" would be called several times during the twenty-four hours to fight the fires; the civilians were not able to cope with the work.

By the third day of the attack, out of the 1,100 houses in Polish hands about 300 had been burned and about 400 completely destroyed. It was a rare exception to find anyone unwounded amongst the defenders. All uniforms were torn and burned and looked like rags. The soldiers' faces were blackened with smoke and wore blank, stony looks which betokened extreme physical and nervous exhaustion.

The Germans were now succeeding in infiltrating our positions, and the stand in Stare Miasto was only made possible by the help which reached us through the sewers from Zoliborz and the centre of the city. After the unsuccessful attempt to break through from Zoliborz, I had recalled Grzegorz. Only very small quantities of arms and ammunition could be smuggled to us by the sewers. For instance, a column of sixty men which left Zoliborz by this route took six hours to reach us and only twenty-four arrived. They brought with them about 300 grenades, two machine-guns and a few

K

tommy-guns. Even this represented valuable help for the fighting garrison. Wachnowski, in consequence, held a lengthy discussion with his small staff before deciding which barricade should get a tommy-gun and which platoons an additional ten grenades. Arms were now so scarce that they could no longer be given to individual soldiers, but had to be allotted to whole positions. For instance, at one change-over at the barricade in St. John's Street there were one machine-gun, two rifles and twelve grenades which had to be passed on to the relieving garrison. A machine-gun-layer at a strongpoint in the vicinity of the Town Hall, decorated for bravery after having repulsed a fierce enemy attack, requested as a reward to be allowed to remain on duty without rest because he was reluctant to pass his gun into other hands. His request was refused. The same night, asleep during his "rest," he was killed by a bomb.

There was something deeply moving about the soldier's attitude towards his arms. Often it would be a weapon which he had captured in an Underground skirmish, kept in concealment and looked after in desperate circumstances. Often it was a legacy from a dead comrade or a war trophy. There was never any need for reprimand for neglected weapons. In one other respect, however, military discipline was not so strong. There were frequent cases of theft and counter-theft of arms, especially those which had been dropped by the R.A.F. Even severely wounded men would refuse to relinquish their weapons. Bodies of the killed were carefully searched for ammunition.

The food of the units was very monotonous. The menu was unvarying for breakfast, lunch and supper. It was always tinned tongue and wine. The wine came from the huge stocks of the Stare Miasto wine-merchants, which were renowned throughout Poland. Often it was easier to get wine than water. The bulk of our food supply came from the German stores at Stawki, which had been captured early in the rising. Among them were thousands of tins of tongue. A week after the attack started, however, all the stocks were buried under the ruins beyond our reach. The tongue ration had then to be replaced by small quantities of cooked barley distributed once a day.

The area controlled by our forces grew daily smaller. My quarters were now in the middle of the battle. The Chrobry

Battalion was fighting in our immediate vicinity, defending Siemens Arcade. Units of P.P.S. militia were also taking part. It so happened that the two political groups who had, until so recently, been divided by strong antagonism were now fighting shoulder to shoulder, for the Chrobry Battalion were soldiers of a right-wing group. The two units got on so well together and their political differences faded so completely in this inferno that later on, when I wished to separate them, they sent a joint deputation to ask me to allow them to remain together. They were commanded by one of our finest officers, Major "Sosna," who was killed about two weeks later. His name was G. Billewicz.

When our units were forced to withdraw from the Ghetto area, they fell back to a line running through Krasinski Square and our machine-guns took up their new positions about 100 yards from my Headquarters, the Ministry of Justice—which had its daily share of bombs and "moo-cows." Fires had constantly to be put out because the attics and upper floors caught fire several times a day. Windows, doors and frames were all shattered. One after another of the four floors met with destruction. At first I occupied the lower floor, while the Government delegate and the Chairman of the Council of National Unity had the second. Some days later, they moved to the basement because the ceiling was rapidly falling on to their heads. Our hair, eyebrows and lashes were white with powdered plaster that fell incessantly from walls and ceilings.

One of my greatest difficulties was to maintain wireless contact with the country, London and the other districts of the city. My responsibilities, of course, covered a far wider field than the actual Warsaw rising. At that time the Home Army was still engaged in fighting in the south and southeast of Poland. Besides this, I had to be in contact with the regional and group commanders of the Home Army throughout Poland. Every day I had to send reports to London on the military situation in Warsaw and in the country as a whole. Every day, too, I had to discuss air supply with London by wireless. Finally, I had to co-ordinate and direct supply for Warsaw organised by Home Army units from outside the city, especially from Kampinos. It was equally important to maintain wireless contact with Monter in the centre of the city. Obviously, it was indispensable to have a thoroughly efficient wireless service, since it was my only means of keeping control.

The transmitters and receivers only functioned properly from the upper floors. If they worked in the basement, they could not be picked up. The incessant artillery fire made the use of wireless more and more difficult. We had big losses in men and equipment. Dust, rubble and the concussions of explosions damaged the sets to such an extent that we had breaks in both transmission and reception of several hours a day. From August 20th onwards, the chief signal officer reported every day that he was down to his last reserves and that at any moment the sets might cease functioning altogether.

We were also dependent on the radio for news of the outside world and of other German fronts. During this time the successful Allied offensive was taking place in France. Every day brought news of fresh advances in the west and of the liberation of more towns by Allied forces. A month before this news would have been a source of joy and optimism. Now it all seemed distant and indistinct—a blurred background to our present inferno. Sometimes the news would prove irritating and irksome—for instance, the announcements of large-scale Allied air attacks on German towns, on Bucharest, Ploesti and Koenigsberg, while a few hundred yards away two armoured trains remained unchallenged as a constant menace to us, day and night; while again within a few miles of Warsaw were airfields and German gun lines which had not been bombed up to now. Irritating, too, was the news of the Soviet offensive which was now developing in Rumania and in the direction of the Bulgarian frontier while Warsaw, lying on the direct road to Berlin, and so near to their positions, was left without help.

But one piece of news moved us. It was picked up by someone in the wireless section and sent in a few scribbled sentences. A rising had started in Paris. Paris had been liberated by units of the Maquis. Then, two or three days later, Allied armies entered the city. Lucky Paris. No one blamed the Parisians for having tried, with their own forces, to co-operate in the liberation of their capital. The analogy was forced upon us, however unwillingly. How different would have been the fate of Warsaw had American and British armies been standing at her gates.

The women of Poland sent a wireless appeal to the Pope:

"WARSAW,
"*August 22nd, 1944.*

"Holy Father, we Polish women are fighting in Warsaw, moved by patriotism and attachment to the land of our fathers.

"We are short of food, arms and medical supplies. We have been defending our fortress now for three weeks. Warsaw is in ruins. The Germans are murdering the wounded in the hospitals. They are driving women and children in front of their tanks. The news that children are fighting in the streets of Warsaw destroying enemy tanks with petrol bottles is no exaggeration.

"We mothers are seeing our sons perish for freedom and for our land.

"Our husbands, sons and brothers, fighting against the mortal enemy of humanity, do not even yet possess the combatant rights to which they are fully entitled.

"Holy Father, no one is helping us. The Russian armies have been standing at the gates of Warsaw for three weeks, but have not taken a step to help us. Help is coming from England, but in negligible quantities.

"The world has no desire to know of our struggle. Only God is with us.

"Holy Father, Representative of our Lord and Ruler, if you hear us, give the blessing of God to us the Polish women fighting for the Church and for freedom.

"THE WOMEN OF POLAND."

Meanwhile, the monitoring of the Soviet and Lublin radios brought us only fresh accusations and insults. In these broadcasts, I was daily attacked as being everything short of a war criminal. Unfortunately, news reaching me from London and from Home Army commanders in the country told of far worse things than mere personal attacks on a single individual or a group of people. They revealed the fate met by Home Army units which had contacted the Soviet authorities.

My appeal to units throughout the country to hasten to the relief of Warsaw met with response both from those in territories west of Warsaw, still under German control, and those already under Soviet occupation.

I received many radio replies from our units which had fought the Germans and now found themselves in territory occupied by the Soviets, announcing that they were coming to our assistance. But all these Home Army units who attempted to reach Warsaw were surrounded by the Russians and subsequently disarmed. All reports were unanimous on the subject.

"LUBLIN DISTRICT,
"*August 26th, 1944.*

"We hear with pain the news of the battle for Warsaw. It is hard for us to sit here idle when our colleagues are perishing there. We are helpless; a number of our units, having failed to cross the front line, have returned in the fear of being disarmed and interned by the Soviets.

"*Commander, Lublin District.*"

The Commander of the 27th Infantry Division sent this message dated September 21st, 1944:

"While executing Burza, the 27th Infantry Division subordinated itself, tactically, to the Red Army. In ordering a march on Warsaw together with a Soviet corps, they drew our division into ambush and disarmed us, directing the men to a new point of assembly. When marching through forests, I gave an order to disperse. Hope to reassemble again in liberated Warsaw. Arrests took place in Lublin and Otwock regions.

"*Commander, 27th Infantry Division.*"

Only after reaching London in May, 1945, did I see a telegram from Lublin, dated October 24th, 1944, and quoting an order of the commander of the 16th Soviet Infantry Regiment, issued on August 24th, 1944. This order quoted my appeal to the people of Poland to hasten with help to Warsaw. I was described as the "commander of the Polish Nationalist Army" supported by the "Polish *Émigré* Government." The Soviet order required that infiltration of Home Army units towards Warsaw should be stopped at all costs by the strict control of roads and traffic. Arms being smuggled to Warsaw should be confiscated and drivers arrested. In addition, it was ordered that all arms dumps and equipment or food stores intended for Warsaw should be seized. Home Army units, if still existent in the area, should be disarmed forthwith and directed to military centres for transfer.

From August 1st, when Soviet fighters fought an air battle

over the Ochota suburbs with the Germans, not a single Russian plane appeared over Warsaw in spite of the close proximity of airfields which they had at their disposal. The only air cover, limited as it was, came from Allied-based Liberators, which had to fly about 650 miles without fighter cover over enemy territory to get to Warsaw from their Italian bases. In such conditions, air operations were far too risky and wasteful to be effective.

After his return from Moscow, Mikołajczyk endeavoured to appeal for help to Stalin (two messages of August 13th and 14th) without any avail. On August 17th Mr. Eden, the British Foreign Secretary, notified the Polish Government that Mr. Churchill had approached Stalin personally to appeal for aid for the Warsaw rising from the adjacent Soviet airfields. Similar action was taken, following ardent requests from the Polish side, by Mr. Roosevelt, who also sent a personal message to Stalin, of which our Ambassador in Washington, Mr. Ciechanowski, was officially notified on the 18th. None of these appeals had any effect at all.

On August 11th the Polish Staff in London submitted a proposal to the British authorities to undertake major action on the "shuttle-bombing" principle, in order to bring the much-needed air support to Warsaw. An operation of this category would have consisted of a major sortie of day bombers, loaded and starting off from bases in the west, landing on Soviet airfields after dropping their bombs. A base specially prepared for this kind of operation was available at Luck behind the Soviet lines, and had already been used for shuttle-bombing raids on Koenigsberg, Gdynia and the Rumanian oil-wells. This proposal, submitted through Mr. Attlee, then Vice-Premier, got the approval of both the Imperial and the U.S.A. General Staffs. On the 15th, the Polish Government was notified that a major American air fleet was ready to take off for Warsaw and was only waiting for notification of approval from Moscow.

The Soviets, however, were in no hurry to give their consent, so Roosevelt and Churchill both sent a mutual personal message to Stalin; this was on August 19th. Five days after that, Mr. Eden notified the Polish Government that the Soviet reply had arrived, but that actually it was tantamount to refusal.

It was only on August 29th that Vernon Bartlett, in the

News Chronicle, disclosed certain details regarding Stalin's reply. Stalin had agreed to aid being given to Warsaw on condition that the leaders of the Home Army in Warsaw were immediately put under arrest. This news caused a sensation throughout the world. There was no British reaction till September 4th, when Mr. Churchill sent a telegram to Moscow, couched in strong terms, asking for the Soviets to reconsider their attitude towards the aid for Warsaw and withdraw their ban against the landing of American planes on Soviet bases. The telegram, moreover, contained the warning that the Soviet attitude was in contradiction to the British-Russian Treaty, and that it might have an adverse effect on the future relations between the two nations. We were given a general outline of this correspondence between the powers and the refusal, on the part of the Russians, to consent to the landing on Soviet bases of American aircraft.

This news, broadcast by the B.B.C., was confirmed by the Polish Government in London, who informed us further that the Russians had even refused to allow damaged Allied planes to land on Soviet-controlled airfields.

We received the news of the Russian refusal at the moment when the street fighting was reaching its climax. The tidings spread swiftly to cellars, shelters and barricades. It was a moment when the Russians had every opportunity to earn the gratitude and friendship of the people of Warsaw and, indeed, of all Poles throughout the country, who were following our tragic struggle with the deepest anxiety. It was a great chance for them to wipe out all the disputes and resentments of the past, accumulated over long periods. When I saw the tribulation of my soldiers and the sufferings of the civilians, I had not the slightest doubt that, had the Russians entered the city then, they would have been greeted with the greatest enthusiasm and hailed as saviours and liberators. By helping the capital, they would surely have been in accordance with the frequently repeated political aim of having in Poland a neighbour friendly to the Soviet Union.

Meanwhile, the prolongation of the fight in the city forced us to more intensive use of the sewers for communication purposes. These dark, underground tunnels, mysterious and forbidding, stretching for miles, were the scene of a human effort of the greatest self-sacrifice—an effort to link up the torn shreds of fighting Warsaw so that all our isolated battles could form one whole and united operation fought in common. The network of sewers carried water and sewage to the Vistula. Built sixty years before, they formed a complicated labyrinth under the houses and streets of the city.

They had previously been used when fighting was going on in the Ghetto, which the Germans had surrounded by a wall and a cordon of police. By this route food, arms and ammunition had been smuggled in. Special organisations were formed at the time and provided with a suitable means of transport to ensure the supply of food for the Jewish population over a period of several months. Handcarts on rubber wheels, built to a width which would allow them to be pushed along the tunnels, were used. During the massacre of the Ghetto, many young Jews managed to flee by the same route.

When the Ghetto had been liquidated and destroyed, the sewers were forgotten, but now that our present fight was continuing, we were obliged once more to use these underground lines of communication. A man who had previously been employed on the sewers arrived in Mokotow announcing that he had come from the centre of the city. All pioneers were volunteers. They went down into the dark underground tunnels of their own free will, appreciating how important it was that liaison should be established. No one was ordered to use the passages, where to lose one's way meant death. Subsequent results were due to the efforts of countless unknown soldiers, both men and women. The final achievement was the establishment of a system of communication linking all our districts in the capital.

At first the Germans did not at all realise that messenger girls and couriers, convoys of wounded and transports of ammunition were passing directly under their positions. One of the most frequented tunnels ran immediately under Gestapo headquarters. The Germans, who for five years had been fighting the Polish Underground movement, little dreamt that Poles had now really gone underground, literally moving under the very earth on which their headquarters stood.

The tunnels were pitch dark, because for security reasons lights were either severely restricted or completely banned. The acrid air was asphyxiating and brought tears to the eyes. The size of the passages varied. The smallest which could be negotiated were 3 feet high and 2 wide. Sharp debris, such as broken glass, strewed the semicircular floor of the passages, making hand support impossible when crawling. The most superficial scratch would have caused septicæmia. Two sticks had to be used as supports and progress was made in short jumps, rather like the motion of a kangaroo. It was extremely tiring and slow. To give an example, one of the routes leading from Stare Miasto to the centre of the city through one of the narrowest tunnels took as long as nine hours to negotiate, although the distance was no more than a mile. To advance along a narrow passage of this sort in pitch darkness, with mud up to the shoulders, often caused stark terror. I knew many men, in no way lacking courage, who would never have hesitated to attack enemy tanks with a bottle of petrol, who nevertheless lost their nerve and were overcome by complete exhaustion after only a few hundred yards in one of these narrow passages. The feeling of panic was increased by the difficulty of breathing in the fœtid atmosphere and by the fact that it was impossible to turn round. If an immovable obstacle was encountered, the only course was to back out.

Some of the tunnels were quite high and people could remain upright in them. But these "comfortable" passages were very rare and their use incurred another danger. They were fed by smaller sewers and were constructed to collect water and sewage from whole districts. The level of mud in them was consequently high. The current was correspondingly strong and progress only possible with the help of a safety rope. In the tunnel connecting Stare Miasto with Zoliborz, a distance of about 20 yards, was one of these high-water danger spots. At this point the sludge, brought into the main channel by many tributary pipes, flowed along noisily at considerable speed. There was no way of avoiding it and the danger was increased by the fact that immediately over it was a manhole in close proximity to a German stronghold. Numerous corpses bore witness to the difficulty of surmounting this obstacle.

Because of the current, it was easier to go from Stare Miasto to Zoliborz (that is, in the direction of the Vistula) than in the opposite direction. Returning from Zoliborz against the current, it was easy to stumble and fall, especially as the rounded bottom of the passage was extremely slippery. Matters were not helped by the fact that soldiers proceeding in this direction carried additional weight in the form of arms and ammunition. It is easy to comprehend the difficulties involved. The soldier had to keep his balance advancing against the current, waist-deep in mud, carrying a load of grenades, a machine-gun or cases of medical supplies. When they reached their destination, people often had to be lifted out of the manholes, so utterly exhausted were they. A fall in this particular passage usually meant death, because the current would sweep bodies away.

As time went on, communication through the sewers improved slightly and some organisation was introduced into the system. The initial sporadic and uncontrolled traffic had been subject to certain regulations. I set up a section on my Staff to be responsible for subterranean communications. Engineers were kept busy; they laid duck-boards, fixed safety ropes, marked danger points and put up warning lights. Day and night sentries mounted guard at the entrances. In view of the importance of the sewers, which were now an essential element in our work, no one was allowed to use them without written orders issued by either a district commander or myself. The sentries refused admittance to anyone not in possession of such a permit. At certain points down below, special patrols checked "travel documents," helped those who had lost their way, and in some instances regulated the level of the water. On the more frequented routes a special time-table was enforced, since the tunnels were used mostly as "one-way streets" and to pass people was out of the question. For instance, columns going from Stare Miasto to the centre of the city left every half-hour from midnight till 3 a.m., while traffic in the opposite direction set out between 8 a.m. and noon. Wherever possible, sappers built dams to regulate the flow of water. For instance, if a column was to leave Stare Miasto to go to Zoliborz in the direction of the Vistula— that is, with the current—the dam at Stare Miasto was closed and the water below the dam fell in consequence. If, on the contrary, a column was moving in the opposite direction, from Stare Miasto to the centre of the city, the dams at the Stare Miasto end were opened to allow the water to drain from the intervening passages.

London played a big intermediary role in the use of the sewers. As I mentioned before, the wireless stations of the district commanders were too weak to contact each other. Weak short-wave sets, on the other hand, were able both to transmit and receive messages to and from high-power radio stations. It was for this reason that hundreds of messages about the use of sewers were sent by all districts to London, where they were retransmitted to the relevant districts; it seemed incredibly foolish that to communicate with a point only a few hundred yards away we had to send a message via London. There was one case where a patrol was sent from Zoliborz to try to find a direct way of communication with the centre of the city. They managed finally to reach their objective and found themselves just beneath the Polish positions, but, to the despair of the scouts, they discovered that the manhole was closed and there was no way of opening it from the inside. After nineteen hours in the sewers they had reached their goal—and could not get to the surface. The men were completely exhausted. With a supreme effort, they returned to Zoliborz, whence a signal was at once sent to London requesting that the central sector be instructed to open the manhole in question.

Messages about this subterranean activity were short and terse, but they well illustrated the true features of the activity developing beneath Warsaw. For example, the centre of the city sent a message through London to Stare Miasto informing us that a signal light had been installed in Swietokrzyska Street (this, of course, referred to the tunnel below the street) and requesting that similar lights be installed by Stare Miasto in Dluga Street. In another Zoliborz was warned to avoid tunnels beyond Wierzbowa Street because strong German units were patrolling there. Zoliborz, in their turn, informed the centre of the city that the laying of telephone wires through to their sector had been stopped by the presence of gas in the sewer. They announced that they would make another attempt on the following day, when the signal-patrol had been provided with gas masks. These are typical of the hundreds of messages which went to and from London.

Great help was given to the traffic now moving along the sewers by women's units. The women who volunteered for it were known as *Kanalarki* (*kanal*, in Polish, is a sewer). They carried messages and orders, reconnoitred new passages and removed obstacles.

In September the tunnels became the route of withdrawal for units being evacuated from overrun positions. Even wounded were transported underground, a proof of the greatest self-sacrifice and devotion on the part of the soldiers who refused to allow their officers and comrades to be left to fall into enemy hands. Telephone cables were laid through the sewers and might successfully have replaced our complicated system of communication through London had it not been for the lack of insulated wire. Only short distances were linked by telephone. In the beginning the Germans did not realise that we were using the sewers. They were as puzzled as they were infuriated to know that isolated districts were in touch and able to help each other and co-ordinate their activities. It took them some time to realise that the means of contact was running just beneath their positions. In fact, their final discovery was due to an accident.

At the beginning of September they started to dig an underground tunnel from their lines in Saxony Park to our stronghold in the Exchange Building, which they intended to blow up. The Exchange was in the immediate vicinity of Saxony Park and was proving a thorn in the enemy side. Neither tanks nor infantry had succeeded in driving out our men. The garrison held on to the ruins with great tenacity, and so the Germans decided to use new tactics in the form of a tunnel. During the digging operations, they came across a sewer 4 feet in diameter; they therefore took their tunnel under it and went on with the work. After a time, however, they heard the rumbling echo of movements in the sewer and soon realised what was going on. It was thus that the fight for the sewers began, characterised by cunning and ruses on both sides.

All the manholes in German-occupied areas were opened and down them were thrown hand-grenades, mines and tins of acrid gas. Other passages were blocked with rubble and bags of cement. Many *Kanalarki* engaged in the work of removing these barriers were drowned in the flood of water which had accumulated behind the obstacles. The enemy hung hand-grenades in the tunnels with the pins removed. If a man, crawling along, hit one of these, he was immediately blown to pieces. These ambushes and other similar tricks were an additional danger to anyone venturing into the passages. In some cases, real battles developed underground against German engineers. The fights went on in the darkness in an incredibly foetid atmosphere between men up to the waist in excrement. They fought within hand-grenade distance, even hand to hand with knives, and failing weapons they drowned each other in the slime.

Finally, the Germans conceived a new method. A few hundred yards from the most frequent crossing-places in the sewers they poured petrol into the tunnels and set it alight. A column with wounded was advancing from Stare Miasto and met this stream of fire flowing toward them. The men at the head of the column leapt for side passages and some managed to save themselves in this way; the rest perished in the flames.

The horror of the sewers was increased by the echo of moans and cries from the wounded and the hysterical laughter of those whose nerves had given way under the experience. The slightest sound was increased a hundredfold and repeated in an endless echo which rolled along and could be heard miles away. The noises were truly terrible. It often happened that a whole convoy would be held up by the man in front who lost his nerve as he approached an open manhole in the German positions. Close to these points the Germans posted men ready to throw down grenades or smoke-bombs at the first sound from the sewer.

Those who refused to go any further were often the victims of hallucination. They would distinctly hear German footsteps when in reality there was nobody there at all. People subject to these illusions became a great danger to the others. They had to be forcibly removed after being gagged by a cloth or rag thrown over their heads from behind.

Battles would often rage around the manholes, as well as down in the tunnels. For instance, units which just before the end of the rising were being evacuated from Mokotow to the centre of the city lost their way underground. To save them, a battle had to be fought against the manholes in the area controlled by the Germans. The effort was successful and most of the men who had lost their way were safely got to the surface. Many of them, however, were blind for several days. The gas given off by the corpses decomposing below endangered the sight of anyone who had to stay down for any length of time.

Thanks largely to the help which reached the defenders by the sewers, Stare Miasto held out for eleven days and nights against the converging German attack which began on August 19th. But conditions there grew more and more difficult for the maintenance of wireless liaison with London and with the rest of Poland. About August 25th the chief signal-officer reported to me that three of our four sets were buried under masonry or damaged. Only one was still working, and this, owing to shocks and concussion, was subject to frequent breakdown. "Kuczaba" warned me that the capacity of this last set was already much reduced and at any moment it might cease working altogether, resulting in a complete break of liaison.

This would, of course, be fatal to us. Wireless liaison, to my mind, meant more than simply a means of carrying out my duties as Commander of all Home Army units. As it became clear that, in spite of superhuman efforts, the defence of Stare Miasto was coming to an end I decided to move my Staff to the centre of the city. With me were the Government delegate and the Chairman of the Council of National Unity. Both were over sixty. The tunnels connecting us with the centre were roughly 3 feet high. To negotiate them was quite beyond the endurance of an elderly man. The question had first been considered when the use of the sewers was in its initial stage; special reconnaissance was made to find a way through which we could all pass, including the two elderly statesmen. The experts made exhaustive efforts to find a more suitable route. From a plan of the city I saw that there was, in fact, a higher tunnel. It ran, it is true, under German positions for nearly half of its length, but this was not the first consideration. In spite of many attempts, the higher route had not yet been used, because the destruction of buildings had at some points completely filled the passages with water. Patrols had to return unsuccessful because they were unable to keep their balance in the swirling mud. The dam blocking the flow to Zoliborz was then opened. The patrol set out again, and this time got through, but on their return about fifteen hours later the men reported that the route was extremely difficult. Indeed, the leader of the patrol had no need to put it into words; it was plain from his appearance. He could scarcely stand and in a faint voice, gasping for breath, he repeated: "Difficult route. Difficult route."

The opening of the dam had, however, produced results. The level of the water fell gradually. Observers in the sewers reported that the fall was at the rate of 1 inch in two hours. The next day at the same hour it would be 12 inches lower. Accordingly, I fixed our departure for the night of August 27th. If only the wireless set would last out the remaining twenty-four hours! The mud was falling a little more rapidly, but a considerable amount remained. The level was still too high for a convoy of thirty or forty people to pass.

After twenty-four hours were up, the guide was still unwilling to lead us through to the centre under present conditions. The fall was still going on at the same rate, but the current was no less strong. It was at this stage that a report came in that the wireless set was only working intermittently. The batteries were running down much more quickly than the mud in the sewers. We had now neither spare parts nor spare batteries. A few hours more and the set would be completely silenced. This put an end to all further hesitation. I ordered my Staff and the defence platoon to be ready to set out that same night.

Late in the evening, I climbed for the last time to the observation point in the upper floor of one of the few remaining buildings. I wanted to have a last look at Stare Miasto. Everything was covered with clouds of smoke and dust from the bombardment. The fire was now less intense. At my feet lay the whole of Stare Miasto—or, rather, the ruins of what had once been the city—enveloped in a pall of dust and smoke. A strong wind from the west was slowly shifting this pall towards the Vistula. For a while I tried to recall where I had seen such a scene before. Then I remembered. It was in some photographs of Stalingrad which a courier had brought from London a few months before.

There to the left I could make out our strongpoint of the Bank of Poland. The Germans had found it the most difficult point to overpower. On the top of the half-ruined dome, shreds of white and red bunting still flew. The building looked like a sieve; through the gaping holes I could see the concrete skeleton. Great holes had been drilled by the 220-mm. guns. On the previous day the Bank of Poland had received seventeen direct hits from this type of shell. It was roughly the normal ration preceding an enemy attack. Seven times the Germans had got inside the building; seven times the left wing was disputed; then the battle went on for the main staircase and consecutive floors until finally the enemy was mopped up in the cellars.

Everywhere round me I could see at rare intervals the skeletons of burnt-out houses standing in a sea of rubble, with an occasional chimney looking like some fantastic amputated limb. The streets and squares of a few weeks ago were now utterly unrecognisable. The ancient houses of Stare Miasto had collapsed across streets, forming gigantic barriers of hundreds of thousands of bricks which even a Goliath could not push aside. The confines of our fortress were marked by the dark lines of trenches clearly defining the background of the Ghetto ruins; further on were the remaining traces of green left in Krasinski Square, a place which had witnessed ceaseless attack and counter-attack; next I saw our stronghold which for ten days had resisted repeated German onslaughts— the ruins of the John of God Hospital and the smashed concrete colossus of the Treasury Printing Building. Nothing but ruins now remained of Warsaw's oldest buildings: the Church of Our Lady, the charred cupola of the Blessed Sacrament Convent, the shell-furrowed roof of St. James's Church in Freta Street and the remnants of the Cathedral tower. The market place was a confusion of craters and rubble.

The destruction of Stare Miasto was the heavy price which Warsaw had paid to be able to hold on. The work of six centuries now lay in ruins. Automatically, I turned my gaze across the Vistula, where, on the horizon, I could just make out in the distance the forests of Wawer, Anin and Radość, through which ran the main eastern front. The silence had now reigned there for twenty-three days, in all that time broken only once or twice by rare artillery fire. Once again I asked myself if and when relief would come. Surely Warsaw's sacrifices could not have been made in vain?

The building of the Ministry of Justice, into which we had moved a fortnight ago, had changed also. Of the four floors only the ground floor remained; one after the other, the roof and the upper floors had been burnt or destroyed by bombs and shells. Above the ceiling of one room there was nothing left but walls.

Before leaving, I had a last talk with Wachnowski. His headquarters were now established in the sacristy of the destroyed Church of St. James. He was the spirit of the defence of the district and was always very calm and spoke in a low voice. We discussed the exact hour of departure for my Staff. He knew that his role was to hold on to the last in what was left of Stare Miasto so as to enable other districts to continue until Soviet help arrived. I knew that this courageous soldier was ready for any eventuality and would not falter, even in the most difficult circumstances.

At 11 p.m. we set out. We had to cross about 200 yards

brightly lit by the flaming buildings. The garrison church was burning nearby. Over the Ghetto German flares went up with a whistling sound. The district was so altered that we had difficulty even in finding our way. Water from a burst main flooded the middle of the street, reflecting the red sky and the shadows of ruined buildings. In places, broken pipes sent up jets of water.

The entrance to the tunnel was in Krasinski Square, within 200 yards of the Germans and covered by their grenades and machine-guns. Only one by one, at varying intervals, could we get into the manhole. The party lined up against the wall of the corner house. Every few minutes a dark shadow would detach itself and dash across to the sandbags round the man-hole. I went down the narrow cement wall, slipping and stumbling on the metal notches which served as steps. After a few steps I was in complete darkness and could see only a small circle of red sky high above me lit by Very lights every few seconds. The fœtid stench made me sick and brought tears to my eyes. I reached a dry ledge above the metal casing. Six feet below, the mud gurgled past. I let myself down into the sewer and found myself thigh-deep in the mud. The current was so strong that I had the greatest difficulty in keeping my balance on the curved bottom. I grasped the rope held by the guide and, clutching it with all my strength, pulled myself forward a few steps to leave room for the next person. We were to start only when the whole party was lined up in the actual sewer. With the rope firmly grasped in my left hand, I kept my right on the shoulder of the man ahead of me. During the whole journey, no light of any kind was permitted and a hold on the next man was the only way of keeping together and avoiding losing the party in the darkness. Should anyone feel too bad and be unable to go on, he had to give three tugs at the rope. The guide would then stop the party.

It took an hour to assemble the whole party in the sewer. My A.D.C. was behind the leading guide and I came after him, with the Government delegate immediately behind. Following him was my messenger girl, Basia. We moved off. After about a dozen paces, I began to get the hang of the thing and discovered how to plant my feet to move forward against the current without losing my balance, how to recognise the direction of the tunnel from the curve of its bottom, and how to use the side of the tunnel without cutting myself. Just before moving off, the guide checked the party once more and reminded everybody of their instructions for the journey: absolute necessity for complete silence—in about 300 yards we would be under the German positions; only he and his helpers who brought up the rear were allowed to use a torch; any alarm must be given by three tugs on the rope; every hour there would be a short rest. We had to go about a mile and a half. This, we hoped, would not take us longer than five hours. Ahead of the column were two soldiers with tommy-guns. We had to crouch because at that point the tunnel was no more than 5 feet high. Suddenly a woman's terrible scream rang out from behind me. Basia had fallen and the current swept her back. In the nick of time the Government delegate managed to grab her and help her to her feet again. It was only thanks to him that she was not swept away. For some minutes her scream echoed along the tunnel, and it rang in our ears even after that had died away. There was something ghastly about the echoes which resounded along these lost caves.

From time to time our route was barred by a stream of water from the roof of the tunnel where it had been damaged by the concussion of heavy shells and bombs. After a couple of these leaks I was soaked to the skin. Once I tried to do a jump through some falling water and collided with my A.D.C., who had stopped a moment after getting through it. I recovered my balance with difficulty, but had to step back, and found myself under the leak again. After an hour's going, we were just underneath the German positions at Krakowskie Przedmieście. Occasionally the sewer was illuminated by light coming through an open manhole; these were the most dangerous spots, because at any moment we could be attacked by grenades. In spite of strict instructions, it was difficult for the whole column to keep silence. Everyone was exhausted and several times people lost their balance and gave the signal for a rest.

The level of the water was now lower, but the mud was thicker and progress no easier. I helped myself along by putting my hands on my knees. I had to find a new technique for advance in order not to cut my legs on the sharp scraps of rubbish lying at the bottom of the sewer. At one point the guide put his torch on for a minute or two. In its light I could see the bodies of cats lying amongst the indescribable filth and excrement. The air was becoming steadily more fœtid. Only below the open manholes could we fill our lungs with comparatively fresh air. At one point we had a longer rest. We could change our positions a bit, but it was, of course, impossible to stand upright. A few moments of immobility made us all chatter with cold. Soon we went slowly on again. Leg-muscles and backs ached intolerably. The guide told us in a whisper than we had another 500 yards to go, rather less than a third of our whole journey. At last, in the distance, I made out the faint glimmer of a blue signal lamp. It looked close, but we still had another 200 yards to go. That last lap was endless. It seemed impossible to reach the flicker of blue light, which cheated us like a will-o'-the-wisp. Then the sewer narrowed and we began to crawl up a slope. Just at the end, my hand found a hanging rope. Soldiers from the manhole ahead hailed me to come up through the small aperture to the surface.

When we emerged into the street through the narrow exit of the sewer, the fresh air made us almost drunk. I personally felt as though I had suddenly been doused with icy water. It was with real difficulty that I gasped the air, while dark spots danced before my eyes. We had to lean against a wall for a time before we could recover. The entrance to the sewer was protected with sandbags and camouflaged. We were at once surrounded by the soldiers who were mounting guard at the opening. They shot questions at us, in quick succession. "Has Bonifraterska Street been badly damaged?" "Is such and such a house in Długa Street still standing?" "Have the Germans taken the whole of Muranowska?" Their families and homes were in Stare Miasto; hence the volley of questions. We were obliged to give evasive replies.

The distance we had covered through the sewers was about 1,700 yards, and it had taken us many long hours in the night. Now our first glance at the centre of the city made a peculiarly strong impression. I had the feeling that I was in a different world. Houses were still standing and here and there were even whole window-panes. Damage, scars, fresh ruins and smouldering ruins were not at first visible. The striking thing was that the streets had retained their former appearance. People were not scuttling along against walls; for the most part they walked along quite normally. Passers-by were still decently dressed, and it was evident that they were still able to wash. Men still wore ties. At first glance it seemed that, in comparison with Stare Miasto, the centre of the city was still living a life of peace, although here too, of course, whole blocks of houses were falling daily victims to bombs and shells. There was one essential difference between the two districts. Here, in terms of time and area, the intensity of danger and fire was considerably smaller. Here, too, there was nothing like the same concentration of people as at Stare Miasto, where in some shelters people were so tightly packed that it was often impossible for them to sit down, let alone stretch out on the ground. Here, in spite of bombs, fires and continuous fighting, it was evident that order was still being maintained; whereas in the hell of Stare Miasto it had somewhat slackened.

We made our way to Monter's headquarters, not along a path which had been trodden through mounds of ruins and rubble, but quite normally, along the street. Monter's staff was located in the massive P.K.O. Bank in Jasna Street. It was famous for its anti-aircraft shelters, which were the deepest and strongest in Warsaw. Most of them had been turned into a hospital. The rest were the Staff's offices. The room I was to occupy was on the third floor; here, it seemed, one could still live on upper floors—another point which struck us. Our clothing was drenched with the slime of the sewers and smelt unbearably of excrement. On arrival, we were given the greatest of luxuries—one bucket of hot water in which to wash. Already a dire lack of water was general throughout the city. Only basement taps still dripped. It was with real pleasure that I got out of my clothes and lay down for a short rest before my meeting with Monter.

A few hours later Monter came to see me. This was our first meeting since the outbreak of the rising. He had been Commander of the Warsaw garrison of the Home Army in the Underground, and now he was directing operations in the city. He was wearing a Home Army uniform and his forage cap was one which had been made during the rising. He was a well-known and popular figure among the soldiers. This was scarcely surprising, as he was always in the thick of the fighting, organised and led attacks personally, inspected the most distant positions almost daily, and often lent a hand in the putting out of fires. In the most critical and dangerous situations, his Slav face never lost its expression of calm self-control.

We exchanged information and discussed plans for future action. With regard to the centre, Monter was more anxious about the situation inside the district than about the position in the front line. The food shortage was rapidly becoming acute and the Germans had destroyed almost all the bakeries. Bread could only last till September 2nd. Owing to lack of milk and constant nervous shocks, mothers were unable to suckle their babies and infant mortality was staggeringly high. Older children, too, were dying in large numbers. The lack of water in Warsaw made fire-fighting impossible and there was also the threat of epidemics. In the shelters dysentery was rife.

The broadcast of the Soviet refusal to grant air bases to the American Air Force caused deep depression among the population, bordering on a collapse of morale. News from across the Vistula was not heartening. A man had managed to get to Mokotów from Rembertów, situated on the Soviet-German front to the east of Warsaw. From his accounts, it appeared that complete quiet reigned on this sector of the front. The Germans had dug themselves in and put out dummy wooden tanks in many places.

We decided that our first aim must be to save the approximately 1,500 defenders of Stare Miasto who were still maintaining their stand in that doomed outpost. At that time the passage of so large a number of people through the sewers seemed impossible. We decided, therefore, to make it possible for them to break through the German wedge which separated our respective positions by about half a mile.

The critical situation of the Stare Miasto was clearly shown by three dispatches sent to the Commander-in-Chief, Polish Forces:

"WARSAW.
"*August 28th, 1944.*

"In the Old Town the enemy has begun to overwhelm our forces by means of tremendous superiority in fire power. The situation on this sector is getting more and more critical. Losses in commanders and in the ranks amount to some 70 per cent. of our original force. It is almost physically impossible to go on enduring the hail of fire and the enemy's technical resources without the means of opposing them. A counter-attack has thrown the enemy out of St. John's Cathedral, inflicting heavy losses. There is no change in the direction of the State Manufactury of Securities. In the Krasinski Palace thirty soldiers were buried without hope of being rescued as the result of a bomb. Strong raids by air, bombardments, and mortar fire.

"Commander-in-Chief, Home Army."

"WARSAW.

"August 28th, 1944.

"Your meagre help makes it impossible to continue the defence of the Old Town further. I foresee that in the next phase Zoliborz may soon fall. The defence of Warsaw requires immediate aid in ammunition and arms and the dropping of essential supplies. . . .

"Commander-in-Chief, Home Army."

"WARSAW.

"August 29th, 1944.

"Stare Miasto: The enemy continues to encircle us and drive us from the bridges and the Vistula motor road. Heavy struggles all day for St. John's Cathedral, which has changed hands three times. . . . During the night the command and detachments of the People's Army [Communist], numbering some 300 men, deserted from their posts here and from the Old Town area. The enemy resorted to propaganda by megaphone, calling for surrender.

"Centre: Shows no change. The enemy has been consistently inactive. Twelve shells of 60-cm. [about 24 inches] calibre fell in the middle of the Centre. . . .

"Commander-in-Chief, Home Army."

Suddenly, while we were talking, we heard the characteristic sound of a "moo-cow." By force of habit formed in Stare Miasto, Grzegorz and I immediately flattened ourselves against the wall to avoid flying glass. Monter remained sitting in the middle of the room, but at the last moment we snatched him over to the wall. We were just in time. That same instant there was a deafening explosion and the whole room was showered with glass and chunks of ceiling. The "moo-cow" had nearly got our building, and several of the men who had come through the sewers with us were buried under debris and wounded by flying glass.

That afternoon I was given a German civilian suit, under-wear and shoes. After that I made an inspection which convinced me that Monter's appraisal of the situation had been in no way exaggerated. I visited one of the several hospitals which had been set up. The sick and wounded lay crammed in the basements; in these underground rooms the air was hot and suffocating. There were small electric fans between the beds, but in insufficient numbers. The pale, sweat-furrowed faces of the wounded bore witness to the lack of air and water. The water situation was upsetting the people more and more. Wells had been dug in courtyards, all the inmates of each building giving a hand, but few produced water—in most cases the only result was a yellow, clayey fluid. Uncertainty, alarm and depression were revealed in the snatches of conversation which I caught while going through the cellars.

On returning to Headquarters, we discussed the situation at Stare Miasto, and Monter worked out basic plans for the withdrawal of the Stare Miasto troops to the centre of the city. They still had sufficient reserves to take part in a com-bined action with the central troops in an effort to break through the German ring. We agreed that the remaining defenders, the wounded and as many of the civilians as possible must be saved at all costs. Although I realised that the fall of Stare Miasto would result in an increase of enemy pressure on the central sector, I knew, too, that the murderous German superiority in men and material was tightening its hold on Stare Miasto daily, and would at any moment result in the annihilation of soldiers and civilians alike.

A plan was completed by Monter for the two-pronged attack on the German ring that divided the city in two. Wachnowski was to decide on the appropriate moment. A messenger was to come via the sewers, giving us twenty-four hours' notice. Wachnowski sent us the signal on the night of August 29th/30th. In the evening of the 30th, the finest centre troops, with the best material we had, took up their positions for the attack from our side. At the same hour the Stare Miasto troops were to attack from the opposite side and, by joining us, cut the German ring. To avoid our own troops shooting at each other as they approached from opposite directions, they were to keep shouting "*Sosna*" (pine-tree) throughout the attack. This was the only way of preventing confusion which would be all too easy in the darkness, especially as most Poles were wearing German helmets and uniforms and the white-and-red armbands would not be easily distinguishable.

Wachnowski was faced with an extremely difficult task. He had to mass all the troops at his disposal for the attack and break-through. After fierce fights, lasting for days, only a few men were left at their posts. Ammunition was so scarce that only by strictest economy would it last for three days at the most. At the same time, the attacking troops had to be so equipped as to have a chance of breaking through. All reserves of ammunition were given out, even down to the last bullet. If the Germans had attacked Stare Miasto that night, they would have reached the centre of the district without any difficulty. Thanks to the fact that the Germans usually attacked only in daytime and were wont to relax their vigilance at night, Wachnowski could risk withdrawing the bulk of his forces from our strongpoints and barricades, leaving only a skeleton defence. He then assembled the main force to strike a blow in an unexpected direction. Due, however, to the crowds of civilians who were anxious to get out of this hell in the wake of the Home Army's break-through, the movement of troops to their positions of sortie was greatly hindered, and for that reason the attack was delayed.

In the first phases of our onslaught the Germans were taken completely unawares and the attack made some headway; after a while, however, the Germans regained their balance and brought a murderous barrage to bear from numerous machine-gun emplacements centred on that sector, simultaneously bringing in tanks on the flank of our wedge, whose fire made it impossible to advance any further.

Wachnowski was waiting for the results of the attack which emerged from the centre of the town, but, seeing that it was impossible for the other side to break through, he decided to withdraw his men to their defence positions, and it was only with the greatest difficulty that he was able to hold on to all his previous positions and get his troops back to their former posts. It was due to his rapid decision and personal energy that at this critical moment a disaster did not ensue.

The attack of the centre troops began at the prearranged hour. They had to blast their way through the walls of burned houses, because the Germans had previously bricked-in all doorways and windows as a precaution against snipers. The attack, which lasted all night, led to a substantial penetration into the German wedge but halfway across it was halted by the fire of twelve heavy tanks. The attempt to free the defenders of Stare Miasto had failed.

Only about seventy men from the Zoska Battalion succeeded in breaking out of the Stare Miasto quarter. Starting as the spearhead of the attack they advanced in one push right to the ruins of Senatorska Street. The remaining part of the battalion was not able to join up with the advance party owing to devastating enemy fire, and the men had to entrench themselves in the Bielanska Street ruins. Dawn was already breaking. The advanced unit stood its ground in anticipation that the rear party would be able to push forward; unfortunately, it was an impossible task to cross the open ground which divided them, owing to the withering flanking fire of the enemy, and so the latter units withdrew as it got light. The Germans took immediate advantage of that move to reoccupy the positions which they had lost in the initial phase. Thus the advanced unit found itself encircled from all sides. In this hopeless situation, Captain "Jerzy" and Lieutenant "Morro" decided to make a dash for the centre of the town through Saxony Park, in which the Germans had their heavy armour.

Using smoke bombs and filipinki, the unit dashed to the other side of the street and were able to reach the Church of St. Anthony, where they surprised a detachment of sleeping S.S. men and thus captured a considerable amount of arms and hand-grenades which they badly needed for further advance. The Germans drew up tanks and machine-guns in great numbers, concentrating their fire on the Church of St. Anthony. The unit, with the majority of its men already wounded, found itself again in a critical situation. By a lucky coincidence, some Stuka squadrons came over and started to dive-bomb nearby objectives, so that the Germans, fearing casualties from their own bombs, went to ground. Jerzy quickly grasped the situation and, unseen by the Germans, led the remaining group of his men over a long stretch of ruins, enabling them to reach the Zamoyski Library, which was occupied by the enemy. They managed to creep into the basement without attracting attention and hid in a passage between the cellars.

The Germans, unaware of this manœuvre, continued to fire into the church for a considerable time, after which they moved in to attack, only to find that there was no one there. They then began to search for the unit, which seemed to have disappeared into thin air; they followed the trail to the Zamoyski Library, but instead of looking into the cellars they were content with merely throwing hand-grenades through the broken windows, which they did for some time without much effect on our unit deep in a basement passage. Our men stayed in their hiding-place from morning till 8.30 p.m., when dusk fell. After dark, they decided on their greatest gamble and, putting on captured German uniforms, they walked out brazenly, pretending to be Germans. A few of the men who spoke fluent German went in front talking loudly and the whole unit marched boldly in the direction of the Polish lines, which were no more than 300 yards away. They were soon stopped in the dark by a German section, whose commander, taking them for a German detachment, told them to behave quietly so as not to attract Polish fire from Krolewska Street or the Stock Exchange area. To crown the whole fraud, they asked the German what routes they should take to avoid mines. Having got the required information, the men from the Zośka Battalion went on and approached the Polish barricade. Having reached the cover of walls of the Stock Exchange they began to call loudly in Polish, "Don't shoot! Radosław's group!" as the fire from one of the Polish machine-guns killed one and wounded two more. When the fire stopped they made a dash for the barricade and climbed over it. They were received with amazement, as they had come from the direction of Saxony Park, which was a German stronghold and therefore a most unexpected area from which to receive a Polish unit!

Only one means of retreat now remained—the sewers. It was doubtful whether it would be possible to lead all of them through the tunnels. To date, the largest number of persons to make the journey at one time had been thirty soldiers. To lead about 1,500 people into the dark underground passages was a matter of the greatest risk. To carry out such a plan, all the barricades would be deprived of their defenders, leaving the way to the ruins clear, and once the people were down in the underground passages there could be no going back, because by then the Germans would have taken over all the abandoned positions at Stare Miasto. It had also to be borne in mind that the people down below would be defenceless.

A few gas-bombs through the manholes or an outbreak of panic in the tunnels would be enough to prevent anyone from getting out alive. Besides, how could the entry of 1,500 into the sewers be concealed when the manhole by which they must enter lay only some 220 yards from the enemy positions? It was one of the most difficult decisions of the rising. For the time being, I ordered the evacuation of the wounded. Luckily, the water level had fallen noticeably, so that it was possible to carry the seriously wounded on narrow, temporary stretchers which had been specially prepared for the purpose. The successful evacuation of the wounded decided the question. Wachnowski received instructions to evacuate the entire district through the sewers.

September 1st. The fifth anniversary of the German attack on Poland was a particularly fierce day for Stare Miasto, for it was then that the enemy made an infantry attack on Krasinski Square. This meant that the last means of retreat, the manhole in the square, was in danger. As all remaining ammunition had been distributed among our troops in Stare Miasto, their counter-attack was stronger than usual. The hungry and desperate Poles attacked with fierce determination; they felt that this time they had nothing more to lose. The German losses were heavy, and in the evening they sent over envoys to propose a few hours' truce for the removal of dead and wounded from the scene of battle. Consequently, the night promised to be a quiet one. Wachnowski decided to take advantage of it. Orders to prepare were issued. Units began moving towards Krasinski Square. By midnight Stare Miasto was completely defenceless. Had the Germans attacked then, they would have met with no opposition at all. Thus began one of the most risky undertakings of the rising. Gradually, about 1,500 people disappeared down the manhole. Speed was essential, because at dawn the enemy would renew his attack. Slowly, very slowly, the queue of waiting people disappeared below ground. When the first had already arrived at the centre of the city, the tail-end was still standing near the manhole. For a long time the whole underground route was literally stuffed with people. Each person held on to the one ahead. The human serpent was about one and a half miles in length. It moved slowly. There was no time for rest periods, because room had to be made for the others who were still waiting by the manhole. It was only with the greatest difficulty that the line moved forward, for the water had now almost completely drained away and the mud had been replaced by a thick slime which gripped their legs up to the calf. The soldiers had had no sleep at all for several days and their only food had been dry potato flakes. The rifles slung round their necks seemed unbearably heavy and kept clattering against the tunnel walls. In addition to their arms, some carried stretchers of wounded. The only ones left behind were those whom the doctors forbade to be moved. Five hundred civilians as well as 100 German prisoners were also evacuated. The last soldier in the queue entered the manhole just before dawn. He was followed by the barricade guards, Wachnowski among them. In the morning the Germans began their usual attack. Stukas, artillery, tanks and, finally, the infantry went into action. The enemy suspected that the silence at the barricades was only a ruse to economise ammunition. General Rcinefarth's forces, which were to have taken the city on August 19th, now, thirteen days later, entered the deserted streets with the utmost caution, suspecting an ambush at every step.

Wachnowski at last reached my quarters. I at once sent a signal to London proposing that he should receive Poland's highest military award, the Gold Cross of the Virtuti Militari. Monter, Radosław and Colonel Juszczakiewicz "Kuba" had got it before him, after the first period of fighting.

The spiritual stronghold of Stare Miasto had been the Jesuit Church, in the cellars of which a Jesuit priest, Father Thomas, had organised a hospital. He was one of the outstanding people whose fine character stood out in sharp relief against the background of the bitter defence at Stare Miasto. When the evacuation began, Wachnowski suggested that Father Thomas should accompany the soldiers, who had grown so accustomed to his help in those days of hardship. But the priest refused. He maintained that it was his duty to remain with the seriously wounded.

What had been going on in Stare Miasto can best be seen from one of my reports:

"WARSAW,
"*September 4th, 1944.*

"To give you some idea of the strength of the attack which the Old Town had to withstand, I send a summary of a captured battle order by the German Lieut.-General of

Police, Reinefarth. In accordance with this order, the Germans began operations on August 19th which led to our abandonment of the Old Town only during the night of September 1st/2nd, i.e. after fourteen days of battle. The order confirmed: The zone of attack to be between the Railway Bridge by the Citadel, Theatre Square and Karowa Street. The direction of the attack: from north and west. The objective to be reached: the western bank of the Vistula. The forces assigned to the attack: ten infantry battalions, two battalions of sappers, one squadron of Tiger tanks (nine tanks with 88-mm. guns), twenty self-propelled guns of 75 mm., fifty Goliaths, six 75-mm. guns, two 28-cm. mortars, two 38-cm. guns, one 60-cm. mortar, one platoon of aerial mine-throwers, a number of flame-throwers, one armoured train (eighteen heavy machine-guns and a battery of 105-mm. guns). Independent of the forces taking part in the main effort, the sector from Castle Square and Powisle (Vistula Embankment) was held by several infantry battalions with tanks, grenade-throwers and mortars. In addition, five to twelve raids were carried out in support of the daily attacks, by Stukas and other types of bombers."

During the last days at Stare Miasto, the B.B.C. broadcast the news that the British Government had accorded combatant status to all soldiers of the Home Army. This was the result of long effort on the part of the Polish Government, achieved on the thirtieth day of fighting.

When this news reached us, I sent the following telegram:

"August 29th, 1944.
"To the Commander-in-Chief, Polish Forces:
"I thank you, General, for the expression of sympathy which you convey in your telegrams. It confirms us in that deep and most sincere devotion which we entertain towards you, General, as Commander-in-Chief. We have been greatly relieved to-day in one respect: Great Britain and U.S.A. have recognised the Home Army as combatants. We have waited a long time for this and we could not understand the delay, but now at least we have that satisfaction.

"Commander-in-Chief, Home Army."

The central district had what seemed to us newcomers to be two exceptional luxuries: a wireless station and a cinema. Shortly after our arrival I was invited to see a film which had been made by a photographic unit in the front line from the very beginning of the rising. It was shown in the German Palladium Cinema, located in the basement of a building no more than 300 yards from the German lines. The film was very like an American short of battle scenes, and technically it was quite good. Watching it, I lived again through the whole operation, beginning with the final preparations and going on through the fights inside buildings and the destruction of enemy tanks.

The wireless station consisted of Błyskawica and the Polskie Radio installation. I used it to speak to soldiers and civilians in Warsaw on September 1st, the anniversary of the German invasion of Poland.

Preparations to make the set ready for the days of struggle had cost an immense effort in the days of conspiracy.

The station was installed on the first day of the rising and started to transmit on August 7th. Unfortunately, during its long burial, its strength had been considerably diminished by damp. The small team of workers, however, did not lose hope and they managed to get it to work three times daily. Three times a day the announcers stood before the microphone and read communiqués on the fighting, as well as appeals for help and arms, and descriptions and stories of the life of the fighting units and the Warsaw people. They searched desperately for persuasive arguments and words sufficiently strong to move world opinion and prompt the arrival of long-awaited help and relief. But all their efforts were in vain. No confirmation arrived from London that the broadcasts were being picked up. Błyskawica could not be heard. Despite this, efforts did not for a moment relax, and the transmission to which nobody was listening went steadily on. Mechanics worked desperately to improve the strength of the sets. The aerials on the roof were under constant enemy fire and were damaged several times a day. They went on repairing them doggedly, though some of them were wounded in the course of the work. This state of affairs lasted for about ten days. And then, just when there really seemed to be no hope of Warsaw ever being heard in Allied countries, the B.B.C. confirmed its reception in London for the first time on August 17th. The joy of all station personnel was unbounded and the elation increased when a few days later reception of Błyskawica and Polskie Radio was confirmed from New York.

On the following day, German artillery was directed on the wireless station. We never knew whether this was a coincidence or if the Germans had really located the radio. In any case, on August 18th a 600-mm. shell, 6 feet in length, hit the six-storied building which housed the studios. It cut through six concrete ceilings like a knife through butter and buried itself in the basement without exploding. People inside were almost asphyxiated by clouds of dust and plaster, but, apart from the inevitable damage to the aerial, the sets were unharmed.

The broadcasts were made in three languages: English, Polish and German. This last was intended for the enemy troops fighting in Warsaw and contained defeatist propaganda.

Throughout my military career I had never, until now, had occasion to speak on the wireless. On September 1st I stood for the first time before a microphone in our studio. It was located at the time in the big Warsaw dance-hall, the Adria. The conditions in which work had to be carried on were, of course, somewhat primitive. Each broadcast was introduced by a few notes of a tune forming the call-sign. It was taken from the national song of 1831, the "Warszawianka"—the same tune that I had heard sung in the streets of Wola. The record was so worn that the melody was almost lost in a hissing noise. Something always seemed to go wrong with the transmitter just before a broadcast, and it had to be repaired against time. A few minutes after a broadcast, German Stukas invariably appeared in the vicinity of the Adria building. They were probably trying to locate the short-wave station. Spotters on the roof warned the studio of approaching planes by telephone. Further transmission was then suspended until the planes had gone.

The way from my quarters in the P.K.O. led through a courtyard and underground passage. My speech was made without enemy interruption. Before I began, a mechanic tapped the microphone once or twice with his finger. He replied to my enquiring look that he was testing whether it was working.

A few days after my broadcast, the Adria building was hit by incendiaries and burned out. Luckily, the station workers managed to get the sets clear, but it was all they were able to salvage from the burning building.

The wireless station was obliged to change its studios several times, but the broadcasts went on without interruption until the last day of the rising. The final transmission was put out from the building which had been the Soviet Embassy before the war. The sets which had by a sheer miracle survived so many trials were finally destroyed by the wireless personnel themselves at the moment of capitulation.

During a Staff meeting, held a few days after our arrival in the centre of the city, Monter handed a small slip of paper to Grzegorz, who read the note and slipped it into his pocket without moving a muscle. In no way did he betray the slightest emotion. The meeting went on as before, and no one guessed the contents of the slip of paper. It was only that evening, when the two of us were alone before turning in for a few hours' rest, that he showed me the note. It contained two short sentences: "On second day of rising 'Kasztan' (Chestnut) seriously wounded in the head during attack on S.S. cadet school. Died later in hospital." Kasztan was his only son.

In those days I was frequently called upon to attend the meetings of the Council of National Unity and make reports on the military situation. It so happened that the majority of the representatives of the political parties and members of the Underground Parliament were present in the centre of the city and could therefore meet. The meetings were attended be representatives of the largest political parties in Poland: the Peasant Party, the Polish Socialist Party, the Christian Democrats' Party, the National Party and various smaller groups which used to send two representatives. Also present were the Vice-Premier and Government delegate, the Chairman of the Council of National Unity, and the three Ministers of the Government who had been appointed to work in Poland. Eight months later, most of the men who attended these meetings were to be arrested by the Russians and put into the dock during the notorious Moscow trial.

The Council of National Unity had at that time to make a very difficult decision. In spite of the fighting going on in the streets of Warsaw, messages were exchanged with the Polish Government in London without interruption. In his messages, the Prime Minister, M. Mikołajczyk, revealed the results of his journey to Moscow, the course of his talks there and personal suggestions as to how relations with the Soviets could be adjusted. He also transmitted the text of the memorandum containing the main principles of agreement which he

L

wished to present to Stalin. The various parties in London added their comments on the document, and the members of the Socialist Party sent a plan of their own. The Council of National Unity had then to express their opinion of the memorandum in the name of the people in Poland. Their conclusions would have a decisive influence on the acceptance or rejection of the project by the Polish Cabinet in London.

Perhaps no parliament in history had ever sat in such dramatic circumstances. On this tiny island of free Polish territory, snatched from the enemy by a superhuman effort and battered ceaselessly from land and air, decision had now to be taken which would affect the whole future of Poland.

The members of the Council were placed in a particularly difficult position. The general conviction in Warsaw at the time was that the Russian refusal to help the capital was due to political reasons. This was understandable. The only elements from which the people of Warsaw could form an opinion were the facts that this bitter fight, which had now been going on for thirty days in the city within a dozen miles of the Soviet positions, had, up to date, not met with the slightest response from the Russians; the refusal of the Russians to allot airfields to Allied air forces; the total lack of help in the form of air supply or of the bombing of German airfields and artillery positions which were costing Warsaw so dear; the intense propaganda campaign directed by the Moscow radio and Press against the leaders of the Underground movement and the Polish Government; and, finally, the Russian failure to reply to any of our repeated offers to establish contact with the Red Army. Many people attributed the Russian attitude to an attempt to impose their own requirements upon Poland by inflicting this physical and moral pressure on both the Polish people and their Government in London.

In his memorandum, Mikołajczyk proposed as a compromise that a new government should be formed which would include the Communists as· a fifth political party. The Communists, at that time, formed a big majority in the "Lublin Committee." The proposed compromise was not easy to accept, in view of Poland's special position. Owing to the close proximity of Russia, the Communist Party was not regarded by the Polish people as an organisation representing political beliefs, but rather as the instrument of a foreign power acting on orders and instructions from outside Poland and subservient to foreign interests. In other words, the Communist was looked on in Poland as a sort of pro-Russian quisling. The war had brought about in Poland—as it had doubtless done elsewhere—a strong swing to the left; but at the same time even the most extreme leftists who had the independence of their country at heart carefully avoided the use of the word "Communist" to describe their political views.

In these circumstances, the members of the Council feared that the presence in the government of Communists—men directly dependent on Moscow and supported by the Red Army operating on Polish soil and the N.K.V.D., the notorious Soviet political police—would deprive the Polish authorities of their freedom of action and defeat the principal aim which led to our rising—namely, the recovery of our independence.

Their fears were also roused by the current political tactics of the Soviet Government. Ever since October, 1943, Mikołaj-czyk had not relaxed his efforts for the renewal of diplomatic relations between the two countries. On their side, the Soviets had consistently produced fresh difficulties and new demands. To begin with, the Russian condition for the renewal of diplomatic relations was Polish acceptance of the Curzon Line as the final frontier between Poland and the Soviet Union. For us this entailed the loss of half the territory of Poland, including two large centres of national culture, Wilno and Lwów. For a nation which had challenged German aggression and staked everything on one card for the defence of Dantzig and Polish Pomerania, the loss of such a vast portion of its territory—at a time when the defeat of Germany was so near—signified the negation of every principle of right and justice in the defence of which it had been fighting against Hitler. At the risk of losing the support and confidence of the vast majority of the Polish people, Mr. Mikołajczyk had, nevertheless, expressed his readiness to discuss with Russia all the questions under dispute. He suggested that a temporary demarcation line be fixed and observed until such time as the definite frontier could be settled after the end of the war with Germany, when the whole subject could be fully explained to the liberated people of Poland.

In reply to this proposal, the Soviet Government advanced new objections. They expressed their readiness to begin discussions at any time, but only with a Polish Government "friendly" to the Soviet Union. The present Polish Government, they maintained, did not comply with this qualification. To support their contention, the Russians cited the alleged "inactivity" of the Polish Underground, accusing it of sabotaging their fight against the Germans and claiming that it resulted from orders by the Polish Government in London. Our experience with the Burza operations and the situation in which Warsaw now found herself clearly showed that our conciliatory step had not produced the expected friendly response from the Soviets. When Mikołajczyk revealed to world opinion the orders given to the Home Army to co-operate with the Red Army, the Russians raised yet another objection, declaring that the presence in the Polish Government and General Headquarters of persons unfriendly to the Soviet Union was impeding the renewal of diplomatic relations. In his talks with Lebiediev, then Soviet envoy to the exiled Allied Governments in London, Mikołajczyk declared his readiness to reorganise his Government so as to ensure friendly co-operation with Russia. The Russians countered with even greater demands, requesting the inclusion in the Government of members of the so-called "Union of Polish Patriots" in Moscow, the Soviet puppet political organisation for Poland. Mikołajczyk was ready to, discuss even this new factor, but when, a few weeks later, he was on his way to Moscow for the purpose, the Russians faced him with a *fait accompli* by appointing, in Chełm, the "Committee of National Liberation," which later moved to Lublin. The occupying Soviet military authorities had entrusted the Committee with the administration of "liberated" Polish territory. An overwhelming majority of this committee were Communists.

The Poles fully understood the necessity for agreement with Russia, but only a reasonable agreement, not one which would mean capitulations to Russia and the loss of unity, liberty and independence. We feared that further concessions on our part would amount to willingness to accept a new form of domination and readiness to renounce our right to a free government of our own. This would have been a tragic betrayal of our sacrifices and losses of the last five years, culminating in the present situation in Warsaw. After steadily expressing for five years our firm decision to recover and preserve our independence, we were certainly not willing to sign it away now. The question as to whether or not members of the Lublin Committee should be included in the Government was not the point on which the political parties disagreed. The difference of opinion arose as to whether Russia should not be requested to recognise the present Polish Government and renew diplomatic relations with it before any new concessions were made. This was the suggestion submitted by the Polish Socialist Party Leaders in London to their colleagues in Warsaw in their plan, which reached us at the same time as Mikołajczyk's memorandum. It was feared that further concessions would only meet with the same fate as previous ones and spur the Russians to yet more demands. Actually, the real difference between the two plans was that Mikołajczyk wanted first to form a new government which would include the Communists and only then apply for the renewal of diplomatic relations with the Soviet Union, while the Socialists proposed that negotiations should begin with Soviet recognition of the Government in its present form and that later on, after the liberation of the capital, it should be reconstructed so as to include the Communists when a treaty of friendship with Russia had been signed.

Mikołajczyk's supporters were the members of his own Peasant Party; the Socialists were supported by the National Party. After considerable debate and some hesitation, Mikołajczyk's plan was unanimously adopted by the Council of National Unity. The representatives of all parties came to an agreed conclusion that in the circumstances their main chance lay in the maintenance of total unity amongst themselves.

In the message addressed to London, the Council of National Unity gave the following reasons for the decision: "That in the fourth week of the rising . . . it has been called upon to make an urgent decision in a matter which constitutes a factual modification of the line of policy hitherto followed by the Government and the authorities at home." It expressed the opinion that the proposal calls for a decisive change in our "foreign policy, rendering possible a retirement on our part from the frontiers determined by the Riga Treaty, and an interference by a foreign power into our internal and military affairs. . . ." The Council also stated that it had been forced to make the decision, "in view of a complete lack of information regarding the basic elements of the international position, in spite of constant demands on the part of the Council and the Government delegate for exhaustive and continuous notification"—and that the said decision has been made "under the pressure of circumstances."

The adoption of Mikołajczyk's plan was, of course, also influenced by the tragic situation of Warsaw. At the time, it was not the independence of the whole country which was alone at stake, but also the survival of the capital of that country, its cultural, educational and political centre; in the balance, too, were the lives of 1,000,000 of its citizens. The debate went on to the accompaniment of Tiger tanks attacking a neighbouring barricade. The constant explosion of shells in the vicinity made the debaters sharply aware of their true position.

When I was acquainted with the Mikołajczyk plan, I made clear my own attitude towards the problem in my message of August 28th, as follows:

"To the Commander-in-Chief and to the Prime Minister:

"I have seen the proposal of the Prime Minister, forwarded here to the Government delegate, as to waiting for the solution of our relations with the Soviets until the occupation of Warsaw by the latter. This plan is total capitulation and envisages a series of capital political issues which are based on the postulation of goodwill on the parts of the Soviets without any prior guarantees from either the U.S.S.R. or the Allies. The plan is a complete reversal of the policy followed up till now and is also a blow to our national independence.

"In this crucial moment for Poland's future, in the face of an impending decision of extreme historic importance, I consider it my duty to state, on behalf of the Polish Home Army which I command and in full accordance with the convictions of the entire patriotically disposed Polish people, that Poland has not fought the Germans for five years under the worst conditions and made the appalling sacrifices she has merely to end up by capitulating to the Soviet.

"Warsaw took up the battle a month ago, with insignificant aid from outside, and is now being crushed to ruin simply to enable the Government to bow to the pressure of circumstance and impose on the nation an attitude of submission to alien force—an attitude which shall be put to shame by history.

"The undaunted attitude hitherto maintained by the Government gives us the hope that it will not give way and that it will seek a solution with Russia based on a promise of independence, full sovereignty and as far-reaching an integrity as possible for the Polish Republic."

Mikołajczyk's offer was countered with the proposal that four seats should be allotted to the four main political parties in a government in which the remaining fourteen seats were to be occupied by members of the Lublin Committee. One year later, most of those who took part in the unanimous vote in besieged Warsaw for the adoption of Mikołajczyk's plan were to find themselves in the dock in Moscow facing trial by a Soviet court.

*   *   *

The Council at that time met in Przeskok Street within a few hundred yards of my quarters in the P.K.O. I used to go there to ensure co-operation between the military and civilian authorities. After the fall of Stare Miasto, the intensity of enemy fire on the centre of the city increased appreciably. It was now impossible to remain in the upper storeys of the buildings. Almost every moment fragments of mines, grenades, shells or phosphorus from incendiaries came flying through the windows. With my whole Staff I moved down into the basement of the P.K.O., where we were crowded into stuffy shelters. The corner of the building was hit by a bomb, one result of which was that the air ducts ensuring ventilation in the basement ceased to function. Through the apertures poured a virulent type of acrid smoke, which forced us to evacuate the building. It appeared that the main ventilation pipe had been partly blown away, setting fire to the cork insulation and sending clouds of smoke into the vents. The soldiers had to pull down the walls to reach the burning cork. By evening, the fire had been subdued and we could return, but, of course, there was now no ventilation at all, with the result that the basement was stuffier than ever. Our faces ran with sweat. At intervals we were obliged to go up to the surface for a breath of fresh air.

On September 4th, when leaving for one of the meetings of the Council, I suddenly got a feeling of acute anxiety. Work was going on as usual in the shelter close to mine; Basia was typing, a few officers were sitting at their desks and a soldier, who an hour before had returned from spotting duty, was strumming a mandolin and humming an insurgent song. In the passages all was as usual, with people going to and fro, messengers and couriers arriving or leaving with reports and orders, but I left the building with a definite feeling of apprehension.

The meeting of the Council was held in exceptionally bad conditions that day. Every few minutes there was a Stuka attack. The explosion of bombs went on non-stop. We all felt acutely depressed. I left early in the evening and as I crossed the threshold I heard the whistle of a 600-mm. shell. These were easy to recognise, and we had had ample opportunity to learn how to distinguish between the different German projectiles. A deafening explosion followed and a shower of bricks, sheets of iron and splintered wood rained down. The whole area was covered by a pall of yellow dust; I could not see further than a couple of yards. Shortly afterwards appeared the cloudy silhouettes of women with stretchers. They seemed to spring from the earth at the first noise of the explosion and rush to the scene of the burst.

During the few hours of the meeting the whole appearance of the streets had been completely altered; walking back the way I had come, I could scarcely recognise any landmarks. Where most of the buildings had stood, only rubble remained, close to the Polish barricades, bricks were piled high in the streets. I passed close by craters filled with water. With difficulty, I reached the P.K.O. and was met by a tragic sight: most of the building had been destroyed and now formed a mound of rubble up to the level of the first floor. The dome of the building had crashed down and lay in the street, looking like a woman's gigantic hat upside down. Not far from it were two large unexploded bombs. I tried to get into the subterranean Staff quarters, but the sentries warned me that there was no way through. The bomb had fallen through the lift-shaft and exploded deep down in the building, two floors below street level, exactly where our quarters had been located. Nevertheless, I tried to get in. Inside it was pitch dark. I switched on my torch; overhead, enormous concrete blocks, detached from their supports, lodged precariously. The staircase leading down was destroyed. With the greatest difficulty, I climbed down on the few remaining ledges, keeping close to the side wall. The blinding smoke got into my mouth and eyes. It was too dense for my torch to pierce it. I went forward almost blindly, stumbling over concrete blocks. Finally, I reached the room in which we used to keep the wireless set and where messenger girls and A.D.Cs. had waited for orders. It was the only room which could be reached. On the floor were bodies, among them the soldier with the mandolin still in his hands, partly buried under the middle of the ceiling, which had collapsed. The only living person I met was one of my messenger girls. She was carefully packing papers and what remained of our belongings. I learned from her that about thirty people had been killed; Grzegorz, Kuczaba and Basia were seriously wounded. Even the way into the room in which we were standing had at first been blocked, and the people inside who were not killed were only saved from asphyxiation by the presence of mind of others outside, who acted promptly and got them out of the premises. I hurried to the neighbouring hospital, where the wounded had been taken. There, too, a bomb had fallen right through the whole building, penetrating the big cement ceiling of the basement in which the hospital was located and killing many of the patients. Conditions there were infernal. Wounded and dying lay close to each other on the floor in passages and rooms; I had to step carefully to avoid them. From all sides came the moaning and choking of the dying. A dozen doctors, nearly dropping with fatigue, went on doggedly operating on one case after another. The stench of gangrene was everywhere. In the crowd of wounded, I finally managed to find Grzegorz. His wound had just been dressed and his head was swathed in bandages. He had been hit in the jaw and his face was full of splinters of wood and stones. Close to him lay the chief signal officer, Kuczaba. Basia, who had been pinned down by a cement block, was dying; one of our group was leaving us—one who at the most difficult moments had managed to cheer us with her imperturbable and infectious cheerfulness. Her real name was M. Piekarska.

During the night I had to transfer the surviving members of my Staff elsewhere. It was not an easy matter. All the buildings still standing were crowded with civilians, either refugees or people burnt out from their houses. The houses near the fighting line were nearly all occupied by soldiers and turned into defence posts. I decided to move into the southern part of the city and instal Headquarters in the Pasta Building in Pius XI Street, freshly captured from the Germans. From previous experience, I had learned that the safest place was often as near as possible to the fighting line. There were chances of less disturbance, because the Germans did not dare to shell or bomb too near their own positions. The Pasta Building fitted this case, as it was within 300 yards of a German post. A special defence platoon was formed from officers and men who were members of the Headquarters Staff, called the Agaton Platoon, after the pseudonym of its commander, who, it will be remembered, had been the first safely to negotiate the sewer between Zoliborz and Stare Miasto. All security measures were taken to ensure the secrecy of the location of Headquarters. In the circumstances, this was essential if we were not to attract a precision bomb from a low-flying plane or a carefully aimed shell, such as the Germans had used with such deadly result on other vital points. As Grzegorz was seriously wounded, I appointed General "Niedzwiadek" Okulicki as my Chief of Staff. All the time, however, Grzegorz was in our vicinity and so I could always be in touch with him.

On September 6th, a week after the fall of Stare Miasto, we received another blow. In spite of the fact that we had not left a single soldier in Stare Miasto, the Germans spent a whole week occupying the sector, house by house and street by street, expelling all the inhabitants from their cellars and shelters. Having cleared the whole district, they then directed their attack on Powiśle, the next district on the river bank. It was clear that their object was to force the Poles from the Vistula. For two days air attacks and artillery bombardment were concentrated on Powiśle; the entire district was ablaze, as the houses burned like matchwood. The inhabitants lived through the same hell that had been the lot of Stare Miasto. After this preliminary deluge of fire, in the early hours of September 6th the Germans rounded up a crowd of women who had fallen into their hands at Stare Miasto and forced them to advance before the enemy troops into the Polish positions. The defenders, misled by the sight of this human herd rushing towards them, held their fire. Recovering, they attempted to fire only at the Germans following behind. It was too late. The women flung themselves on the barricade and, from the rear, the Germans forced their way over. Once the people saw Germans inside the barricade, panic spread throughout the entire district. Refugees fled toward the centre of the city, taking with them sick and wounded. The main part of the city, between the Kierbedz and Ponia-towski bridges, fell into enemy hands. The continuation of the fight hung precariously in the balance. Monter gathered all his available reserves and organised counter-attacks. He succeeded in halting the German advance on the line of Nowy Swiat, one of the main arterial roads of the city. Here once more the battle changed into a fight for positions—from cellar to cellar and from staircase to staircase.

In Powiśle there were mass shootings of prisoners. In the few hospitals which could not be evacuated the medical personnel, both doctors and nurses, were forced to bring out all the sick and wounded and lay them down round huge bomb craters. There the Germans killed the helpless patients with bursts from machine-guns and rolled the bodies into the craters.

The headlong flight of the population from Powiśle threatened the spread of panic, which would have made further defence impossible. By superhuman efforts, we tried to restore order in the terror-stricken crowd. The stream of fugitives had to pass across two wide streets covered by enemy grenades, tank and machine-gun fire: the Nowy Swiat and the Sikorski Aleje (formerly Jerozolimskie Aleje). In Nowy Swiat the only shield against enemy fire was provided by a few fragile barricades. These were constantly battered by grenades and tank-fire. The people had to crawl along, a fact which considerably slowed up their progress and threatened to cut off those still waiting their turn. Some kind of organisation was soon achieved. Each person crawling along carried one brick. When he reached a gap in the barricade, he threw in his brick and in this way it was filled up. Soon a few men from the crowd volunteered to stand at the barricade and take the bricks from the people to rebuild the barrier in a more satisfactory fashion. In a short time it was repaired, but only until the next shell tore another gap.

The other broad thoroughfare which had to be negotiated before the refugees could reach a safer place was the widest street in Warsaw, Sikorski Avenue (so named by the Underground movement). The houses on both sides had been burned by the Germans and the walls of the destroyed dwellings were now partly in Polish and partly in enemy hands. The opposing positions formed a chess-board, defended by snipers deployed on both sides. In addition, the Avenue was under fire from two German strongholds: the Central Station and the Bank of National Economy. A railway tunnel running beyond the Aleje made it impossible to dig a passage under the street like those which had been constructed in other parts of the city covered by enemy fire.

In the first week of the rising, couriers and messengers had risked dashes across open streets. This was done mostly after dark, but, of course, if the message was very urgent and important it was even attempted in daylight. The number killed in this way reached a total of over twenty per day. Later on, some safeguards were improvised. At night engineers built up sandbag cover to a height of 8 feet between which messengers could dash from one side to the other. German tanks used to knock down these screens several times a day, and then the traffic had to stop until fresh cover could be rebuilt on the following night. An improvement was made by digging a trench 4 feet deep. The difficulty lay in the water and gas pipes, which ran across the trenches; it was not easy to move quickly with such obstacles in the path. Trenches became, during the whole rising, very vital arteries; messages, orders, ammunition and troops all passed along them.

After the fall of Powiśle and the threat to the northern part of the city, one of them was used by thousands of refugees and wounded evacuees. This was only possible thanks to a carefully organised traffic control. The approach to the Aleje from both sides led through cellars and courtyards of burnt-out houses; several thousand people waited there patiently for their turn to cross. Couriers, soldiers on duty and doctors were provided with priority cards for the use of the trench. In the corridors, arrows and soldiers on duty showed the way and regulated the traffic. The people had to dash across the trench at 10-yard intervals; on the other side, a rapid checking of documents and passes insured against the infiltration of German spies or snipers. During the peak period of the evacuation, the traffic across the Aleje reached the figure of 3,000 people a day. The Germans probably counted on using the railway tunnel running beneath the Aleje for their traffic to the eastern front later on, for they did not use heavy projectiles on this street. They contented themselves with shelling the Aleje from tanks, but this was quite sufficient to stop all passage until the sappers had repaired damage.

The loss of Powiśle considerably worsened our position.

The people fell prey to deep depression bordering on despair and there was nothing to indicate an end to their agony. Since September 2nd there had been no bread. Most of the warehouses had been destroyed. I ordered the distribution of remaining supplies among the units. Each platoon, from then on, had to be fed from its own reserves of food. This decreased the risk of destruction of large stocks, but made rationing more difficult and ran the risk of too swift consumption of such food as was left. The ammunition position was also bad—a dozen cartridges for each soldier was all that remained. Grenades were less scarce, thanks to our own production, which was able to keep up the supply at a level almost equal to the demand. Day after day I never ceased to request supplies by air, but in my heart of hearts I never believed they would come. Too many appeals had passed unnoticed, too many promises had remained unfulfilled. After the three memorable days in mid-August and the few drops in Kampinos Forest, air supply over the city stopped completely, with the exception of an occasional plane or two.

No less catastrophic was the question of health. The hospitals located in the cellars were terribly overcrowded; they were a living inferno for the wounded, whose numbers ran into thousands. The Warsaw electric plant, heroically defended and kept running for forty-five days under German artillery fire, was utterly destroyed and turned into a heap of rubble on September 4th. This meant that from then onwards darkness reigned in the cellars where people lived and hospitals were located. Munition workshops which depended on electric power had to cease production. The wireless station Błyskawica was temporarily silenced. After a few days, however, some petrol-driven motors were found and enough current was produced by dynamos to get the sending sets working again. The production of munitions was also reorganised and restarted, but necessarily on a much smaller scale.

Realising the extreme precariousness of the whole situation, I made a careful personal inspection of our positions. I tried also to look into the living conditions of the civilians. The sufferings of these people had very nearly reached the limit of human endurance. For five weeks, women, children and aged people had been living in dark, damp cellars. Lack of water and the impossibility of changing clothes had resulted in plagues of vermin of every type. Dysentery had increased to an extent that might well develop into a general epidemic at any moment. The appearance of the people, with their ashen faces, hollow cheeks and reddened eyes, spoke for itself. Refugees from bombed houses were white with plaster, which added to their ghostly aspect. Hunger, thirst and disorder, together with the necessity for remaining in darkness and humidity, had strained their nerves to breaking-point.

The morale of the soldiers was still unimpaired. My pride in them was perhaps even greater now, in these days of defeat and misfortune, than in the first days of success and enthusiasm. The crowd of workers, artisans, college students and civil servants, which in one day had turned into a fighting army, showed an astonishing endurance and vitality. Defenceless against bombing attacks, they clung tenaciously to shattered front-line houses, ready at any moment to oppose the entire weight of enemy superiority with poor weapons and dwindling ammunition. In some positions they did not leave their posts for several nights on end. Hungry, sleepless and in rags, they still hung on. Going along the front line, I passed through long rows of houses, some half destroyed and some demolished to the ground floor. Firing positions were mostly located at basement windows or behind holes and cracks made by blast, screened by sandbags hurriedly flung together for cover. Positions were reached by climbing primitive ladders or crossing planks laid over gaping holes. Only rarely did stair-cases to the first floor still exist. On the ground floor, behind barricaded doors, spotters observed the foreground and, behind them again, protected by a wall, a few men stood ready with filipinki or bottles of petrol to oppose the advance of tanks. If upper floors were still standing, they were posted with men armed with tommy-guns and anti-tank weapons. Every house had its commander and reserve party ready at any moment to resist a sudden attack. A company occupying more than one house kept its reserves as far back as possible. A system of co-operation between the various service branches, adapted to the special conditions, had been evolved during the five weeks of street-fighting. Liaison was maintained by women. During the day, artillery and grenade fire was too fierce to allow any movement, so that supplies of ammunition could only be taken in after dark. Special athletic agility was required of those who had to pass from one place to another by shaky ladders, temporary planks or places open to enemy observation.

In some sectors there was relative calm. The only activity would be confined to the mutual hunting of men who revealed themselves to the other side. In other sectors, there were continuous attacks and counter-attacks. Fighting would go on at a few yards' range inside isolated houses. Often a hand-to-hand struggle would ensue. Continuous mutual under-mining, in an attempt to blow up the opponent's position, would go on. On every soldier's face I certainly saw fatigue, but readiness for further fighting and capacity for endurance were equally apparent. But the lack of ammunition, the declining food reserves and the deterioration in health of the civilian population did not permit any illusions about the merciless approach of the end. One thought alone held me to my decision to continue the fight: the hope that the following day would bring a Soviet offensive and, with it, a complete change on the Russian front facing Warsaw, but there was nothing to indicate that such a change was impending. Each day brought fresh disappointments.

One Sunday I was present at mass celebrated in the hall of our H.Q. Crowds of soldiers were kneeling in prayer when suddenly German bombers appeared over the city and began bombarding our own and the neighbouring buildings. The walls were shaken to the foundations and it looked as if the ceiling of the whole hall might come down upon us at any moment. The priest did not even stir; he simply went on with the service as if he were in a peaceful country church. Taking example from him, the people paid no attention to the threatening danger and quietly went on praying.

I quote this one instance remembering the heroic behaviour of the priests, who not only fulfilled their duty to the last, but were an example to everyone and often undertook the most difficult tasks.

Several times during the fighting the Germans had attempted to open talks for an armistice. This they had done either by leaflets dropped from aircraft or by envoys sent over to various sector commanders. I gave instructions that these approaches should be ignored. On September 5th they sent several officers to one of the barricades in the centre of the city to propose a few hours' truce to allow the removal of decomposing corpses. They took the opportunity to suggest that representatives of the Polish Red Cross should be sent to make an agreement with them on steps to be taken for the protection of the civilian population. Together with the Government delegate, I agreed that the requested party should be sent. Two representatives, Countess Tarnowska and M. Wachowiak, reported to the German commander at the appointed hour. The German authorities then suggested that all civilians and the sick and wounded should be enabled to leave the city. For this purpose, the Germans proposed a cease-fire on certain sectors at definite times.

My fears and suspicions of the Germans and their methods remained unchanged. To deliver oneself to the Germans was always coupled with the risk of annihilation, regardless of promises and assurances to the contrary, but in view of the threat of destruction which faced all in this part of the city, I found it impossible to reject the enemy proposal completely. I therefore gave orders that the hours of cease-fire should be published in the Press along with names of points at which people were to be able to cross over. To these were added the German conditions. I made it clear that any wishing to do so were at liberty to leave on their own responsibility without the least hindrance from our side.

Response was small. Out of the several hundred thousand people crowded in the centre of the city, only a few hundred availed themselves of the opportunity. Their mistrust of the Germans was stronger than their horror of the infernal conditions in which they were existing and the continual danger with which they were faced. An overwhelming majority considered that to be left to the mercy of the Germans was a greater danger than to face their artillery or bombs.

I was well aware that in making this proposal the Germans were inspired by other than humanitarian motives. Sure enough, during the talks with our Red Cross delegates, the commander of the German sector, General Rohr, requested that I should send across my representatives as the German command wished to transmit certain proposals to me. I decided to hear what they had to say, and accordingly sent one of my Staff officers, Lieut.-Colonel "Zyndram," to the next talk of the Red Cross delegates. I instructed him to confine himself to a hearing of the German proposals. I forbade him to give any explanations, to answer any questions or to assume any obligations. Soon after the Polish delegation crossed over to the German side, General Rohr invited Zyndram to his quarters for a talk, which was carried on in the presence of two interpreters. General Rohr made a long speech in which he tried to convince Zyndram of the folly of further fighting in Warsaw. With great eloquence, he held forth on the dangerous prospects of Communism for Poland and the whole of Europe. He was at pains to prove that the Soviet Army was unwilling to help fighting Warsaw. He threatened the whole city with the destruction which had befallen Stare Miasto and, in the name of humanity, urged me to commence talks for the laying down of arms. Zyndram replied that he would report the talk to me. General Rohr finally asked that my answer should be brought to him next day at 8 p.m.

We had already discussed the question. At one of the conferences of the delegates of the National Council, at a moment of general mental depression following the loss of our foothold on the embankment and the appalling ordeals of the civilian population, a resolution was taken that I was to begin capitulation talks with German emissaries. The whole conference took place in very pessimistic mood. After very arduous discussion on my part, I eventually managed to persuade the gathering to empower the Government delegate and myself to take up capitulation talks at the moment which we would both consider most favourable, and that the existing circumstances were hardly opportune.

I therefore decided not to reject the German proposal immediately, but to play for time and delay the talks as long as possible, in the hope that a Soviet attack would be launched at last.

When, at the hour fixed, the German envoys approached our barricade, they were told that my answer would be given only on the next day. The following day I sent over Zyndram accompanied by two other officers. They had instructions to receive concrete proposals from the Germans, but not to hold discussion of any kind. Their visit to the German Headquarters was similar to that of the previous occasion. General Rohr tried to impress the delegates just as he had two days before, talking of the Soviet menace, showing the senselessness of the fight and making all kinds of threats. At the end of his speech he handed over a letter, addressed to me, containing the conditions for surrender. These guaranteed that the Home Army would receive combatant rights in captivity and that the civilian population would be evacuated with adequate assistance and assured of safety and the means of of existence. General Rohr requested an answer that same evening.

This took place on September 10th, and the same day something occurred for which we had been waiting for forty-two days. From across the Vistula came the thunder of powerful Soviet artillery. At the same time, the first Soviet planes appeared over the city. I decided to formulate an answer in such a way as to cause further delay and to await further developments from across the Vistula.

I duly sent my answer to General Rohr in the evening, pointing out that he was only commanding a sector of secondary importance and was therefore not in a position to guarantee that the terms of the agreement would be kept. I accordingly required that his conditions should be confirmed by the Commander of the 2nd Army at least. My second condition was that all the terms for surrender and the obligations undertaken by the Germans should be broadcast to the world over the German station Deutschlandsender, since this only could give me adequate assurance that the German conditions would be adhered to.

General Rohr, on reading my letter, raged with fury. He declared that I should be satisfied with conditions made by a German general—even if he was only a sector commander; that he was speaking in the name of the Army Commander, that the Army Commander would give no other assurances and that this was his last word. In this tone, General Rohr wrote me another letter declaring once more his unwillingness to conduct further talks if the Polish side rejected the conditions which he had already offered.

We spent the night of September 10th full of apprehension and nervous tension lest the artillery barrage across the river, which had caused me to break off talks with the Germans, should once more relapse into silence. But in the early hours of the morning the Soviet guns did not relax their fire—on the contrary, the barrage appeared to be approaching the suburbs of Praga. At 2.30 p.m. the first shells from the east fell on Praga. They caused big fires around the Orthodox Church and at several other points. Soviet fighters reappeared, and for the first time in forty days we watched air battles over the city. The result was immediate: Stukas and Junkers disappeared from the Warsaw sky. There could be no doubt now. This was a big Soviet offensive on Praga from the south-east. I had observers posted on the tops of the highest buildings still standing, with instructions to maintain continuous watch on events developing across the river.

The Russians had declared that the rising in Warsaw had started too early. When street fighting now began in Praga, I thought the moment had arrived when the Russians would find it appropriate to establish contact with us for purposes of co-operation. On September 11th, when I realised that the Soviet artillery barrage was not merely an isolated duel, but a preliminary to operations of a bigger scale, I sent a message to Marshal Rokossovsky by the only available route—through London.

"WARSAW.

"*September 11th*, 1944.

"To Marshal Rokossovsky—via London and Moscow:

"The news received to-day from Premier Mikołajczyk of prospective collaboration between us in the fight for Warsaw induces me to ask you, Marshal, to send us assistance and to co-ordinate our efforts. Please accept greetings in my name and that of the soldiers of the Home Army to the Soviet Army and the Polish detachments included in it, now approaching the gates of Warsaw.

"From telegrams sent to you by Captain Kaługin on 6.8 and by General Monter on 8.8, you will know our general situation. It has not changed much since then, except that we have lost the Old Town and the Powiśle area. On the other hand, we hold the city centre with Mokotów in the south and Zoliborz in the north. Reinforced by arms dropped last night, we are continuing the struggle, but further supplies of German ammunition and more arms are badly needed. Drop what you can along the axis Marszałkowska Street from Swiętokrzyska Street to the Saviour's Square, and along the Sienna Street axis from Napoleon Square to Towarowa Street. The people of the city are suffering terribly under German artillery fire of the heaviest calibre and under attacks by dive-bombers; I urgently ask you to neutralise these two methods of attack.

"Knowing how slender our resources are, you must not expect any outstanding co-operation from us, as owing to the lack of heavy artillery, our attacking forces are weak. None the less, if you will indicate the direction which is important to you, and if you will first reinforce us with heavy weapons, we can concentrate all our strength there to aid the Soviet Army's decisive blow for Warsaw. Please supply wireless parts to us so that we can make direct radio contact. I await an answer and send you soldierly greetings.

"BOR,

"*Lieutenant-General, C.-in-C., Home Army.*"

Independently of this message, Monter selected special groups to cross the Vistula as soon as the Soviet troops reached the opposite bank and make contact with the Soviet Army.

At the sound of Red Army artillery and the sight of Soviet planes, soldiers and civilians alike were filled with tremendous elation. Any thought of surrender disappeared in a flash. Crowds of people emerged from shelters and cellars. True, the German grenade-throwers, the "moo-cows" and artillery were still hammering at the city, but what did this matter when Stukas had ceased dive-bombing and when, at last, hope of liberation was revived? The population was infected with a general surge of optimism. From their bright faces, it was difficult to believe that these people had been through six continuous weeks of hell. To the man in the street, liberation seemed to be as close as Stalin's guns thundering across the river.

But I personally felt the greatest anxiety. Although the Germans had noticeably decreased their air and artillery activity, they had correspondingly increased their tank and infantry pressure on the positions by or near the river which were still in our hands. I felt the deepest concern for Czerniaków, Mokotów and Zoliborz. The garrisons of these areas had to oppose increasing pressure from German units using the most modern weapons. I knew how desperate was the plight of the Polish defenders. It was always the same: fatigue, hunger and shortage of ammunition, and an all-day fight against overwhelming German superiority. Desperate calls for ammunition still came in from all sides. I could see the possibility of the fight breaking down at the very moment when our goal was within reach. I sent one more message to London—I had lost count of the number I had already sent—one more S.O.S. I received the answer that, as the result of strong intervention on the part of Roosevelt and Churchill, the Russians had agreed to allow the Americans to use their bases once more, and that a large-scale operation of about

100 bombers had been planned to take place in the course of the next few days. The announcement for this operation would be the tune, "One More Mazurka To-day," broadcast by the B.B.C. in its Polish programme.

I realised, though, that every hour might prove decisive and that help could easily arrive five minutes too late. I dispatched to Czerniaków the remnants of our reserve of ammunition and grenades, as well as my spare units under the command of Radosław. Communication with Czerniaków was becoming more and more difficult. At about nine on the morning of September 12th, a force of some eighty Soviet bombers flew over Praga. Air battles went on all day. Russian artillery started to shell our bank of the Vistula, directing their fire on the citadel, the fort of Traugutt and Gdańsk Station. In Praga, raging fires were now clearly visible. The Soviet attack developed along the river, forcing the Germans to withdraw from the south in a northerly direction, towards Jabłonna and Modlin. The enemy was not choosing to retreat through Warsaw, but further to the north; everything pointed to the fact that the Soviet offensive was going well. By the evening of September 12th we could see Soviet units occupying Gocławek and reaching the southern perimeter of Praga.

On September 13th the Germans withdrawing from Praga blew up the eastern ends of both the Poniatowski and railway bridges. This, however, did not worry us unduly. We still held the four districts of Mokotów, Zoliborz, Czerniaków and the centre of the city. Two of these, Zoliborz and Czerniaków, lay on the Vistula and could be used as a Soviet bridgehead for the landing of Russian units. For five weeks there had been a drought, and the level of the river was unusually low; from observation posts, stretches of sand could be seen which narrowed the river at some places to a width of about 250 yards. I recalled that the Red Army had crossed the lower Dnieper during the spring thaw, when it was three times the present breadth of the Vistula. In the meantime, however, the areas which we held on the river were daily being reduced; the bridgehead in Czerniaków was being pressed by the enemy from all sides. The Polish garrison was putting up a desperate defence for every house, but the German superiority was overwhelming.

That day I sent a message to London:

"Warsaw.
"September 13th, 1944.

"Under the gigantic enemy fire and his technical superiority, we have yielded terrain in Czerniaków and the Frascati area. We are holding on with our last effort. After dropping ammunition successfully, you must drop us food, as from to-morrow, September 14th, we shall cease to distribute even hunger rations of food. The Soviet attack on Praga is developing successfully.

"Commander-in-Chief, Home Army."

On the same day Soviet reconnaissance aircraft dropped metal tins over the centre of the city containing the announcement that they were about to make a trial dropping operation. A request was included that targets be indicated by lights in the form of stars. And, indeed, the first Soviet air supply took place that night. The supplies were dropped in bags, without parachutes. The contents were American canned food and rifle ammunition. They all fell into our hands, but most of them were damaged as they hit the ground.

One of the bags of canned food may have fallen on the German side. In any case, that night a German Storch plane dropped bags of biscuits poisoned with arsenic over our illuminated targets. Many cases of poisoning were reported. The Germans' aim was clear. They wished us to believe that the Russians were dropping poisoned food. It was not the first time the Germans had used poison. Two days before, in one of the houses from which a German unit had been repulsed, our soldiers had discovered bottles of wine containing arsenic, which caused a few deaths. It was hard to understand why an enemy with such vast superiority in men and modern weapons should have recourse to a subterfuge of this kind.

On September 14th I went myself to the observation post to watch the course of the battle raging before our eyes. There were actually two battles going on: one between Russians and Germans in the streets of Praga and the other for Czerniaków between our units and German Panzer groups. Czerniaków had now been completely cut off, and there was no sewer connecting it with the centre of the city. The only means of access was by sewer through Mokotów. With the naked eye, I could see Soviet tanks across the Vistula moving along the river embankment in the sector of Saska Kępa.

In the northern part of Praga, the Germans were still blowing up barracks, flour-mills, factories and the larger buildings. Our wireless station picked up a new Soviet appeal, broadcast by the Lublin Committee. It was made on September 14th, at 8.30 p.m., and ran as follows:

"To fighting Warsaw: The hour of liberation for heroic Warsaw is near. Your sufferings and martyrdom will soon be over. The Germans will pay dearly for the ruins and blood of Warsaw. The first Polish Division Kościuszko has entered Praga. It is fighting side by side with the heroic Red Army. Relief is coming. Keep fighting! Whatever may have been the motives of those who started the rising prematurely, without agreement with the High Command of the Red Army, we are with you with all our hearts. The whole Polish nation is with you in your self-sacrificing struggle against the German invaders. A decisive fight is now taking place on the banks of the Vistula. Help is coming. Victory is near. Keep fighting!"

On the following night, more, and this time bigger, Soviet supplies were dropped. We received two heavy machine guns, fifty tommy-guns, eleven grenade-throwers, with 500 grenades and, in addition, bags of *kasha* (groats)—all without parachutes. Unfortunately, it turned out that the ammunition was useless, as the Russian bullets did not fit our rifles, which were either British or German. The ammunition we were using was largely German. Weapons and ammunition dropped without parachutes were seriously damaged. The bullets were twisted and the most valuable weapon often looked like scrap metal after impact with the ground. From September 14th onwards, Soviet planes made nightly drops.

The Soviet technique differed considerably from the Allied in this respect. The R.A.F. operations over Warsaw lasted no more than a dozen minutes, whereas the Soviet drops were repeated several times during the night because they were made by planes of small capacity which, on the other hand, were able to make several short flights from their bases near the city. This forced our reception points to remain illuminated all night, with the result that German grenade-throwers would start up, causing big losses among soldiers awaiting the supplies, as well as among the inhabitants of surrounding houses. Consequently, the lighting up of reception points became the signal for mass civilian flight to safer places.

Although, owing to these technical imperfections, the usefulness of Soviet supplies was inferior to their weight, the moral effect of the operations was enormous, and the spirit of the defenders rose accordingly. Nightfall was awaited with impatience, since it brought the characteristic drone of the Soviet planes bringing supplies. They were known to the soldiers as the Flying Taxis.

By September 15th the whole of Praga was in Soviet hands. From that moment onwards only a shrunken river separated Soviet positions from Polish units in Czerniaków.

After the capture of Praga, I renewed my attempts to make contact with Marshal Rokossovsky and tried once again to establish tactical co-operation. My idea was to arrange with the Soviet Command as soon as possible for a common plan of attack on German positions, to be made simultaneously from both inside and outside the city. In accordance with my instructions, Monter sent three groups of men across to the Russians. They were to cross the Vistula, taking with them quartzes, ciphers and all indispensable elements for the establishment of direct radio liaison. They also carried a precise report on our positions, the location of our units, targets for bombardment, reception points for dropping operations and so on. One of these groups failed to reach the Vistula and returned without accomplishing its task. Both the others got safely across the river on two consecutive nights, September 14th and 15th.

In a fourth group, charged with the same task, Monter included Captain Kaługin—the same Soviet officer who had reported to us in the early days of the rising as liaison officer—together with two envoys from the People's Army. This group took with it exactly the same elements as the previous ones had done. On the night of September 18th they safely crossed the Vistula by boat and beached on the Soviet side.

I received no answer to the message I had sent to Marshal Rokossovsky through London on September 11th. But I was not discouraged and continued to try for new means of contact.

Warsaw had a common telephone system serving both sides of the river. The central exchange had been destroyed during the fighting, but we still used the cables, connecting our field telephones to them; in this way we managed to maintain liaison between a few of our sectors. The cables crossed under the Vistula to the opposite bank, where the Russians were already in control. With the Soviet occupation of Praga, there was therefore a possibility of establishing telephone contact with them. To this end, I now sent a signal girl across the river with a precise explanation as to how it could be done. She was to explain that one of the cable terminals was in a certain manhole in Saska Kępa, now taken by the Russians. The manhole was 50 yards from the corner of Washington Square on French Street. In the manhole, three cables formed a triangle, and the upper one was being used by us. The first cable of a field telephone had to be attached to all twenty-four wires of this main upper cable. The second one had to be grounded. I requested the Soviets to branch their telephone in this way so that we should be in direct contact. I informed them that my telephonist would be on duty from 8 p.m. on September 18th onwards, and proposed that contact should be established to improve our means of communication in such a way as to exclude interception.

In view of the importance of telephonic liaison with the Red Army, I sent an identical description and proposal to London for transmission through British channels to Moscow. Unfortunately, I received no reply from the Soviet side on this question up to the end of the rising, and thus an extremely simple means of contact was left idle.

On September 16th we could plainly hear Soviet loudspeakers broadcasting propaganda in German across the Vistula, but there was still no contact between us and the Russians. Finally, ten days after the start of the battle for Praga, two Soviet parachutists were dropped between five and six in the morning and landed in Wilcza Street. One of them landed on some railings and was seriously hurt. Both were wearing Soviet uniforms. They were brought to the Palladium, to Monter's headquarters, with the unconscious man on a stretcher. The other declared that he had come from Marshal Rokossovsky to Monter. He had been provided with a wireless set which, however, had been damaged in the fall. He reported that he had been ordered to make contact with the commander of the Warsaw garrison and the Home Army, to inform Marshal Rokossovsky of our needs and to tell him of our situation in the city. Monter asked whether Rokossovsky would also inform him of the position of Soviet forces and of the intentions of the Soviet command, which would render tactical co-operation possible. He received a negative answer. The Soviet officer stated that his instructions only concerned the passing of reports from Warsaw to Rokossovsky.

The wireless operator, who had suffered concussion, died a few days later. Our mechanics managed to repair the set, and the other Soviet officer sent a signal in his own cipher with the help of one of our girl wireless operators. In agreement with me, Monter sent a proposal, through the Soviet officer, for a combined Soviet and Polish attack. On the strength of his information regarding the location of German units, Monter proposed that the Russians should attack from the northern and southern sectors of the capital, starting from Jablonna in the north and Falenica and Otwock in the south. He expressed his readiness to co-operate in the establishment of a bridgehead across the Vistula by bringing in the Polish partisan units concentrated in the Forest of Kampinos. He declared also that the Home Army units in the capital were ready to support the Soviet forces when they fought their way across the Vistula towards Zoliborz, Mokotów and the centre of the city, and at any other point on which the Russian attacks would be directed.

This message was sent on September 22nd. Like the previous ones, it was never answered. Through the intermediary of the Soviet officer, Monter sent regular informative communiqués in which he gave the exact position of our troops and those of the enemy. In every case (including the message of September 22nd) these messages were repeated to London as well.

At about the same time—that is, about September 20th— two more Soviet parachutists landed on Zoliborz and two others in Mokotów. They declared to the respective district commanders that their exclusive task was artillery observation. They said that they had not been authorised to establish any tactical liaison. The ciphers they carried were suitable only for the correction of artillery fire and the indication of enemy targets.

Efforts at liaison through the groups which I had sent over previously produced results only thirteen days after the battle for Praga started—that is, the ninth day of the Soviet occupation of the suburb. Apparently one of our groups had reached the Soviet command. At 12.15 on September 24th, the Soviet wireless answered our call signals for the first time. The message which reached us was drafted in Polish and signed by Berling.

The exchange of messages went on at the rate of ten a day. Berling confined himself to discussion of technical matters on the dropping of supplies and artillery fire. All proposals made by Monter and myself regarding tactical co-operation and the crossing of the Vistula were ignored.

After the Russians had taken Praga, the Germans renewed their attacks on our two bridgeheads, Zoliborz and Czerniaków, on the left bank of the Vistula. The situation became more and more critical. The Czerniaków defenders held on to a few houses and a short length of the bank by dint of super-human effort, fighting in the conviction that the fate of the whole city lay in their hands. It was perfectly clear that it was no longer airborne supplies which were needed, but detachments of troops. Otherwise our resistance would be broken by the Germans any day. Consequently, the commander of Czernia-ków sent a patrol to the commander of the Soviet sector in order to put before him the tragic position of the Czerniaków defenders, who were already cut off from the rest of the city, and to request that help be sent immediately.

There was at that time, on the other side of the river, the division of Poles formed by the Russians under the command of Berling, who in September, 1939, had been captured by the Russians and put in a prisoner-of-war camp. Even before the outbreak of war between Germany and Russia, Berling contacted the Soviet authorities and expressed his willingness to enter their service. As a result of this, he was freed from the camp and underwent special political training at a school near Moscow. When war between Germany and Russia broke out, Berling re-entered Polish service under General Anders. However, this did not last long. When General Anders's army left Russia for the middle east, and later for Italy, Berling remained in the Soviet Union. He then joined the Union of Polish Patriots.

After relations between the Polish and Soviet Governments were broken off, Berling, who had been a colonel in the Polish Army, was promoted by Stalin to general. The Russians then appointed him commander of the division which they had formed from the Poles who had been detained in the Soviet Union. After their entry into Poland, Berling's division was transformed into an army, which thus consisted of Poles who had been forcibly enlisted.

In reply to the Czerniaków demand delivered by the

insurgent patrol, Berling sent a battalion of his men, numbering approximately 500, across the Vistula. A similar detachment was sent to Zoliborz at the same time. The commander of the Berling battalion was a Russian, Major Latyszonow. The battalion had its own radio station, by means of which it was possible to conduct conversation, which, of course, had to be in code. The battalion was well armed, particularly in anti-tank weapons and *pepeszki* (Russian automatic pistols). In the equipment lay the main value of this help. The troops were Polish peasants who, a few weeks before, had been forcibly conscripted in the Lublin region. They were, therefore, recruits who had had little or no training and no battle experience. Finding themselves suddenly dumped into the hell which Warsaw, and particularly Czerniaków, then was, they proved of little use in the fighting and were unable to put up much resistance to enemy attacks. To depend on them was difficult and to entrust independent sectors to them proved extremely risky, since they were apt to flee at the sight of attacking German tanks. They were finally used in such a way that each "Berlinger" was doubled by one of our men, even taking his arms if necessary.

I found the fact that this battalion had crossed the Vistula without great losses very heartening. It clearly indicated that the crossing was possible and led us to expect that other detachments would be sent in their wake. Together with our troops, they could then widen the bridgehead and facilitate the Russian occupation of the city.

I watched the battle scene almost daily from the rooftops of the highest buildings. My H.Q. at 19 Pius XI Street was only 2,000 yards from the Soviet positions as the crow flies. It was no exaggeration to say that the whole of Warsaw awoke each morning with the hope that that very day would see the liberation of the capital. The food situation and sanitary conditions became daily more appalling. When the battle for Praga had ended, the Germans renewed their systematic destruction of the city. The sky over Warsaw now lay within range of Soviet anti-aircraft guns on the opposite bank, and, thanks to this and to Soviet planes, German air activity had almost ceased. But after a few days of reduced activity, the heaviest enemy artillery, along with grenade-throwers and " moo-cows," now resumed their work of destruction with increased intensity. The population continued to live in hopes of the freedom which still seemed so very near at hand.

As for medical supplies, ammunition and food, I was counting on the help which we had been informed would be provided by a large-scale American operation. Day after day I received messages from London declaring that more than 100 aircraft were ready to take off. The departure of airborne supplies was scheduled for to-day, then to-morrow, then the day after. Each day the operation was postponed till the next.

One night a short announcement was made at 11 p.m. and repeated after midnight. A force of Flying Fortresses was to take off at dawn. The prearranged melody of "*Jeszcze Jeden Mazur Dzisiaj*" (One More Mazurka To-day) was played at the end of the B.B.C. Polish programme. Not one member of the Staff shut an eye that night. Gathered at the radio receivers, we all awaited the next programme. Would the melody be repeated or not. If in its place the "*Marsz Piechoty*" (Infantry March) were played, it would mean that the expedition had been cancelled. Its cancellation or confirmation would be heard at 9 a.m. Sick with excitement, we heard the programme out. Then, after the announcer's final words, the tune of "*Marsz Piechoty*" rang out. The expedition had been cancelled.

The following night brought the same news. Several hours after the cancellation, I received a message explaining that the aircraft had taken off, but, after getting as far as Holland, had been obliged to turn back owing to bad weather. Night after night we waited in vain to hear "*Jeszcze Jeden Mazur Dzisiaj*." Finally, on the night of September 17th/18th, the announcement of the operation was twice confirmed. It was with fears and doubts that we waited for the morning programme. This time "*Jeszcze Jeden Mazur Dzisiaj*" was repeated, and a message came in at the same moment announcing that the expedition was due to reach Warsaw between 11 a.m. and noon. The autumn day was sunny and fine, with a cloudless sky. The population, of course, neither knew nor suspected the advent of the operation. But it was the sound of cheering and shouts of joy on all sides which told me that the aircraft were coming over. The whole sky was filled with planes flying in at a great height from the west. They left behind long trails of white dots. It took a long moment to realise that the dots were parachutes. German anti-aircraft fire opened up, but was unable to reach the planes at that altitude, though shrapnel bursts pierced individual parachutes. Once more Warsaw lived through a moment of indescribable enthusiasm. With the exception of the sick and wounded, everyone had emerged from the cellars. Basements and cellars were deserted; courtyards and streets were jammed with people. Everyone able to stand on his own legs had rushed into the open. At first the people were quite certain that they were watching parachutists coming down.

Disappointment and depression followed the few short moments of exaltation and joy. I must admit that it was probably one of the worst moments I experienced during the rising. We had seen a splendid exhibition of Allied air power—but the majority of the containers fell beyond our lines, on the very places which, a week or ten days before, had been held by the Home Army. The vast crowd of people who had been shouting and cheering bowed their heads and returned to their cellars and shelters after the planes had disappeared. We had been eyewitnesses of the scale of help we might have received had it arrived sooner. Had the 1,800 containers been dropped in the first days of the rising, when two-thirds of the city was in our hands, they would certainly all have been collected by us, and might then have decided the outcome of the battle. With this substantial supply of arms and ammunition in the hands of the insurgents, the whole of Warsaw would undoubtedly have been freed of the enemy. Unfortunately, help had come when we retained only small patches of the city. It is very difficult to carry out precision dropping from so great a height. We could merely witness the massive exhibition of power and think of what might have been, had this help reached us sooner.

Other disappointments followed. Days had passed since the taking of Praga, and not only did Soviet activity not increase, but, on the contrary, each day seemed to grow less. From September 19th onwards the Soviet Air Force once again considerably reduced their activity over the city. Instead, after a ten-day interval, German Stukas in small groups again began to circle over the capital and to bomb it from the air. Doubts as to whether the Russians had intended to cross the Vistula and take Warsaw in the near future were expressed more and more openly. Soviet policy might have been directed against the Polish Government, against me, or

against a certain group of Polish people, but it was difficult
to imagine that this policy would be opposed to their own
interests. Such would be the case if they missed the opportunity
offered by our hold on Warsaw to capture, without difficulty
or losses, so powerful a bridgehead and at the same time
increased the distrust of the population towards them in
encouraging it to undertake a fight which, in view of their
lack of support, they had condemned to hopelessness. For six
weeks they had had bridgeheads on the western bank of the
Vistula, they now had Praga in their hands, and our rising
provided them with diversionary activity right in the heart
of the German lines; here, then, was every condition favourable
for the capture of Warsaw by an encircling movement from
the south in conjunction with a frontal attack.

It was in this frame of mind that I gave an interview to
the British airman, John Ward, who was sending short news
reports by radio to the British Press. Ward had been captured
by the Germans three years before, had escaped, and got
through to Warsaw, where, together with a great many other
British prisoners of war in hiding, he lived among the Polish
people and took an active part in Underground work. Ward
was a courageous young man. He was the only foreign
correspondent in Warsaw and also took an active part in the
fighting. I awarded him the Cross of Valour.

From the moment when we transferred our headquarters to
Pius XI Street, I received repeated warnings that the Communists were preparing a *coup d'état* with the intention of liquidating
me, allegedly encouraged by the accusations which Soviet
propaganda was pouring out against me through its radio.
I was advised not to go out into the town without armed
escort, but I did not pay much heed. Our headquarters were
under the competent eyes of the reliable Home Army Command defence squad, and out in the street no escort would be
of any avail if anyone wished to have a shot at me. On the
other hand, I did not fear an attempt to kidnap me, as I
always carried a revolver handy; moreover, our soldiers, in
whom I had implicit faith, were available in practically every
spot where I went, ready to come to my aid if necessary.
I nearly always went alone, whether to my daily meeting
with the Government delegate or to a conference with representatives of the National Council. If, however, I was going
to see Monter on the other side of the Jerozolimskie Aleje or

to inspect some unit or detachment, I was always accompanied by someone from the Staff or my aide-de-camp.

These journeys were not always easy; detours had to be made to cross sectors which were under enemy fire, either through backyards, intercommunicating basements of houses or even tunnels which had to be dug specially for that purpose. The street on which our headquarters stood was under constant enemy automatic fire, sometimes also from enemy tanks; in order to get there, one had to make a rapid crossing from the backyard of a crescent-shaped house opposite between two breastworks built of sandbags which were often blown to pieces by shells from enemy tanks.

Soviet propaganda had not for a moment relaxed its attacks on me and other commanders of the rising. Soviet and Soviet-controlled radio stations accused me unceasingly of being a war criminal and announced that I should have to stand trial for having evoked the Warsaw rising. In spite of this, I decided to make my real name known as well as those of the commanders fighting in Warsaw. I divided all the Home Army detachments in Warsaw into three divisions and appointed Monter as their army corps commander. (It was at this time that his nomination to the rank of general came through from London.) The purpose of this move was to give assurance that we were acting openly as commanders of detachments which formed part of the armed forces of one of the Allied nations.

Therefore, when it was suggested to me from London that I should think it over carefully before I decided to reveal myself personally to the Soviet authorities, because they were referring to me as an enemy, I answered:

"September 1st, 1944.

"C.-in-C., Polish Forces,

"I am completely aware of what I have to expect from the Russians, but for the sake of the cause I think it better that even this last card should be played. When thousands die around us, the death of one man means nothing. I intend to reveal my identity, that of my deputy, and of the Chief of Staff.

"Commander-in-Chief, Home Army."

Our eyes were constantly turned towards Czerniaków, which, though cut off from us, was our most forward position on the Vistula—closest to the Soviet lines. The noise of battle in Czerniaków could still be heard, but judging by the area of fire—the diameter of which was steadily shrinking bit by bit—the territory held by the defenders was diminishing day by day. On September 18th we made an attempt to renew contact with Czerniaków, and the Frascati district was retaken, but further advance failed. Czerniaków had sewer-contact only with Mokotów. By this means, some of the defenders retreated to Mokotów on September 20th, with Radosław at their head. His report, in which he described the situation at Czerniaków, was sent through the sewer-passage from Mokotów to the centre of the city. The battalion of Berlingmen which Berling had sent from Praga to Czerniaków was no longer a help. Without Russian help in food, ammunition or artillery support, it became a dead weight; our men had to share out their own rations, and these were soon exhausted. In the German hurricane-shell fire 70 per cent of the Czerniaków defenders lost their lives. Some Berlingmen and insurgents retreated with Radosław through the sewers to Mokotów. The remainder, one platoon of the Zośka Battalion, was left at Czerniaków. (It will be recalled that this was the battalion which forced its way from Stare Miasto to the centre of the city.) The remainder of the Berlingmen, under Major Łatyszonow, also remained. The Zośka Battalion stayed on at Czerniaków for the purpose of holding a bridgehead which would make the landing of further Soviet help possible; it was cut off from the entrance to the sewer and had only one remaining retreat to the right bank of the Vistula. It held several houses which defended a small stretch of the river bank. Rooftop observers watched from dawn to nightfall and listened to the noise of battle reaching them from the direction of Czerniaków. The question on everyone's lips was: "Are our men still fighting?" This state of affairs lasted until September 23rd. On that day final silence fell upon Czerniaków.

Towards morning on September 24th, a wounded officer on crutches made his painful way to the commander of a sector in the centre of the city. He had with him a messenger girl and two soldiers. One of the soldiers was a Berlingman. All four were in a state of complete nervous and physical collapse. It was with some difficulty that the officer was recognised to be Jerzy (Captain Białous), Commander of the Zośka Battalion. "Where are the rest of you?" everyone asked.

M

Jerzy shook his head sadly. They had fallen on the way; these four were the only survivors of the whole detachment. Jerzy could say no more that day. He was utterly exhausted, wounded and hungry; he had no more strength left. He was permitted to rest, and it was not until the next day that he told the story of his own experiences and the history of the Czerniaków battles.

The remainder of the Zośka Battalion had held on tenaciously in the few houses and on the river embankment to the bitter end. They had had to withstand several tank and infantry attacks each day and daily suffered fresh losses, but the Germans were unable to force them to the river. In this terrible plight their will to fight was sustained by the same idea which upheld the whole of Warsaw—the delusive proximity of the Soviet positions on the eastern bank of the river. They found it impossible to decide on capitulation knowing that so close to them—only 250 yards of river-bed away—was the great, conquering power which had thrust the Germans all the way from the Volga to the Vistula, battering the enemy and crossing so many obstacles greater than the Warsaw river. There were still quite a few Berlingmen with the battalion, including their commander, Łatyszonow, who still had his radio set with him. Jerzy and Łatyszonow shared headquarters in the kitchen of a half-ruined house. The radio station was also located there, and through it pleas were sent the whole day long for food, ammunition, artillery fire and troops. The Russians, however, sent neither food, ammunition nor troops. They confined themselves to accurate artillery fire directed on the German positions indicated by the insurgents, which helped to sustain the defenders in their ordeal from day to day. Nor did the Russians send accumulators for the radio, for which our men asked in vain, and thus their last means of contact with the outside world was broken off; but as several torch and field telephone batteries were found, the set was once more put into operation on September 22nd. The Czerniaków defenders had to fight not only German tanks and infantry but also the fires with which the Germans tried to smoke them out of the few half-ruined buildings still in their hands. The enemy was unable to wipe them out, but in the end hunger overcame them. The soldiers, wounded and civilians had had nothing to eat for four days.

At 6 a.m. on September 23rd Jerzy held a general conference with Łatyszonow and Father Peter, the courageous chaplain of the Zośka Battalion, who had accompanied it through all its battles. Jerzy decided to transfer his detachment, the wounded and the civilian population to the other side of the Vistula. He arranged the sequence of the crossing, the plan of action and the guards. Łatyszonow made contact with Soviet headquarters and presented Jerzy's requests. Jerzy asked for help for the crossing to be made at 8 a.m. He requested artillery fire on the German positions covering the Vistula and a smoke-screen on the river and pontoons, without which the crossing would be out of the question. The Commander of the Soviet 5th Division promised to give the requested aid at 9 a.m. He would send 100 pontoons, each of which would carry twenty persons. He was unable to arrange for a smoke-screen over the whole river, but it would be made in sections. The hearts of the defenders were filled with hope. Patiently they awaited nine o'clock and prepared for the crossing, but at the appointed hour no help came.

It was not until some hours later that the Russians declared that the crossing could not take place during daylight and that the promised aid would be given at 8 p.m., after dusk. In reply to Jerzy's request that food be dropped, they instructed his men to spread out large signal-sheets on the ground and promised that airborne supplies would be dropped within the next few hours. Jerzy's men immediately pulled out towels and bedsheets and spread them on the ground in the form of a large square, but no food was dropped. On the contrary, the spreading of signal-sheets attracted fierce grenade fire from the Germans. Throughout the day the Germans renewed their attacks many times and set fire to one of our buildings. About midday they sent out envoys with proposals of surrender. Jerzy, in the hope that the crossing would be made, rejected the proposal. He agreed only to evacuate such civilians as chose captivity in preference to the risk of the crossing. By evening all the buildings held by the defenders were on fire. Eight o'clock, the time indicated for the crossing, was approaching, but still no help came. Jerzy demanded direct communication with Soviet headquarters. He then had a conversation with Berling, who again renewed all the Soviet guarantees, claiming that the crossing had been delayed owing to technical difficulties, but that it would definitely take place at nine o'clock. He stated that the 100 pontoons were all ready and that everything would be well organised.

In spite of these assurances, after the two delays, doubts began to grow in the minds of the defenders as to whether the Soviet aid would come at all. At nine o'clock the detachments marched out in small groups in the direction of the river. There they waited until eleven o'clock. Just before midnight, two sapper boats crossed to our side. In one of them was an officer who declared that Soviet headquarters had altered their plans and that, instead of sending 100 pontoons at one time, fifteen sapper boats would be sent each evening. This blasted all hope of evacuation to the other side. Despair overcame the waiting people; some of them tried to swim across, others began to throw rafts together. About sixty, under the command of Jerzy, tried that very night to break through in the direction of the Polish positions in the centre of the city. Of those, four succeeded. Such was the end of the defence of Czerniaków. The fall of this bastion on the Vistula, which was held for so long at the price of such great losses, ended all hope of real and effective aid for Warsaw.

Starting on September 18th—that is, after the final occupation of Praga and the repulse of the enemy to the north along the river—operations on the Soviet front died down once more and silence reigned, broken only by a desultory exchange of artillery or anti-aircraft fire. Soviet planes flying over the city became rarer and rarer. Air supplies continued, but on a much smaller scale than during the battle for Praga. Soviet inactivity, of course, resulted in a renewal of Luftwaffe activity. German air squadrons became more audacious and their appearance more frequent. The Junkers and Stukas which bombed the city used to ground at night on airfields far to the rear in the neighbourhood of Toruń and Grudziądz, whence they would fly in the early morning to the Warsaw airfield at Ok cie, which they used as a base for the many bombing trips they made daily over the capital. The Germans were well aware of danger of the Russians getting to the other side of the Vistula with such ease, because the city was in the hands of the Home Army; for that reason they concentrated their efforts in preceding phases of the battle on reducing our position to a minimum, their most determined attacks being directed at our positions along the river from both north and south.

Then, emboldened by Soviet inactivity on the other side of the river, they switched all available forces to wipe out all our strongholds in the vicinity of the western bank and push back our forces to the centre of the town, thus cancelling altogether the danger of a Soviet crossing on sectors held by the Home Army. With that object in mind they brought all the heavy equipment they had at their disposal to bear on our positions lying near the embankments: heavy artillery, armour, flame-throwers, mortars of all types and air bombing and strafing. In order to keep our forces in the centre of the town engaged, they kept up a ceaseless bombardment by the heaviest guns (the ones which were used to destroy the Sevastopol fortifications), with simultaneous attacks along various points of the perimeter.

The fighting was incredibly fierce, our men holding on to positions with unprecedented determination. After many fruitless assaults, the Germans had to resort to air bombing (which they could do with the utmost precision, as we had no anti-aircraft defences) and swarms of heavy bombers virtually pulverised whole blocks of buildings, annihilating and burying the defenders under mountains of rubble. Then the tanks moved in. Our perimeter was being slowly reduced, the wastage in men was cruel and our ammunition supplies were dwindling and required careful hoarding.

The food situation had become desperate. On September 14th the last rations had been distributed to the soldiers. From that day onward there was no question of any regular allotments of food, even in very small quantities. Each unit depended on the initiative and imagination of its commander. It happened more and more often that men did not eat for several days; fainting from hunger and exhaustion was common. The reports from Żoliborz and Mokotów were particularly alarming. In the centre of the city the last source of supply was some wheat and barley in the warehouse of the Haber-busch and Schiele Brewery. It had miraculously avoided destruction and the stocks were now divided between soldiers and civilians. Long lines of them waited to be handed a little of the grain; a handful of wheat or barley, cooked in half a pint of water, was now the only fare for breakfast, lunch or dinner. The wheat was milled in private coffee-grinders and used for a sort of soup which was nicknamed *Plujka* (from the word *pluć*, which means spit). When eating this soup, the husks had to be spat out at every mouthful. By about September 20th, these last reserves of wheat and barley had been completely exhausted. Such horses as had been in the city had been killed and eaten long since. Now it was the turn of dogs, cats and pigeons, which were systematically hunted.

Besides hunger, there was a dire lack of water, even for sick and wounded. German grenade-throwers found good targets in the long queues of men and women who lined up at the few wells in which a little water could still be found. Water was no longer rationed by pots, but sometimes by glasses. Special wells, guarded by sentries, were reserved for the use of the hospitals.

The state of the hospitals were indescribable. Wounded poured in all day and every day. The doctors could hardly cope with the work. Surgical operations were carried out without anæsthetics, in cellars, by the light of a few candles or in exceptional cases carbide lamps. Where dressing materials were short, paper was used to stop hæmorrhage. Exhaustion reached such a pitch that even the first-aid service, which hitherto had worked very well indeed, slackened. People became indifferent to everything—even to the cries of those buried in the basements of destroyed houses. Strength had been used up and there were no more men to clear the rubble. In the cellars, where altruism reached the extreme point of sharing the last pound of wheat, a few men, utterly devoid of scruples, would part with a scrap of food for gold or jewels to people ready to pay any price for something to eat. Babies who managed to survive till the end of September were rare exceptions.

With the renewed silence on the Russian front, the Germans once more renewed their proposals for surrender. This time, they sent envoys to Zoliborz and Mokotów. Those at Mokotów proposed a meeting between von dem Bach and myself on neutral ground. The commanders of both districts rejected the offers. The Zoliborz commander, Colonel Zywiciel-Niedzielski, who was appealed to by General von dem Bach in the name of humanitarian feelings, cited in his answer the inhuman treatment which was being meted out to civilians by the Germans. He gave, among others, the case where our units found in a recaptured dwelling the naked bodies of women and children who had been tortured and murdered with the utmost bestiality.

A dive-bombing attack on Mokotów by Stukas on September 24th was the beginning of an encircling attack on the district, supported by intensive artillery fire. The attacking forces were composed of the 73rd Infantry Division and elements of the Herman Goering, Viking and Frankonien Sudeten Panzer divisions. The Mokotów commander, Colonel "Karol" Rokicki, requested, through his two Soviet artillery observers, fire support from Berling. Once again, he received a series of promises which were never kept. On September 25th, Rokicki sent me this short radio message: "Situation very serious. Lack of help from Soviet artillery." On September 26th, his next message said: "No fire from Soviet artillery." On 27th, the last news came from the Mokotów commander, informing me that his units had now been pressed into an area covering only a few streets. He estimated the losses in soldiers and civilians at 70 per cent. This was among the highest proportion of losses which we had yet suffered. Mokotów fell that same day.

On receiving the news of the loss of Mokotów, I called a full Staff meeting with Monter, and invited the Government delegate as well. Each person present reported on the situation. They were all agreed that civilians and soldiers alike were suffering from hunger, a state of affairs which made the situation untenable for more than three or five days at the most. Either the enemy or hunger would overwhelm us in that time; this was the time limit for the arrival of help from outside. Surrender was the only alternative. I once more recapitulated all our previous efforts and attempts to establish co-operation with the Russians. I recorded that numerous messages sent by Monter, Kaługin and myself, through London or directly to Rokossovsky, had failed to produce tactical co-operation between us and the Soviet command. Equally ineffective were the attempts of the liaison groups sent across the Vistula. The Russians had confined themselves to air supplies made by a few planes nearly every night, but every one of our proposals to organise a combined attack by Polish and Soviet forces on the German positions and to agree on its date and direction had been left unanswered by the Soviets. The Russians had kept us in complete ignorance of their intentions and of the probable date of their attack which would lead to the occupation of this side of Warsaw; they had left us to make our own assumptions and to draw our own conclusions from a series of facts. They had allowed the

Germans to liquidate the bridgehead at Czerniaków defended by our troops, despite the fact that the battle there was fought out before their very eyes. Only one conclusion could be reached from this: that the Soviet commander had no intention of crossing the Vistula in the near future. True, the question arose as to what was their motive in broadcasting the appeals, "Keep fighting," and in supplying us by air. There could be only one explanation. The brief Russian help was only a concession to political opinion in the west, and had no connection with a plan to relieve Warsaw, its defenders and its people.

As further evidence to contribute to an impartial judgment of the events which accompanied the Warsaw rising, I think that it is not irrelevant to quote the testimony given by two German generals, who were arrested after hostilities had ceased—namely, General Guderian, Chief of Staff of the German land forces on the eastern front, and General von dem Bach. To-day their statements throw adequate light on several hazy points and clarify the doubts which we had at the time as to reasons for the pause in the Soviet offensive when it reached the Vistula.

General Guderian's testimony has been already mentioned.

General von dem Bach stated the following:[1]

A. From the Point of View of Material. The movement of troops to the front was hampered and the supply of material had to be switched on to a detour, which not only increased the distance, but also the wastage of valuable fuel. Further consequences were the tying down of several regiments of troops and strong artillery units which were diverted from the fighting on the Praga sector. Furthermore, the engagement of one of the best Panzer divisions, so badly needed on the front, for over fourteen days; the loss through fire or capture by the insurgents of very important army equipment and food stores; finally, the loss of all army ordnance and repair depots which were irreplaceable.

B. Nor should the effect of the rising on the morale of the enemy be under-estimated. The [German] troops fighting east of the Praga suburb felt their rear constantly menaced by the rising. Primarily, the front-line troops, already unmercifully battered and in retreat, felt their line of withdrawal in constant jeopardy of being cut, *with the simultaneous threat of a big push*

[1] *National Memorial Institute Quarterly*, Vol. I, Part 2 (Warsaw, 1947).

impending from the Red Army. It was to this feeling of insecurity that we can easily ascribe *the rapid fall of Praga under the Russian attack, even though it came so much later than expected, in view of the fact that German rearguards were mainly concerned with keeping open their communication with the bridges over the Vistula lying north of the city, and beat a hasty retreat in that direction.*

In the light of this evidence from German generals, does not the official statement of Soviet spokesmen—that the German counter-attack launched in the beginning of August upset the Red Army schedule regarding the capture of Warsaw, which finally took place after four months—seem to give rise to some serious doubt?

Von dem Bach says quite plainly that the Germans were awaiting a great Russian offensive to coincide with the Warsaw rising, in the place of which came, after long delay, merely a local push at the Praga suburb east of the Vistula! It seems therefore that the "great Russian offensive," which only developed after four months, had been awaited by the Germans at the very beginning of the Warsaw rising. Thus is seems fairly clear that other factors were influencing the Russians and not merely a Red Army setback, as they alleged; all the more so as the condition of the German forces east of the Vistula was so bad that their "only concern was to keep open their line of retreat to the bridge [over the Vistula] lying to the north of the town, so as to permit a rapid withdrawal."

A certain light is also thrown on the Russian intentions with regard to the Warsaw rising by a statement of Osóbka-Morawski,[1] which appeared in the Warsaw *Robotnik*, of August 1st, 1946: "Having obtained the necessary information, on leaving Moscow I gave a code message by radio to my political associates [in Warsaw] that they are no longer to count on help and should endeavour to save as much human life as possible." Thus it can be seen that Osóbka was very well aware, during the Warsaw rising, that the Soviets were not going to give any help. But his code message was not sent to the defenders of Warsaw.

At this meeting in the evening of September 27th we decided that the fighting must stop, since it was hopeless. It had become obvious that the Soviets were not willing to cross the Vistula and to take Warsaw. We had to save the rest of the

[1] The former Prime Minister of the so-called Provisional Government of Poland.

civilian population. So we reached the decision that talks with the Germans should be started on the following day. In the centre of the city alone there were still over 300,000 people. We wished to spare them the fate of the civilians at Stare Miasto, Powiśle, Czerniaków and Mokotów.

I sent one more message to Rokossovsky. In it, I briefly described the desperate situation of the civilians and the Army and declared that hunger and German pressure could even then be endured for a further seventy-two hours. If we neither received relief within this period nor the promise of the arrival of such relief within the next few days, then I should be forced to stop the fight.

So the decision whether we were to continue fighting or surrender would depend on the answer of Marshal Rokossovsky.

In the early hours of September 28th our wireless station succeeded in contacting the Russians and transmitted the text of my message. The Russians confirmed its reception.

On the same day I sent a telegram to London as follows:

"WARSAW.
"*September 28th, 1944.*
"Mokotów fell on September 27th. Further struggle in two isolated sectors may become impossible. Hunger. If we do not receive the effective aid of a Soviet attack by October 1st we shall be compelled to cease the struggle. We are informing Rokossovsky directly of the possibility that we shall be unable to hold on.
"*Commander-in-Chief, Home Army.*"

In the greatest suspense, we awaited the answer from Rokossovsky. Every moment someone would burst into the Staff room asking if anything had come in. But for twenty-four hours no answer reached us. Instead, during the night, a few Soviet planes flew over and dropped their usual load, a few bags of ammunition and several sacks of *kasha*. The latter burst on landing, spreading their contents over a wide area. People rushed from all sides, however, collecting it to the last grain.

Beginning at dawn on September 29th, intensive German artillery fire was reported from Zoliborz. This was the usual forerunner of a German attack. All the next day and the following night was spent in vain expectation of a Soviet reply. Nothing came. Accordingly, on September 29th, I sent envoys to the Germans. They were to ask General von dem Bach what he suggested, in view of his many requests and proposals to meet me.

He proposed the evacuation of the civilian population and then, pointing out the uselessness of further fight, he laid down his conditions for surrender in which soldiers of the Home Army would be treated with the rights due to combatant troops. I decided to open the talks with the question of the evacuation of the civilians. I still refrained from taking the decision to surrender, in the hope that an answer might yet arrive from the Russians. The wireless operators remained on duty, in turns, for seventy-two hours, but the answer never came. Each hour made it more and more certain that Warsaw would never see the arrival of its relief.

The general German attack on Zoliborz started on September 29th. They used all their available aircraft, artillery, infantry and two Panzer divisions. Zywiciel reported that the Germans were suffering heavy losses in tanks and armoured units, but their superiority was overwhelming and the position of his units, confined in a small area, was desperate. On September 30th, I gave up all hope of a Soviet reply. I considered the position of the defenders of Zoliborz to be absolutely hopeless and, unable to send them help of any kind, I ordered fighting at Zoliborz to cease.

Meanwhile, talks on the evacuation of the civilian population had reached an agreement, which was signed by the Polish Red Cross for our side. The people of Warsaw were to be allowed to leave the city during October 1st, 2nd and 3rd. Two barricades were designated as exit points for the evacuation and hours were fixed for a cease-fire at these points for both sides. The Government delegate published these conditions in the Press and on posters. But on October 1st, it appeared that there were still very few volunteers ready to leave Warsaw for the camp at Pruszkow, where they were to be sent. The Germans had even prepared a dozen horse carts to drive those unable to walk the eight miles to Pruszkow. Of course, it was merely a symbolic gesture from the German side with a view to convincing us of their humane feelings. The number of wounded and others unable to walk ran into tens of thousands—the few carts were certainly no solution to their transport problem; and yet, on that first day, the German carts waited in vain until 5 p.m. and had to withdraw empty.

Instead, the people of Warsaw used the opportunity afforded by the cease-fire for a very different purpose. Thousands of civilians, mostly women, went out on the Mokotowska Race-course, which during the war had been turned into garden allotments, and searched for potatoes, tomatoes, carrots, onions and so on. In the evening the German sector commander of Mokotowska Racecourse sent an envoy to remind them that the cease-fire had been arranged in order that they might leave the city and not for the purpose of food excursions. He announced that next day he would fire at anyone approaching the German trenches to dig up vegetables under the very noses of his soldiers. It was clear that, in spite of hunger, the population had no wish to leave Warsaw so long as its defenders still went on fighting. This was understandable since in every family there was a son, wife, husband, father or daughter in the ranks of the Home Army.

Late on the night of September 30th, weary after long talks with my Staff, I turned in to my quarters for a rest. In the next room a carbide lamp was burning. Agaton, commanding the security platoon, was on duty at the wireless. Tired out, I immediately fell asleep. An hour later, Agaton woke me up; his face was showing great excitement. I leapt off the bed, thinking in a flash that news must have come from the Russians.

"Sir," he burst out, "just a moment ago the B.B.C. broadcast the news that you had been appointed Commander-in-Chief of the Polish armed forces."

At first I thought Agaton had gone mad. Nothing was less expected or seemed less probable than this news at such a moment. In the early hours, I received official confirmation in a message of appointment from the Polish President in London:

"With effect from September 30th, 1944, according to Article 13 of the Constitution, I appoint you Commander-in-Chief, Polish Armed Forces. You will assume your rights and duties on arrival at the present seat of the highest Polish authorities.

"*(Signed)* Władysław Raczkiewicz."

With the name of General Sosnkowski, the Commander-in-Chief now leaving office, was linked a fine tradition dating back to the early days of the present Polish Army. General Sosnkowski's dismissal, together with the fate of Warsaw, presented the morale of the Polish forces with a severe test. In those difficult days, President Raczkiewicz had doubtless tried to put forward a symbol which would unite all Poles. This symbol was Warsaw. I understood my appointment as a tribute to my soldiers in Warsaw.

Expecting to be obliged to surrender in the next few hours, I issued last instructions. Outside Warsaw there was still the remainder of the Home Army operating on German-occupied territory; I expected to be in German hands myself in a few days, and these men could not be left without orders. The surrender of Warsaw should not be identified with the surrender of the whole Underground movement, which had to carry on as long as there were Germans in occupation of any part of Poland. I appointed General Okulicki my successor as Commander of the Home Army. A few months before, Okulicki had left Italy to be parachuted into Poland. The Gestapo as yet knew nothing of his presence in Poland and there were chances that, at the surrender, the Germans would not notice his disappearance. He prepared his departure from the city and chose a small group of Staff officers. Each of them had to leave Warsaw individually after agreeing on their ultimate meeting place in the country.

At the same time, I appointed two couriers who were to reach Great Britain and report to the Polish Government on the events which had taken place in Warsaw. Two others were appointed by the Government delegate. We expected that at least one of the four would succeed in reaching London. In fact, only one of them, Captain J. Nowak, reached London after a long and difficult journey.

As in the night of October 1st/2nd there was no answer from the Russians to my last message, I decided to renew my talks with the Germans regarding an armistice. For the purpose, I appointed a delegation, with Colonel "Heller" (Iranek Osmecki) in charge. Together with my Staff, I worked out an agreement in which the conditions for surrender were formulated in such a way as to be as favourable as possible for the Poles. Above all, I wished combatant rights to be accorded, not only to the soldiers of the Home Army, but also to all those who had fought in our ranks and agreed to accept my tactical orders. This meant combatant rights also for the Communist Armja Ludowa. The next condition which I considered essential was that no one among the

Home Army or civilians should be held responsible for his or her participation in the Underground Movement either during the period of fighting or in the preceding period. I sought assurance of combatant rights for the numbers of women who had fought in our ranks. This last condition would, of course, be without precedent; equally unprecedented was the employment of women for front-line duty during both the Underground days and the actual rising. Further conditions related to the evacuation of the civilian population and its welfare, and the right of the Polish Red Cross and other charitable institutions to assist. In briefing the delegation, I gave its members exact instructions defining the limits of the concessions which they could make in their talks.

The delegation reached the German barricades facing the Polytechnic School at 8 a.m. on October 2nd. Thence it was conducted to the H.Q. of General von dem Bach, which was situated on the Ozarów estate, about six miles out of Warsaw to the west. He introduced himself to the delegation with his full title: "Obergruppenführer S.S. und General der Polizei von dem Bach." They all sat down with the General at a round table. In the background, at a desk, sat the General's Chief of Staff, and a major. Von dem Bach read my letter authorising the delegates to discuss and sign an agreement for an armistice. Then he rose to his feet and very ceremoniously made a short speech, carefully enunciating each phrase.

Von dem Bach declared that he was unable to hide his satisfaction over the decision of General Bor to stop the fighting. He was glad that in this hopeless position I had taken what was, it was true, a tragic decision, but the only right one. On this point he admitted that he had been the only optimist, not only among the members of his own Staff, but in Army Group and Berlin circles as well. Nobody but he, indeed, had believed in the possibility of any kind of parleying with the Home Army which could result in a cessation of the fight.

"It will be a big surprise for all of them," he said, "when I inform them that we have started discussions. But permit me, gentlemen, only to inform the Army Group and Berlin when our agreement has really taken shape in the course of our talks."

Further on, von dem Bach paid manifold compliments to the fighting valour of the Home Army units and described the serious difficulties which he had had to overcome when fighting against us.

After this peroration, the gathering sat down and discussions for the agreement began. The principal difficulty was apparent from the start. General von dem Bach required that German forces should immediately occupy the part of the city held by the Home Army. This, he stated, was because the German command must have a guarantee that the Poles would not break off the talks should a Soviet attack be made meanwhile. In addition, von dem Bach continued, from the operational point of view the communication arteries running parallel with the Vistula were of vital importance. The blockade of these communication lines by the Home Army, as well as the presence of their units in the centre of the city, would render the transfer of reserves and artillery from one point to another very difficult in the event of a Soviet attack. He therefore requested that, on that same day, we should agree to have these arteries occupied by German units.

The Polish delegation rejected this request because the presence of Polish and German units in the same area would irrevocably lead to incidents and even to an outbreak of fighting in view of their deep, mutual antagonism. Von dem Bach obstinately insisted, however, that some point of agreement must be reached which would provide sufficient guarantee to the German Army Group Commander that talks for an armistice would not be broken off by the Polish side.

As the application of these conditions required the issue of immediate orders, Zyndram returned to Warsaw, where, after agreement with me on the subject, it was decided that that same day one barricade, on Sniadeckich Street facing the Polytechnic School, would be removed. This should be accepted as a satisfactory sign that talks would not be broken off.

Before going any further with the discussions, the Polish delegation declared that they had brought with them a prepared text for the agreement. This somewhat astonished the Germans, but they agreed to accept it as a basis for discussion and, with only very minor amendments, all the Polish proposals were accepted by both sides as a binding agreement. That afternoon, the Polish delegation, together with the German officers, put on to paper the final text of the agreement.

Meanwhile, talking with Heller, General von dem Bach said that the highest interest had been awakened in leading

German spheres by the part played by Polish women in the organisation and in the fight in Warsaw. It had so astonished the Germans that even the Fuehrer "himself personally" had become interested in it, and von dem Bach, on his last visit to Berlin, had been summoned to inform the Fuehrer personally as to his experiences and opinion in the matter.

The incident which had most impressed him was when a messenger girl had been taken prisoner in Bank Square. On the night of September 1st, when the Stare Miasto garrison was evacuating to the centre of the city, a Polish major, accompanied by a messenger girl, had fallen into German hands. The major was killed, but, when the German soldiers approached the messenger girl, she killed several of them with the revolver she had snatched from the hand of the dead major. More Germans arrived, but only after further firing and when she had run out of ammunition was she taken prisoner. The girl's courageous defence was reported to the General, who decided to interrogate her himself. During this, his admiration was increased by her self-assurance, tenacity and faith in the justice of the cause for which she was fighting. Realising that she was clever and had chances of contacting my H.Q., von dem Bach, who was still clinging to his idea of parleying with me, tried to persuade her to return to the Polish lines with a letter for me. At first she refused, but the General pointed out that if she returned, she would be able to go on fighting, which, he presumed, was just what she wanted.

This succeeded, and the girl decided to return. He stipulated, however, that she should read the letter she was to carry to me. In it, he had made proposals for an end of the fight and the surrender of arms. When she had read this, she declared that she could not take it upon herself to deliver it. True, she said, this letter would in no way influence the decision of General Bor; nevertheless, she would never accept such a mission.

After these personal confidences, loaded with compliments for us, von dem Bach passed on to political matters. He expressed the certainty that the end of the war would find the Germans on the winning side, because, quite apart from the V1 and V2, they had many other new secret weapons in process of preparation which would radically tip the scales in their favour.

At 8 p.m. on October 2nd, the surrender agreement was signed at von dem Bach's headquarters. For the second time in this war, Warsaw had to give way to the superiority of the enemy. At the beginning and end of the war the capital of Poland had fought alone. Yet the conditions in which fighting had gone on in September, 1939, were very different from those of 1944. Five years earlier, the Germans had been at the summit of their power. The weakness of the Allies had made it impossible for them to help Warsaw. The fall of Warsaw in 1939 was the first in a long series of German victories; but in 1944 the situation was reversed. The Germans were declining towards their fall, and we all had a bitter feeling that the failure of the rising would probably be the last German victory over the Allies. History would perhaps show one day why Warsaw had been left this second time without relief.

Heller reported to me late in the evening, bringing me news of the agreement which had been reached with von dem Bach and repeating his statements to me. It was not difficult to guess that the "flirtation" of the Prussian S.S. man concealed other, deeper intentions and motives. I knew von dem Bach's past too well to nurture any illusions about the sincerity of his pro-Polish emotionalism. I knew, too, that after the occupation of Poland in 1939 it was he who, as commander of the S.S. and Polizei in Polish Upper Silesia, was responsible for the ruthless repression which occurred there. The methods adopted by the Germans during the rising alone were sufficient to reveal the true character of the German commander. It was more difficult to discover the actual motives for such a sudden change in German tactics. From von dem Bach's attitude it was evident that the Germans wished to end the fight as soon as possible, and in order to do so were ready to recognise our combatant rights. A few weeks earlier, they had already mentioned it over the radio. In view of the deterioration of the German situation on the whole front and the approach of their inevitable defeat, we had some hopes that the surrender conditions would be adhered to. Perhaps another reason lay behind this new German attitude. It was at that time that they had formed the new Home Guard, the *Volkssturm*, which was also intended for partisan activity in the rear of the armies of their enemies when operating in Germany. In according us the rights of official combatants, the Germans probably wished to create a precedent which would apply, later on, to their own partisans.

The most important points in the agreement were as follows:

"I. . . . 5. . . . Soldiers of the Home Army are entitled to the rights of the Geneva Convention dated August 27th, 1929, concerning the treatment of prisoners of war. Soldiers of the Home Army taken prisoner in the area of the city of Warsaw in the course of the struggle which began on August 1st, 1944, shall enjoy the same rights.

"6. Those non-combatant persons accompanying the Home Army, within the meaning of Article 81 of the Geneva Convention on the treatment of prisoners of war without distinction of sex, are entitled to the rights of prisoners of war. This affects in particular women workers. . . .

"8. Persons being prisoners of war in the sense of the aforesaid articles shall not be persecuted for their military or political activities either during the period of struggle in Warsaw or in the preceding period. . . .

"9. In regard to the civilian population who were in the city of Warsaw during the period of struggle, collective responsibility shall not be applied.

"No person who was in Warsaw during the period of struggle shall be persecuted for functioning in time of war in the organisation of administrative or judiciary authorities. . . .

"10. The evacuation of the civilian population from the city of Warsaw which the German Command has demanded shall be carried out at such a time and in such a manner as shall save the population superfluous suffering. . . .

. . "II. . . . 2. The Home Army Command will deliver to the German lines all German prisoners of war. . . .

"8. The evacuation of the wounded and sick soldiers of the Home Army, as also of medical material, will be determined by the Medical Head of the German forces in consultation with the Medical Head of the Home Army. . . .

"9. Soldiers of the Home Army shall be recognised by a white-and-red arm-band or pennons, or a Polish eagle. . . .

(*Signed*) {
VON DEM BACH.
COLONEL HELLER.
LIEUT.-COLONEL ZYNDRAM.
}

The following is my last order to my troops:

"WARSAW.

"*October 3rd, 1944.*

"Soldiers of Fighting Warsaw!

"Our two months' struggle in Warsaw, which has been a chain of heroic actions on the part of the Polish soldiers, is fraught with dread, yet it is a solemn proof, above all, of our mighty striving for liberty. The valour of Warsaw is the admiration of the whole world. Our struggle in the capital under the blows of death and destruction, carried on with such tenacity by us, takes first place among the glorious deeds achieved by Polish soldiers during this war. By it, we have proved our spirit and our love of freedom. And although we have not been able to gain military victory over the enemy, for the reason that during these two months the general development of military events on our soil has not favoured our cause, none the less these two months of struggle for every inch of the streets and walls of Warsaw have achieved their political and ideological end. Our struggle will influence the destiny of our nation, because it is an unparalleled contribution of devoted valour in the defence of our independence.

"To-day the technical superiority of the enemy has succeeded in forcing us into the central part of the city, the only district still in our possession. The ruins and rubble are crowded with civilians co-operating valiantly with the soldiers, but already exhausted beyond measure by the ghastly conditions of existence on the field of battle. There is not sufficient food even for bare existence, and there is no prospect of a final conquest of the enemy here in the capital. We are now confronted with the prospect of the complete destruction of the population of Warsaw and the burial of thousands of fighting soldiers and civilians in its ruins.

"I have therefore decided to break off the struggle.

"I thank all soldiers for their magnificent bearing, which did not succumb even when conditions were at their worst. I pay due tribute to the fallen for their agony. I express the admiration and gratitude of the fighting ranks of the army to the population and declare the army's attachment to them. I ask the people to pardon the soldiers any transgressions committed against the population during the long and protracted struggle.

"In agreeing that military operations shall terminate, I have endeavoured to ensure to the soldiers all rights due to them after the cessation of the struggle and to the civilian population such conditions of existence and protection as shall best save them from the cruelties of war.

"You soldiers, my dearest comrades in these two months of fighting, one and all of whom have been to the very last moment constant in the will to fight on, I ask now to fulfil obediently such orders as arise from the decision to cease fighting.

"I call to the population to comply with the evacuation instructions issued by me, the city's Commander, and the civil authorities.

"With faith in ultimate victory of our just cause, with faith in a beloved, great and happy country, we shall all remain soldiers and citizens of an independent Poland, faithful to the standard of the Polish Republic.

"KOMOROWSKI, *Lieutenant-General,*
"*Commander-in-Chief, Home Army.*"

At that time I received various suggestions that I should escape and try to get to London, but of course I refused bluntly; it was clear to me that I could not leave my men at that moment but had to share their fate. My escape would have been looked upon by the Germans as a breach of the agreement I had signed with them, and would undoubtedly have had repercussions on the fate of both soldiers and civilians. I could only have attempted an escape once I had been sent to a P.O.W. camp. Then I should have been responsible only for myself as an individual; but this, later on, proved to be quite impossible, as I was too well guarded.

On October 3rd, in the early hours of the morning, dead silence reigned over the city. After sixty-three days of non-stop fighting, the hush sounded ominous. The news that talk had begun for the capitulation of the army had spread like wildfire among the civilians, even on the previous day. Waves of people, pale and hungry, moved from their cellars and shelters towards the barricaded exits—women, children and old people, carrying on their backs the remnants of their salvaged belongings. In nearly every family there was someone who was unable to leave the city without help.

Parents and friends helped the aged. The wounded were carried on hurriedly improvised stretchers or even in a comrade's arms. It was a tragic journey of hundreds of thousands

of people to an unknown destination. All we knew was that
the evacuated people were being directed to an assembly
camp at Pruszkow. No one knew what would become of
them afterwards. Although the Germans had promised that
safety, work and food were assured, no one had the slightest
confidence in their promises. Even greater uncertainty was
felt by the insurgents, who remembered that the Germans
had been calling them "bandits" not so long ago and had
shot their comrades who had been taken prisoner.

All through these days I lived in constant fear and anxiety
over the fate of my wife and child. I was aware of the mass
murders of civilians which the Germans were perpetrating on
the inhabitants evacuated from the captured parts of the city.
I spoke to no one about my worries, knowing how well they
were shared by most of my men and fearing that I might
adversely affect their spirit and determination to fight.

I shall never be able to describe the relief which I felt on
receiving that short—but how eloquent!—radio message in
the last days of our ordeal. One of my area commandants
radioed the following dispatch: "Bor's wife and both sons
safe. . . ."

How much that message meant to me! Not only that my
family had got out safely into one of the provincial areas, but
also that, at the very time of the fighting, my wife had safely
given birth to a second son!

After signing the surrender agreement, von dem Bach
transmitted to me, through Zyndram, an invitation to meet
him at his H.Q. at Ozarów on October 4th, to discuss with
him all the additional measures to be taken in connection with
the surrender and fate of the civilians. He also invited me to a
lunch at which would be present all the heads of the German
Army and the civil administration. I refused to be present at
the lunch, but agreed to discuss with him the fate of the
population of Warsaw and the problem of improving the
conditions of evacuation. I would, therefore, visit him on
October 4th at noon.

At a fixed hour, I went through the barricade with Heller
and an interpreter; two German cars awaited us on the other
side. We crossed the street between rows of burnt-out houses.
The district through which we drove had never been engulfed
in the fight. On our side the streets were blocked by the rubble
of houses and ploughed up by shells, and at every step craters

had to be negotiated, but on this side the roads were untouched. The cars met no obstacles, and yet all the houses and the whole district had been systematically burned down. There was no sign of life anywhere. On all sides emptiness gaped from the black holes which had once been windows. Only German sentries could be seen amid the ruins. We passed artillery positions which had so recently been shelling the city. Half an hour later, the car stopped in front of a house at Ozarów, built in the Polish country style. In the hall, the German Chief of Staff drew Heller aside. Another German officer tried to do the same with my interpreter, "Sas," but I ordered him to remain with me. I wished to have a witness at the talk, and accordingly announced to von dem Bach that, although I spoke German, it had got rusty through lack of practice and I preferred to use an interpreter. My German opponent was the living personification of the Prussian Junker type. He was tall, broad of shoulder, aged about fifty, wearing gold-rimmed glasses; he was dressed in S.S. uniform, and the insignia of a Knight of the Iron Cross hung round his neck. His demeanour showed self-assurance and satisfaction covered by elaborate politeness. He spoke in a very loud voice and with great distinctness, in the fashion which seemed to characterise Nazi Party leaders. He opened the talk with a series of compliments and tributes to the courage and fighting value of the defenders of Warsaw. Then he switched to politics. He first expressed his sympathy at our fate, saying that he was fully aware of the bitterness which the Home Army and civilians alike must feel for Russia and their western Allies. He had not the least doubt that, after this last experience, the Poles could have no further illusions on the unfriendly intentions of Soviet Russia or the lack of real support from the other Allies. Germany and Poland, he went on, were now facing a common danger and had a common foe. Both nations should, therefore, cease their quarrels and go forward together, shoulder to shoulder.

My reply to this speech was brief. I wished to avoid any misunderstanding, and before discussions went any further I wanted to make it clear just how we stood. I had signed the surrender of the Home Army units in Warsaw and I was ready loyally to adhere to its execution. The surrender had not in any way changed the attitude of Poland towards Germany, with whom we had been at war since September 1st, 1939.

General von dem Bach, however, did not give up. He agreed completely that Germans had committed a series of great mistakes towards the Poles. He, himself, he said, had always been personally opposed to the policy of oppression and terror which had been adopted in Poland. He considered, however, that there was still time to repair these errors and to undertake anti-Soviet activities together in a common interest. I again declared that he could expect nothing from me which would be opposed to my conception of honour or to my allegiance and fidelity to my own authorities.

Von dem Bach then switched to another proposal: that I should occupy a villa which he had had prepared for me. Only a token sentry would be posted there, and he suggested that I should relax after the hardships of the fighting. This, he said, would enable me to supervise, with him, the evacuation of the population of the city.

I refused this proposal as well. I thanked him for the suggestion that I should rest, but was unable to accept different conditions from those of the other prisoners. Neither could I supervise the evacuation with him if it was to be carried out by German military or police units. I expected that the German side would put into effect their commitments embodied in the agreement with regard to the civilian population, but I could not share with the German authorities the responsibility towards the Polish nation for the execution of that agreement.

Von dem Bach then made one last proposal. He suggested that the armistice signed in Warsaw should be applied to all units of the Home Army operating in the part of Poland under German occupation, in order to avoid further useless bloodshed. He considered this to be the only sensible solution, in view of the present political situation of Poland, and he was ready to treat such a secret agreement with complete discretion.

Once more I refused. We had fulfilled all our obligations as an Allied nation for five years, and we were certainly not going to default on the eve of victory. "But, General," smiled von dem Bach, "you and your compatriots are quite wrong. You are being unduly influenced by a temporary German setback. The future will bring surprises of which nobody has dreamed. German victory is absolutely certain. You will remember my words. Final victory in this war will be ours." I answered that my opinion on the subject was quite different.

After he had assured me that the civilians would not be expelled from Warsaw, except for reason of military necessity, and had promised he would see to this personally, our talk ended. I then had no idea that masses of civilians from the district conquered by the Germans during the fighting had been taken to concentration camps. I discovered that only after my liberation in 1945. Our talk had lasted nearly an hour. Von dem Bach's leave-taking was considerably colder than his greeting had been.

Leaving the house, I brushed aside the crowd of German cameramen and got into the car which took me back to Warsaw. The march-out of the Poles from Warsaw was scheduled for the following day, October 5th, at 9.45 a.m.

During the rising I had appeared once or twice in a uniform which was a sort of home-made battle-dress made from a captured German material of light blue. I decided not to use it and to leave the city in civilian clothes with a white-and-red armband, because a high percentage of the Home Army men had never had a uniform, and their only distinguishing mark was their armband. We feared that perhaps the Germans would interpret the Hague Convention by according combatant rights only to those in uniform. I wished to demonstrate that an armband and an identity card of the Home Army was sufficient to prove military status.

The last hours were hard for all of us. It was not easy to give up the last bit of the city on which we had lived for sixty-three days as free men and where, beneath the ruins, now lay so many of our comrades of the Underground days.

On the previous evening, Błyskawica had broadcast its farewell programme. Broken with emotion, the voice of the speaker had announced: ". . . We have been free for two months; to-day once more we must go into captivity, but at least the Germans cannot take Warsaw again. All that is left is a heap of rubble. . . . Warsaw no longer exists." At the end of this broadcast, the personnel destroyed the sets and equipment which had continued to appeal for help throughout the rising.

The last messages, giving the terms of surrender, were sent, and the short-wave station was silenced as well. One of the messages was addressed to those soldiers who, in far-off England, had taken part in our struggle, working ceaselessly day and night at their receivers to pick up signals from Warsaw.

My last message to the President of the Republic of Poland in London read:

"WARSAW.

"*8 p.m., October 4th, 1944.*

"To the President of the Republic of Poland:

"I report that, in fulfilment of the capitulation agreement, which I concluded on the 2nd inst., the troops fighting in Warsaw will lay down their arms to-day and to-morrow.

"It is quite impossible that I should not go into captivity in view of the repressive measures that otherwise might be taken against the Home Army and the civilian population. I am surrendering with the troops to the Germans to-morrow, the 5th inst., before noon. To-day I visited General von dem Bach, with whom I concluded the agreement for capitulation. I was invited to a lunch, at which representatives of the German military forces and civil authorities were to be present. I refused to take part in the lunch, but settled with General von dem Bach all questions connected with securing the best possible conditions for the prisoners of the Home Army and the civilian population of Warsaw. In this last telegram which I send as a free man to you, Mr. President, I desire to offer you my deepest respect and to express to the highest representative of the Republic my warmest wishes for the attainment by our country of freedom, greatness and happiness.

"The conduct of our troops is magnificent. It arouses the admiration of the enemy.

"TADEUSZ KOMOROWSKI, *Lieutenant-General.*"

In the course of the two months of extremely heavy fighting in Warsaw, the Home Army's battle casualties were serious. It is not possible to give exact figures, as the fighting took place in circumstances which precluded the keeping of accurate records. We assessed our losses at roughly 15,000 killed, missing and seriously wounded; it would be impossible to count lighter casualties, as they actually continued to be on active service; in fact, there were very few of us who went through the whole duration of the rising without sustaining some sort of injury or wound. Casualties among the civilians are still harder to assess, as it would not be possible to give even an approximation of the number of people buried under the ruins or the victims of German terror in the captured districts. German propaganda and, in its wake, Russian assessments speak of 200,000; I consider this number exaggerated. German casualties in the Warsaw rising were 10,000 killed, 7,000 missing and 9,000 wounded, thus exceeding the losses of the Home Army.

On October 5th, at 8 a.m., I inspected for the last time my security platoon, which had been with me for so long, taking part in the fight for Wola and Stare Miasto. Its survivors now stood in two files in the courtyard of what was my last Headquarters. The order rang out: "Attention!" The commanding officer reported to me: "Thirty-six soldiers parading, sir." I remembered that in the first days of August there had been 128 on parade. The inspection was carried out in complete silence. Passing along the files, I was struck by the scarcity of their arms, which, even for us, was rather below standard. For instance, I could not see one tommy-gun. I asked the officer for an explanation. He was silent a moment, a little uneasy, and finally admitted that the men had buried most of their arms during the night to avoid handing them over to the Germans.

Just before we left, a woman from the Underground, Anka, whom I knew well, came up to me. "I am staying in Warsaw as a civilian," she said. "I shall leave with the civilians. Where is your wife? Have you something I can take to her?" I gave her the money I had on me and my fur coat, which I had taken from my flat the day before. I asked her to give all this to Renia. Several hundred yards divided us from the last barricade to be crossed before we reached the enemy side. To get through, we had to march in single file, weaving along the pathways through the ruins. Crowds of civilians were moving slowly and laboriously towards the points opened for them.

By 9.15 the Polish detachments from the centre of the city were ready to march and had lined up in a column. In accordance with the terms of surrender, the soldiers carried their arms; they had previously surrendered their remaining ammunition. Such part of the population as had not yet had time to leave Warsaw crowded on either side of the street. Suddenly a woman in mourning emerged from the crowd. She came up to me and, handing me a medal, said: "General, please accept this souvenir of the 1863 rising." Before I had time to thank her, she had disappeared into the crowd again. The appointed hour approached. I began singing the Polish national anthem, "*Jeszcze Polska nie Zginęta*" (Poland is not yet Lost), which the troops and civilian population at once took up. On the other side of the barricade, the Germans listened. I could clearly see the uniforms of the S.S. men awaiting us beyond the barricade, 200 yards away. When the last words of the anthem had died away, the command "Left turn" was given. The chaplain at the barricade, holding the Blessed Sacrament in his hands, made a cross in benediction over the departing troops and the gathered crowds. We passed through the barricade and marched towards the German guards over the smooth surface of the undamaged streets. The Polish and German positions had been so close to each other at this point that the Luftwaffe had had to leave it alone for fear of destroying German units. Very soon we were surrounded by a cordon of German soldiers and the cars and motor-cycles of German police, whose automatic rifles were at the ready. Tanks and armoured cars were patrolling street crossings. We entered the wide courtyard of the Military Technical Institute. The Home Army detachments gave up their arms. The German colonel in command approached and asked me to enter the waiting car. I took leave of my Staff and, together with a designated group of five generals, six orderly officers and five batmen, I moved towards the cars. All their licence-plates bore the mark "POL" (*Polizei* = Police). I was now alone except for two German policemen. I took a last farewell of the detachments of the Home Army, which were standing at attention, and the row of cars at once set off at full speed.

In an hour's time, we arrived at Ozarów Station, where General Chruściel joined us. General von dem Bach was waiting there. Closely surrounded by a large number of guards, we boarded the train, which pulled out immediately. Our carriage was in the middle of the train, with carriages containing our escorts before and behind us. At each compartment was posted a guard with an automatic rifle, who accompanied us even to the toilet. All the guards were S.S. men. We had no idea where we were being taken. All we knew was that, for the time being, we were going in a westerly direction. *En route* the Germans gave us breakfast, and for the first time in a month I tasted bread.

At Sochaczew Station the commander of the convoy informed me that the commander of the 9th German Army,

General von Luttwitz, wished to speak to me. Together with Heller, I alighted, and after a few minutes' car ride we arrived at a nearby Polish country house. There General von Luttwitz awaited me in full regalia, with his Staff officers. Standing stiffly to attention, General von Luttwitz declared: "From now on, General, you and all your soldiers who have been taken prisoner in Warsaw are under the protection of the Wehrmacht, which is responsible for ensuring that your treatment is in accordance with international conventions and those of the Ozarów surrender." This declaration over, we exchanged stiff bows and returned to the train in Sochaczew.

At dusk the train turned northwards. When night had fallen, a guard with an automatic rifle entered each compartment. They had orders to remain with us until dawn. At each stop the carriage was surrounded by guards, and at the large stations police in plain clothes could be seen. At daybreak we found ourselves in East Prussia and, finally, at the little station at Kruglanken, we were told to alight. A cordon of fifty armed S.S. men now surrounded our small party of twenty unarmed and utterly weary men. Cars took us to a Waffen S.S. camp, where we were led to the huts assigned to us. We went to bed immediately. As I lay down, I was conscious of the complete physical and nervous fatigue of the previous days. It was hot and stuffy in the hut, so I got up to open the window and at once a torch was flashed right in my eyes. Apparently, in addition to the regular camp watch, guards had been posted, not only at the doors, but also at the windows of our huts.

*   *   *

The following day General von dem Bach appeared in the hut to inform me that that afternoon he would take me to Hitler or Himmler, who were nearby at German G.H.Q. However, he did not reappear. Two days later, four S.S. men, carrying machine-guns, conducted me to a neighbouring barracks, where a German Air Force major and a Lieutenant-Colonel with the letters S.D. on his sleeve were waiting. They explained that German G.H.Q. wished to speak to me on the phone and that they were now trying to put the call through. Headquarters wished to have it made clear whether the capitulation of Warsaw, which I had signed, applied only to the troops which took part in the battle for the capital or to all the detachments of the Home Army under my command. I replied that the answer was contained in the text of my surrender, which clearly stated that only the detachments which fought in Warsaw had surrendered. The officers then asked whether, in view of this, I would now be willing to give orders for the cessation of hostilities and to negotiate a "discreet" laying-down of arms? I replied: "I shall issue no such order. And even if I did, it would not be obeyed, because the whole of Poland knows that I am now in German hands, and my subordinates would understand that I had done so under pressure. Consequently, all such proposals are useless." When the telephone call came through in two hours' time the German major repeated my answer, and with that I was escorted back to the huts. The scheduled meeting with Hitler or Himmler did not take place. Instead, on October 10th we were transferred to Berlin, where we spent twenty-four hours in the *Reichssicherheitsamt*, supposedly waiting for Himmler.

The terrible devastation of Berlin made us optimistic, I admit. We thought the end must be very near. There was an air-raid alarm that night, followed by the arrival of Mosquito planes. The talks were therefore again postponed, and the next morning we continued on our way, this time going to the large prisoner-of-war camp, Oflag 73, in Langwasser, near Nürenberg. It had typical wooden huts, surrounded by barbed wire. In addition to the stockade which surrounded the entire camp, our huts were hurriedly hemmed in after our arrival by extra barbed-wire barriers 10 feet high. Guards with spotlights were stationed at the corners, and there was a guard at the entrance. Thus we were isolated from the rest of the prisoners. We were not permitted to converse with anyone on the other side of the wire. Even members of the German camp personnel had to have a permit signed by the Camp Commander in order to enter the area of our huts. It looked as though our conspiratorial skill had been definitely overrated by the Germans in this instance. The whole foundation of the huts was hollowed out to form an empty space under them. This was daily sprinkled with yellow sand. A very fat Abwehr corporal had to crawl across this space under our huts every day to look for evidence of attempts at escape. Evidently the camp personnel had heard a bit about our use of sewers, because the manhole to the sewer nearest the camp was reinforced with iron bars and fitted with a big lock, which was inspected with great frequency. Day and night German officers and non-commissioned officers paid us visits to make sure we were still there. At night we were awakened and checked many times. I learned later that each respective camp commander and Abwehr officer had been warned that should any of us escape he would pay for it with his life.

These safety measures and restrictions amused us at first, but later they grew irksome. They were so stringent that General Grzegorz-Pełczyński, whose wound was still festering, was not permitted to go to the camp hospital, for fear he might make friendly contacts and succeed in escaping from there. The wound threatened to develop into blood-poisoning and his health deteriorated every day. It was not until I had sent a sharp protest to German H.Q. that Grzegorz was finally transferred to the hospital, where he was placed in a room with barred windows and watched by two guards, one of whom stood at the window and the other at the door. Only once was I allowed to visit him, and then I was accompanied by an escort consisting of one officer and two soldiers with guns. An interpreter was present throughout our conversation.

The Germans applied far more stringent rules to me than to the other prisoners. They treated me, admittedly, as a general, but did not allow any of the privileges usually applicable to prisoners of that rank. I was not allowed to leave the barracks nor the little yard adjacent to it. At first they did not allot any Red Cross parcels to us, without which it was difficult to make the starvation prison ration suffice; it was only after the personal intervention of a representative of the International Red Cross from Geneva that this was corrected. We were constantly searched and our small pile of personal belongings ransacked; we were not allowed to contact anyone, and for that reason could not even attend Sunday service. Our civilian clothes were taken away and old, worn-out Italian uniforms issued instead. The barracks in which we were confined was bitterly cold; the wind blew through the cracks in the walls and water in the buckets froze practically every day.

It was the Germans who informed us judiciously about the occupation of Warsaw and Cracow by the Russians, without adding, naturally, that the Germans had, on evacuation, dynamited and burned all the remaining buildings in the centre of the city.

Time dragged in the monotony of camp life. After two months of hunger in Warsaw, the effects of camp diet began to make themselves felt. A glass of bitter soup extract and 250 grams of rye bread for lunch and supper, with the addition of a plate of turnips for lunch, was all we got. I felt myself growing weaker and weaker.

At the beginning of November the boredom of camp life was broken by one further visit. Quite unexpectedly, the Camp Commander and two civilians turned up in my hut. Even at the first glance, there could be no mistake; they were Gestapo agents. The camp commander introduced them as employees of the *Reichssicherheitsamt* (State Security Bureau), who had come at Himmler's request to converse with me. The purpose of these talks was clear after the first few phrases. The same propositions to co-operate against the Russians which I had heard from General von dem Bach were now repeated. To support it, they made use of a whole series of worn-out clichés, familiar to everyone who had read the Goebbels Press. They maintained that the Germans still had enormous forces in reserve, that they were unconquerable, that they were preparing new weapons which would enable them to conquer, not only Russia, but also the western powers.

I listened in boredom and kept repeating the same answers again and again. After two hours the Germans went to lunch, announcing that they would return in the afternoon. But after lunch the conversation made no better headway. This time they once again proposed a secret armistice with the Home Army detachments in the provinces. I answered as before, but I must admit that I listened to the proposal with a certain satisfaction, because it was obvious from all this that the Home Army was still active and making itself felt. Even in this little propaganda show we could detect the utter hopelessness of the Reich's military situation.

At one point, one of my German visitors (as I learned later, his name was Harro Thomson) asked me if there was anything I wanted. In reply, I asked about the fate of my predecessor, General Grot Rowecki, who had been arrested in Warsaw on June 30th, 1943. The Gestapo man admitted that he had been in charge of the case and interrogated Rowecki in the Gestapo headquarters in Berlin. "General Rowecki showed the same senseless obstinacy which we are now meeting with from you," he said.

As I knew that Rowecki's health was far from good, and had grown worse because he had received no parcels from Poland since the rising started, I asked to be allowed to send him the next Red Cross parcel which came for us. The Gestapo man agreed and, in my presence, he ordered an Abwehr officer to redirect it. After some weeks we received the first Red Cross parcels and I pencilled the full rank and name: Lieut.-General S. Rowecki (he had been promoted to Lieutenant-General during captivity). Two months later, I heard quite by chance that the parcel was still in the cupboard in the Abwehr officer's room. He confided to a soldier, who later repeated it to me, that he was very annoyed to have had to keep a parcel for two months from General Komorowski for a friend of his who had been dead for a long time.

It was only in the spring of 1948 that Harro Thomson, interrogated by the Western powers, revealed that General Grot Rowecki had been shot at Sachsenhausen. This took place on special order of Himmler in the first days of the Warsaw rising.

From camp we had a grand-stand view of two terrific air raids on Nürenberg, both of them at night-time; the noise of the approaching formations of bombers was impressive. Soon the first flares lit up the whole area and the bombs followed practically immediately. The scene was stupendous and quite unforgettable: we all stood in front of opened windows in spite of bitter cold and fragments falling in a hail all around, hammering on our roof. Some bombs which fell close shook the barracks to the very foundations; doors and windows were being blown in, flares made the scene as light as bright sunshine, and every now and then enormous pillars of fire rose up in fantastic fountains around us. The noise cannot be described; the bomb explosions and anti-aircraft artillery seemed to fill space in an endless, deafening roar.

On February 5th, 1945, after about four months in the Langwasser camp, we were suddenly told to pack our belongings and were transferred by rail, under strong escort, to another prisoner camp, Colditz. It was located in an old castle of the Kings of Saxony. There were more than 300 prisoners, mostly British, some French from de Gaulle's army, a dozen Czechs from the R.A.F. and a few Americans. We had pleasant meetings. The British prisoners included four officers who had previously escaped from a camp in Poland and had been with us for a long time in Warsaw until they were recaptured and sent to Colditz. The camp sheltered many important inmates: The Germans called them "prominent" prisoners. They were Captain I. Elphinstone, nephew of Queen Elizabeth; Lieutenant Lord Lascelles, nephew of King George VI, Captain Lord Haig, Lieutenant Michael Alexander, nephew of Field-Marshal Alexander, Lieutenant John Winant, son of the United States Ambassador in London, two relations of Winston Churchill and others.

Life in the camp had been well organised by the prisoners. They had a wireless set kept in safe hiding which all the efforts of the Abwehr never succeeded in disclosing, and it worked non-stop. For the first time in a prisoner-of-war camp I was thus able to get regular news of the outside world. Here, too, we had a badly needed change of clothes. Our fellow prisoners, on their own initiative, replaced our tattered Italian uniforms and provided us with some shirts and underwear.

I again shared a room with my former Chief of Staff and Deputy Commander, General Pełczyński. We were in a separate wing of the castle, reserved for the "prominent." During the day, I was allowed to meet and mix with other prisoners. At eight o'clock in the evening, the officer on duty used to lock the door, and sentries were posted there and under the window. It was here that we were dealt our most painful blow, not from the hand of the enemy, but from those whom we considered faithful friends. This blow was the conclusion of the Yalta Agreement, the conditions of which we learnt through our colleagues who listened to the B.B.C.

There was not the slightest doubt that Soviet Russia was unfavourably disposed towards the true independence of Poland. It was perfectly clear that her willingness to rebuild a "strong and independent Poland" applied only to a Communist Poland (potentially the Seventeenth Republic of the Soviet Union), or at least to a "Communised" Poland, entirely subservient to the Kremlin's command. The Russians had supplied enough proof of this, the ultimate being their attitude towards the Warsaw rising, in which they stood by impassively and watched the Germans deal with almost the whole actively patriotic element of the country. But it was entirely incomprehensible to us why the Allies were giving up to slavery and partition their most faithful and oldest ally of the war.

N

Their decision erased and tore to bits all the principles of the Atlantic Charter and allowed brute force and violence to be inflicted on Poland—the "inspiration of nations"—and to prevail over right and justice. Poland was to give up 46 per cent. of its pre-war territories, while a clique of usurpers and Kremlin agents, "supplemented" by "members of other parties" in a manner devoid of any practical effect or meaning were to be imposed on the nation as a government by the three signatories of the Yalta Pact. Moreover, these decisions were made with complete disregard for the existence of the body of legal Polish authorities, as well as of the wishes of the nation itself.

It was clear to us that Yalta was tantamount to blotting out our country's independence. This blow, so heavy and unexpected, shook us to the core. Our allied colleagues seemed perplexed and embarrassed by this unexpected turn of events regarding Poland's fate. Most were openly ashamed when they met us; some of them asked quite plainly whether we would still be inclined to shake hands with them after the blow which their governments had inflicted on us.

During the first few days at Colditz I received another German proposal; this time it proved to be the last. I was taken to a private room in the camp command offices, where a well-dressed civilian was waiting for me. He introduced himself as Counsellor Benninghausen. He began by declaring that he had come from Berlin on the authorisation of very good friends of his, members of the pre-war German-Polish Association. He said that he, as well as all his friends, had always been opposed to the bad treatment meted out to the Poles. He fully realised that an unfortunate policy had been adopted towards Poland, and he thought that the mistakes could be rectified. The Polish nation belonged to the West and was now faced with a serious menace from the East. As I probably knew, the whole of Poland was now under Soviet occupation. In these circumstances, I would probably wish to continue my Underground fight, this time against the Russians. The German Government was ready to help me. I would be released at once with such officers as I selected; I should receive every help in both money and arms, and I should be transferred to Polish territory in the rear of the Soviet front to start an underground movement against Russia. Such a plan would be co-ordinated with the German authorities and its aim would be far-reaching in its attempt to oppose the Russians and their policy to sovietise Europe. I told the Counsellor that he was merely wasting his time, because I had already refused more than once to discuss any co-operation, and I had in no way altered my mind. The visitor asked me if this were my last word. He said he was ready to stay for three or four days to give me time to think the whole matter over. I replied again that every minute he spent in the consideration of these things was sheer waste of time, and only then did he depart.

In mid-April, military operations took a new turn. The advancing American armies were approaching Saxony, and the increased nervousness of the Germans clearly showed us that the time of our liberation was near. Throughout those days we lived from one wireless communiqué to another, hearing at the same time the sounds of approaching battle and expecting to see Americans at the gates of our camp every day. Just when liberation seemed so close, on April 13th, all the "prominent" group, as well as my Polish comrades, were suddenly roused in the night and evacuated from the camp. Those who were to stay behind felt very anxious about us, because it looked as though we were to be treated as hostages and taken to "Hitler's fortress."

We were taken to Koenigstein, east of the Oder. We were to have remained there, but after twenty-four hours we were moved on again. They took us across Czechoslovakia into the mountains of Tyrol to a civilian internee camp at Laufen. We made energetic protests against the internment of officers in a civilian camp, and as a result were transferred to Titt-moning, a camp for Dutch prisoners.

One of the British prisoners succeeded in escaping from there. The Germans were furious and kept us in the courtyard the whole night. Meanwhile, the Gestapo pursued its search with the help of police dogs, turning everything upside down. The next day, with fully five times more guards than before, their tommy-guns at the ready and trained on us, we were taken back to Laufen. There we were confined in some rooms on the third floor.

We could hear the first sound of distant artillery; the American forces were approaching Laufen. Allied planes appeared overhead. The civilian internees at Laufen—mostly British and American, with a few Poles—made contact with us by bribing a German soldier. Using their own channels, they informed the Swiss Minister, who was in the vicinity, of our arrival in Laufen. The Minister arrived immediately, requesting the German guards to allow him to see us in accordance with his rights as representative of the protecting power.

Minister Feldscher, the Swiss envoy, and his attaché, Buchmueller, were permitted to see two of us, the senior officer of the British group and myself. The German general who was in charge of all the camps in southern Germany had come from Munich and was also present. He assured the Swiss envoy that we should be left in the camp regardless of the situation on the front, even if the Allies occupied the area. Twelve hours later, we were once more taken in lorries, under heavy guard, deep into the Tyrol, to a camp at Markt Pondau. We were isolated in a separate building, but our guardian angel, Minister Feldscher, to whose indefatigable care and energy we owe so much, turned up only a few hours after our arrival. In the area, all the remaining German authorities were gathering from all parts of Germany, especially from Berlin. Amongst them was found to be Himmler's deputy, S.S. Obergruppenführer General der Polizei Berger. He occupied a very high position both in the Gestapo hierarchy and the list of war criminals. He was in a state of almost complete nervous collapse. Feldscher succeeded in convincing him that, for the sake of his own skin, he should hand us over to the care of the protecting power, i.e. Switzerland.

On May 4th Berger walked into my room. He was a large, corpulent German covered with every variety of the Iron Cross and other decorations. He was obviously under great nervous tension and made a very pompous speech: "General Bor," he said, "you are in great danger. Stalin has put a high price on your head. In the German ranks, Communism is developing—a Communism far more dangerous than that of 1918. Soviet agents are ambushing you on all sides. In the circumstances, I can no longer accept responsibility for your safety and therefore I have decided to hand you over to the care of the Swiss authorities." He then went out and made a similar speech to the British in the next room.

A few hours later we were installed in cars, flying large Red Cross and Swiss flags, and sped towards the Swiss frontier, through Innsbruck. During the night of May 5th we passed numerous routed German Army columns withdrawing in disorder to the east.

The same night, we passed the last German guard posts on the road to Innsbruck; we then followed an empty road lined with overturned German vehicles. After twenty minutes, a turn in the road brought us in sight of a small town. In the middle of the road stood a soldier. His uniform was unfamiliar —not field grey any more. He stopped us. On his left arm he wore the badge of his division—a cactus tree on a yellow-and-white ground. The only American among us was Winant. He leapt from the car and threw his arms round the American soldier, shouting: "Oh, boy! You're the finest fellow I ever met in my life."

I fully agreed.

It was the 103rd American Infantry Division; its staff was located at Innsbruck, to which we were immediately directed.

In a charming tourist hotel on the top of a hill, with a breath-taking view down to the winding valley of the Inn, we were at last able to enjoy full rest. Our feeling of gratitude for the hospitality and goodwill shown to us by the command and troops of the 103rd Division can scarcely be described. We met there, by chance, the French Generals Weygand—also his wife—and Gamelin, both released at the same time from German captivity. I had never met them before. They came straight up to us with words of sincere admiration for the effort our country had made in its battle with the Germans, stressing, from the point of view of military value, their appreciation and high assessment of the Warsaw rising. I was deeply moved by their kind words and sympathy.

Next day a group of us, comprising Captain Elphinstone, Lieutenant Lord Lascelles, Lieutenant Winant, myself and my aide-de-camp, was sent off to the Army Group Command, from where we were to be flown to the Supreme Command H.Q.

It so happened that both the Army Group G.O.C. and the Chief of Staff were absent on duty; we were therefore cordially received by an American colonel in charge with truly American hospitality, after which we spent the night in a hotel. Next day we were given further travelling instructions, and found military cars waiting for us in the morning. The two British officers of royal parentage and the American Ambassador's son were taken off to the airfield, while my A.D.C. and I

N*

were directed to the reception point of former Polish prisoners of war at Murnau. We drove in a jeep for several hours across the colourful subalpine countryside until we reached Murnau, where I not only rejoined my prison colleagues from whom we had parted only the day before, but also quite a number of former officers and men from the Home Army and some pre-war fellow officers, most of whom had been in prison since 1939. Soon after, I left from a nearby airfield for Paris and some days later I arrived in London, where our President and the Polish Government were living.

All the time I was very much concerned with the fate of my wife and children, who had remained in Poland. Not till October, 1945, did I hear that my wife had arrived in the U.S. Zone in Germany, and a few days later learnt that she had flown with the children to Brussels. She escaped from Poland across the so-called "green frontier." She organised the whole crossing to the western side of the Iron Curtain entirely by herself. It had never occurred to me that she could risk such a venture with two small children, one of whom was no more than a baby.

From Brussels she sent me a letter briefly describing her experiences since the beginning of the Warsaw rising until her departure from Poland. As that letter gives a picture of the awesome days of fighting in our capital, seen from the quite different angle of one of the members of the civilian community, I am quoting it:

". . . Those unforgettable days of the outbreak of the rising—the moving sight of our boys, with their arm-bands, on the barricades; the first free Press which we read with a breathless suspense; our home, which alas! was between the lines, with its entrance on Foch Street under enemy fire; the Poles from Theatre Square facing the Germans on the Marshal's Place. But in spite of all this and even in so limited an area, we breathed the air of freedom, unknown for so many years. We had a Polish outpost on the corner of Theatre Square, on the opposite side of the street; I crossed over there from time to time by tunnels cut through the basements of the houses, in order to listen to the radio. We watched the movements of the Germans from our attic windows, and we also saw the Polish flag, unseen for so long, flying from the top of the sky-scraper on Napoleon Square and the Town Hall. We once went to the shelter underneath the Opera, but after that I only went down to the ground floor for the night. I hate shelters. An enemy shell went clean through the flat over ours—plaster came down, but that was all. The baby got quite accustomed to the firing: we walked about in the yard although fragments kept falling around; he was only very much afraid of the diving Stukas and the bombs. At night we had the spectacle of the incendiary shells, which was magnificent, though we were in constant danger from the fires.

"After some days, a messenger from our outpost summoned me to see Anka, to whom I gave the card which she was to take to you; I threw it to her across the street tied to a stone on a piece of string. She promised to take it. Some days later she came again at 8 p.m. and asked me whether I would like to get out of the hole we were in, and cross over to the part of the town occupied by our troops. I had to decide at once. I had a moment of uncertainty; it meant that I should have had to cross the enemy fire on the run across the street; I should never have been afraid for myself, but in my eight-months state I could not carry Adam. I feared that even if I crossed over safely myself, Adam, carried by someone else, might be killed. Then too there was the old military principle: never endanger others to ensure your own safety, sit tight wherever you are and trust your lucky star. So I told her that I preferred to stay where I was, though I did promise that I would go down into the shelter at night. . . . I went down with the baby and the nanny.

"Suddenly, at 2 a.m. there was a great commotion—shots, shouting and running footsteps. I heard someone calling: 'Escape! Germans in the shelter.' We jumped up, but what was the use? There was nowhere to escape! We settled down again to await what would happen. There was a terrible lot of noise, shooting, German commands, every sound magnified by the acoustics of the shelter. A poor old man hobbled by; said he was feeling faint and would probably die. In a corner I found a man sleeping like a log under an umbrella! Later we found out he was an Englishman; I sometimes wonder what happened to him. And so we waited. After a while things got somewhat quieter, only occasionally there were more German orders and shots, but nobody came in our direction. This went on till seven o'clock in the morning, when I ventured out to reconnoitre. All I saw was a dead man

lying in the yard; then I heard a German soldier approaching
and hid behind a wall. I decided to get back home, traversing
one backyard after another on the run. The house was empty;
there was nothing warm to give the child to eat—no gas—
and I was afraid to make a fire in the stove for fear of betraying
my presence by smoke coming from the chimney. Out in the
yard, we heard steps and shouts—Germans walking about
everywhere; the nanny was half-crazy with fear. All day we
just waited, not knowing what for.

"At 6 p.m. someone banged on the door—a German with
revolver: '*Was machen sie hier?*' (What are you doing here?).
I laughed in his face. Here I was, pregnant, another woman
and a baby. He barged in, looked into the cupboards, under
the bed and shouted, '*Raus!*' (Get out!). The house was going
to be set on fire in ten minutes. We had barely time to put
something warm on the baby, wrap him in a shawl, and
grab a small case and a rug before we were out. I luckily
carried on me those few valuables we had. I did not even
have time to put on a coat, nor a scarf on my head.

"They took us by back yards to King Albert Street, where
we found quite a large crowd of people driven in from all
the adjacent houses. Young drunken S.S. men were running
amok, tearing rings off fingers, hitting men in the face and
breaking window-panes. In the bottom shelter, where I had
only by luck avoided spending the night, quite a number of
people were shot, and the remainder driven out into the
streets and forced to advance at the head of tanks against our
own barricades. Many were killed. How is one not to believe
in Divine protection?

"From King Albert Street, they drove a crowd of several
hundred of us into Marshal Square, thence into Saski Park.
Night came, but it was uncannily light; everything around
was afire—Królewska Street, the Iron Gate, Senatorska
Street. Flames were bursting high, and every now and then
we heard the rumble of a house collapsing.

". . . The Germans were running wild. We heard curses,
heavy blows and from time to time a shot muffled at the
barrel-end. Quite close to me, one German put his rifle against
the breast of a man and pulled the trigger; the man groaned
and slumped to the ground. He was shot because he had
dallied too long in joining the male group, having stayed
behind to say farewell to his wife. I sat down on the ground;

little Adam fell asleep on my knees. About midnight, a command was given for everyone to get up, form ranks and start marching. Nanny took the baby in her arms. I threw the little case over my shoulder, unfortunately breaking the thermos bottle with the last drop of milk for the child. They drove us on over the freshly captured Iron Gate and along Chłodna Street, over crumbled barricades, ruins and dead bodies. The infernal heat was almost unbearable and smoke stung our eyes. Little Adam looked at all this in wide-eyed astonishment and from time to time pointed to the flames. Along the streets we passed rows of German soldiers, sooty, dirty and looking worn out. At the Church of St. Charles Borromeo some of us were stopped and ordered to enter. We were told that we should continue next morning; I was afraid that it would probably end with the firing squad. I cannot say that I felt any fear for myself. I thought of you, that when you were told of the plight of the civilians it might break your heart. However, I kept faith in your inflexibility.

"The worst tribulation was the intolerable thirst. Our tongues were literally drying up. People were throwing themselves on buckets of filthy water from ponds. The baby had parched lips and I had nothing to give him. I saw a German standing by and asked him what was going to happen to us. He told me that two days before they drove the people out into the yard and shot them, but that probably we should merely be convoyed out and taken to Germany. I asked him whether they also shot the children? . . . He shrugged his shoulders. 'They did whatever was ordered.' . . . A young S.S. man came in and started with the announcement that everyone had to be punished because we were equally responsible for those 'bandits who are fighting us: it is all the dirty work of Jews.' He ended with the words: 'And the worst criminal of the lot is this one'—pointing to the figure of Christ on the ruined altar.

"We tried to get some rest on a piece of ripped-down tapestry. People were sitting and lying wherever they could. The church was partially ruined. Heaps of junk and abandoned suitcases were lying all about. A dead woman covered by a sheet lay at the foot of the altar. There was the unceasing din of artillery fire, automatic arms and tanks passing. We slept. At dawn they roused us and drove us on. A halt was called: we saw a lorry with great cans of coffee for the soldiers. I thought to myself, 'I do not care. I must get something for the baby.' I found an empty bottle in the street and took it along. They gave me a little coffee for the child; I rinsed the bottle and poured some in—how he loved it. After that they drove us on along Wolska Street and over Wola, towards the Western railway station. Along the side streets we could see barricades with our boys behind them. In certain sectors the Germans were taking advantage of the cover which our march provided and were bringing up ammunition wagons. When we reached the station, they crowded us into cars bound for Pruszkow. We continued to suffer from searing thirst. The day was beautiful—hot sunshine. Luckily, we did not stay long in the Pruszkow camp [horror camp set up for transit of Warsaw refugees]. My eight months pregnancy and the baby got me out comparatively quickly.

"I should never have thought that a baby of little Adam's age could have reacted so readily to our release from the camp. When we left the dismal crowd and the gates behind us and were walking free along a foot-path across the fields, the child suddenly started to roll in the grass with squeals of joy, regardless of fatigue—just like a little animal released from its cage. I stayed in the town of Pruszkow for two days with some friends, and after that went to some people I knew in the country. I left there two days before childbirth, as I did not want to cause undue trouble for my hosts, who were accommodating lots of people, all refugees.

"I went to one of those little pseudo-hospitals, where I was told that there was not even a midwife available; there were at least some benches and clean sheets. A gynæcologist lived some three miles away. The child was born at midnight with no one to help except a nurse who knew practically nothing and did not even want to tie the umbilical cord. The doctor arrived an hour and a half after. The baby was extremely weak the first few days; I had very little milk owing to an infectious diarrhœa which I had contracted and from which many people then suffered. Besides, there was very little food, but thank goodness we pulled through somehow. I was up after six days and got home after a fifteen-mile drive in a rickety cart. The baby began to be ill with terrible skin-burn, owing to lack of clean diapers; the most I had was five very small towels. There was no doctor or medicines to be had. So I decided to go to Cracow—two days before Warsaw's capitulation. The baby was grievously ill for nearly two months and gained practically no weight; I did all I could and tried every method of treatment, but his recovery took a very long time. In Cracow we underwent a short air and artillery bombardment when the Russians stormed the city. After their entry, I changed my address three times, after warnings that the N.K.V.D. was on my trail; I also changed my name twice. The last two months I spent in a small village outside the town, living in a tiny, picturesque, thatched cottage. The situation was worsening from day to day; arrests of Home Army men without any reason given; all administrative posts slowly being taken over by Communists or Soviet agents; increasing difficulties in finding work; and the prices rising all the time. I felt the noose tightening round my neck. Escape was essential.

"By sheer luck, it was quite easy on the whole, and, apart from brief moments, I did not encounter any major difficulties. In spite of the security thus achieved, and joy at the prospect of seeing you again, the saddest moment came to me when I realised, on reaching this side, the extent of tragic abandonment in which Poland was left. Everyone there still strongly believed that it was merely temporary; they live only by that hope. The darkest and most terrible moments in the Underground now seem beautiful and happy compared with the present day, because we had faith in victory and a happy end, while to-day . . ."

*   *   *

To-day the scales have been turned against us once more. The long years of strife and struggle and faith in the victory of a just cause, the loss of so many lives, the untold tragedies born with fortitude—all this seems to have been in vain. Germany fell defeated, but Poland did not gain the freedom for which she had paid such heavy toll.

The Yalta Agreement shattered our justified expectations. In consequence of the decisions taken there, Europe has been divided into two spheres of influence, and Stalin—who in 1939 had helped Germany to launch the Second World War—could at last grasp the booty which, according to the secret clause of the Molotov-Ribbentrop Agreement, he was to have shared with Hitler. This time he received his prize from the hands of our own allies.

The Western powers, in their eagerness to settle down to a

peaceful existence, let themselves be led astray by the hope of Soviet Russia's co-operation in a political and economic reconstruction of the world. This wishful thinking was followed by a policy of concessions to Stalin, with the result that central-eastern Europe passed under Communist domination. Poland was one of the victims.

However, the people of Poland cannot forget that a thousand-year-old tradition links them to Western civilisation and the Western way of life. Against all odds, they still believe that Poland's war effort and the sacrifices suffered for a common victory have not been wasted. Putting their trust in the future, they can only conceive it in a close union with the Western world, fully aware that the present artificial division of our continent will not stand the test of life and that in reality western and central-eastern Europe form one whole. The Polish people fighting for independence wished to see Poland take its place, together with other free countries, in a future central-eastern European bloc. Only such a bloc would be capable of maintaining a proper balance in that part of the world, safeguarding it against any possible aggression from those who in their imperialistic drive are apt to absorb smaller states.

To construct world peace at the expense of injustice and wrong done to smaller nations is a dangerous experiment. It can only result in acute political tensions and a perpetual smouldering of grievances—a most precarious state of international affairs, so clearly demonstrated by our present times.

INDEX

WARSAW
Centre of the City

0 ————————————— 1000

-- Sewers from the Old Town to
   to the centre of the city.
⊙ Successive HQ. of the C.i.C. Home
   Army during the Warsaw
   Rising.

POWĄZKI

Former Jewish District

Pawiak Prison

Goods Stn.

Central Stn.

Water Supply Stn
"Filtry"

OCHOTA

Based on the Map 1:25.000 drawn up by the Geograph